The corporation under Russian law, 1800–1917
A study in tsarist economic policy

Thomas C. Owen
Louisiana State University

Studies of the Harriman Institute

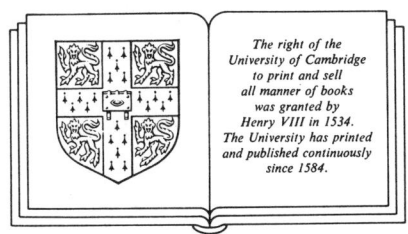

Cambridge University Press

Cambridge
New York   Port Chester   Melbourne   Sydney

Published by the Press Syndicate of the University of Cambridge
The Pitt Building, Trumpington Street, Cambridge CB2 1RP
40 West 20th Street, New York, NY 10011, USA
10 Stamford Road, Oakleigh, Melbourne 3166, Australia

© Cambridge University Press 1991

First published 1991

Printed in the United States of America

Library of Congress Cataloging-in-Publication Data
Owen, Thomas C.
The corporation under Russian law, 1800–1917 : a study in Tsarist economic policy / Thomas C. Owen.
    p.   cm. – (Studies of the Harriman Institute)
Includes index.
Includes bibliographical references.
ISBN 0-521-39126-1
1. Corporation law – Soviet Union – History. I. Title.
II. Series.
LAW
346.47'066 – dc20
[344.70666]   90-36148
                                                                       CIP

British Library Cataloguing in Publication Data
Owen, Thomas C.
The corporation under Russian law, 1800–1917 : a study in Tsarist economic policy – (Studies of the Harriman Institute).
1. Russia. Companies. Law, history
I. Title II. Series
344.70666

ISBN 0-521-39126-1 hardback

The corporation under Russian law, 1800–1917

Studies of the Harriman Institute

Columbia University

Founded as the Russian Institute in 1946, the W. Averell Harriman Institute for Advanced Study of the Soviet Union is the oldest research institution of its kind in the United States. The book series *Studies of the Harriman Institute*, begun in 1953, helps bring to a wider audience some of the work conducted under its auspices by professors, degree candidates, and visiting fellows. The faculty of the Institute, without necessarily agreeing with the conclusions reached in these books, believes their publication will contribute to both scholarship and a greater public understanding of the Soviet Union. A list of the *Studies* appears at the back of the book.

To Sue Ann

Contents

List of tables	page ix
Preface	xi
Abbreviations	xvii

1 *Zakon* (The law), 1800–1856   1

    The international context   1
    Russian corporate law before 1836   6
    The law of 1836 and its inconsistencies   15
    Minor amendments under Nicholas I   24

2 *Birzhevaia goriachka* (Stock-exchange fever), 1856–1870   30

    The flurry of incorporation   32
    The railroad boom   35
    The stock market under Reutern   45

3 *Proval reformy* (The failure of reform), 1860–1874   55

    The need for reform   56
    The Butovskii Commission   65
    Recommendations from business organizations   72
    The abandonment of the Butovskii bill   75

4 *Opeka* (Tutelage), 1865–1890   79

    Rationalization of the concession system   81
    Restrictions on conflict of interest   86

	Manipulation of the banking system	97
	Professor Mendeleev's dilemma	111
5	*Proizvol* (Arbitrary acts), 1880–1905	116
	Restrictions on foreigners, Jews, and Poles	118
	Ambivalence toward cartels	132
	The Tsitovich Commission and its failure	137
	The law of 1901	150
6	*Bezobrazie* (Outrage), 1905–1914	155
	The need for reform	156
	The Timashev Conference	161
	The reactionary counteroffensive	171
7	*Tupik* (Dead end), 1914–1917	181
	Half measures during the wartime emergency	182
	The aftermath: corporate legislation of the Provisional Government and the Soviet regime	189
8	Autocracy, corporate law, and the dilemma of cultural delay	198
Selected bibliography		220
Index		228

Tables

2.1	Selected stock values established by the Ministry of Finance, 1865–1872	*page* 46
2.2	Median capitalization and par value of shares issued by new companies founded in St. Petersburg and Moscow, 1866–1870	52
2.3	Share ownership in the Moscow Merchant Bank, 1869–1885	53
4.1	Banks in the Russian Empire, 1864–1900	106

Preface

This book is about a seemingly irrelevant subject: capitalist institutions in a society composed mostly of illiterate peasants, where industrialization, initiated by an autocratic monarchy, continued after World War I under a regime fervently opposed to capitalist principles. The number of companies founded in the Russian Empire before the Bolshevik revolution of October 1917 scarcely surpassed six thousand (including approximately fifteen hundred founded during World War I), and the number of corporations in existence on the eve of the war fell far short of corresponding figures for Britain and France.[1] The number of individuals who deserved to be called capitalist entrepreneurs remained tiny by European standards. Although many aspects of Russian urban history have yet to be clarified, preliminary studies suggest that the vast majority of merchants held to Russian cultural traditions, distrusted secular Western education, and preferred to carry on their businesses in family firms rather than in large, impersonal corporations.

Accordingly, much of the entrepreneurial and managerial elite of the tsarist economy had to be recruited from the slim stratum of Russians or Russified foreigners who had acquired a university or technical education. This process was impeded, moreover, because most members of the landed gentry, the civil and military bureaucracy, and the professions (law, journalism, medicine) evinced strongly anticapitalist attitudes, despite their

---

[1] Iu. K. Grinval'd, "Uchrezhdenie aktsionernykh obshchestv vo Frantsii," *Promyshlennost' i torgovlia*, 3, no. 6 (Mar. 15, 1910), 379, and "Uchrezhdenie... vo Soedinennom Korolestve," *Promyshlennost' i torgovlia*, 3, no. 11 (June 1, 1910), 722–6, noted that in France 5,944 companies had been founded between 1900 and 1905 and that 40,995 companies existed in Great Britain in 1906, with a total capitalization of over 2 billion pounds sterling. For Russian numbers, see footnote 4 to this preface. Note: Dates in Russian documents before February 1918 in the text, notes, and bibliography are given according to the Julian (Old Style) calendar, in use within Russia until the Bolshevik government adopted the Gregorian (New Style) calendar on February 1, 1918.

differences of opinion on other questions. As a spokesman for Russian iron producers complained with bitter sarcasm in 1905,

> In the "cultured" language of our dear country, employed by former owners of serfs, the word "industrialist" has somehow become a synonym for "swindler," "bloodsucker," "exploiter," and other, no less flattering, definitions. And the industrialists? They kept quiet, keep quiet, and apparently intend stubbornly to keep quiet forever and ever, as if to confirm the correctness of our kindhearted public opinion.[2]

Little more than six decades elapsed between the first important episode of corporate entrepreneurship, after the Crimean War (1853–6), and the Bolshevik seizure of power. The development of technically advanced heavy industry in Russia dated only from the 1880s. Soviet historians boast that the so-called socialist system of central planning has proved more efficient than capitalism as a means of utilizing the great material wealth of their country. Some critics of the Soviet autocracy argue that a nascent capitalist system sturdy enough to develop without state tutelage was beginning to emerge in the economic boom of 1909–14 and that only the war and the Bolshevik coup prevented the development of a new society based on a free economy and constitutional democracy. Others stress the capacity of the tsarist government to respond creatively to new social and economic challenges after 1905. All sides would agree, however, that Russian capitalism remained chronically weak before the accession of Sergei Iu. Witte to the post of minister of finance in 1892 and that the paucity of serious scholarship on the Russian corporation is justified by the insignificance of the subject.

These are strong arguments. They cannot be contested by the claim that Russian capitalism had more vitality than has previously been supposed, although some recent econometric work has given a slightly more optimistic picture of Russian economic growth, particularly in the "autonomous," or non-state-directed, sectors than earlier scholars had admitted.[3] On the whole, the rudimentary statistics now available demonstrate the relatively slow pace of corporate development in the Russian

---

[2] Adol'f A. Vol'skii [Adolf Wolski], *Proizvoditel'nye sily i ekonomichesko-finansovaia politika Rossii*, 2nd ed. (St. Petersburg, 1905), 2.

[3] See Paul R. Gregory, *Russian National Income, 1885–1913* (Cambridge, 1982), for the more favorable growth figures and Fred V. Carstensen, "Foreign Participation in Russian Economic Life: Notes on British Enterprise, 1865–1914," in Gregory Guroff and Fred V. Carstensen, eds., *Entrepreneurship in Imperial Russia and the Soviet Union* (Princeton, 1983), 140–58.

Empire. It is precisely this phenomenon that presents the greatest interest, however. Once the race for economic power in the age of steam had begun, the link between industrial development and military success became clear to the most obtuse tsarist bureaucrat. Following the ignominious defeat of the Russian navy and the capture of its Black Sea ports in the Crimean War, the Russian government took steps to promote economic development. However, a close examination of the tsarist corporate law shows that even Witte, the most energetic proponent of state-sponsored industrial progress, proved no less reluctant than his predecessors to relinquish the regime's legislative and administrative control and to tolerate a genuinely free market.

The major theme of this study, then, is the interplay between the tsarist legal system and modern capitalism, as represented by the institution that was particularly sensitive to both legislative decrees and market forces: the modern corporation. Essential to an understanding of capitalism under the tsarist regime is an appreciation of the unique duality of the imperial corporate law. Through a myriad of legislative acts, the bureaucrats strove to promote the development of capitalist institutions: banks, stock exchanges, consultative organizations of businessmen in every region and sector, and of course the corporation itself. At the same time, the tsar's servitors ingeniously hampered this development by a no less impressive series of laws that mandated dozens of social and ethnic restrictions and other obstacles to the free play of market forces. The emphasis on the primacy of the political factor in Russian history is a familiar enough concept, but it deserves to be reiterated in the context of the economic and social changes that accompanied the expansion of capitalist institutions in the late imperial period.

From its inception until its collapse in World War I, the tsarist autocracy viewed itself as standing above society, subject to no restraints by countervailing social or political institutions. It claimed the right to implement major social and cultural transformations from above, even after it surrendered some of its prerogatives to elected and semi-elected representative bodies in 1906. Despite the economic irrationalities engendered by this attitude of autocratic intransigence, the regime refused to reform the law in response to changing economic conditions in the twelve decades from the accession of Paul I to the fall of Nicholas II.

As for the larger political ramifications of our subject – the Soviet claim of the inevitability (*zakonomernost'*) of the allegedly "socialist" Bolshevik revolution, or the influential liberal view that capitalism and democracy were steadily gathering strength within the interstices of the decaying tsarist order – the study of capitalist institutions offers a good deal of fresh evidence to fuel the debate. At issue is the degree of institutional accommodation that occurred between the tsarist regime and the corporate elite. To what extent did the relationship between the state and the various business interests engender political cooperation or conflict? To this question we shall return in the concluding chapter after the evidence for generalizations has been presented. Suffice it to say that the history of the corporation under the tsarist government provides copious evidence to contradict both the teleological Soviet view and the optimistic liberal one, while offering new insights with which to construct a more nuanced and comprehensive account of the relationship between capitalism and politics under the tsarist regime.

This study of corporate law originally took shape as the introductory chapter of a monograph on corporate entrepreneurship, of which no detailed work yet exists in the embryonic field of Russian business history. The larger project is well under way, in the form of a machine-readable database containing statistical information on corporations and their founders and managers from 1700 to 1914.[4] The database is intended to provide the raw material for a rigorous statistical analysis of the geographical distribution of industry, ethnicity and social status of founders and managers, and other patterns that are not yet clear. It soon became apparent, however, that the evolution of the government's policies toward the corporation could not be relegated to a short chapter. Apart from the complexities of the law itself, its function as both a symptom of bureaucratic attitudes and an obstacle to economic growth made corporate law a subject deserving of extended treatment.[5] Moreover, without justifying the repressive nature of the tsarist regime, the present study highlights as well

---

[4] "RUSCORP: A Database of Corporations in the Russian Empire, 1700–1914" (hereafter RUSCORP), compiled with support from the National Science Foundation (grant no. SES–8419943) and available from the Inter-University Consortium for Political and Social Research, Ann Arbor, Michigan (database no. 9142). The database contains profiles of 4,539 corporations chartered by the imperial government to the end of 1913 and of 2,118 Russian and 262 foreign corporations operating in 1914. New domestic and foreign corporations chartered from the beginning of 1914 to the end of September 1917 totaled 1,973, of which 310 were created in the first seven months of 1914. Leonid E. Shepelev, *Aktsionernye kompanii v Rossii* (Leningrad, 1973), 309–10, 329, 333.

[5] A preliminary discussion of corporate law appeared in Thomas C. Owen, "Four Episodes of Corporate Law Reform in the Russian Empire, 1836–1914," *Research in Economic History*, 11 (1988), 277–99, based on a paper delivered to the American Association for the Advancement of Slavic Studies in Kansas City, Missouri, in October 1983. Although that article and this monograph develop similar themes, they were written separately. The permission of the editors of the journal to reprint occasional passages from the article is gratefully acknowledged.

the social and cultural peculiarities of Russian capitalism, particularly the abuses of stock-exchange speculation and managerial malfeasance, in an effort to explain why the bureaucracy considered strict regulation the best means of protecting the financial interests of investors, the public, and the state itself. The examination of tsarist policy from this new, cultural perspective reveals the dual nature of the law itself, both as a reflection of the traditions of the society in which it grew and as a set of principles to be implemented for the public good, however differently the goals might have been defined by officials of the autocratic state and by business leaders who sought a new and more rational social order.

The idea of using Russian words for chapter headings is borrowed from Norman Davies, who used Polish words to excellent effect in his highly acclaimed history of Poland.[6] The Russian words remind the reader of the exotic cultural milieu to which the European corporation was transplanted in the last century, and they highlight the peculiar problems that corporate entrepreneurs encountered under tsarist rule. The visceral repugnance expressed by these men in the words *opeka, proizvol,* and *bezobrazie* is inadequately conveyed by their English counterparts: "tutelage," "arbitrariness," and "outrage."

Besides the staffs of the Lenin Library and the Historical Library in Moscow and the Saltykov-Shchedrin Library in Leningrad, several individuals deserve special thanks for sharing their expertise and facilitating my research in Soviet libraries and archives in 1980: Valerii I. Bovykin, Andrei G. Golikov, Nina S. Kiniapina, Vladimir Ia. Laverychev, and Nikolai I. Tsimbaev in Moscow and Boris V. Anan'ich, Galina A. Ippolitova, and Leonid E. Shepelev in Leningrad. The unpredictable nature of Soviet life in the late Brezhnev era brought to the foreign researcher occasional episodes of personal warmth, intellectual sustenance, and professional competence. All these helped to mitigate the frustrations of working in Soviet archives, where, according to state policy, foreigners were denied access to the inventories (*opisi*) of collections.

Useful support was also provided by the staffs of other libraries in the past decade. These include the Helsinki University Library Slavic Collection, the School of Slavonic and East European Studies at the University of London, the British Library, the Library of Congress, the New York Public Library, and the university libraries at Harvard, Columbia, Stanford, California at Berkeley, Wisconsin at Madison, and Washington

---

[6] Norman Davies, *God's Playground: A History of Poland,* 2 vols. (New York, 1982).

(Seattle). The Slavic Reference Service at the University of Illinois Library in Urbana acted as an international clearing house of last resort for many obscure sources. At Louisiana State University, Paul Wank and his staff in the Inter-Library Loan office processed difficult requests with unfailing professionalism and courtesy. Marc Harris, Alexandra Sparks, Randy Hebert, and Katharine Paine gave essential instruction in the use of text-processing equipment.

For generous financial assistance between 1979 and 1981 I am grateful to the LSU Council on Research, the International Research and Exchanges Board, the Kennan Institute for Advanced Russian Studies in Washington, D.C., and the Russian Institute (now the W. Averell Harriman Institute for Advanced Study of the Soviet Union) at Columbia University. Paul Lerner provided essential help in arranging publication in the Harriman Institute's monograph series. Needless to say, although the institutions and persons named above contributed to this project, I remain responsible for any errors of fact or interpretation in the chapters that follow.

To my wife, Sue Ann, I owe special thanks for her constant encouragement and moral support during our travels to faraway libraries and throughout the no less daunting composition process in Baton Rouge.

T.C.O.
September 1990

Abbreviations

Archival sources

BAREEHC	Bakhmeteff Archive of Russian and East European History and Culture, Columbia University (New York)
GBL-OR	Gosudarstvennaia biblioteka SSSR imeni V. I. Lenina, otdel rukupisei (Moscow)
GPB-OR	Gosudarstvennaia publichnaia biblioteka imeni M. E. Saltykova-Shchedrina, otdel rukopisei (Leningrad)
HIA	Hoover Institute Archives, Stanford University (Stanford)
LOII	Leningradskoe otdelenie instituta istorii Akademii nauk SSSR (Leningrad)
TsGIA	Tsentral'nyi gosudarstvennyi istoricheskii arkhiv SSSR (Leningrad)
TsGIAM	Tsentral'nyi gosudarstvennyi istoricheskii archiv v Moskve (Moscow)

Published sources

MERSH	*Modern Encyclopedia of Russian and Soviet History.* Ed. Joseph L. Wieczynski.
PSZ	*Polnoe sobranie zakonov Rossiiskoi imperii.*
RBS	*Russkii biograficheskii slovar'.*
SURP	*Sobranie uzakonenii i rasporiazhenii pravitel'stva.*

Organizational names (dates of founding indicated in parentheses)

AIT	Association of Industry and Trade (Sovet s″ezdov predstavitelei promyshlennosti i torgovli) (1906)

MEC	Moscow Exchange Committee (Moskovskii birzhevoi komitet) (1839, new charter 1870)
MSRIS	Moscow Section of the Russian Industrial Society (Moskovskoe otdelenie Obshchestva dlia sodeistviia russkoi promyshlennosti i torgovle) (1884)
PEC	Petersburg [Petrograd from 1914 onward] Exchange Committee (Sankt-Peterburgskii [Petrogradskii from 1914 onward] birzhevoi komitet) (1831, new charters 1832 and 1875)
PSMFO	Petersburg [Petrograd from 1914 onward] Society of Mill and Factory Owners (Petersburgskoe [Petrogradskoe from 1914 onward] obshchestvo zavodchikov i fabrikantov (1906, an employers' union)
RIS	Russian Industrial Society (Obshchestvo dlia sodeistviia russkoi promyshlennosti i torgovle) (1867)
RSSP	Russian Society of Sugar Producers (Vserossiiskoe obshchestvo sakharozavodchikov) (1887; called the Biuro predstavitelei sakharozavodchikov, or Bureau of Sugar Producers' Representatives, 1887–97)
SRCIA	South Russian Coal and Iron Association (Sovet s″ezdov gornopromyshlennikov iuga Rossii) (1874)

The corporation under Russian law, 1800–1917

СОБРАНІЕ УЗАКОНЕНІЙ И РАСПОРЯЖЕНІЙ ПРАВИТЕЛЬСТВА,

ИЗДАВАЕМОЕ ПРИ ПРАВИТЕЛЬСТВУЮЩЕМЪ СЕНАТѢ.

2 ЯНВАРЯ № 1. **1895.**

СОДЕРЖАНІЕ:
Ст. 1. Объ утвержденіи устава товарищества мануфактуръ Герасима Разоренова и Ивана Кокорева.

ВЫСОЧАЙШЕ УТВЕРЖДЕННОЕ ПОЛОЖЕНІЕ КОМИТЕТА МИНИСТРОВЪ.

1. Объ утвержденіи устава товарищества мануфактуръ Герасима Разоренова и Ивана Кокорева.

Государь Императоръ, по положенію Комитета Министровъ, Высочайше повелѣть соизволилъ разрѣшить потомственному почетному гражданину Ивану Александровичу Кокореву и женѣ потомственнаго почетнаго гражданина Аннѣ Герасимовнѣ Кокоревой учредить товарищество на паяхъ, подъ наименованіемъ: «Товарищество мануфактуръ Герасима Разоренова и Ивана Кокорева», на основаніи устава, удостоеннаго Высочайшаго разсмотрѣнія и утвержденія въ С.-Петербургѣ, въ 9 день декабря 1894 года.

На подлинномъ написано: «Государь Императоръ уставъ сей разсматривать и Высочайше утвердить соизволилъ, въ С.-Петербургѣ, въ 9 день декабря 1894 года.
Подписалъ: Управляющій дѣлами Комитета Министровъ, Статсъ-Секретарь *А. Куломзинъ*.

УСТАВЪ
ТОВАРИЩЕСТВА МАНУФАКТУРЪ ГЕРАСИМА РАЗОРЕНОВА И ИВАНА КОКОРЕВА.

Цѣль учрежденія товарищества, права и обязанности его.

§ 1. Для содержанія и распространенія дѣйствій бумаготкацкой и отдѣлочной фабрики, принадлежащей женѣ потомственнаго почетнаго гражданина Аннѣ Герасимовнѣ Кокоревой и находящейся Костромской губерніи, Кинешемскаго уѣзда, въ селѣ Тезинѣ, учреждается товарищество на паяхъ, подъ наименованіемъ: «Товарищество мануфактуръ Герасима Разоренова и Ивана Кокорева».

Примѣчаніе 1. Учредители товарищества: потомственный по-

I

Zakon (The law), 1800–1856

> It is well known that the laws describe, so to speak, the internal life of the state. In them we see how its moral and political energies have come into being, taken shape, grown, and changed. Consequently, without knowledge of the laws, the history of the state can be neither clear nor authentic; and by the same token, laws without history often remain incomprehensible. Thus, the more promptly the laws are published, the more the sources of history will be available to contemporaries and the more authentically they will be made known to posterity.
>
> – Mikhail M. Speranskii[1]

It is one of the many ironies of Russian history that, as the tsarist empire gained influence in European political life by virtue of its diplomatic and military achievements, it gradually fell further behind Europe in terms of economic development. This process of increasing relative economic backwardness appears to have gathered momentum in the reigns of Catherine II (1762–96), Paul I (1796–1801), and Alexander I (1801–25). All three monarchs prided themselves on their bold vision and admiration for certain aspects of Western European culture: enlightened administration, Prussian military efficiency, and the Napoleonic reforms to 1811, respectively. However, the problem of economic backwardness apparently escaped their notice entirely. Russian armies marched triumphantly across Europe in 1799 and 1814, but economic output increased so slowly that the Russian economy failed to keep pace with that of the other major European powers.[2]

The international context

These patterns may be explained largely by the persistence of institutional obstacles to modern commercial practice under tsarist rule. The Russian

---

[1] Mikhail M. Speranskii, in Preface to Russia, *Polnoe sobranie zakonov Rossiiskoi imperii, sobranie 1*, 46 vols. (St. Petersburg, 1830–9), vol. 1, xvii.
[2] The following comparative figures are drawn from B. R. Mitchell, *European Historical Sta-*

merchant, although shrewd and diligent, relied more on intuition and the aid of loyal friends and relatives than on rational calculation and an understanding of trends in the world market. Double-entry bookkeeping, bills of exchange, and forecasts of economic trends remained mysteries to the ordinary merchants of the Russian provinces outside the ports of the Baltic and Black seas. English and American merchants in Russia in the early nineteenth century marveled at the skill of illiterate Russians in the use of the simple abacus, but they noted also the merchants' reliance on other hallmarks of their traditional culture: secrecy, cheating, and evasion in dealing with strangers. Such techniques proved more likely than honesty to win a tidy profit in the absence of a modern banking system, of strong legal guarantees of the right of private property, and of governmental policies favorable to commerce and industry. One British merchant noted the pride with which Russian merchants turned a dishonest profit: "A dextrous theft in the way of overreaching is regarded by them as the very triumph of their genius."[3]

As the industrial age began, the highly developed system of European commercial practices provided a firm organizational foundation for the emergence of the modern corporation. The international commodities markets managed the flow of cotton from the American South through the ports of New Orleans, Savannah, and Charleston to Liverpool and thence

tistics, 1750–1975, 2nd rev. ed. (New York, 1981), 412–13, 418; British figure for 1720 from B. R. Mitchell and Phyllis Deane, *Abstract of British Historical Statistics* (Cambridge, England, 1962), 131:

Russian and European pig iron production, 1720–1830 (thousands of metric tons)

Year	Russia	Great Britain	France	Germany
1720	10	25	—	—
1730	16	—	—	—
1740	25	—	—	—
1750	33	—	—	—
1760	60	—	—	—
1770	84	—	—	—
1788	125	69	—	—
1796	123	127	—	—
1806	146	248	—	—
1818	127	330	113 (1819)	—
1824	140	462 (1823)	198	85
1825	158	591	199	95
1830	187	688	266	110

[3] Peter Putnam, ed., *Seven Britons in Imperial Russia, 1698–1812* (Princeton, 1952), citing reports by John Carr (1804), William Coxe (1801), and Robert Kerr Porter (1805–7), 286 note 41, 274–5, 313 (quoted).

to spinners and weavers throughout Europe, including St. Petersburg and the Moscow region. Central to this system was the smooth functioning of expert brokerage houses, often staffed in the major cities by trusted friends and relatives of the senior partners in London, Paris, or Hamburg. Alfred D. Chandler stressed that this form of pre-corporate capitalism, based on the family firm or partnership, had evolved out of the late medieval mercantile practices of Italian and Flemish traders. In the early nineteenth century it still rested on the same devices that had emerged more than five centuries before: market reports, expertise in handling exchange rates among major currencies, and double-entry bookkeeping.[4]

However, it is no less important to note that this sophisticated worldwide system had made scarcely any imprint on the Russian merchants as late as the reign of Nicholas I (1825–55). Following the destruction of Novgorod and its Hanseatic German community by Moscow in 1494, could Russian merchants even have dreamed of emulating the entrepreneurial talents of the merchant adventurers of England, whose trade in woolen cloth in Norway, Spain, Prussia, and the Netherlands began in the late fourteenth century and lasted for centuries thereafter? Could the most cosmopolitan of Russian cities, St. Petersburg, have rivaled Amsterdam, which, since the seventeenth century, had functioned as a center of commercial information throughout the world?[5] As the French say, to ask the question is to answer it.

To this impressive system of international commerce the major European powers added the corporation. The essential feature of the corporation, the principle of limited liability of investors, enabled this form of enterprise to dominate the market-oriented economies of the modern world. This principle attracted massive amounts of capital into commercial, financial, and industrial projects too large for an individual or a partnership to undertake safely. To be sure, the participation in a single business venture by hundreds of persons unknown to one another also carried special risks: the dangers of fraud and speculation practiced by managers against the interests of the stockholders and the public. The

---

[4] Alfred D. Chandler, Jr., *The Visible Hand: The Managerial Revolution in American Business* (Cambridge, Mass., 1977), chap. 1: "The Traditional Enterprise in Commerce," describes these institutions of world trade on the eve of the industrial age.

[5] The early history of the merchant adventurers is described in Eleanora M. Carus-Wilson, *Medieval Merchant Venturers*, 2nd ed. (London, 1967), chap. 3. On Amsterdam as an major information exchange, see Woodruff D. Smith, "The Function of Commercial Centers in the Modernization of European Capitalism: Amsterdam as an Information Center in the Seventeenth Century," *Journal of Economic History*, 44, no. 4 (Dec. 1984), 985–1005.

restrictive corporate legislation passed by the major European governments in the wake of the South Sea Bubble of 1720 can best be understood as an effort to encourage the beneficial effects of corporate activity while minimizing the harmful ones. Strict controls persisted throughout the eighteenth century. In France, the revolutionary National Assembly briefly outlawed all companies with unnamed shares, which were susceptible to speculation, and required that all corporations henceforth receive legislative approval.[6]

However, as the benefits of corporate enterprise became clear in the early industrial era, restrictions gradually fell away. In England, all enterprises except banks were allowed to incorporate freely under the Companies Act of 1844, and their investors obtained limited liability in 1856. Faced with the strict provisions of the Commercial Code of 1807, which required that each new corporation (*société anonyme*) receive a special charter from the national government, French entrepreneurs adapted to the needs of the modern economy the limited partnership, or *société en commandite*, whose investors (*commanditaires*) but not partners (*commandités*) enjoyed limited liability. In the early nineteenth century, a new, quasi-public corporation became popular, called the *société en commandite par actions*, the shares of which were bought and sold publicly. Like the simple and limited partnership, it was managed by partners, who bore full liability for the debts of the enterprise; however, as in the *société anonyme*, its basic capital was divided into shares (*actions*), which circulated freely on the stock exchange. These stockholders did not participate in the management of the company, even to vote, but they did enjoy limited liability. This arrangement allowed the full partners to maintain control of the enterprise while attracting needed capital from the public. Despite public concern prompted by episodes of stock-exchange speculation in the 1830s, a bill to outlaw the limited partnership failed in the National Assembly in 1838. Following the implementation of restrictions on the *commandite* in 1856, the legislature in 1867 allowed the establishment of the *société anonyme* by registration instead of state concession, a change that opened the way for hundreds

---

[6] A good discussion of the South Sea Bubble and the Bubble Act of 1720, which made incorporation difficult and led English businessmen to devise the unincorporated joint-stock company, is Armand B. DuBois, *The English Business Company After the Bubble Act* (New York, 1938; reprinted 1971). The restrictions on corporations decreed at the height of the French Revolution (Aug. 24, 1793–Nov. 1, 1795) are discussed by Charles E. Freedeman, *Joint-Stock Enterprise in France, 1807–1867: From Privileged Company to Modern Corporation* (Chapel Hill, 1979), 9–10.

of new corporations and consigned the *commandite* to obscurity.[7] Prussia followed suit in 1870.[8]

By the middle decades of the nineteenth century, therefore, the major European economies had adapted to the dynamism of the corporation. Before turning to the fate of the corporation under Russian law, we must examine another feature of economic history in the modern world. In the felicitous terminology of the comparative historian Douglass C. North, variations in the economic performance of different countries in the past several centuries reflected more than the operation of trends susceptible to neoclassical economic analysis. It is essential to apply "a theory of property rights that describes the individual and group incentives in the system"; also needed are "a theory of the state, since it is the state that specifies and enforces property rights," and "a theory of ideology that explains how different perceptions of reality affect the reaction of individuals to the changing 'objective' situation." In early modern Spain, for example, in contrast to the Netherlands and Britain, the lack of firm property rights hindered entrepreneurship.

> The widely reported observation that the hidalgos had an aversion for trade and commerce and a preference for careers in the church, army, or government suggests that they were rational men. The structure of property rights that evolved in response to the fiscal policies of the government simply discouraged individuals from undertaking many productive activities.[9]

These three qualitative aspects of economic history – property rights, state policy, and ideology – deserve special attention in the Russian case as well. In the first category may be included various obstacles to the emergence of a vigorous merchant class in Muscovy and the Russian Empire, such as the ban on the ownership of populated land by merchants until 1861 and the perpetuation of communal ownership of land by peasants until the early twentieth century. The most capable finance ministers, from Egor F. Kankrin to Sergei Iu. Witte, imposed a bewildering variety of economic restrictions that proceeded logically from the state's autocratic power to define and manipulate, largely for its own fiscal purposes, the social

---

[7] Freedeman, *Enterprise*, esp. chaps. 5–6.
[8] The law of June 11, 1870 in the North German Confederation is discussed in Hans Würdinger, "Aktiengesellschaft; Recht der AG; Geschichte und Struktur," in Ervin von Beckerath and others, eds., *Handwörterbuch der Sozialwissenschaften*, 12 vols. (Stuttgart, 1956–65), vol. 1, 124.
[9] Douglass C. North, *Structure and Change in Economic History* (New York, 1981), 7–8, 151–2.

estates (*sosloviia*) that it ruled. Finally, the ideology of the bureaucrats must be contrasted to that of the commercial-industrial elites, with particular attention to the conflicts over economic policy in the final decade of the imperial period.

In the chapters that follow, North's analytical approach will prove useful in illuminating several crucial aspects of corporate development under the last four Russian emperors. Restrictions on the right of corporations to own certain kinds of property severely constrained the development of the economy from 1863 onward. The state imposed these and other fetters on corporations within the framework of the particularly repressive corporate law of 1836; it refused to enact significant reforms of this law in the following eight decades, despite increasingly vociferous demands by capitalist leaders throughout the empire; and it continued to the very end to exercise a form of tutelage over corporations that acted as a distinct disincentive to corporate entrepreneurship. The ideological preconceptions that underlay this policy met a serious challenge from the Russian corporate elite, which, by 1905, had matured sufficiently to articulate its own vision of a freer and more rational economic policy toward corporations. However, the state refused to modify its essentially arbitrary and inconsistent laws in the interest of rationality and positive incentives, despite the deleterious consequences of such laws. This autocratic impulse remained remarkably constant over the centuries, an element of continuity in tsarist policies toward the corporation from the era of Peter the Great to the very eve of World War I.

Russian corporate law before 1836

Neither the benefits nor the shortcomings of the corporation were much appreciated in Russia before 1825, owing to the infinitesimal number of companies chartered by the imperial government.[10] Following the example of the Western European governments in the eighteenth century, Russian policy makers required that every corporation receive a special charter from the state. The advantages of this so-called concessionary system of

---

[10] The only substantial studies of these companies are N. N. Firsov, *Russkie torgovo-promyshlennye kompanii v pervuiu polovinu XVIII stoletiia* (Kazan, 1896); Aleksandr S. Lappo-Danilevskii, "Russkie promyshlennye i torgovye kompanii v pervoi polovine XVIII veka," *Zhurnal ministerstva narodnogo prosveshcheniia*, 320, no. 2 (Dec. 1898), part 2, 306–66, and 321, no. 2 (Feb. 1899), part 2, 371–436 (reprinted as monograph, St. Petersburg, 1899); and A. I. Iukht, "Torgovye kompanii v Rossii v seredine XVIII v.," *Istoricheskie zapiski*, 111 (1984), 238–95.

incorporation were several. First, only those projects that promised substantial benefits to the state and the economy would be permitted. Second, the number of applications was bound to be small, in view of the considerable time and expense required to take the draft charter through the bureaucratic maze. Third, the clauses regarding the financial structure of the company strictly defined the responsibilities of the managers toward investors so as to minimize opportunities for fraud. Finally, the prestige of the state would stand behind the new enterprise, thereby helping to coax capital investments out of the pockets of a public unused to capitalist institutions imported from Western Europe.

From the reign of Peter the Great (1682–1725) to the early nineteenth century, however, the Russian law remained vague in the extreme. In a decree dated October 27, 1699, Peter encouraged merchants to organize "trading companies [*torgovye kompanii*], as in other states," to export raw materials from Archangel, Astrakhan, and Novgorod. Unfortunately, this document left undefined the very meaning of "company" and failed to mention the principle of limited liability. Firsov explained Peter's inattention to such details by advancing the plausible supposition that the monarch's main purpose in fostering foreign and domestic commerce was to increase the revenues of the state; it did not occur to him to establish rational incentives for the merchants who were called upon to bear the risks of such undertakings.[11]

Peter's decree typified both his enthusiastic admiration for European technology and his disdain toward European legal norms such as the inviolability of private property. The energetic autocrat, who terrorized underlings by wielding his famous staff (*dubina*), had no patience with market forces. He knew all too well the traditional secretiveness and acquisitive spirit of the Russian merchants and apparently failed to realize that these precapitalist attitudes were unfortunately reinforced, if not caused, by the state's penchant for arbitrary taxation and its refusal to allow anyone but the gentry (*dvorianstvo*) to purchase land populated with

---

[11] Peter's decree appears in *PSZ* 1–1706. Avgust I. Kaminka, *Aktsionernaia kompaniia: iuridicheskoe issledovanie* (St. Petersburg, 1902), 377, described several ventures launched by influential statesmen in the eighteenth century; he argued that such enterprises enriched not the stockholders but the promoters. The index to the first series of the *PSZ* mentions no corporate charters under the headings "trading company" (*torgovaia kompaniia*) and "trading partnership" (*torgovoe tovarishchestvo*); has no entries at all for other words denoting "company" – *aktsionernoe obshchestvo, kompaniia, obshchestvo,* or *tovarishchestvo;* and lists factories and plants (*fabriki i zavody*) only by function, usually with reference to state-owned armaments plants.

serfs.¹² Peter's reliance on brute force was illustrated by the text of one of the earliest documents that can be considered a charter (*ustav*) of a merchants' partnership. Although this decree, issued in 1711, mentioned neither limited liability nor the public sale of shares, it authorized the transfer of a state-owned linen factory in Moscow to a group of merchants. Peter promised to reward them with his imperial favor (*milost'*) if the enterprise prospered; but if it failed, each partner would be fined a thousand silver rubles.¹³ A less effective incentive for entrepreneurship could hardly be imagined.

Catherine the Great (1762–96), although better educated than Peter, likewise showed little solicitude for corporate enterprise. Her practice of lavishing state wealth on a small circle of courtiers represented a continuation of the policy of Empress Elizabeth, who had allowed treasury officials like Count Petr I. Shuvalov to amass a fortune from such privileges as the monopoly on fishing rights on the White Sea. The empresses' favoritism apparently had a hidden economic cost.¹⁴ Merchants complained in vain that as bearers of the risks and of state taxes associated with commerce and industry, they should enjoy a monopoly on such activities instead of being forced to compete in the market against gentry landlords, who bore no taxes and benefited as well from their monopoly on unpaid serf labor. Successful entrepreneurs might grow rich under such a system; but even the largest undertakings, like those of the remarkable Demidov family, ironmasters in the Ural mountains, did not take the form of the corporation.¹⁵

---

¹² A. Leroy-Beaulieu, *L'empire des tsars et des Russes*, 3 vols. (Paris, 1881–9), vol. 1, 304–5; Aristide Fenster, *Adel und Okonomie im vorindustriellen Russland: Die unternehmerische Betätigung der Gutsbesitzer in der grossgewerblichen Wirtschaft im 17. und 18. Jahrhundert* (Wiesbaden, 1983), esp. chap. 5 on the conflict between the gentry and merchants over the right to engage in industrial enterprises. Fenster's bibliography contains many useful references to recent scholarship on this important issue. A detailed study of the merchants' legal disadvantages, including the gentry's exclusive right to own land populated with serfs, is Manfred Hildermeier, *Bürgertum und Stadt in Russland 1760–1870: Rechtliche Lage und soziale Struktur* (Cologne, 1986). Part I, chap. 4, *Standesflucht*, describes the striving of prosperous merchants to rise into the gentry estate to receive its legal advantages, thus weakening the merchant estate still further.

¹³ *PSZ* 1–2324, dated February 28, 1711.

¹⁴ On P. I. Shuvalov (1710–62), *RBS*, vol. 23, 490–503. A thorough study of aristocratic entrepreneurs, complete with tables of major enterprises in various sectors, is Fenster, *Adel und Okonomie*.

¹⁵ "Rukavkin, Danila," in *RBS*, vol. 17, 435. An informative account of the obstacles to merchant entrepreneurship under Catherine is Wallace C. Daniel, "Grigorii Teplov and the Conception of Order: The Commission on Commerce and the Role of the Merchants in Russia," *Canadian-American Slavic Studies*, 16, nos. 3–4 (Fall–Winter 1982), 410–31. See Nikolai I. Pavlenko, *Istoriia metallurgii v Rossii XVIII veka: zavody i zavodovladel'tsy* (Moscow,

Catherine herself seemed unaware of the economic benefits of a firm legal order. Although she founded the great port of Odessa in 1794, granted tracts of land to German Mennonite farmers, and encouraged the Free Economic Society, she destroyed institutions of self-government in Riga and other Baltic ports and thereby earned the everlasting resentment of the German merchants there.[16] She issued no general law to encourage or regulate corporations. Her only mention of them occurred in a decree enumerating the powers of the police to enforce the regulations of each "society, partnership, brotherhood, or similar institution," and to "destroy and ban" any that injured "the general welfare." During Catherine's entire reign, the state chartered only four corporations, two of which were to export a raw material, grain, to Europe.[17]

In 1799, Paul I approved the creation of the Russian-American Company, formed by the merger of two partnerships of merchants active in the fur and fishing trades along the Siberian and Alaskan coasts. However, this company enjoyed so many governmental privileges, including a monopoly on the sale of furs, that it can best be understood as a mechanism by which the state sought to derive tax revenues from the eastern frontier of the empire. In fact, a third of the company's profits passed to the state, and its leading figure, Aleksandr A. Baranov (1747–1819), functioned as the de facto governor of Alaska. The corporate form of organization had the singular benefit of placing the natural resources of Alaska in the hands of merchants, not bureaucrats, but after Baranov's death the company earned ever smaller profits. Only in 1821 did its investors begin to enjoy limited liability. Eventually an enormous drain on the treasury, the Russian-American Company fell under direct state control in the 1840s. It perished quietly after the sale of Alaska to the United States in 1867.[18]

1962), esp. chap. 8, section 3, on the movement of successful metal producers into the gentry estate. On the Demidov family, *RBS*, vol. 6, 209–32; and Hugh D. Hudson, Jr., *The Rise of the Demidov Family and the Russian Iron Industry in the Eighteenth Century* (Newtonville, Mass., 1986).

[16] See G. G. Marazli, ed., *Iz proshlogo Odessy: sbornik statei*, comp. L. M. de-Ribas (Odessa, 1894); and Patricia Herlihy, *Odessa: A History, 1794–1914* (Cambridge, Mass., 1986). On the Baltic cities, an especially vigorous indictment of Russian rule is Julius Wilhelm Albert von Eckardt, *Bürgerthum und Bürokratie: Vier Kapitel aus der neuesten livländische Geschichte* (Leipzig, 1870), viii–ix. C. Mettig, *Geschichte der Stadt Riga* (Riga, 1897), also idealized the medieval system of self-government and criticized the diminution of the city's liberties in the eighteenth century.

[17] *PSZ* 1–15379, dated April 8, 1782, articles 64 and 65. The corporate charters appear in *PSZ* 1–12904, dated June 1, 1767, and *PSZ* 1–13886, dated October 18, 1772. Only four corporate charters appear in the *Polnoe sobranie zakonov* under Catherine II, but it is possible that others were approved without being published.

[18] This company has received more attention from historians than any other in Russian

The first general decree to uphold the principle of limited liability for investors appeared in Russia in 1805. Emperor Alexander I, still in his relatively enlightened period, before the epic clash with Napoleon, issued a decree that cited a legal decision of the previous month, according to which the founders and stockholders of a bankrupt shipbuilding company were not to be held personally liable for the debts of the enterprise. To allow creditors to collect the company's debts from individual stockholders, it announced, would be "completely contrary to the very essence of this kind of company." In an implicit reference to the charter of this company, issued in 1782, the decree reiterated "the rule that a joint-stock company is liable only for the capital invested in it [*pravilo, chto aktsionernaia kompaniia otvechaet odnim skladochnym kapitalom*] and that in case of failure [*pri neudachakh*] none of its stockholders shall lose any more capital than he has invested in the company."[19]

Less than two years later, a statute dated January 1, 1807, clearly demarcated joint-stock companies from smaller enterprises that neither provided limited liability for investors nor required confirmation by the tsar.[20] The terminology employed in the law of 1807 remained in use for more than a century.

Under the system of social estates by which the autocratic state ordered Russian society from 1649 to 1917, merchants enjoyed the right to engage in commerce and industry as well as certain privileges, such as freedom from military duty and corporal punishment, in exchange for an annual guild membership payment and unpaid service in various elective municipal posts.[21] Although exceptions to these rules in favor of the gentry had

---

history. See Mary E. Wheeler, "The Origins of the Russian-American Company," *Jahrbücher für Geschichte Osteuropas*, N.S., 14, no. 4 (Dec. 1966), 485–94. On Baranov, see the article by S. Ogorodnikov, *RBS*, vol. 2, 478–9; and Alton S. Donnelly, "Baranov, Aleksandr Andreevich," in *MERSH*, vol. 3, 88–92. Three informative studies of the company's operations are Semen B. Okun', *The Russian-American Company*, trans. Carl Ginsburg (Cambridge, Mass., 1951); Richard A. Pierce, ed., *Documents on the History of the Russian-American Company*, trans. Marina Ramsey (Kingston, Ontario, 1976); and P. A. Tikhmenev, *A History of the Russian-American Company*, trans. and ed. Richard A. Pierce and Alton S. Donnelly (Seattle, 1978). Since 1972, Pierce has published an impressive series of monographs and documents on Russian America at his Limestone Press in Kingston, Ontario. A useful overview, with bibliography, is Alton S. Donnelly, "Russian-American Company," in *MERSH*, vol. 32, 38–44. On limited liability, *PSZ* 1–28756 (1821).

[19] *PSZ* 1–21900, dated September 6, 1805. The charter of this company does not appear in the *PSZ* volumes for 1781, 1782, or 1783 and presumably was never published as an imperial statute, as it should have been.
[20] *PSZ* 1–22418.
[21] Historians employ the word "estate" to denote the Russian *soslovie*, although in Muscovy and imperial Russia the estates enjoyed far fewer rights of self-government than did their counterparts in Europe: the French *états* and the German *Stände*. The Russian word *kupets*

severely eroded the merchants' nominal monopoly on trade and manufacturing,[22] the law of 1807 reiterated these privileges and specified the various kinds of enterprises in which merchants were to pursue their businesses and from which persons in all other estates were to be excluded. These were, one, the simplest form of business firm, composed of a single merchant enrolled in one of the three urban guilds; two, a "full partnership" (*polnoe tovarishchestvo*), in which all the partners, members of the same merchant guild, assumed full liability for the debts of the firm; and three, a "limited partnership" (*tovarishchestvo na vere*), composed of full partners and outside investors of any social estate. Only the last enjoyed limited liability.[23] These two forms of partnerships, called "trading firms" (*torgovye doma*; singular, *torgovyi dom*), did not require the approval of the central government. They were established by the full partners through the signing of a contract, which was then presented to the municipal clerk. The many thousands of such firms in Russia lie outside the scope of the present study.[24]

is generally translated as "merchant," but under Russian law the merchants (*kuptsy*; collective noun, *kupechestvo*) could own and operate manufacturing enterprises as well. Some informative recent works on the impact of the estate structure on Russian urban life are Hans-Joachim Torke, *Die staatsbedingte Gesellschaft im Moskauer Reich: Zar und Zemlja in der altrussischen Herrschaftsverfassung 1613–1689* (Leiden, 1974); J. Michael Hittle, *The Service City: State and Townsmen in Russia, 1600–1800* (Cambridge, Mass., 1979); Alfred J. Rieber, *Merchants and Entrepreneurs in Imperial Russia* (Chapel Hill, 1982); Manfred Hildermeier, "Was war das meščanstvo?: Zur rechtlichen und sozialen Verfassung des unteren städtischen Standes in Russland," *Forschungen zur osteuropäischen Geschichte*, 36 (1985), 15–53; and Hildermeier, *Bürgertum und Stadt*. Gregory L. Freeze, "The *Soslovie* (Estate) Paradigm and Russian Social History," *American Historical Review*, 91, no. 1 (Feb. 1986), 11–36, esp. 14–21, addresses the semantic problems associated with the application of the term *soslovie* to eighteenth-century Russia.

[22] See the laws on "trading peasants" (*torguiushchie krest'iane*), which allowed the gentry to receive dues called *obrok* in cash or kind from serfs engaged in trade: *PSZ* 1–10486, dated December 1, 1755; *PSZ* 1–14275 of March 17, 1775; *PSZ* 1–24992 of February 11, 1812; *PSZ* 1–25113 of May 22, 1812; and *PSZ* 1–25302 of December 29, 1812.

[23] For an intelligent discussion of these forms of enterprise, see V. Maksimov, *O tovarish-chestvakh*, 2nd ed. (Moscow, 1911), 7–28; and the relevant articles in the Commercial Code, 2126–2138, reproduced in Maksimov, 58–66.

[24] The number of trading firms grew from 1,625 in 1892 to 3,593 in 1905, 5,801 in 1911, and 9,202 in 1914, but their aggregate economic importance remained minor. In 1914, for example, the entire basic capital stock of over nine thousand trading firms amounted to 333.1 million rubles (an average of 36,199 rubles), while the 2,263 corporations, excluding railroads, in the empire in that year were based on stock worth 4.6 billion rubles, an average of over two million per company. Leonid E. Shepelev, *Aktsionernye kompanii v Rossii* (Leningrad, 1973), 232–3; Shepelev, "Chastnokapitalisticheskie torgovo-promyshlennye predpriiatiia Rossii v kontse XIX-nachale XX vv. i ikh arkhivnye fondy," *Informatsionnyi biulleten' Glavnogo arkhivnogo upravleniia MVD SSSR*, 1958, no. 10 (Oct.), 79. Valerii I. Bovykin, *Formirovanie finansovogo kapitala v Rossii, konets XIX v.–1908 g.* (Moscow, 1984), 111–19, provides precise statistics showing the relative shares of total production by joint-stock companies, share partnerships, and trading firms in various sectors.

The law of 1807 devoted only two sentences to the corporation. Part 1, article 1, noted that members of any free estate – notably the gentry – were entitled to participate in a corporation without joining the merchant estate.[25] However, because corporations enjoyed the privilege of limited liability and could be established only for undertakings of national economic importance, their creation required the permission of the tsar himself. Further than this the laws of 1805 and 1807 did not go. No reference was made to the internal structure of a corporation or to the rights and responsibilities of its managers and stockholders. Such details appeared only in the charter of each new company, which functioned essentially as a separate statute in the absence of a general corporate law.

Unfortunately, even the uncomplicated decrees of 1805 and 1807 allowed a certain terminological confusion to develop, one that was destined to persist to the very end of the tsarist period. The law of 1807 differentiated the corporation from the full and trust partnerships by calling it, somewhat awkwardly, a "partnership with shares" (*tovarishchestvo po uchastkam*), such shares to be sold to investors under the principle of limited liability. Various charters granted to corporations in the preceding decades had employed other names for the corporation, based on either French or Russian words. The terms *aktsioneroe obshchestvo* and *aktsionernaia kompaniia* derived from the French words for "company" (*société* and *compagnie*) and for "share" (*action*), either through translation (*obshchestvo* for *société*) or direct borrowing (*kompaniia* for *compagnie*; *aksiia* for *action*). The Russian words *tovarishchestvo* (partnership) and *pai* (share) also appeared in tsarist documents, as in the phrase *tovarishchesvto na paiakh* and *paevoe tovarishchestvo*. (Strangely enough, the official term *tovarishchestvo po uchastkam* occurred only rarely in the charters themselves.) These inconsistencies continued in later years. In 1826, for example, one charter referred to the enterprise as a *torgovaia kompaniia* in the title and a *torgovoe obshchestvo po aktsiiam* in the text.[26]

It is essential to note that, whatever name a given company happened

---

[25] Articles 6 and 7 did mention, however, that a law dated November 4, 1802, confirmed the right of a member of the gentry not on active military duty or in civil service to enroll in the first or second merchant guild as a wholesale trader without losing his gentry privileges. The gradual decay of the estate system in the century before 1917 under the influence of decrees such as these remains to be examined in detail by historians. Hildermeier, *Bürgertum*, makes this phenomenon one of his major themes, for example, in his discussion of "the crisis of the guild merchants" at the end of Catherine's reign and "the de facto dissolution of the urban estates" under the impact of guild reforms promulgated in 1863 and 1865.

[26] *PSZ* 2–145, dated February 13, 1826.

to bear, all enterprises distinguished by their imperial charter and guarantee of limited liability to investors operated for the next century under a single system of corporate law. In the chapters that follow, the English words "corporation" and "company," essentially synonyms, will apply to them all. When it becomes necessary to make finer distinctions, the term "joint-stock company" will be used for the *aktsionernoe obshchestvo* or *aktsionernaia kompaniia*, and "share partnership" will denote the *tovarishchestvo na paiakh*.

The rudimentary nature of the law of 1807 may be seen as an indication of the government's lack of interest in corporate enterprise, even in the post-Napoleonic era, when corporations began to develop rapidly in Europe. One of the leaders of the rebellion against autocracy in December 1825 blamed the government for having stifled the entrepreneurial spirit within the Russian merchant elite:

In the first two [merchant] guilds there are many well-trained, capable, and rather enterprising people whose character bears the imprint of the Russian national spirit [*russkoi narodnosti*], ... but, lacking encouragement from the government, they remain restricted to the most paltry activities; without sufficient capital to create companies, they have left all the benefits of external commerce to foreigners and content themselves with enterprises of limited significance.[27]

This critic grasped the essential incompatibility between traditional methods of autocratic rule and the modern capitalist economy, in which the corporation occupied a central position. In Weberian terms, the proponents of corporate enterprise from the 1820s onward advocated "rational-legal" norms of bureaucratic policy and administration, which would promote the development of capitalist institutions. In contrast, the tsars and their ministers adhered to their familiar mode of behavior, best described as "military-autocratic." Strictly speaking, the Romanov monarchy qualified as a "traditional" regime in Weber's terminology because it drew its legitimacy from tradition, but this term obscured the reforming zeal with which tsarist ministers, often endowed with superior education and impelled by the highest ideals of state service, mandated sweeping

---

[27] Aleksandr I. Iakubovich, "Pis'mo k imperatoru Nikolaiu Pavlovichu," dated Dec. 28, 1825, in A. K. Borozdin, ed., *Iz pisem i pokazanii dekabristov: kritika sovremennogo sostoianiia Rossii i plany budushchego ustroistva* (St. Petersburg, 1906), 79, quoted in A. I. Klibanov, "Aleksandr Ivanovich Iakubovich: deistvitel'nost' i legenda," *Istoricheskie zapiski*, 106 (1981), 234. Klibanov noted that Iakubovich, who had met representatives of the British East India Company in Tiflis, may have had that great company in mind when he criticized the Russian government for its apathy.

changes in the social and economic order, principally for the sake of military power.[28]

As he entered the second decade of his reign, Emperor Nicholas I was forced to recognize the enormous costs of maintaining a legal system that discouraged corporate enterprise. In 1836, his ministers promulgated a statute on corporations, modeled on European laws, that was destined to last as long as the Romanov dynasty itself. Although the short debate surrounding the creation of this statute was conducted in the dry and abstruse language of bureaucrats – no merchants were consulted by the legislators – this episode constituted a drama of the greatest importance. As Richard S. Wortman has noted, the Russian legal reform of 1864, based on Western norms of jurisprudence, constituted a major anomaly in the tsarist system of government. "For the Russian autocracy to accept an independent judiciary required that it betray its essence and cease to be the Russian autocracy."[29] Mutatis mutandis, as economists say, the importation of the European principle of corporate entrepreneurship under Nicholas I, like that of an independent judiciary under Alexander II, posed at least an implicit challenge to the pretensions and prerogatives of the absolutist state in Russia. By what legislative measures would the tsarist ministers seek to promote the growth of the corporation in the interests of economic development, while at the same time regulating and constricting that growth so that the state would not, in Wortman's words, "betray its essence"?

---

[28] On the rational-legal type of authority, the classic definition is that of Max Weber, in *The Theory of Social and Economic Organization*, trans. A. M. Henderson and Talcott Parsons, ed. Talcott Parsons (New York, 1964), 329–41, esp. 338–9: "Capitalism is the most rational economic basis for bureaucratic administration and enables it to develop in the most rational form, especially because, from a fiscal point of view, it supplies the necessary money resources." In the same work, 193, Weber described the specific cultural context most conducive to the emergence of capitalist institutions: "The extraordinary importance of the highest possible degree of calculability as the basis for efficient capital accounting will be evidenced again and again through the discussion of the sociological conditions of economic activity. It is far from the case that only economic factors are important to it. On the contrary, it will be shown that the most various sorts of external and subjective barriers have existed to account for the fact that capital accounting has arisen as a basic form of economic calculation only in the Western World." By the same token, the notoriously insensitive and arbitrary Russian state, despite its impressive administrative complexity, does not deserve the Weberian label "bureaucratic," which connotes an enlightened and efficient state apparatus organized along rational lines. "The bureaucratic state order is especially important; in its most rational development, it is precisely characteristic of the modern state." Max Weber, "Politics as a Vocation," in *From Max Weber: Essays in Sociology*, ed. Hans H. Gerth and C. Wright Mills (New York, 1958), 82.

[29] Richard S. Wortman, *The Development of a Russian Legal Consciousness* (Chicago, 1976), 285.

The law of 1836 and its inconsistencies

Despite the strong element of continuity in tsarist policies toward the corporation over the centuries, the personalities of tsars and their ministers occasionally left a profound impression on the provisions of the law. This was especially true in the case of the corporate law of 1836, whose principal author, Minister of Finance Egor F. Kankrin (1774–1845), imparted to this landmark legislation its peculiarly repressive coloration.

Of Kankrin's dominance over economic policy in the reign of Nicholas I there can be no doubt. He served an unusually long term, from 1823 to 1844. His many projects for financial reform rested on a firm understanding of economic theory that was all the more remarkable for his failure to finish the undergraduate course of study at the University of Giessen. Having distinguished himself as a military quartermaster during Napoleon's invasion of Russia, Kankrin retained throughout his term as finance minister his youthful habits of frugality and caution. It was as if he continued to act as the quartermaster of the entire Russian state for the sake of its vast military institutions. As "the most influential of the Tsar's advisors on economic policy," Kankrin "knew perhaps better than anyone else how weak the economy actually was, if only because it consistently failed to supply the revenue the state needed for its operation." He encouraged domestic manufacturing by such inexpensive measures as protective tariffs, industrial exhibitions, and councils of manufacturing and commerce in the 1820s; he stabilized the weak Russian currency by replacing the grossly inflated assignats with a new paper currency (1839–42); and he promoted technical education. However, as early as the mid-1830s he viewed with alarm the first signs of industrial overproduction in the shallow domestic market. Throughout his long career, he refrained from any plan to shift the Russian economy from an agricultural to an industrial foundation.[30]

Kankrin's most famous statement betrayed his ignorance of the benefits of railroads in the largest country in the world. "Railroads do not always result from natural necessity, but are more often an object of artificial need or luxury. They encourage unnecessary travel from place to place, which is entirely typical of our time, and also fleece the public of excess

---

[30] Walter M. Pintner, *Russian Economic Policy under Nicholas I* (Ithaca, 1967), quotations from 253.

funds."[31] Especially troubling to this dour architect of Russian economic policy was the specter of social unrest that swept European capitals in 1830. Determined to shore up the financial structure of the state and even to give mild encouragement to domestic manufacturing, Kankrin remained tenaciously devoted to that most elusive goal of Russian statecraft, the preservation for yet another generation of the traditional social and political order that was threatened by new forces building strength in the more dynamic West.

These concerns were clearly reflected in the law on corporations that emerged, after a year of discussions and compromises, from the Committee of Ministers and received the tsar's confirmation on December 6, 1836. Because the work of Leonid E. Shepelev constitutes an example of competent and unbiased Soviet scholarship in the field of tsarist economic history, his findings, based on exhaustive research in the archive of the Ministry of Finance,[32] may be summarized briefly. Two purposes were to be served by a general law. On the one hand, the minister of internal affairs, Dmitrii N. Bludov, sought to encourage the kind of corporate entrepreneurship that was producing impressive rates of economic growth in Western Europe. (It must be pointed out, however, that Bludov misunderstood the essential nature of the modern corporation, believing incorrectly that it consisted in the sale of shares to the public rather than

[31] Quoted from his annual report of 1838 by Nina S. Kniapina, *Politika russkogo samoderzhaviia v oblasti promyshlennosti* (Moscow, 1966), 156.
[32] Leonid E. Shepelev, "Iz istorii russkogo aktsionernogo zakonodatel'stva (zakon 1836 g.)," in N. E. Nosov, ed., *Vnutrenniaia politika tsarizma (seredina XVI–nachalo XX veka* (Leningrad, 1967), 168–96; and Shepelev, *Kompanii*, 46–55. Shepelev's monograph contains much, but not all, of the useful material published in his earlier articles on this subject. Besides the article of 1967, these are Shepelev, "Tsarizm i aktsionernoe uchreditel'stvo v 1870–1910-kh godakh," in N. E. Nosov and others, eds., *Problemy krest'ianskogo zemlevladeniia i vnutrennei politiki Rossii: dooktiabr'skii period* (Leningrad, 1972), 274–318; and Shepelev, "Aktsionernoe zakonodatel'stvo Vremennogo pravitel'stva," in N. E. Nosov and others, eds., *Issledovaniia po sotsial'no-politicheskoi istorii Rossii: Sbornik statei pamiati B. A. Romanova* (Leningrad, 1971), 369–80. Shepelev, an archivist as well as an historian, has spent his career plumbing the riches of TsGIA, the imperial governmental archive in Leningrad. His work, well documented with archival citations, is also filled with generous quotations from the ministerial reports and minutes of conferences. It is no exaggeration to say that the present account, although hardly congruent with Soviet scholarship, depends heavily on the work of Shepelev and his colleagues at the Leningrad Branch of the Institute of History for archival information that would not otherwise be available. Other useful Soviet works on the subject of corporate law are Iurii Ia. Rybakov, *Promyshlennoe zakonodatel'stvo Rossii pervoi poloviny XIX veka (istochnikovedcheskie ocherki)* (Moscow, 1986); Vladimir Ia. Laverychev, *Tsarizm i rabochii vopros (1861–1917 gg.)* (Moscow, 1972); and the works cited therein. Two short treatments in French that add little to the accounts by Soviet historians also deserve mention: Alexandre Krimmer, *Sociétés de capitaux en Russie impériale et en Russie soviétique* (Tunis, 1934); and F. Mallieux, *La société anonyme d'après le droit civil russe* (Paris, 1902).

in the guarantee of limited liability to investors.)[33] On the other hand, the law also contained numerous restrictions because Kankrin, the finance minister, feared the economic effects of volatility in the corporate securities market in the early 1830s.

The tsarist government itself bore much responsibility for these problems. In order to stimulate investment in corporations, the state's Commercial Bank had lowered its interest rate on deposits from 5 to 4 percent in 1830. A brief spurt in the founding of new companies was followed by a dramatic rise in stock prices as some unscrupulous men manipulated the market to victimize the unsophisticated public. The Ministry of Finance defined stock-exchange speculation (*birzhevaia igra*) as "transactions with shares for a certain period" (*sdelki s aktsiiami na srok*) or agreements for "delivery of shares at a certain time at a definite price."[34] A related abuse, called "stock jobbing" (*azhiotazh*, from the French *agiotage*), was practiced by founders who, according to the ministry, set up new companies solely in order to make a quick profit by selling appreciating shares to the naive public, regardless of the eventual damage to the enterprise itself. The inevitable decline in stock prices in the mid-1830s produced several corporate bankruptcies that ruined not only small investors but also leading figures on the nascent Russian stock exchange.[35]

In response to a query from the Petersburg Commercial Court in 1835, the Petersburg Exchange Committee (PEC) admitted that corporate stocks and bonds had been traded illegally on the exchange. It was "a common occurrence" for the buyer and seller to sign a note (*nadpis'*) that specified the price of a packet of shares on a future date. Even if the note passed to another buyer, the terms of the deal, essentially a futures transaction in stocks and bonds, remained binding on the seller of the stock. Such deals "on delivery and on time" (*na raznost' i na srok*) appeared "perfectly correct" to the Petersburg merchants, despite their openly "speculative character," the more so because European governments, out of respect for the law of supply and demand, had abandoned their previous prohibition of this practice.[36]

The bureaucrats saw the matter differently, however. Although the state never outlawed futures trading in commodities,[37] speculation in

---

[33] Shepelev, *Kompanii*, 50, 48.
[34] Shepelev, *Kompanii*, 28, quotation from 41.
[35] Shepelev, *Kompanii*, 35; *azhiotazh* defined in note 41.
[36] Aleksandr G. Timofeev, *Istoriia S.-Peterburgskoi birzhi, 1703–1903 gg.* (St. Petersburg, 1903), 140–1.
[37] Timofeev, *Birzha*, 141.

stocks and bonds appeared too dangerous to be condoned. In their initial drafts of the corporate law, both Bludov and Kankrin explicitly prohibited "the purchase and sale of shares... not for cash and with delivery at a certain time [*k isvestnomu sroku*] and at a certain price."[38]

Kankrin was especially determined to quell the epidemic of stock jobbing by stifling economic development in general, if need be, in the hopes of winning public confidence for the few corporations that received the tsar's blessing. As he wrote to Bludov in March 1835,

> I cannot conceal the fact that the dubious successes of several companies founded in our country threaten to dissuade the public from all participation in them, all the more so because a small number of people have already been ruined by stock jobbing [*ot azhiotazha*]. For this reason, the government must exercise more care in the future. In this regard it is better to reject ten companies that fall short of perfection than to allow one to bring harm to the public and to the enterprise itself.[39]

The dilemma was clear to all. Excessive bureaucratic meddling could easily stifle the growth of corporations, but without firm regulation by the state, innocent investors faced scandalous treatment at the hands of mischievous dealers in the stock exchange. The major provisions of the law of 1836 can be understood only in terms of its pursuit of two essentially contradictory principles: the encouragement of corporate capitalism on the current West European model and bureaucratic regulation in the traditional Russian style. (Parenthetical references indicate the articles in the law of 1836 and the corresponding articles in the imperial Commercial Code, or *torgovyi ustav*.)[40]

In order to attract capital and entrepreneurial talent into solid corporations, the law guaranteed limited liability for investors and managers (articles 1 and 33; 2139 and 2172). Central to the new law was a concession system in which proposed charters underwent review by the appropriate ministries and the Committee of Ministers (from 1905 onward, the Council of Ministers) before being submitted to the tsar for his signature (article 2; 2140). The legislation also provided for the granting of special privileges and favors, such as monopoly rights, tax exemptions, and financial support, by the State Council to a new company for a specific period of time if it

---

[38] Quoted in Shepelev, *Kompanii*, 53.
[39] Quoted in Shepelev, *Kompanii*, 35.
[40] See *Polnyi svod zakonov*, vol. 10, part 1, in various editions, for example, 1857 and 1900. A convenient compilation of these articles, with references to the law of 1836 and later amendments up to 1911, is Maksimov, *O tovarishchestvakh*, 29–53; see also 66–102 for the text of Commercial Code articles 2139–2198 (plus appendices to 2158).

exploited a newly patented device or undertook a project of state significance, for example, a railroad, shipping line, or water supply system (articles 3–9, 21; 2143–2147, 2159).

These three principles remained in force to the end of the tsarist period. Although the idea of limited liability constituted the essential feature of the modern corporation in all countries, the two other requirements reflected the peculiar concerns of the regime. The bureaucrats' insistence on the concession system of incorporation testified to their distrust of spontaneous economic activity, an attitude held by all the Russian autocrats from Peter the Great to Stalin. Paradoxically, however, corporations gained an indirect benefit from the restrictive nature of the concession system. Although the law explicitly denied that the state endorsed any particular company or guaranteed its success (article 4; 2142), the tsar's signature on the corporate charter allowed the managers to claim that their enterprise had been "confirmed by the tsar" (*vysochaishe utverzhdennyi*). This bit of imperial favor tended to attract investors who might otherwise have remained indifferent to the stock market. The granting of monopolies and other privileges represented another distinctive feature of Russian economic life since the reigns of the Muscovite tsars, namely the dependence of private entrepreneurs on the overwhelming financial power of the state. Both the concession system and the issuing of special favors figured prominently in the policies of European states in the 1820s and 1830s, but nowhere did these principles persist with such force into the twentieth century as in the Russian Empire.

Many articles of the law reflected the fact that Kankrin feared the negative consequences of free enterprise more than the dangers of excessive regulation. Among the provisions intended to protect the public from fraud and poor management was the stipulation that no company could begin operations until all shares were sold and all payments for shares were collected within the period specified in the charter (article 16; 2154). The owner's name was to be inscribed on each share, and after the sale the new owner's name must be entered both on the share and in a special book at the company's headquarters (articles 22 and 29; 2160 and 2167). Partial payment for shares (i.e., the purchase of shares "on margin") was allowed only for companies that were small enough to begin operations without amassing the full amount of basic capital (article 23; 2161), and the minimal amounts of capital necessary for this purpose had to be specified in the charter (article 24; 2162). Article 27 (2165) prohibited founders from purchasing more than one-fifth of the total share capital, so as to prevent them from seizing financial control of the company, increasing the price of stock artificially, and then selling the overvalued securities to the unsuspecting public. To minimize the danger of embezzlement in the crucial period between the announcement of a company's confirmation by the tsar and the first general assembly of stockholders, articles 27 and 28 (2165 and 2166) required that the founders record all full and partial payments for shares in a special "sealed book" (*shnurovaia kniga*).

To guard against arbitrary action by the managers, the law placed primary authority in the hands of the stockholders. At its first meeting, the general assembly of stockholders (*obshchee sobranie aktsionerov*) created the company by electing the managing board or board of directors (*pravlenie*), composed of at least three directors (*direktory*).[41] Founders could be

[41] A semantic problem arises at this point. In the largest Russian companies, the stockholders elected both a council (*sovet*), composed of members (*chleny*), and a group of managers (*pravlenie*), composed of directors (*direktory*). In his informative study of French and Belgian corporations operating in Russia, McKay followed the Western terminology, rendering *sovet* as "board of directors" and *pravlenie* (corresponding to the French *directoire*, apparently the source of the Russian word, derived from *pravit'*, "to direct") as "the management team... which actually directed" the enterprise. John P. McKay, *Pioneers for Profit: Foreign Entrepreneurship and Russian Industrialization, 1885–1913* (Chicago, 1970), 369, note 4. In the present study, *sovet* will be called "council" and *pravlenie*, "board of directors." This scheme has two advantages. First, it allows for a direct translation of the Russian words *sovet* and *direktor* as "council" and "director." Second, it provides for a "board of directors" in every company, not just the largest ones, which had both a council and a board. In the vast majority of cases, the directors elected one of their number to be the "executive director" (*direktor-rasporiaditel'*), who bore primary responsibility for day-to-day operations. (Occasionally, especially in large companies, the executive manager – *rasporiaditel'* – was hired.) The semantic difficulty resides in the fact that the directors of Russian companies tended to take a more active role in the management of their enterprises than do members of the board of directors in the typical American corporation, where the chief executive officer and his hired staff perform this function. See William J. Grange and Thomas C. Woodbury, *Corporation Law: Operating Procedures for Officers and Directors*, 2nd ed. (New York, 1954), chaps. 9, 13, 14; and Charles N. Waldo, *Boards of Directors: Their Changing Roles, Structure, and Information Needs* (Westport, Conn., 1985). In Germany after 1870, in contrast to British and American practice according to Jürgen Kocka, the law "prescribed a dual board structure." An elected supervisory board (*Aufsichtsrat*) met only a few times a year, but "made the most basic decisions" regarding investment policy and the hiring of managerial personnel. By 1914, up to 20 percent of all board members were representatives from banks; the Deutsche Bank in 1913 had 186 men sitting on the boards of various companies, although many of these were salaried managers, not elected. In a typical corporation, the executive board (*Vorstand*), which was appointed by the supervisory board (and not elected, as in Russia), "actually ran the company." After 1900 the technical complexities of industrial production allowed the "salaried employees who worked full time as directors, department heads, and executives of the corporation" to gain influence at the expense of the supervisory board, while self-financing by large corporations reduced the financial power of the banks over industry, in contrast to Hilferding's famous theory of *Finanzkapital*, appropriated by Lenin. Jürgen Kocka, "The Modern Industrial Enterprise in Germany," in Alfred D. Chandler, Jr. and Herman Daems, eds., *Managerial Hierarchies: Comparative Perspectives on the Rise of the Modern Industrial Enterprise* (Cambridge, Mass., 1980), 91–2.

elected to the board (article 36; 2175). Members of the board must transact the business of the company by majority rule (article 40; 2180) and must share responsibility for any illegal acts performed in the company's name (article 41; 2181). At the annual assembly, the stockholders set general policy (article 42; 2182) and elected the directors by a three-fourths majority of those voting, according to the number of shares owned by each individual (article 44; 2184). An elected audit commission (*revizionnaia komissiia*), composed of stockholders not on the board, was to examine the company's records, take an inventory of its property, and present its findings to the annual general assembly (article 45; 2185). A company could be dissolved only upon the decision of the general assembly. The owners of shares could participate in a division of the assets only if the corporate resources exceeded its debts to third parties (article 48; 2188).

The primary legal weapon against speculation on the stock market was the strict ban on futures agreements. Article 29 (2167) categorically stated the following:

Any agreement among private persons, whether on the exchange or outside it, regarding the purchase and sale of stocks or notes [*rospisok*] not for cash, and with delivery at a future date and at a certain price, is absolutely forbidden. Furthermore, if such agreements are made known in court, they shall be considered null and void, and those individuals convicted of having made such agreements shall be punished under the law against games of chance [*azartnye igry*]. Brokers or notaries who dare to conclude such agreements shall be dismissed from their posts.[42]

Besides its encouragement and regulation of corporate enterprise, the law also pursued another purpose: to defend the interests of the state itself. The point deserves special emphasis because even such a skilled Soviet historian as Shepelev tended to overlook this aspect of the law of 1836, owing to the chronic underestimation, in Marxist social theory, of conflicts between the wealthiest members of a given society and its governmental agencies. The concerns of Kankrin and Bludov in this regard were illustrated by the vague language that specified the kinds of companies undeserving of a charter: "companies whose purpose is clearly unprofitable, or contrary to the laws, to morality, to good faith in trade and to public order, or, finally, which would cause significant detriment to the state's

---

[42] Quoted by Timofeev, *Birzha*, 141, from article 2167 of the Commercial Code of 1887. This provision remained in force until abrogated on June 8, 1893.

revenues or harm to industry" (article 13; 2151).⁴³ Such a formulation could be used by a tsarist bureaucrat to deny a charter to any group of entrepreneurs deemed unworthy, for whatever reason, of the privilege of forming a corporation.

On balance, the law of 1836 tended toward regimentation at the expense of free enterprise.⁴⁴ Jealous of its power, the tsarist government required that all companies confine their activities to those specified in the corporate charters. Nor could the charter be changed by the general assembly of stockholders. If, for example, the expansion of a corporation's activities necessitated an increase in the size of the basic capital, the permission of the Finance Ministry must be secured. Stockholders could make "not a single change in its rules without new permission from the government, except in those articles relating to details of clerical work, etc., in which the charter explicitly permits changes by the board of a company or by the general assembly of stockholders" (article 15; 2153). There was no appeal from the state's rejection of a charter (article 57; 2198). Shepelev correctly noted that during the debates over the bill in 1835 and 1836, the principle of concession was never challenged; indeed, "it constituted the essence of the law." Until 1917, therefore, "the fate of every company remained in the hands of the bureaucracy."⁴⁵

As the only comprehensive corporate law ever promulgated by the tsarist government, the law of 1836 exerted a strong and lasting influence on the subsequent history of capitalist institutions in Russia. Its fifty-seven articles formed the basis of the section of the Commercial Code that governed corporations for the next eight decades. Although rulings of the Governing Senate (acting as the supreme court of the empire) occasionally supplemented the code, they overruled only two of its articles, minor ones at that.⁴⁶

One of the most confusing consequences of this legislation was its perpetuation of the various names of capitalist institutions. The title of the law and the relevant section of the Commercial Code mentioned both

---

⁴³ In his discussion of the final version of the law, Shepelev, *Kompanii*, 45–55, did not mention this article.
⁴⁴ This assessment is shared by two American historians who had occasion to comment briefly on the law. Pintner, *Russian Economic Policy*, 103, called the legislation "highly restrictive." Wortman, *Legal Consciousness*, 285, noted in passing that "the government remained averse to the reforms in credit and commercial law necessitated by the new industrial economy."
⁴⁵ Shepelev, *Kompanii*, 55.
⁴⁶ Articles 11 (2149) and 47 (2187); see Maksimov, *O tovarishchestvakh*, 70 and 98.

"share partnerships" (*tovarishchestva na paiakh*) and "joint-stock companies" (*kompanii na aktsiiakh*). Although a certain consistency can be seen in the use of the terms *kompaniia* and *aktsiia* in the text of the law (the Ministry of Internal Affairs had unsuccessfully proposed the application of these terms only to companies with special privileges obtained by ministerial confirmation and the relegation of all other corporations to the less formal laws on trading firms),[47] the titles of new companies in ensuing years used all three words for "company" and both words for "share" (see the section on Russian corporate law before 1836). In 1878, the Senate ruled that no legal differences existed between companies with different names, and in 1898 it declared *pai* and *aktsii* to be essentially the same under the law,[48] so that the tsarist system remained unique in its abundance of synonyms in corporate legal terminology. In practice, a slight difference did exist: The purchaser of an *aktsiia* received two sheets of paper, one the share proper and the other a set of coupons to be submitted for annual dividends, whereas the owner of a *pai* simply inscribed his name in the book of shareholders.[49]

Although the framers of this statute strove to include clauses that reflected the latest word in European corporate law (for example, the principle of limited liability), their desire to encourage capitalist enterprise was tempered by the strong habit, second nature to tsarist bureaucrats, to limit, define, and constrain the activities of all institutions subordinate to their rule. The irony was that, in one sense, the law of 1836 was totally unnecessary. Every corporate charter bore the emperor's signature, and thus it was regarded by most jurists as having "the force of law." Logic dictated either that a comprehensive corporate law be issued and then revised as necessary, so that prospective founders of a company need not petition for the imperial confirmation of their particular charter, or that the vacuum in the Commercial Code before 1836 be filled with separate charters, one for each company, all having the force of law because they had crossed the emperor's desk. But this was the Russian Empire under the notoriously arbitrary autocrat Nicholas I, who insisted on perfect order only on the parade ground. Historians have detected in this reign the emergence of a small cadre of professional jurists and "enlightened bu-

---

[47] Shepelev, *Kompanii*, 42.
[48] Maksimov, *O tovarishchestvakh*, 59, 29, 31, 109.
[49] Maksimov, *O tovarishchestvakh*, 29, 31; G. F. Shershenevich, *Kurs torgovogo prava*, 4th ed., 4 vols. (St. Petersburg, 1908–12), vol. 1, 417.

reaucrats" who drafted and implemented the reforms of Nicholas's son, Alexander II,[50] but in matters economic, Bludov and Kankrin left a legacy of confusion that weighed heavily on the entire subsequent history of Russian capitalism.

Minor amendments under Nicholas I

By the mid-nineteenth century, the term "corporate law" in the major European countries embraced a broad spectrum of legal issues, from legislation regulating the process of incorporation to the finer points of case law that occupied lawyers and jurists. Primarily, however, the phrase denoted the basic legal framework defining the status and operation of the corporation: requirements for incorporation, regulations regarding the minimum size of basic capital and minimum price of shares, mutual rights and responsibilities of directors and shareholders, and procedures designed to ensure the financial soundness of the enterprise and to prevent fraud by managers against stockholders and the public.

In Russia, virtually all discussions of the subject following the promulgation of the law of 1836 centered on the laws by which the tsarist state defined the nature of the corporation and set limits on its functions. The activities of lawyers and judges in such matters as torts and contracts introduced only minor clarifications of the corporate law of 1836 in the remainder of the tsarist period. Furthermore, the profession of "corporate lawyer" scarcely existed in nineteenth-century Russia; the only individual who distinguished himself in the use of legal expertise to draft charters and other specialized documents for corporations was the notorious Nikolai N. Sushchov (see Chapter 2). Finally, the failure of the tsarist government to modify the outmoded law of 1836 during the era of the "Great Reforms" provoked perennial demands from business leaders for a thoroughly new law based on the latest European models. The central issue in such debates was the very nature of the corporation within the autocratic legal and political system. This question remained unresolved because the tsarist bureaucracy resisted the establishment of firm legal norms and preferred to operate according to the dictates of its arbitrary will.[51]

---

[50] Wortman, *Legal Consciousness;* W. Bruce Lincoln, *In the Vanguard of Reform: Russia's Enlightened Bureaucrats, 1825–1861* (De Kalb, Ill., 1982). Lincoln, 54, 33, 89, 171, excluded from the ranks of the "enlightened bureaucrats" both Bludov and Kankrin, the principal authors of the corporate law of 1836.

[51] The small number of civil cases involving the corporation as an institution is clearly indicated in the index to the decisions of the imperial appeals court from the 1860s to

The several refinements added to the restrictive law of 1836 by the tsar and his advisors in the following two decades are therefore of little interest except as indications of the government's persistent paternalism toward the merchants. This approach to social issues was especially evident in a series of decrees that addressed problems engendered by the new industrial system, such as price inflation caused by the concentration of workers in cities and the pollution of air and water by manufacturers. Like his father, who had simply forbidden polluting factories to operate upstream from cities and had banned from Petersburg and Moscow provinces any factory that employed a large labor force or consumed substantial quantities of wood fuel, Nicholas I entrusted solutions to the police. None of the decrees of Alexander I or Nicholas I signified the elaboration of a coherent or effective policy, however; problems of air and water pollution and deforestation remained acute to the end of the tsarist period (see Chapter 6).

Typical were three decrees. In 1826, provincial governors received instructions to move all sources of industrial pollution downstream from cities in the next ten years. Seven years later, factories that posed serious pollution or fire hazards were banned from populated areas of the city, and other, less dangerous, enterprises – iron foundries, pottery factories, and sugar mills – were given ten years to meet minimum standards. In 1849, all new spinning mills, iron foundries, and factories that used flammable chemicals were banned from Moscow district; other factories were allowed only with the permission of the governor-general; and the number of workers and machines in each enterprise was to be reported semi-annually to the police. Many decades later, a merchant leader recalled bitterly the

---

1900. Only one and a half of its 1,529 pages deal with shares (*aktsii*), the corporation (*aktsionernoe obshchestvo*), and shareholders (*aktsionery*); another one and a half pages list cases involving all kinds of partnerships (*tovarishchestva*), including unincorporated ones. L. M. Rotenberg, *Predmetnyi alfavitnyi ukazatel'* to the annual series *Resheniia grazhdanskogo kassatsionnogo departamenta pravitel'stvuiushchego senata* (St. Petersburg, n.d.), 15–16, 1396–8. The fine points of these decisions are summarized in Ivan A. Gorbachev, *Tovarishchestva . . . aktsionernye i paevye kompanii: zakon i praktika s senatskimi raz"iasneniiami* (Moscow, 1908), 137–42, 235–7. Thus, there is virtually nothing in Russian law to compare with the rich and diverse legislation and case law regarding corporations in the United States, discussed in William W. Cook, *The Principles of Corporation Law* (Ann Arbor, 1925), and Edward M. Dodd, *American Business Corporations until 1860, with Special Reference to Massachusetts* (Cambridge, Mass., 1954). Cook's bibliography contained over two thousand cases, and Dodd's lists of laws and cases filled eleven pages each. The main principles of American and European corporate law were outlined in Frank E. Horack, *The Organization and Control of Industrial Corporations* (Philadelphia, 1903), a survey of legislation in the forty-eight states that advocated a standard federal law; Grange and Woodbury, *Corporation Law*; and S. N. Frommel and J. H. Thompson, eds., *Company Law in Europe* (London, 1975).

absurd requirements that the governor-general, Count Arsenii A. Zakrevskii, imposed on manufacturers, such as the storage of a pile of peat by each factory in order to demonstrate a commitment to the reduced consumption of wood fuel. As usual, merchants resorted to monetary persuasion to obtain exemptions from the law of 1849; the standard bribe ranged from one hundred to three hundred rubles, depending on the intermediary.[52]

Changes in the corporate law also reflected the inconsistencies of the police mentality. To be sure, the procedural requirements of the law were obeyed by all corporate entrepreneurs, for they had no choice but to submit a draft charter and, following its confirmation by the tsar, to observe its formal provisions in the management of the enterprise. In this sense, the law of 1836 and the charters that were based on it established a firm framework for corporate enterprise, one that presumably stifled all but the most determined founders, so time-consuming were the formalities of incorporation by concession. At the same time, however, the concessionary system persisted as a kind of administrative action carried out by legislative means. The confusion of the two categories tried the patience of legal scholars.

In an effort to clarify the relationship between corporate charters and the law, some experts argued that charters lacked full legal force because they did not supersede the law of 1836 when they diverged from it and because disputes arising from judicial interpretations of a charter's articles were not subject to appeal but were handed down by judges according to the law of contracts.[53] However, numerous decisions of the Senate specified that charters should indeed be considered laws of the empire. In 1884, for example, the Senate declared that corporate charters could contain "changes, supplements, and even exclusions" to articles 2159–88 of the Commercial Code and that these articles, which dealt with the internal structure and finances of a company, should not be assumed to apply unless reiterated in the charter itself.[54] Whatever the legal status of corporate

---

[52] *PSZ* 1–20881, dated August 2, 1803, on pollution; *PSZ* 1–21791, dated June 13, 1805, on work force and fuel consumption; *PSZ* 2–366, dated May 24, 1826, on pollution; *PSZ* 2–6431, dated September 22, 1833, on factories in Petersburg; and *PSZ* 2–23358, dated June 28, 1849, on factories in Moscow. These and other factory laws are discussed in Rybakov, *Promyshlennoe zakonodatel'stvo*. A vivid portrait of the arbitrary and vindictive Zakrevskii by a prominent Moscow merchant is Nikolai A. Naidenov, *Vospominaniia o vidennom, slyshannom i ispytannom*, 2 vols. (Moscow, 1903–5; reprinted Newtonville, Mass., 1976), vol. 1, 88–103; on bribes, 97.

[53] Shershenevich, *Kurs*, vol. 1, 441–4; Maksimov, *O tovarishchestvakh*, 38–9.

[54] Maksimov, *O tovarishchestvakh*, 100–2; Shershenevich, *Kurs*, vol. 1, 441.

charters, there is no question that serious divergences soon developed between the law of 1836 and the various charters issued by the tsarist government after that date.

A good example of the contradictions that arose between the general law and specific charters can be seen in the gradual obsolescence of article 22 (2160), which required that each share bear the name of its owner. After the sale, the new owner was to write his name on the face of the share and to inform the company of the transfer (article 29; 2167). Far more easy to sell than named shares were shares made out "to the bearer" (*na pred'iavitelia;* literally, "to the person who presents it"). Bludov and Kankrin had, in fact, favored the legalization of such shares in 1836.[55] After more than a decade of being permitted in various charters, these were finally legalized in a decree promulgated on June 14, 1848. In subsequent editions of the Commercial Code, article 2160 continued to state that "unnamed shares are forbidden," but from 1887 onward note 1 to this article blithely admitted that "the charters of several joint-stock companies permit exceptions to the general regulations set forth in this and following articles"![56] True to form, Russian legislators never dealt with the obvious implication of this change, namely the need for procedures to defend the rights of stockholders in cases when shares made out to the bearer were lost or stolen, as did, for example, French legislation enacted in 1872 and 1902.[57]

Although certain articles in the charters superseded the law of 1836 in this way, the argument against regarding charters as full-fledged laws rested on another peculiarity of the Russian concessionary system: the tendency of charters to undergo periodic modification. Constant changes in the charters were necessary because the original document typically defined the enterprise in very specific terms. Most common was an increase in the size of a company's basic capital, a change that allowed it to issue more stock. Every alteration, even one as small as this, required the approval of the ministers and the tsar. Although such permission generally was granted, the fact that the charters evolved, even with imperial permission, undermined the notion that they constituted genuine laws.[58]

---

[55] Shepelev, *Kompanii*, 53.
[56] *PSZ* 2–22363; Shershenevich, *Kurs*, vol. 1, 421; Maksimov, *O tovarishchestvakh*, 81.
[57] Shershenevich, *Kurs*, vol. 1, 430–1.
[58] Shepelev, *Kompanii*, 56. In 1897, the Senate reiterated that "a corporate charter confirmed by the tsar constitutes a law, and therefore a corporation may not go beyond the limits imposed upon it by the charter" (quoted in Maksimov, *O tovarishchestvakh*, 100). See, however, Shershenevich, *Kurs*, vol. 1, 442–4, who stressed the essentially administrative,

In the decades following the promulgation of the general law, the government made three minor changes that illustrated the almost absurd intricacies of the tsarist legislation. In the early 1840s, companies were freed from the obligatory purchase of annual business certificates, as if an exemption from a fee of several hundred rubles could, as the law declared, "attract private enterprise into joint-stock companies" and thereby stimulate economic growth.[59] The law of June 14, 1848, allowed corporate stocks to be used as collateral in loans, a change that significantly increased their attractiveness to a handful of wealthy merchants but had little measurable impact of the pace of corporate activity. Finally, the bureaucracy introduced a new procedure intended to prevent embezzlement by the founders of a new company in the period of its greatest vulnerability: after the tsar's approval of a new charter but before the first general assembly. Under this amendment to article 2166 of the code, dated December 28, 1853, founders were required not only to record all stock purchases in a special sealed book (*shnurovaia kniga*), as stipulated in the law of 1836, but also to account for the money thus collected in another book and to leave both books open for public inspection on the premises of the local municipal government until the subscription of shares had been completed.[60] It is doubtful that this decree significantly reduced the scope of corporate fraud in succeeding decades. Thus, despite its tendency to reach into every cranny of corporate life, this legislation did as little as the law of 1836 to address the structural impediments to corporate entrepreneurship in Russia.

The nebulous state of the law and the contradictions in it prompted tsarist ministers to violate the letter and the spirit of the law of 1836 in many interesting ways. The avowed purpose of the law remained to promote the founding of corporations that would make a major contribution to the economic growth of the empire (*po vidam gosudarstvennogo khoziaistva*). However, in practice all sorts of small firms that engaged in the production of textiles, leather, or flour and were owned entirely by the members of a single family received permission to incorporate. As for the capital to be accumulated by a new company, the law mentioned only

---

not legislative, nature of the tsarist incorporation procedure. He especially questioned the statutory nature of corporate charters promulgated after the constitutional reform of 1906, when the tsar began to share his legislative power with the State Duma and State Council, neither of which examined corporate charters before their confirmation by the tsar. Shepelev, "Chastnokapitalisticheskie," 94, stressed the latter point.

[59] Shepelev, *Kompaniia*, quoting a document in TsGIA, f. 40; it does not appear in the *PSZ* index in the early 1840s.

[60] *PSZ* 2–27810; Shepelev, *Kompanii*, 58; Maksimov, *O tovarishchestvakh*, 83–6.

the issuing of stocks (*aktsii* and *pai*), but over the decades the public sale of bonds (*obligatsii*), essentially a long-term debt at a fixed rate of interest, became an important source of corporate funds. Moreover, article 23 (2161) of the law of 1836 required that a certain portion, up to 100 percent, of the basic capital be raised through the sale of shares before operations began, but as early as 1838, the Dnepr Steamship Company received a charter that set no minimum at all, and many others began to function after selling as few as one-fifth of their shares.[61]

By the 1850s, corporate founders had learned a clever way to benefit at the expense of the stockholders: to bestow upon themselves, free of charge, a large portion of the corporation's initial stock as compensation for their entrepreneurial efforts. Having invested nothing of their own, they could dispose of the company quickly, taking a profit on the sale of their shares to the public. Even when the founders of a timber company appropriated 20 percent of the stock without paying for it, the Ministry of Internal Affairs refused to act. Free from the threat of criminal punishment, other founders launched what one scholar called "a whole series of corporate enterprises that were inflated [*dutykh*] to a significant degree, created by the [state's] desire to establish a corporation no matter what."[62] The cautious Kankrin passed from the scene in 1844, to be succeeded by other finance ministers less fearful of corporate dishonesty, but the policy of excessive permissiveness could no more resolve the logical dilemma than could Kankrin's insistence on near perfection in every new charter.

The rigidities, contradictions, and absurdities of the Russian corporate law under Nicholas I should not cause us to overlook the abuses that swept through the French stock exchange in the 1830s. In the wake of periodic crises, French and Prussian legislators delayed approving incorporation by registration until 1867 and 1870, respectively. The crucial difference was that by midcentury, European corporate law had shown itself flexible enough to accommodate the growing energies of industrial capitalism, while the Russian government held firmly to the outworn legislation of 1836 long after the need for fundamental reform had become apparent in the reign of Alexander II.[63]

---

[61] Kaminka, *Kompaniia*, 380 (quoted), 381, 384.
[62] Kaminka, *Kompaniia*, 386, 387 (quoted).
[63] Freedeman, *Enterprise*, chap. 3. For a useful overview of Russian law that stresses the government's ambivalence toward economic development under the last three tsars, see William G. Wagner, "Tsarist Legal Policies at the End of the Nineteenth Century: A Study in Inconsistencies," *Slavonic and East European Review*, 54, no. 3 (July 1976), 371–94.

2

Birzhevaia goriachka (Stock-exchange fever), 1856–1870

> The whole system [of merchant taxation in Russia] seems most elaborately devised to destroy all enterprise, and to depress as much as possible the spirit of trade, in a country which naturally possesses it in but a very limited degree; and it must be long ere the resources of the country can be properly developed while the government seeks its own aggrandisement regardless of the prosperity of the community, since the protection it affords to home manufactures, by the duty on foreign goods, is effectually neutralized by the expenses attendant upon the sale and manufacture of the home product itself.
> – Laurence Oliphant, traveler (1852)[1]

Having surveyed the intentions of the tsarist policy makers, we must now shift the focus of our discussion from the law itself to the object of the law: corporations and their managers. The efforts of Finance Minister Reutern and his successors to reform the corporate law of 1836 can be understood only in the context of the persistent abuses that marred the corporate economy in the early decades of the reign of Alexander II. It is, of course, impossible to review all aspects of economic development in this period, but several episodes well illuminated in the memoir literature and other primary sources may be cited to show the interplay between the law and trends in corporate development.

The law of 1836 succeeded perhaps too well in achieving its primary goal of limiting stock jobbing and speculation. Indeed, the antispeculative provisions of the law, particularly the prohibition against future sales of shares at a fixed price and the requirement that all stock sales be in cash, appear to have contributed to the slowing of the pace of corporate development by the late 1830s. This is not to deny the importance of perennial impediments to economic development in Russia – insufficient credit, poor transportation, the weak domestic market – but only to suggest that the

---

[1] Laurence Oliphant, *The Russian Shores of the Black Sea in the Autumn of 1852* (New York, 1854), 27–8.

failure of corporate managers to continue in the 1840s the impressive rate of incorporation that marked the mid-1830s had administrative as well as purely economic causes, as Oliphant noted in the epigraph.[2]

In the mid-1850s, the major economic problem facing the tsarist regime was not speculation but the familiar curse of economic backwardness. The defeat of Russian troops on their own soil in the Crimean War demonstrated to tsarist policy makers the futility of the repressive mechanisms characteristic of the reign of Nicholas I. The finance ministers of Alexander II (1855–81) – Petr F. Brok (1852–8), Aleksandr M. Kniazhevich (1858–62), and Mikhail Kh. Reutern (1862–78) – encouraged the development of new corporate enterprises not only because private initiative was essential to harness the latent productive forces of the empire, but also because the state itself faced a crisis in the collection of its revenues.[3]

Just as this motive for reform appeared familiar (when has the Russian state ever received taxes it considered sufficient?), so the proposed remedies echoed the vague pronouncements of the energetic autocrats Peter I and Catherine II. For example, Kniazhevich asserted that the solution to the economic emergency caused by the rapidly rising state debt and the outflow of specie to Europe and Asia lay in a vigorous program to encourage industrial development, specifically in coal, mechanical engineering, cotton and silk textiles, and railroads.[4] Recent scholarship has revealed the importance of the fiscal motive as an impetus to the so-called Great Reforms of Alexander II, especially the emancipation of the serfs. Stressing this element of continuity in autocratic policies, several recent studies have shown conclusively that the temptation to apply the label "liberal" to the political and economic innovations of Alexander's reign must be resisted out of respect for the facts.[5]

---

[2] Generalizations based on statistical evidence are impossible at this stage of research in Russian economic history because the numbers themselves vary widely in the secondary literature. Citing tsarist sources, Leonid E. Shepelev, *Aktsionernye kompanii v Rossii* (Leningrad, 1973), 63–4, gave the figure of seventy-four new companies founded from 1837 through 1856, or 3.7 per year on the average, but the RUSCORP database, a survey of corporate charters published in the *PSZ*, yielded a far larger number for these years: one hundred, or an annual average of five. Both data sets showed a sharp decrease beginning in 1839.

[3] Jacob W. Kipp, "M. Kh. Reutern on the Russian State and Economy: A Liberal Bureaucrat during the Crimean Era, 1854–60," *Journal of Modern History*, 47, no. 3 (Sep. 1975), 437–59.

[4] Iosif F. Gindin, *Gosudarstvennyi bank i ekonomicheskaia politika tsarskogo pravitel'stva (1861–1892 gody)* (Moscow, 1960), 29.

[5] On the fiscal implications of the emancipation, see Daniel Field, *The End of Serfdom* (Cambridge, Mass., 1976). The issue of liberalism is cogently examined in Daniel Field, "Kavelin and Russian Liberalism," *Slavic Review*, 32, no. 1 (Mar. 1973), 59–78. The same critical

The history of Russian corporate law in this period adds new evidence to support this contention. Despite the efforts of numerous well-educated and patriotic bureaucrats to promote capitalist development, the legal and institutional framework that they put into place did not significantly promote the expansion of political and economic freedom. Indeed, the methods by which the reforms were implemented remained the same as before: the promulgation of a new policy after secret deliberations among experts in the chanceries of St. Petersburg. Because the bureaucrats took the initiative, they could only hope that their innovations would be welcomed and used wisely by merchants. However, the latter in turn displayed many of their traditional wiles, including cunning and trickery, to pluck a quick profit from new opportunities. In the context of an emerging corporate economy, such theoretical reforms from the top, coupled with the immaturity of the merchants, could only produce a repetition of the unhappy experience of the 1830s. Following the Crimean War, the outburst of corporate speculation and dishonesty differed from the previous episode only in the greater flair and audacity of the entrepreneurs.

The flurry of incorporation

Although Russian industry had begun to flourish during the Crimean War in response to the sharp increase in prices (twenty-five new companies were founded in 1853–6, an average of over six per year),[6] the main impulse for the corporate boom of the late 1850s came from a dramatic shift in the state-controlled credit market. Shepelev drew a parallel between the 1850s and the 1830s: In both cases, the state lowered the interest rate on deposits in its credit institutions, thereby encouraging individuals to withdraw their savings and to invest them in corporations, which promised a higher rate of return. To be sure, Finance Minister Brok had good financial reasons of his own for lowering the interest rate from 4 to 3 percent. The bank received few applications for new loans at five per cent because the landed estates of the gentry were already heavily mortgaged, and the

---

approach is evident in the richly detailed study of restrictions on municipal self-government by Valeriia A. Nardova, *Gorodskoe samoupravlenie v Rossii v 60-kh—nachale 90-kh godov XIX v.: pravitel'stvennaia politika* (Leningrad, 1984). Walter Hanchett, "Tsarist Statutory Regulation of Municipal Government in the Nineteenth Century," in Michael F. Hamm, ed., *The City in Russian History* (Lexington, 1976), 91–114, esp. 99–106, discusses the debilitating provisions of the municipal statute of 1870. The law of 1892 introduced further restrictions: Hanchett, "Regulation," 107–113.

[6] RUSCORP database.

payment of 4 percent on steadily increasing deposits, mainly those of merchants, caused a net drain on the bank's assets. In the summer of 1857, the state's bank lowered its rate on both deposits and loans by a full percentage point, in effect reducing them by 20 and 25 percent respectively.

This change had an immediate and powerful effect on Russian corporations, especially in St. Petersburg, where a genuine capital market already existed. In June 1857, Brok had worried about an excess of deposits over loans amounting to 145 million rubles, but the new law caused a swift reversal. Between August and December 1857, withdrawals surpassed deposits by 48 million rubles; from January through June 1858, by 25 million; and from July through December 1858, by 86 million.[7]

By 1859, deposits had fallen to such a low level – 20 million rubles – that the specter of the state's bankruptcy led the Ministry of Finance to propose the phasing out of all loan operations, the encouragement of privately owned banks, and the establishment of a new State Bank. On May 31, 1860, the new bank received its charter, and on July 1 the Commercial Bank closed its doors. A new era – of private banking under the supervision of the State Bank – had begun.[8] A careful observer of corporations in the early reign of Alexander II stressed the importance of changes in the interest rate, not only in the banking system but also in the market for interest-bearing bonds issued by the state.

> One is easily convinced by the consequences that the raising and lowering of the interest rate on state securities [*gosudarstvennye bumagi*] strongly affected the fate of corporations. The lowering of rates prompted the formation of many companies and allowed them to sell their shares successfully, while the raising of rates dealt a blow to corporations.

For example, any government bond that paid an annual return of over 5.25 percent drew investment capital away from corporations.[9]

In the wake of the drop in the interest rate, a veritable "fever" (*goriachka*)[10] swept through the imperial capital. As the Ministry of Finance reported to the State Council a decade later, many investors with more "credulity" than financial acumen "had only one concern at first: how to

---

[7] *PSZ* 2–32082, dated July 20, 1857; Shepelev, *Kompanii*, 67–74.
[8] P. Kh. Spasskii, *Istoriia torgovli i promyshlennosti v Rossii*, 4 parts in 1 vol. (St. Petersburg, 1910–11), part 2, 8–9; Gindin, *Bank*, chap. 1.
[9] L. Rozental', *Ocherk deiatel'nosti russkikh aktsionernykh obshchestv v techenii 1862 i 1863 gg.* (St. Petersburg, 1865), 10.
[10] Spasskii, *Istoriia*, part 2, 8.

participate in these joint-stock enterprises. To this end they exerted every possible effort. When subscriptions [to new stocks] were opened, they ordered huge blocks in order to receive at least a portion of the shares when they were distributed." The economist Vladimir P. Bezobrazov noted "a sudden, huge development" in corporate activity, "into which people from all social classes rushed headlong." "Joint-stock companies constitute one of the most vigorous topics of Russian life at the moment, at least in the capital," wrote another expert. "People of every rank and status have been crowding into joint-stock enterprises."[11]

As for the corporate entrepreneurs themselves, they understood all too well the mechanisms by which ignorant investors could be parted from their money. A government memorandum dating from the late 1850s gave a classic description of stock jobbing (*azhiotazh*). Founders of new companies, it noted,

often were concerned only with their own advantage. They would reserve for themselves a certain portion of the shares, sell them at profitable prices, and then withdraw from the enterprises. Those who had spent their money [on the stocks] later lost it, partly because of unscrupulous activities and partly because of improper conduct by the founders. Many corporate stocks that were initially sold at prices far above par value later fell to the very lowest prices.[12]

In early 1859, the government began to perceive the same negative effects of the corporate boom as in the 1830s. Now it was illogical, however, to seek an end to abuses in the promulgation of restrictive legislation, for the law of 1836 already gave the government full authority to deny a charter to a questionable new enterprise. The Committee of Ministers could only instruct the various agencies to scrutinize carefully all petitions for a corporate charter. Approval was to be granted "only to those from which the state or the public could positively expect to derive benefit and interest, with due attention, at the same time, to the trustworthiness of the founders."[13] This statement of good intentions had little, if any, impact, owing to the bureaucrats' inability to evaluate the true economic potential of new companies from an examination of their draft charters. By mid-1859, in fact, the first episode of stock-exchange fever had abated

---

[11] Quotations from works by Bezobrazov and Leon Rozental', cited by Shepelev, *Kompanii*, 67–8.
[12] Memorandum in the Ministry of Finance archive, quoted by Shepelev, *Kompanii*, 68.
[13] Shepelev, *Kompanii*, 76, 69 (quoted).

naturally, owing to the lack of new sources of capital available for investment.[14]

The railroad boom

In the absence of a solid study of Russian corporate development in the 1850s and 1860s, it is difficult to assess the impact of the stock-exchange fever on the major sectors of the Russian economy and even more difficult to make meaningful comparisons with similar episodes in Western Europe. The major effects of financial speculation are apparent, however, in at least one sector, that of transportation. The largest companies formed in the empire were those devoted to the construction of railroads and the establishment of steamship lines. The state took a special interest in such enterprises because of their obvious economic and strategic importance. The greatest scandals of the 1860s occurred in the transportation sector, probably because the huge size of these companies and the concomitant possibilities of large profits attracted more than their fair share of unscrupulous entrepreneurs. To be sure, some of the most active figures in these giant corporations acted out of unselfish and patriotic motives: the engineers Andrei I. Del'vig and Stanisław Kierbedź; the silkworm cultivator and Slavophile publicist turned railroad manager and banker, Fedor V. Chizhov; and the all-purpose corporate promoters Nikolai A. Novosel'skii, Vasilii A. Kokorev, and Heinrich Marc.[15] Yet even these men found it difficult to realize the potential benefits of corporate entrepreneurship in a cultural and political milieu in which mass ignorance, primitive market conditions, and bureaucratic corruption still predominated over European norms of business practice. Particularly vexing was the perennial dilemma

---

[14] Shepelev, *Kompanii*, 69. In the five-year period from 1856 through 1860, the finance ministry counted 109 new corporate charters, whose yearly totals inscribed a sharply rising and falling curve: 8, 15, 43, 26, and 17. Shepelev, *Kompanii*, 66, citing ministry data. In RUSCORP, the corresponding figures are 9, 15, 36, 27, 17. The higher figure for 1858 in the ministry's version is at least partly due to the erroneous identification – as new companies – of two that received charter renewals and of two existing steamship companies, Caucasus and Mercury, that merged in that year.

[15] On Del'vig, Baron A. I. Del'vig, *Moi vospominaniia*, 5 vols. (St. Petersburg, 1913). On Kierbedź, *Polski słownik biograficzny*, vol. 12, 419–20; and M. I. Voronin, *St. V. Kerbedz, 1810–1899* (Leningrad, 1982). On Chizhov and Kokorev, Thomas C. Owen, *Capitalism and Politics in Russia: A Social History of the Moscow Merchants* (Cambridge, 1981), chaps. 2–3; and Alfred J. Rieber, *Merchants and Entrepreneurs in Imperial Russia* (Chapel Hill, 1982), chaps. 4–5. See also Paula Lieberman, "V. A. Kokorev: An Industrial Entrepreneur in Nineteenth-Century Russia," doctoral dissertation, Yale University, 1981, on railroads (chap. 4) and banks and oil (chap. 5).

of Russian economic development: Vigorous state action appeared necessary to force new paths out of economic backwardness; but such leadership by the state, even when carried out by skilled men whom W. Bruce Lincoln has aptly named "enlightened bureaucrats," carried with it intrinsically deleterious effects of overcentralization, arbitrary actions, and the stifling of initiative and market rationality.

The dimensions of this dilemma may be illustrated by a brief look at the history of the Russian Steamship Company (commonly called ROPIT, after its Russian name, Russkoe obshchestvo parokhodstva i torgovli). Founded in 1856 by Nikolai A. Novosel'skii, who later served as the mayor of Odessa, and Nikolai A. Arkas, an aide-de-camp of the emperor who held the naval rank of first captain, this huge company, originally capitalized at 6 million silver rubles, became the first Russian steamship line to maintain scheduled service from Russian ports on the Black Sea to Constantinople, Athens, Smyrna, Rhodes, Alexandria, Beirut, and Jaffa. The enormous costs of such service could be sustained, however, only with the aid of a generous state subsidy. Financial support from the imperial treasury seemed warranted as an investment in Russian economic influence in the eastern Mediterranean, but it also drained the resources of the state and kept in place a monopoly inimical to the development of other, less favored, shipping companies.

The published history of this firm's operations, a dry chronological account that avoids almost all important questions of managerial decision making, unfortunately obscures the benefits and shortcomings of this particular state-supported monopoly,[16] but numerous observers pointed out its negative economic effects. A British businessman who worked briefly for the company commented years later:

Although nominally a company with a large share-capital, its existence depended almost entirely (during many years after its inception) on a subsidy from the Government of so liberal a character that it was commonly reported that the vessels could sail backwards and forwards to and from the various ports [without passengers or freight] and still pay a reasonable dividend to the stockholders.

[16] Sergei I. Ilovaiskii, *Istoricheskii ocherk piatidesiatiletiia Russkogo obshchestva parokhodstva i torgovli* (Odessa, 1907). See also the company's annual reports from 1857 onward: *Otchet Russkogo obshchestva parokhodstva i torgovli* (St. Petersburg, annual, 1858–1917); Werner E. Mosse, "Russia and the Levant, 1856–1862: Grand Duke Constantine Nicolaevich and the Russian Steam Navigation Company," *Journal of Modern History*, 26, no. 1 (Mar. 1954), 39–48; and Peter Weisensel, "The Russian Steam Navigation and Trade Company," *MERSH*, vol. 32, 166–70, with full bibliography. Mosse, "Russia and the Levant," 46–7, noted the financial losses on all service to foreign ports except those in England.

The subsidy, however, was gradually diminished as the vessels became self-supporting.[17]

A spokesman for the Russian Industrial Society (Russkoe obshchestvo dlia sodeistviia russkoi promyshlennosti i torgovle, RIS), Nikolai A. Shavrov, complained that such monopolies only hurt the Russian economy by stifling the growth of healthy competition in the shipping business in the Black, Azov, and Caspian seas and the major Russian rivers.[18] Whatever the economic cogency of Shavrov's patriotic rhetoric, the tsarist government's use of direct administrative measures to promote an economic trend considered desirable for strategic reasons strikes the student of Russian corporate law as an all too familiar phenomenon. In any case, the several charters issued to ROPIT by the government and the voluminous decrees by which the Ministry of Finance increased and reduced the company's per-mile subsidies for its various routes are of interest both as a convincing proof of the company's financial dependence on the state and as evidence that the bureaucrats in Petersburg failed to conceive an alternative to the old policy of pursuing economic development through legislative decrees.

This policy operated with particular force in the new railroad companies that sprang up after the Crimean War. Many of them proved susceptible to the same abuses that Shavrov bemoaned in the shipping industry: waste, mismanagement, and bureaucratic inertia perpetuated by favoritism at the highest levels of government.

Although the need for some kind of governmental action to promote railroad development became obvious to all educated Russians during the war in the Crimea, in the two decades before the war, Nicholas and his ministers had approached the issue cautiously. At the time of the great railroad booms in the 1830s and 1840s in Britain, France, and the United States, only two railroad companies were established in Russia, one to serve the imperial resort at Tsarskoe selo (1836) and the other to transport freight on horsedrawn wagons between the Volga and Don rivers (1843). (The railroad linking Warsaw to Vienna was approved by Nicholas I in January 1839, but the charter was not published in the *PSZ* until the company was reorganized in 1857.)

The st   itself undertook to build the first major railroad in Russia

---

[17] George Hume, *Thirty-Five Years in Russia* (London, 1914; reprinted New York, 1971), 33.
[18] Nikolai A. Shavrov, *Vidy pravitel'stva i vidy subsidiruemogo pravitel'stvom Russkogo obshchestva parokhodstva i torgovli* (Moscow, 1883) and Shavrov, *O merakh dlia razvitiia torgovogo morekhodstva v sviazi s razvitiem otechestvennogo sudostroeniia, pri sovremennom ekonomicheskom polozhenii Rossii*, 2 vols. (Moscow, 1895–6).

proper, between St. Petersburg and Moscow, in 1843–51, having begun a serious study of the project in 1841. It also took over construction of the Warsaw-Vienna railroad in 1843 when that company encountered financial difficulties. The government's lack of enthusiasm for railroads was reflected in its rejection of all but a handful of the eighty-six proposals from individuals (including sixteen in 1856 alone) that it received from 1834 through 1860. The bureaucrats sought to keep the transportation system firmly in their own hands. They saw in the various proposals evidence of poor planning, which carried the danger of financial disaster and potential expense to the state in the future.[19] Although the Petersburg-Moscow line was named after Nicholas I, the old autocrat remained suspicious of modern transportation technology.

The Crimean War demonstrated, however, that without a national railroad network, the Russian Empire would remain mired in economic backwardness. It was said that British soldiers in the Crimea received mail from home more quickly than did the Russian defenders there. Although the tsar's troops at Sevastopol might well have suffered defeat owing to the obsolescence of their flintlock muskets whether their supplies and reinforcements had been brought by rail instead of by oxcart,[20] the public blamed the defeat on the lack of modern transportation links among the major economic centers: Moscow, Warsaw, Kiev, and Odessa. In terms of the time needed to haul freight, the grain-producing Black Earth region lay farther from the imperial capital than did India from England. Sailboats traveling up the Volga River spent three months in transit from Astrakhan to the late summer fair at Nihznii Novgorod and four months more on their way to Petersburg through the canal system.[21] In 1855, the Russian Empire contained only 1.5 percent of the world total of 67,000 kilometers of railroad lines, compared to 29,600 in the United States, 13,000 in Britain, 8,300 in Germany, and 5,500 in France.[22]

[19] The charters of the two railroad companies are in *PSZ* 2–9009 and *PSZ* 2–17007, respectively. On railroad policy under Nicholas, see Nina S. Kiniapina, *Politika russkogo samoderzhaviia v oblasti promyshlennosti (20–50-e gody XIX v.)* (Moscow, 1968), 150–96, figures from 187; and William L. Blackwell, *The Beginnings of Russian Industrialization, 1800–1860* (Princeton, 1968), part 4: Transportation.

[20] Aida M. Solov'eva, *Zheleznodorozhnyi transport Rossii vo vtoroi polovine XIX v.* (Moscow, 1975), 61–2. For the debate on this point between Vasilii A. Kokorev and Vasilii A. Poletika, see Poletika's article, "Po povodu 'Ekonomicheskikh provalov,'" *Russkii arkhiv*, 2, no. 8 (Aug. 1887), and Kokorev's verbose response in *Russkii arkhiv*, 3, no. 9 (Sep. 1887), 13–128.

[21] Kiniapina, *Politika*, 154.

[22] Solov'eva, *Transport*, 63. Jacob Metzer, *Some Economic Aspects of Railroad Development in Tsarist Russia* (New York, 1977, a photoreproduction of his doctoral dissertation, Uni-

In 1865, Finance Minister Reutern expressed the government's determination to build a modern transportation system. He stressed not only the strategic role of steam and rails but also their economic importance.

In the last few years newly formed capital, the result of savings, has flowed into productive expenses, primarily railroads. This seems to me to represent the only possible way out of our financial and economic difficulties. Unless the exports of our goods abroad are increased by means of railroads, we cannot increase our monetary circulation or maintain the rate of our bills of exchange, an improvement of which is essential if we are to attract foreign capital. Only the railroad can secure adequate prices for our products, prices that are more stable [than in the past] and that reward individuals for their labor. Such compensation is necessary if our lands are to provide a sufficient income and, consequently, bear a real price [in the market]. The railroad will strengthen our productive forces and thus increase the revenues of the state treasury. Finally, the railroad, more than any other factor, will augment the political strength of Russia.[23]

To build a railroad system in Russia required massive amounts of investment capital, so huge were the distances separating major cities even in the so-called European part of the country. The tsarist government poured millions of rubles into new railroad companies, but the opportunities for mismanagement and corruption multiplied in proportion to the subsidies. The railroad boom of the 1850s and 1860s produced not only a network of rails but also a legacy of inefficiency and speculation that led the state to acquire the bulk of the rail system by the end of the century.

The worst example of waste and mismanagement can be seen in the activities of the largest company ever chartered by the tsarist government: the Russian Railroad Company (Glavnoe obshchestvo russkikh zheleznykh dorog or La grande société des chemins de fer russes). Established in 1857, the company obligated itself to build four major rail lines totaling 4,000

versity of Chicago, 1972), argues that railroads contributed only "about 5.6 per cent of GNP in 1907" because of the availability of cheap alternative methods, such as water transport and overland drayage. However, his use of data from only a single year (1907) and his numerous errors in the citation of Russian sources cast doubt on his methodology. Any econometric study of the impact of railroads on the Russian economy must balance the obvious benefits of speedy transportation of bulk goods in all weather conditions and the stimulation of heavy industry against the deleterious effects of waste, corruption, high construction and operating costs, and the role of political rather than economic considerations in the choice of routes. A fine introduction to the economic effects of railroads in the Russian Empire, from the finances of separate lines to their impact on industry, agriculture, and resettlement in Siberia, is Oskar Mertens, "Dreissig Jahre russischer Eisenbahnpolitik," *Archiv für Eisenbahnwesen*, 7 sections in vols. 40–2 (1917–19). Mertens served as secretary of the Riga–Dünaburg Railroad.

[23] A. N. Kulomzin and V. G. Reitern–Nol'ken, *M. Kh. Reitern: Biograficheskii ocherk* (St. Petersburg, 1910), 136–7, quoted in Shepelev, *Kompanii*, 82.

versts (2,680 miles) in the following decade: from Petersburg to Warsaw and thence to the Prussian border; from Moscow to Nizhnii Novgorod; from Moscow to Feodosiia in the Crimea, via Kursk and the lower Dnepr River; and from Kursk or Orel to the Baltic port of Libau, via Dünaburg (Russian Dinaburg, renamed Dvinsk in 1893, now Daugavpils in Soviet Latvia). The founders set the basic capital at the phenomenal figure of 275 million silver rubles. The first issue of shares, which sold for 75 million rubles, far surpassed the size of any other company chartered by the tsarist government, before or since, including relatively large enterprises typical of the late 1850s, like the Riga-Dünaburg Railroad (10.2 million), the Volga-Don Railroad (8 million), and the Moscow-Saratov Railroad (10 million). Especially generous to managers and investors alike was article 6 of the charter, according to which the Russian state guaranteed an annual return of 5 percent to stockholders, whether or not the company produced a profit from its operations. In return for its financial largess, the state enjoyed the right to recoup its losses, eighty-five years after the completion of construction, by acquiring without cost the entire railroad system constructed and managed by the company.[24] Even a cursory reading of the charter reveals numerous opportunities for profitable mismanagement of the enterprise by unscrupulous directors.

The most prominent banker in St. Petersburg, Baron Alexander L. Stieglitz (Shtiglits in Russian, 1814–84), headed the list of founders. Stieglitz, whose father Ludwig had helped to organize the first Russian fire insurance company in 1827, had furnished funds for the construction of the Petersburg–Peterhof Railroad, successfully completed in 1857, and served as president of the PEC from 1846 to 1859.[25] Other participants included the venerable banking houses of Baring Brothers in London, Hope and Company in Amsterdam, Isaac and Emile Pereire in Paris, and Mendelssohn and Company in Berlin. These foreigners may not have had as their primary purpose the extraction of exorbitant profits from a financially

---

[24] *PSZ* 2–31448, dated January 26, 1857.
[25] Kiniapina, *Politika*, 192; Aleksandr G. Timofeev, *Istoriia S.-Peterburgskoi birzhi, 1703–1903 gg.* (St. Petersburg, 1903), 191. The family also owned technologically advanced sugar plants and linen and cotton mills. On the careers of Ludwig and Alexander Stieglitz, see Blackwell, *Beginnings*, 255–61; Count Aleksandr A. Bobrinskoi, *Dvorianskie rody, vnesennye v obshchii gerbovnik vserossiiskoi imperii*, 2 vols. (St. Petersburg, 1890), vol. 2, 644–5; and the articles by A. G. in *RBS*, vol 23, 427–8 and 425–7. Ivan G. Andreev, *Nevskie priadil'shchiki: kratkii ocherk istorii priadil'no-nitochnogo kombinata imeni S. M. Kirova* (Leningrad, 1959), 5, 12, noted that the steam engine named Faith still produced power for the cotton-spinning mill in 1927. With two others, called Hope and Charity, it had been installed in 1834!

unsound corporation, but it soon became apparent that the association of these illustrious bankers with the new enterprise did not prevent an epidemic of poor management. The managers and engineers who arrived from Europe to supervise the construction of the railroad impressed many patriotic Russians as haughty, spendthrift, and incompetent. The council (*sovet*) of the company, consisting of ten Russians and ten other persons, mostly Frenchmen, maintained its headquarters in Paris and therefore could hardly have been expected to exert tight control over construction operations on the Russian plain. So profligate was the managerial style of Colignon (Kolin'on), the chief construction engineer, that the company spent in 1858 all the funds collected in the initial stock subscription of 75 million rubles. It became necessary to raise an additional 35 million rubles by selling seventy thousand bonds paying 4.5 percent interest.[26] Even as the lines from Petersburg to the Prussian border and from Moscow to Nizhnii Novgorod were nearing completion in July 1860, the company admitted to the Railroad Committee that it could not fulfill its other obligations. A new charter, issued less than five years after the original one, deleted the requirement that the company construct the lines to Feodosiia and Libau and set the beginning of the eighty-five-year concession at January 1, 1867.[27] A second bond issue of 2.4 million rubles (18,877 bonds priced at 125 silver rubles paying 4 percent) proved necessary.[28]

As a recent American study of this episode has shown, Finance Minister Reutern and other proponents of the influx of foreign capital failed to anticipate the negative consequences of the grandiose financial scheme. The Russian Railroad Company suffered from all the disadvantages of foreign

---

[26] Shepelev, *Kompanii*, 75. A vivid memoir of the "robbery of the company's funds committed by the Frenchmen" hired by Colignon is Andrei A. Auerbakh, "Vospominaniia," *Istoricheskii vestnik*, vol. 101 (Sep. 1905), 672–81, quotation from 676. Auerbakh worked as a bookkeeper for the company as it surveyed the Moscow–Feodosiia line, abandoned in 1860. His brother, Aleksandr Andreevich, was a prominent mining engineer.

[27] *PSZ* 2-37589, dated November 3, 1861.

[28] Oskar Matthesius, "Russische Eisenbahnpolitik im neunzehnten Jahrhundert von 1836 bis 1881," *Archiv fur Eisenbahnwesen*, vol. 26 (1903), 1229, gives Latin spellings of the European bankers who launched the company; financial details are on 1230. His survey of Russian railroad history from 1836 to 1903, several hundred pages long, appeared in 14 sections in vols. 26–32 of the *Archiv* (1903–9). On the failure of the company to meet its original contractual obligations and the negotiations that led to the confirmation of the second charter on November 3, 1861, see also V. M. Verkhovskii, ed., *Istoricheskii ocherk razvitiia zheleznykh dorog v Rossii s ikh osnovaniia po 1897 g. vkliuchitel'no*, 2 vols. (St. Petersburg, 1898–1901), part 1, 93–7. Besides the works of Solov'eva, Matthesius, Mertens, and Verkhovskii, well-documented surveys of the development of Russian railroads are Nikolai A. Kislinskii, *Nasha zheleznodorozhnaia politika po dokumentam arkhiva Komiteta ministrov: istoricheskii ocherk*, ed. Anatolii N. Kulomzin, 4 vols. (St. Petersburg, 1902); and J. N. Westwood, *A History of Russian Railways* (London, 1964).

control, including the absurdity of locating the council on the banks of the Seine. At the same time, the Russian economy derived little financial benefit from the participation of European bankers because shares in the company were purchased mainly by "unsuspecting Russian investors."[29] One expert on the history of Russian finances drew some comfort from the fact that the government's reduction of the interest rate on its securities succeeded in channeling private investment capital into the new companies, including the largest.[30] Nor did the Russians who purchased stock in the Russian Railroad Company deserve pity; they received their dividends from the state treasury, as the corporate charter mandated, whether the company posted a profit or not. Indeed, it was not the primary purchasers of the shares who paid the price of French mismanagement, but those who became stockholders in hopes of riding the crest of speculation to ever higher levels. As the railroad expert Pavel P. Mel'nikov complained, the founders "cared not so much for the economical construction of railroads, to be managed at a profit guaranteed by the government, as for making a profit on the sale of their stocks and bonds." Whether or not all the founders harbored such dark motives, the fact remains that after the founders sold out, the company's indebtedness to the state increased steadily. Technically bankrupt at the time of its second chartering in 1861, the company continued to lose money. By 1868, it owed 135 million rubles to its creditors, including 92 million to the state, although its entire stock capital remained at the original level of 75 million rubles.[31]

It is not at all clear, however, that the largest railroad concessionaires were the most incompetent or that financial success necessarily followed diligent work. As Witte pointed out, few railroad contractors were able to repeat the rise of Pavel G. Derwies (Derviz) to fortune in the 1860s because as time passed, the state imposed various financial restrictions on railroad contractors. Meck (Mekk), Derwies's main engineer on the Kursk-Kiev line, lost a great deal of money in his next venture, a railroad from Libau to Romny. A "very correct German" like the frugal Meck might suffer enormous losses, although he left his widow a sufficiently large income to permit her to support the musical genius Petr I. Chaikovskii.

---

[29] Alfred J. Rieber, "The Formation of La Grande Société des Chemins de Fer Russes," *Jahrbücher für Geschichte Osteuropas*, N.S., 21, no. 3 (Sep. 1973), 382.
[30] Pavel P. Migulin, *Russkii gosudarstvennyi kredit, 1769–1899*, vol. 1 (Kharkov, 1899), 266, quoted by Shepelev, *Kompanii*, 75.
[31] A. P. Pogrebinskii, "Stroitel'stvo zheleznykh dorog v poreformennoi Rossii i finansovaia politika tsarizma (60–90-e gody XIX v.)," *Istoricheskie zapiski*, 47 (1954), 151, quoting Verkhovskii, *Ocherk*, part 1, 110.

One of the Mecks' sons wasted his youth on extravagant night life and died prematurely, but another served as the president of the Moscow–Riazan and Riazan–Kozlov railroads in Moscow.[32] The most dramatic event of this time, a great railroad crash in which Emperor Alexander III and his family narrowly escaped death (October 1887), owed more to the carelessness of the engineers and traffic managers than to the wily machinations of capitalists in Petersburg. (Witte, who had incurred the tsar's displeasure shortly before the crash by warning of the danger of excessive speed, enjoyed thereafter a series of promotions to offices of great power.)[33]

The state itself had found it difficult to construct railroads efficiently. Even by using conscript labor it could not reduce the per-verst cost to ten thousand rubles, as Anatolii N. Kulomzin had prescribed in 1865, and in any case it lacked the financial resources to build a complete rail network.[34] For both technical and financial reasons, the tsarist bureaucracy preferred to let private companies do the actual construction and management and to provide sufficient financial guarantees to attract the desired amount of entrepreneurship into this new field of endeavor. For example, Derwies's contract to build the Riazan–Kozlov line stipulated that if, at the end of the concession period, a debt remained to be paid to the state by the company, funds must be withdrawn from its reserve capital fund for this purpose, but in case the fund were too small the debt would simply be canceled.[35] Because the government signed this document, Derwies hardly bore sole responsibility for the large debts that accumulated under these favorable terms.

Thus, although the system of railroad concessions certainly promoted profiteering and waste, the tsarist government as a whole, not just the officials who benefited from corrupt deals with favored companies, preferred it to all other possible policies. In a rare moment of lucidity, the Soviet historian Pogrebinskii noted that the government used the funds derived from the foreign sale of railroad bonds to alleviate its serious balance-of-payments

---

[32] Sergei Iu. Witte, *Vospominaniia*, 3 vols. (Moscow, 1960), vol. 1, 122, on P. G. Derwies; 157, on I. G. Derwies; and 122–3, on Meck and his sons; see also editor's note, 519. On the musical patronage of Nedezhda von Meck, see David Brown, *Tchaikovsky: The Early Years, 1840–1874* (New York, 1978); and Brown, *Tchaikovsky: The Crisis Years, 1874–1878* (London, 1982). The career of P. G. von Derwies is surveyed in *RBS*, vol. 6, 261–2.

[33] Witte, *Vospominaniia*, vol. 1, 191–8, on the crash; 203–8 on promotion to directorship of the Railroad Department in the Finance Ministry; and 250–6 on being named minister of transportation in early 1892.

[34] Pogrebinskii, "Stroitel'stvo," 153, 159.

[35] Pogrebinskii, "Stroitel'stvo," 159.

problem. In 1866–75, the negative trade balance with Europe, which stood at 306 million rubles, might well have reached 850 million without the placement of bonds abroad. Such a development would have caused "a complete financial catastrophe" because the tsarist government lacked sufficient gold reserves to cover its trade deficit, to say nothing of the enormous financial burden of the war with Turkey (1877–8).[36] Moreover, in defense of the managers, it must be stressed that the structure of freight rates limited corporate income. Managers saw no benefit in covering costs as long as the state guaranteed a steady profit. Eventually the Baranov Commission (1876–85) endorsed a system of low freight rates with the force of law, which prevented companies from charging customers sufficiently high fees to produce a profit.[37]

Both inefficient management and the state's faulty legal-administrative system contributed, therefore, to the sorry state of railroad company finances in the 1860s and 1870s. Arrears mounted steadily as the state paid out huge sums to meet its pledge of a guaranteed return (usually 5 percent on stock) to investors. Even the fiercely independent merchants and Slavophiles who had launched the Trinity Railroad without the slightest financial aid from the state in 1859, in order to demonstrate the capabilities of Russians in the face of the Russian Railroad Company's scandalous waste, were obliged to turn to the treasury for a guarantee of 5 percent as they issued 12 million rubles' worth of additional stock to extend the line from the Trinity Monastery northward toward Iaroslavl in 1868.[38] By the mid-1880s, only six railroad companies (including the Moscow-Iaroslavl, the Moscow-Riazan, and the Warsaw-Vienna) owed the state nothing; five companies (including the Riazan-Kozlov) had debts of up to 50 percent of their stock capital; six (including the Russian and Baltic), of up to 100 percent; four, of up to 200 percent; ten, up to 300 percent; and eight, between 300 and 394 percent![39]

In an effort to limit the drain on the treasury, Reutern in 1872 shortened the guarantee period for some new railroads to as little as fifteen years, but this proved so drastic that he agreed two years later to provide payments

[36] Pogrebinskii, "Stroitel'stvo," 160–2, quotation from 162.
[37] A law of March 8, 1889, ended rate competition among railroad companies and made all rate schedules subject to governmental approval. Russia, Ministerstvo finansov, *Ministerstvo finansov, 1802–1902*, 2 vols. (St. Petersburg, 1904), vol. 2, 246–7, 568. Witte recounted his role in drafting this law in his *Vospominaniia*, vol. 1, 203–7, 245.
[38] *Moskva*, July 3, 1868, 2.
[39] P. I. Georgievskii, *Finansovye otnosheniia gosudarstva i chastnykh zh.-dorozhnykh obshchestvakh v Rossii i v zapadno-evropeiskikh gosudarstvakh* (St. Petersburg, 1887), 292–3.

for the full period of the concession. The state took upon itself the task of selling railroad bonds abroad, in the form of consolidated loans, for which the companies paid a nominal fee, an interest rate, and amortization. It also paid construction costs, provided loans for rolling stock, paid guaranteed dividends to investors, and even purchased railroad securities left unbought by the public, for a total of 846 million rubles between 1867 and the end of 1883. As early as 1876, however, such payments had exhausted the special railroad fund. On September 1, 1883, Bunge merged all assets and liabilities of the fund into the general state treasury. As the decades passed, it became clear that the weakest railroad companies would never repay their huge debts. The state then took over the operation of their lines. "At the turn of the century the entire capital of the railroads in the country amounted to 4.7 billion rubles, of which approximately 3.5 billion rubles belonged to the government."[40]

A British observer considered the entire system of railroad concessions a colossal mistake. By stipulating that the assets of a railroad company would revert to the state free of charge at the end of the concession period, the bureaucracy virtually invited railroad managers to exploit their enterprises in the interest of short-term gain and to leave only an empty shell to be inherited by the state.[41]

The stock market under Reutern

Railroad companies, because of their great size, fell victim to many of the worst abuses in corporate finances. However, the stock market underwent renewed speculation in the late 1860s after a respite of several years during the "cotton famine" occasioned by the American Civil War (1861–5). The rapid spread of the stock-exchange fever to new strata of the population and the ever greater dimensions of the speculation threw into bold relief the failure of repressive legislation to regulate the speculative mania. Memories of this episode would haunt tsarist policy makers in future decades and would serve as a vivid example of the dangers of liberalizing the commercial code. If such abuses could run rampant under the repressive concession system implemented in 1836, how could a less restrictive cor-

---

[40] Ministerstvo finansov, *Ministerstvo*, vol. 1, 583–4; quotation from Peter I. Lyashchenko [Petr I. Liashchenko], *History of the National Economy of Russia to the 1917 Revolution*, trans. L. M. Herman (New York, 1949), 534.
[41] William H. Beable, *Commercial Russia* (New York, 1919), 29.

Table 2.1. *Selected stock values established by the Ministry of Finance, 1865–1872 (rounded to nearest ruble)*

Corporation	Nominal values	Semi-annual periods									
		65-1	65-2	66-1	66-2	67-1	67-2	68-1	68-2	69-1	72-1
Russian Railroad Co. (4½% bonds)[a]	500	336	342	347	358	347	326	313	311	319	351
Russian Railroad Co.[a]	125	89	90	92	95	92	87	83	87	91	102
Riga-Dünaburg RR[a]	125	83	83	84	91	88	83	81	88	93	119
Volga-Don RR[a]	100	195	195	56	59	54	49	51	56	61	62
Moscow-Riazan RR[a]	100	50	51	50	63	68	73	90	123	141	202
Caucasus & Mercury	250	67	62	65	89	96	87	94	105	112	94
ROPIT	150	160	176	178	196	183	176	202	245	298	328
St. Petersburg Fire Insurance Co.	200	71	52	56	54	65	63	92	92	103	115
Moscow-Iaroslavl PR	150	—	75	75	75	75	75	75	75	113	141

[a]Stock or bond guaranteed by the state.
Source: PSZ 3-41754, 42314, 42907, 43483, 44181, 44872, 45430, 46173, 46703, 50420.

porate law be expected to provide protection against the evils of speculation?

This is not to imply that the Ministry of Finance passively accepted the proliferation of poorly financed corporations. Indeed, one of Reutern's most creative acts was the semiannual publication, begun in October 1862, of a list of corporate securities that specified the value that the state would place on the stock if it were offered by the owner as an installment payment for liquor excise taxes. Prices on the stock market during the previous six months were to be taken as the norm, but in no case could the value be set in excess of three-quarters of the value of a guaranteed security (and one-half for unguaranteed ones). In the absence of a comprehensive rating system for corporate stocks and bonds, this list functioned as a crude but effective measure of the financial strength of the largest corporations in the empire, particularly because it had the force of law.

Although an analysis of these semiannual lists would take us far from the theme of corporate law, Table 2.1 shows the sorry state of corporate finances in the 1860s. (Notable are the slump in the value of the securities issued by the largest railroad companies and the high marks accorded to the competence of the Riga Germans and of the Muscovites who controlled the Trinity Railroad.) At least one observer bemoaned the depressant effect of these lists on stock prices,[42] but the historian reaps an important benefit: an impartial and precise semiannual ranking of corporate managements.

For all the efforts of tsarist bureaucrats to interject an element of stability into the corporate stock market, a new episode of speculative fever erupted in the late 1860s. Once more, the state played an important role in directing the public's money into corporate securities. In 1865, Finance Minister Reutern cautioned against the issuing of additional state interest-bearing bonds, on the grounds that "government loans divert all available capital away from private enterprises and industry and provoke justified complaints of a lack of cash. One cannot expect private enterprise and private credit to recover and grow strong as long as the government strives with all its might to attract available funds to itself."[43]

Reutern's enlightened encouragement of private investment in corporations did not lead immediately to a flourishing of a modern stock market. Part of the problem lay in the institutional backwardness of the markets themselves. Despite their name *birzha*, which could mean either "exchange" or "stock exchange," those in even the largest cities – Petersburg, Moscow, Warsaw, Kiev, Odessa, and Riga – had functioned for many decades almost exclusively as commodity exchanges, where raw cotton, tea, coal, coke, and other products were bought and sold at prices arranged by brokers (*maklery*). The grain exchange in Petersburg and the coal and iron exchange in Kharkov functioned as separate institutions after their establishment in 1895 and 1902, respectively. The trading of corporate shares, hampered from 1836 onward by the prohibition against futures sales on margin, developed slowly. In Petersburg, hand-written price lists circulated in the 1830s. Published reports appeared later, but only in French, "and finally, from January 1, 1884, onward, in Russian."[44] Outside the relatively cosmopolitan capital, modern forms of stock trading appeared even later. In Moscow, the hub of the empire's domestic sales network, the organized buying and selling of corporate stocks began only in 1864, when the founders of the Moscow Merchant Bank (which was finally founded in 1866) began offering its shares (*pai*) to the public and the government issued tickets for its first "lottery loan" (*vyigryshnyi zaem*). As late as 1866, the Moscow exchange simply posted stock prices received

---

[42] Rozental', *Ocherk*, 36. The earliest publication of these values occurred in the *PSZ* in February 1865; see Table 2.1 of the present volume.
[43] Quoted from a report in 1865 by Shepelev, *Kompanii*, 82.
[44] Timofeev, *Birzha*, 142 note 1.

from Petersburg. Weekly quotations of stock prices in Moscow began in 1867, followed by daily ones in 1870.[45]

Paradoxically, the emergence of European methods of stock trading in Petersburg before other cities in the empire did not foster the spread of honesty and caution there. Instead, it was in the northern capital that the worst episodes of speculation occurred. The most egregious example of defiance of the law occurred when a young man in a room at the Hotel Demuth began trading stocks there in the mornings in early 1869. As prices rose, ever larger crowds of people flocked to his room. Soon the prices of lottery tickets and shares in large companies like the Rybinsk Railroad reached unprecedented levels, driven ever higher as investors engaged in wild speculation, gambling on the sale of huge blocks of stocks and bonds with no cash at all (*in blanco*). As one economist observed a decade later, "For a time this operator held in his hands the fate not only of private companies but also of the state's bonds." Again the tsarist government stepped into the marketplace, this time to dampen the speculative mania. An issue of 15 million rubles, in bonds paying 5 percent, proved sufficient to burst the bubble. By the end of the summer, many investors had lost heavily in this "famous stock-exchange massacre [*pogrom*] of 1869."[46]

Among the losers were prominent businessmen, including bankers. Members of the Petersburg Mutual Credit Society had borrowed so heavily for speculative purposes that in August 1869, its vault contained no cash at all![47] An anonymous author in the weekly newspaper of the RIS castigated as "completely unwarranted" the easy loans granted by this credit society for stock-exchange gambling. This and other institutions made large loans for which the only collateral was the corporate shares, that is, the object of speculation itself, which had little intrinsic worth and whose price was certain to fluctuate all the more after such loans were made. The writer called upon the State Bank to restrict the supply of credit; it "should threaten to refuse further aid if such [harmful] activities continue."[48] The flawed assumption behind such advice was that the spec-

---

[45] Nikolai A. Naidenov, ed., *Moskovskaia birzha, 1839–1889* (Moscow, 1889), 45–7.
[46] Evgenii I. Lamanskii, "Iz vospominanii E. I. Lamanskogo," *Russkaia starina*, December 1915, book 12, 404–5; Leopol'd Nisselovich, *O birzhakh i birzhevykh ustanovleniiakh* (St. Petersburg, 1879), quoted in Timofeev, *Birzha*, 143–4.
[47] Isaak I. Levin, *Aktsionernye kommercheskie banki v Rossii*, vol. 1 (no more published) (Petrograd, 1917), 186.
[48] "Po povodu voprosa ob otmene zapreshcheniia prodazhi na srok fondov i aktsii," *Torgovyi sbornik*, 1869, no. 39 (Sep. 27), 459–60.

ulators in the stock exchange bore all the blame for the feverish gambling, while the bureaucrats stood above the bacchanalia. In fact, Evgenii I. Lamanskii, the director of the State Bank, sat on the board of the Petersburg Mutual Credit Society as well, but failed to impose restraints on speculative loans.

The fever of 1869 demonstrated once again the inability of tsarist legislation to curb the dishonest behavior of capitalists impatient to make a quick profit. Although Reutern successfully ended the speculative episode by issuing the 5 percent bonds, he apparently did not discipline Lamanskii and other high officials whose irresponsible actions contributed both to the potency of the financial boom and to the severity of the inevitable crash. The underlying cause of such shortsighted speculation remained the relatively low level of business ethics among merchants, bankers, and bureaucrats in Petersburg. This cultural fact, a product of the centuries of Russian isolation from the European business world in the medieval and Early Modern period, could not be removed by the autocrat's signature on a carefully drafted law. On the other hand, the distressing tendency of business leaders to victimize the public seemed to justify the tsarist bureaucrats' determination to keep in force the restrictive corporate legislation of Nicholas I.

In the absence of detailed biographical studies of the principal figures whose dubious sense of propriety allowed the speculative mania of 1869 to reach ruinous proportions (Lamanskii's memoirs are silent on this issue), the historian must remain content with memoirs that illustrate the dishonesty of "wheeler-dealers" (*del'tsy*) close to the tsarist bureaucracy. One such man, the legal expert Nikolai N. Sushchov, had been dismissed from his post as chief procurator of the Senate for unethical behavior, having represented both sides in a lawsuit. He retired with the mellifluous title of privy councilor and commanded huge fees for his skillful phrasing of corporate charters acceptable to the ministers and the tsar. Sushchov, the only individual in the reign of Alexander II worthy of the title "corporate lawyer," displayed all the worst tendencies of a shrewd former bureaucrat in the business world. For years he enjoyed lucrative directorships that paid from sixty to eighty thousand rubles per year in ROPIT, the Russian Railroad Company, the Russo-Belgian Metal Company, the Russian Bank for Foreign Trade, and other large enterprises. Whether or not he engaged in the speculative frauds of the late 1860s, he shamelessly extracted huge fees for writing the simplest legal clauses. For a charter twenty pages long, he charged from five to forty thousand rubles; and for rewording a few clauses he received twenty thousand, "an honorarium that is enjoyed by no writers of genius, not only in Russia but probably in the whole world!" The image of this "inebriated, insolent, red-haired, pink-cheeked, and fat-bellied man" in the memoirs of the corporate director Vitmer corroborated other portraits by such diverse observers as the merchant Naidenov, the aristocratic entrepreneur Wrangel, the engineer Fenin, and the minister Witte. Sushchov also served as the model of the shrewd but dishonest corporate director Salamatov (from *salo:* lard, tallow, fat) in the novel *Del'tsy* by Petr D. Boborykin (1872). The antithesis of a frugal European bourgeois, he died penniless, having squandered his many millions on "eating, drinking, cards, and loose women."[49]

Amid the distressing phenomena of stock-exchange speculation by men of high rank, the development of new corporations did in one sense show the gradual maturation of the Russian commercial-industrial leadership. Here again, however, the familiar pattern of Russian economic history may be discerned: A major change occurred in the marketplace owing to the revision of a single provision in the Commercial Code. It will be recalled that many corporations established after the promulgation of the law of 1836 were not entirely new enterprises, but previously existing full or limited partnerships newly incorporated under the concessionary system. The primary advantage of incorporation consisted in the acquisition of limited liability for the managers and investors. Before Reutern assumed the duties of finance minister, the full partners who wished to avail themselves of this benefit faced an important deterrent to incorporation because article 27 in the law of 1836 required that the founders of a new company distribute among themselves no more than one-fifth of the initial share offering. Those manufacturers and traders who intended to limit the circle of shareholders to their family and friends avoided incorporation, as they

---

[49] On his dismissal, Baron Nikolai E. Vrangel', *Vospominaniia (ot krepostnogo prava do bol'shevikov)* (Berlin, 1922), 139–41. On directorships, *Ob"iasnitel'naia zapiska k otchetu R. O. P. i T. za 1860 g.* (St. Petersburg, 1861), 77; ROPIT journal for 1901 [sic], TsGIA, f. 107, op. 1, ed. kh. 2466; *Otchet soveta upravleniia Glavnogo obshchestva rossiiskikh zheleznykh dorog za 1870 g.* (St. Petersburg, 1871), xv; and A. I. Fenin, *Vospominaniia inzhenera: k istorii obshchestvennogo i khoziaistvennogo razvitiia Rossii (1883–1906 gg.)* (Prague, 1938), 66–8. On fees, Nikolai N. Naidenov, *Vospominaniia o vidennom, slyshannom i ispytannom*, 2 vols. (Moscow, 1903–5; reprinted Newtonville, Mass., 1976), vol. 2, 108–9, who specified 5,000 rubles for the Moscow Merchant Bank charter, confirmed on July 1, 1866 (*PSZ* 2-43360); Vrangel', *Vospominaniia*, 141, on the 20,000-ruble clause; Aleksandr N. Vitmer, "Otryvochnye vospominaniia," *Istoricheskii ocherk*, year 32, vol. 125 (Sep. 1911), 862, 870 (quoted); Witte, *Vospominaniia*, vol. 1, 338–9, on 25,000 to 30,000 as the price of one of Sushchov's charters; and Boborykin, *Del'tsy*, vols. 7–8 (Moscow, 1885–6) of his *Sochineniia*. Final quotation from Vrangel', *Vospominaniia*, 140.

disliked the loss of control that would have resulted from selling four-fifths of the stock to the public at large. Contrary to article 27, however, in the 1860s the Committee of Ministers began to allow the incorporation of solid "family firms" that did not sell shares to the public. Such enterprises acquired the benefits of limited liability without altering their familial structure. Whether Reutern and his advisors realized the wisdom of their illegal policy, the results seem to have been positive, not least for the state itself, because reorganized family firms proved less susceptible than giant new undertakings to the dangers of speculation and financial mismanagement.[50]

By 1870, the rapid increase in both new enterprises and reorganized partnerships created a unique, dual system of corporations, one that has scarcely been noted by historians[51] despite its importance for an understanding of the economic and cultural peculiarities of Russian capitalism well into the twentieth century. As mentioned in Chapter 1, several different names for companies appeared in the earliest legislation. Although the law of 1836 stipulated no structural peculiarities, under Reutern the pattern of structural differentiation had become clear.

The typical joint-stock company (*aktsionernaia kompaniia* or *aktsionernoe obshchestvo*), newly formed for a large undertaking like a railroad, steamship line, or bank, raised its basic capital in the sale of a large number of shares, called *aktsii*, commonly priced at 100, 200, or 250 rubles. In contrast, a moderately sized share partnership (*tovarishchestvo na paiakh*), typically established to provide limited liability for an existing enterprise such as a cotton-textile factory, raised less capital than did the giants and did so by selling to a small circle of the partners' relatives and friends a relatively small number of shares (*pai*), often priced at between 500 and 25,000 rubles each. *Aktsii* were often issued "to the bearer" (in defiance of article 22 of the law of 1836), but *pai* almost always displayed the name of the owner. Moreover, in many cases they could be sold to outsiders only after being offered to other shareholders for a period of from two weeks to several months, as specified in the corporate charter.

As might be expected, joint-stock companies flourished in St. Petersburg, where a vigorous capital market existed. In contrast, the share partnership

---

[50] Shepelev, *Kompanii*, 79, 122.
[51] The distinctions discussed here are ignored by Kiniapina and Blackwell. They receive brief mention in Shepelev, *Kompanii*, 21–2; Iosif F. Gindin's article, "Moskovskie banki," on Moscow companies in *Istoriia Moskvy*, 6 vols. (Moscow, 1952–9), vol. 4, 213–15; and Valerii I. Bovykin, *Formirovanie finansovogo kapitala v Rossii, konets XIX v.–1908 g.* (Moscow, 1984), 111.

Table 2.2. *Median capitalization and par value of shares issued by new corporations founded in St. Petersburg and Moscow, 1866–1870*

	St. Petersburg		Moscow	
	Aktsiia	Pai	Aktsiia	Pai
Number of companies	31	7	7	5
Median capitalization	2,000,000 r.	800,000 r.	5,602,000 r.	500,000 r.
Median par value of shares	128 r.	500 r.	200 r.	1,000 r.
Median number of shares issued	12,500	2,000	13,986	500

Source: RUSCORP database.

remained relatively more popular in Moscow, where capital markets remained weaker and merchants preferred somewhat smaller family firms, which they expanded gradually by reinvesting profits from year to year. A full study of the corporate charters has yet to be undertaken, but a preliminary statistical analysis reveals marked differences between corporations headquartered in Petersburg and Moscow. As Table 2.2 shows, this tendency, already perceptible before the Crimean War, had become firmly established by 1870.

The Petersburg Discount and Loan Bank, founded in 1869, typified the usual joint-stock company. Its initial stock offering of 5 million rubles consisted of 20,000 shares (*aktsii*), priced at 250 rubles to facilitate their purchase by the public. In contrast, the cotton industrialists who founded the Moscow Merchant Bank in 1866 gave it the characteristic features of share partnerships headquartered in the central region. Chartered with a basic capital of 1.26 million rubles, the bank issued 252 shares (*pai*) priced at 5,000 rubles each. Although the restricted number of stockholders appeared quite unusual for a bank (and numerous other banks founded later in Moscow adopted a less exclusive structure), this pattern accorded perfectly with the old merchant tradition of solid, cautiously managed, family-centered businesses. The Soviet scholar Gindin drew from the archives of this bank fascinating statistical information, presented in Table 2.3, that demonstrated the persistence of the old family ties over the decades. Moreover, most shares remained in the families of the original founders. In 1876, all the packets of more than ten shares belonged to only twenty-three families, and in 1885 to only twenty-five.[52]

[52] Gindin, "Moskovskie banki," in *Istoriia Moskvy*, vol. 4, 213–15. The table on 214 reads

Table 2.3. *Share ownership in the Moscow Merchant Bank, 1869–1885*

	1869	1876	1885
Number of stockholders	77	178	200
Total shares	252	700	1000
Average number of shares owned by each stockholder	3.3	3.9	5
Number of shares in packets of more than ten shares (nominal value: above 50,000 r.)	167 (66%)	600 (86%)	644 (64%)

Source: Iosif F. Gindin, "Moskovskie banki," in *Istoriia Moskvy*, vol. 4, 213–16.

These patterns suggest that corporate entrepreneurs made rational choices to maximize their benefits under the existing corporate law. At the same time, the painful experiences of the stock-exchange fevers early in the reign of Alexander II made clear the need for the reform of tsarist corporate legislation, coupled with measures to raise the distressingly low level of entrepreneurial probity. The most perceptive observer of corporations in the late 1850s bemoaned the loss of "up to hundreds of millions of rubles" in the speculative mania of that time, but he asserted that the very reasons for the losses – "the present lack of the spirit of enterprise and the shortage of prominent capitalists" – made it imperative to create joint-stock companies, the only practical form of "large enterprises built upon aggregated capital."[53]

The period between 1855 and 1870 revealed the persistence of the old relationship between capitalists and the tsarist state, particularly the limited success of governmental efforts to borrow West European institutions before the cultural prerequisites for successful adaptation had developed. The history of Russian corporate law reflected the familiar dilemma that had faced tsarist policy makers from Peter's time onward: Excessively strict legislation entailed economic stagnation, but the relaxation of controls opened the way to abuses by the capitalists. As a consolation, the historian finds in the laws devoted to corporations in this first episode of Russian large-scale entrepreneurship a rich documentary record of the interplay between the positive and negative features of both the tsarist autocratic mode of government and the dynamism of capitalist institutions. Besides the corporate charters themselves, the list of corporate securities

"100" for the total number of shares in 1876, an obvious error not corrected, however, in the list of errata inserted at the end of the volume.

[53] Rozental', *Ocherk*, 4, 3.

issued twice a year from October 1862 onward by the Ministry of Finance provided a fascinating record of the government's own changing opinion of the financial condition of the largest companies in the empire. This index exerted, in turn, a direct influence on the public perception of the strength of these enterprises. We are left, therefore, with a restatement of the familiar role of law in the tsarist system: It not only provided a record of policy makers' attitudes toward current economic issues, but it also acted, in true Russian fashion, as a major factor in the shaping of the economic trends themselves.

3

Proval reformy (The failure of reform), 1860–1874

> To be sure, we see efforts to introduce reforms; commissions and subcommissions are appointed, and bills written; but these never reach the point of confirmation and implementation. This is the characteristic feature of the Russian bureaucracy: that bills prepared on every aspect of the law subsequently pass [directly] into the archive.
>
> – Józef Kaczkowski, legal historian (1908)[1]

The great surges in corporate activity after the Crimean War appear all the more impressive, notwithstanding the illegalities, absurdities, and excesses of the stock-exchange fevers, when we recall that no major reform of the corporate law of 1836 occurred to precipitate the rush to incorporation. In contrast to the Russian experience, some of the economic dynamism of Western Europe can be explained by the gradual loosening of the law to accommodate the needs of large-scale undertakings. By the early 1870s, after the great panic of 1873 had swept through the stock exchanges of London, Paris, and Vienna, fundamental differences between European capitalist institutions and those of the Russian Empire had become clear. In Europe, legislation to allow unstable corporations appeared less harmful than restrictions that would hobble the growth of the entire economic system, and if the occasional panics swept away the weakest firms, a resilient structure of corporate capitalism remained.

In Russia, the bureaucracy saw the matter differently. Although the shortcomings of the law of 1836 caused the tsarist policy makers to consider numerous reforms, by 1874 all such plans had succumbed to the bureaucrats' more elemental impulses: inertia and fear of change. The reign of Alexander II, especially the period before 1866, has often been called "the Era of the Great Reforms," but the corporate law of the empire remained

---

[1] Józef Kaczkowski, "Towarzystwa akcyjne w państwie rosyjskiem: studyum prawno-ekonomiczne," *Ekonomista*, 8 (1908), no. 1, 104.

as much in need of reform in 1881 as in 1860. The familiar pattern may be discerned here, in the work of the "enlightened bureaucrat" Mikhail Kh. Reutern,[2] as in other aspects of public life under Alexander II: the drafting of an impressive reform by a panel of experts; the submission of suggestions by various business organizations, which illustrated the sectoral and regional conflicts among these institutions; and the ultimate abandonment of the reform by the minister of finance.

The need for reform

At the end of the 1860s, the differences between the corporate laws of the major Western European nations and those of the Russian Empire were clear to all. Just as the trend toward incorporation on demand reflected the growing political power of business interests in Europe, the lack of such a trend in Russia testified to the political impotence of the merchants. Corporate law first evolved toward entrepreneurial freedom in Great Britain, as mentioned in Chapter 1. The French law of July 24, 1867, introduced essentially the same principles as those legislated by the British Parliament: abolition of the concession system for the largest corporations (1844), limited liability for managers and investors (1855–7), and the extension of these reforms to banks and insurance companies (1862).[3] Soon, most other European countries adopted the same legislation: Portugal in 1867, Spain in 1868, Prussia in 1870, Belgium in 1873, Italy in 1882, and Switzerland in 1883. Only Rumania and Austria retained the concession system (authorization in the latter country to be given by the court, not the economic ministry), and only Holland, Turkey, and Russia required preliminary authorization in the form of a separate law.[4]

In Germany prior to 1870, the port of Hamburg had allowed anonymous companies with limited liability to be established without a special law. Legislation establishing the corporation (*Aktiengesellschaft*) passed in the Prussian Landtag that year brought the British and French reforms of the 1860s to Prussia. The German counterpart of the French limited part-

---

[2] W. Bruce Lincoln, *In the Vanguard of Reform: Russia's Enlightened Bureaucrats, 1825–1861* (De Kalb, Ill., 1982), 207, noted that Reutern deserved this label for his approval of consultations with elected representatives of the zemstvos in the drafting of legislation.
[3] Norbert Horn, "Aktienrechliche Unternehmersorganisation in der Hochindustrialisierung (1860–1920): Deutschland, England, Frankreich und die USA in Vergleich," in Norbert Horn and Jürgen Kocka, eds., *Recht und Entwicklung der Grossunternehmen im 19. und frühen 20. Jahrhundert* (Göttingen, 1979), 128; Charles E. Freedeman, *Joint-Stock Enterprise in France: From Privileged Company to Modern Corporation* (Chapel Hill, 1979), 142–4.
[4] *La Grande Encyclopédie*, 31 vols. (Paris, n.d.), vol. 30, 134.

nership, known as the *Kommanditgesellschaft auf Aktien*, had begun to operate in Germany during the nineteenth century, but in 1892 it was superseded by the limited-liability partnership (*Gesellschaft mit beschränkter Haftung*, or GmbH), which, unlike the *commandite*, gave full partners limited liability without the sale of shares on the stock market.[5]

These reforms did not go unnoticed in Russia. In an important speech at Kharkov University in 1861, the legal expert Semen Pakhman (Pachmann) analyzed, often critically, the corporate law of the major European countries and proposed the reform of the Russian law. Peter the Great's bureaucracy had grown inordinately powerful: "We lived a long time under its yoke." Now, however, even the state itself urged society to become more active. Pakhman quoted from the journal of the Ministry of Internal Affairs in 1858 a criticism of the tradition of state tutelage (*opeka*) over industry, a habit that "teaches the people to hope, to expect, and to demand everything from the government, while the people remain inactive, having lost the ability to think about itself."[6]

According to Pakhman, the primary failing of the Russian corporate law of 1836 lay in its inability to recognize "the principle of freedom for industrial joint-stock activity." The many "formalities" of the law created two evils: "centralization of companies and the huge size of enterprises, which inhibits the freedom of enterprise." The first and most basic reform would be the creation of two categories of corporations. The concessionary company would continue to exist, as under the current law, with special state permission and financial support, to manage a few massive undertakings of national economic significance. All other corporations, however, should be freed from the concessionary system. Citing the English law of 1856, Pakhman urged that all firms of moderate size, namely, those with twenty or more partners or investors, be granted limited liability upon simple registration with a local governmental authority.[7]

Professor Pakhman had little use for the French *société en commandite par actions*, despite the praise that it received from the future finance minister, Bunge, and other experts, who saw in it a way for small enterprises to avoid the concession system imposed by the law of 1836.[8] The principle

---

[5] *Encyclopedia Britannica*, 14th ed., vol. 6, 151.
[6] Semen V. Pakhman [Pachmann], *O zadachakh predstoiashchei reformy aktsionernogo zakonodatel'stva* (Kharkov, 1861), 43 (quoted); 44 (quotation from *Zhurnal ministerstva vnutrennikh del*, without reference).
[7] Pakhman, *O zadachakh*, 48, 75–6.
[8] Pakhman, *O zadachakh*, 30, gave incomplete citations to Bunge's article in *Zhurnal dlia*

of unlimited liability for managers was supposed to ensure high standards of honesty and competence, but recent French practice had shown that few honest men would consent to act as founders and managers under such onerous conditions; instead, scoundrels gladly accepted the burden of unlimited liability, indulged in all sorts of fraudulent deals, and then absconded with the company's funds when financial disaster threatened. Pakhman concluded that the Russian law on limited partnerships (*tovarishchestva na vere*) should not be amended to allow free circulation of their shares on the stock market, a change that would have made them the equivalent of the much-abused *commandite* in France. Rather, like the English government, which refused in 1853 to allow the division of shares in a partnership, the Russian authorities should keep the existing forms – partnerships, limited partnerships, and corporations – while modifying the law of 1836 to allow local registration for all but the largest of corporations. As for the abuses that had shocked the world of corporate finance after the Crimean War, Pakhman called for a reduction in government favors to companies. He endorsed the views of the economist Ivan K. Babst, who denounced the state subsidies lavished on the Russian Railroad Company and approved the British Parliament's refusal to rescue mismanaged corporations.[9] The path to improvement lay in what might be called the democratization of the corporation: the abolition of the ban on unnamed shares; the maximum possible participation of stockholders in the decision-making process within each company; and the issuing of large numbers of shares, only part of which should be owned by the founders. "Open discussion" (*glasnost'*) and "responsibility" (*otvetstvennost'*), two catchwords among liberals in the early reign of Alexander II, constituted Pakhman's recipe for progress. Democratic ideals were in the air, and their benefits appeared obvious to economists like Pakhman who were familiar with European institutions.[10] Was the corporation not a miniature democracy, composed of citizens (stockholders) and elected public servants (the management)?[11]

aktsionerov, 1857, no. 26; and to *Russkii vestnik*, 1860, no. 20, section *Sovremennaia letopis'*, pp. 417–20.

[9] Pakhman, *O zadachakh*, 88, citing unspecified articles by Babst in *Vestnik promyshlennosti*, 1860, nos. 6, 7, and 3. On the crucial role of this journal in the alliance between the Moscow merchants and Slavophile intellectuals, see Thomas C. Owen, "The Moscow Merchants and the Public Press, 1858–1868," *Jahrbücher für Geschichte Osteuropas*, N.S., 23, no. 1 (Mar. 1975), 26–38.

[10] Pakhman, *O zadachakh*, 77–81, 86–8, 94, 103 (quoted), 104, 125–6.

[11] Cynical observers opposed to abuses of the democratic form of government noted that

Business groups joined economists in calling for fundamental reform of the Russian corporate law. The main newspaper of the merchants in the northern capital, *Birzhevye vedomosti* (Stock-exchange news), stated in an editorial in 1867: "The laws that we have now do not promote the widest development of the principle of association. By stipulating a multitude of formal conditions, the law [of 1836] does more to hinder than to help the formation of joint-stock companies."[12]

However insistent these calls for reform may have been, the Russian bureaucracy remained institutionally immune from public control. Soviet historians tend to portray the tsarist regime as the defender of the gentry's economic interests and the sponsor of an industrialization program that enriched a handful of capitalist millionaires, but the state had strong priorities of its own. In the realm of industrial policy, Reutern, the most talented and dynamic minister of finance under Alexander II, appears to have pursued neither economic development for its own sake nor policies designed to benefit a particular group, but rather the restoration of the economy as a revenue-producing mechanism for the state itself.[13] For example, tariff reductions promised an increase in imports and a net rise in revenues, so Reutern, following the policy of his predecessors in 1850 and 1857, proposed a dramatic reduction in duties in 1867. He was overruled only by the State Council, which heeded the demands of Russian merchants for moderate protection of the textile industry.[14]

To be sure, Reutern proved susceptible enough to the new spirit of *glasnost'* to consult periodically with business leaders, to allow the estab-

---

corporations were not at all immune. As Werner Sombart noted, in *Der moderne Kapitalismus*, 6 parts in 3 vols. (Munich, 1924; reprinted Berlin, 1955) vol. 3, part 2, 735, "The joint-stock company is the mirror image of modern democracy: the people (stockholders) are said to rule, but power is really held by a tiny clique that forms in the company from time to time." ("Die AG ist das Spiegelbild der modernen Demokratie; in der Fiktion herrscht das Volk (Aktionäre), in Wirklichkeit ein kleiner Klüngel von Machthabern, der in der AG verschieden zusammengesetzt ist.")

[12] Quoted in Vladimir Ia. Laverychev, *Krupnaia burzhuaziia v poreformennoi Rossii (1861–1900 gg.)* (Moscow, 1974), 42.

[13] See Joseph W. Kipp, "M. Kh. Reutern on the Russian State and Economy: A Liberal Bureaucrat during the Crimean Era, 1854–60," *Journal of Modern History*, 47, no. 3 (Sep. 1975), 437–59; and Oliver S. Hayward, "Official Russian Policies Concerning Industrialization during the Finance Ministry of M. Kh. Reutern, 1862–1878," doctoral dissertation, University of Wisconsin, 1973.

[14] M. N. Sobolev, *Tamozhennaia politika Rossii vo vtoroi polovine XIX veka* (Tomsk, 1911), 222, 240–1, 271–7, 290–4, 302, 417–19; and Nikolai A. Naidenov, *Vospominaniia o vidennom, slyshannom i ispytannom*, 2 vols. (Moscow, 1903–5; reprinted Newtonville, Mass., 1976), 65–8, 84–90.

lishment of new consultative organizations like the Russian Technical Society (1866)[15] and the RIS (1867),[16] and in 1872, to replace the moribund Commercial and Manufacturing Councils of Nicholas's day with a slightly more representative Council of Trade and Manufacturing, to which its Moscow Section and several regional committees were subordinate.[17] He also made several regulatory changes in an effort to encourage economic activity in the 1860s. Although the three episodes discussed here may seem minor in the context of the great challenges facing Russian society in the wake of the Crimean War and the emancipation, they appeared appropriate to policy makers accustomed to controlling social and economic processes by issuing edicts from the chanceries on the Neva.

A decree signed into law by Alexander II on January 1, 1863, undermined the traditional system of social estates (*sosloviia*) by granting to all Russians, and even to foreigners, the right to engage in industry and commerce, functions associated in the past with the merchant estate (*kupechestvo*), though peasants had long been allowed to engage in petty trade and handicrafts as a way of increasing their economic worth to landlords. If merchants were to be deprived in 1863 of their nominal monopoly on large-scale commerce and manufacturing, logic would have dictated the abolition of the entire estate structure at this point in Russian history. However, as in the emancipation of the serfs, the tsarist regime refused to jettison all facets of the estate system. Like a huge block of carved ice melting in the summer sun, it grew smaller and lost many of its originally sharp outlines, but to the very end of the tsarist period, it still hampered social mobility and accentuated social frictions that exploded in revolutionary anger in the early twentieth century.[18] Naturally, many anomalies

---

[15] Harley D. Balzer, "Russian Technical Society," *MERSH*, vol. 32, 176–80; and N. G. Filippov, "Nauchno-tekhnicheskie obshchestva dorevoliutsionnoi Rossii," *Voprosy istorii*, 1985, no. 3 (Mar.), 31–45, devoted primarily to the Russian Technical Society; and the works cited therein.

[16] Thomas C. Owen, "The Russian Industrial Society and Tsarist Economic Policy, 1867–1905," *Journal of Economic History*, 45, no. 3 (Sep. 1985), 587–606.

[17] The history of merchants' organizations under the tsarist regime remains to be written. Preliminary descriptive and analytical works include Leopol'd Nisselovich, *O torgovo-promyshlennykh uchrezhdeniiakh* (St. Petersburg, 1882); *Torgovo-promyshlennye s'ezdy v Rossii* (St. Petersburg, 1896); A. Gushka [pseud. of Osip Arkad'evich Ermanskii, né Kogan], *Predstavitel'nye organizatsii torgovo-promyshlennogo klassa v Rossii* (St. Petersburg, 1912); E. S. Lur'e, *Organizatsiia i organizatsii torgovo-promyshlennykh interesov v Rossii* (St. Petersburg, 1913); and Ia. I. Livshin, "'Predstavitel'nye' organizatsii krupnoi burzhuazii v Rossii v kontse XIX–nachale XX vv.," *Istoriia SSSR*, 1959, no. 2 (Mar.–Apr.), 95–117.

[18] A stimulating discussion of the estate system and its significance is Gregory L. Freeze, "The *Soslovie* (Estate) Paradigm and Russian Social History," *American Historical Review*, 91, no. 1 (Feb. 1986), 11–36. Freeze appears excessively critical, however, of the traditional

developed as the estate structure underwent gradual decay. Merchants gained admittance to the hereditary gentry; aristocrats, generals, and high bureaucrats headed giant corporations; peasants received university degrees; impoverished noblemen became bookkeepers; and until 1874, when military service was extended to merchants for the first time since the reign of Peter the Great, many townspeople without any commercial or industrial pretensions enrolled in the merchant guilds as a means of avoiding the draft.

The law of January 1, 1863, contributed directly to this confusion. In the interest of economic development, it opened the fields of commerce and industry to nonmerchants. In so doing, this legislative act explicitly severed the traditional connection between guild membership and personal status because, as article 21 announced, certificates granting the right to trade were henceforth to be issued "to persons of both sexes, Russian subjects of all ranks [*vsekh sostoianii*], and foreigners." Article 18 required anyone engaged in commerce to buy an annual certificate, no matter what his or her social status. Even corporations (except, of course, those exempted by special provisions of their charters) now assumed this obligation. A first-guild certificate allowed a person or company to conduct wholesale and retail commerce, to maintain a factory (*fabrika*) or plant (*zavod*), or to produce articles of handicraft (article 32). A second-guild certificate entitled the holder to engage in local retail trade, factory management, and handicraft production, without any limit on the number of enterprises owned, as long as each had a separate certificate and none produced goods worth more than fifteen thousand silver rubles per year (article 33). The owner of every plant or factory equipped with machinery, or powered by steam, or manned by more than sixteen workers must also purchase a first- or second-guild ticket (*bilet*) for each such enterprise (article 34). (Machinery, steam power, or a work force of sixteen or more remained until 1917 the official criteria for classifying a productive unit as a factory or plant, as opposed to a small workshop.) The largest enterprises – joint-

---

liberal Russian historiography, which viewed the estate structures and its various juridical antecedents as a means by which the autocratic state regimented Russian society from the seventeenth century onward. The present study endeavors to show that, at least for managers of large corporations from 1856 onward, it is hardly correct to say, as does Freeze, 25, that "particular ministries tended to articulate the interests of a subordinate or closely associated group," for example, "the Ministry of Finance for townspeople." Although the Ministry of Finance devoted relatively more efforts to economic development than did the Ministry of Justice, Freeze's formulation ignores the finance ministry's obsession with raising revenues for the state and its political and even psychological insulation from the merchants, a pattern rooted in the undemocratic nature of tsarist institutions.

stock companies and share partnerships – and banks were required to obtain a first-guild certificate (article 36). A further rationalization consisted in the abolition of the third merchant guild, in which numerous urban inhabitants of limited means, both small-scale traders and those without any commercial occupation, had traditionally clustered to take advantage of the privileges of the merchant estate: exemption from taxation and the military draft.[19]

Having abolished the juridical link between membership in the merchant estate and commercial or industrial activity by its members, the law blithely reiterated a crucial feature of the old estate system: All family members enjoyed the rights bestowed upon the head of household by the purchase of an annual guild or business certificate (article 57). Even as it opened the economic field to nonmerchants, it maintained the previous structure of urban merchant "guilds," created by Peter in a vain attempt to implant the European burgher ethos in the Russian merchant estate. To this quaint echo of medieval town law, imposed by an autocratic state on its recalcitrant merchants without benefit of urban self-government, the law of 1863 attached numerous requirements dictated by the nature of rural Russian society. Although peasants who engaged in petty trading in the villages remained exempt from the requirement to enroll in a merchant guild and were free to trade in grain and other foodstuffs (articles 4–5), they were obligated to buy inexpensive "business certificates" (*promyslovye svidetel'stva*) (article 15) each year.[20]

Perhaps the most significant aspect of the guild reform of 1863 was the resistance to it mounted, quite without success, by the merchants themselves, who feared that the loss of their privileged economic position might cause a reduction in their financial strength. In fact, the leading merchant families in Moscow and other major cities enjoyed a marked prosperity in following decades, so that their protests can best be understood as a

---

[19] An excellent survey of this legislation and the social context in which it appeared is Manfred Hildermeier, *Bürgertum und Stadt in Russland 1760–1870: Rechtliche Lage und soziale Struktur* (Cologne, 1986), part 2, chap. 5.

[20] This system of annual payments persisted for decades thereafter. For example, on the eve of the introduction of the first corporate income tax in 1885 (see Chapter 5, this volume), merchants paid 565 rubles for a first-guild certificate or between 40 and 120 rubles for a second-guild certificate, depending on where they lived. Nonmerchants paid between 10 and 30 rubles for a petty trade certificate. In addition, members of the first guild paid from 20 to 55 rubles for a ticket for each enterprise; members of the second guild, 10 to 35 rubles; and petty traders, 2 to 10 rubles. *PSZ* 3–2282, dated June 5, 1884, section *shtaty i tabeli*, 195.

measure of their devotion to the old estate system, in which they sought to rise to an honored place next to the gentry.[21]

Another social group found its traditional privileges curtailed by the state in the interest of industrial development. The Cossacks who inhabited the region along the Don River had for centuries enjoyed special rights under tsarist rule. In the nineteenth century, these included the practice of commerce in the Don Military Region (oblast' Voiska Donskogo) without the purchase of guild certificates. In the Grushev area of the region, moreover, no one but a Don Cossack was permitted to work the rich coal deposits, whether as an individual or as an investor or manager of a corporation. Finally, in late 1863, the Ministry of Finance overruled the objections of the local authorities (*voiskovoe pravlenie*) and abolished the Cossacks' monopoly on coal production in this area.[22] Far from demonstrating a bias toward the gentry, in accordance with the monotonous Soviet claim that governmental actions invariably enhanced the position of the "ruling class," this policy change represented only a minor step away from the traditional estate system, in which Cossacks enjoyed exclusive control of their steppelands. Reutern stopped far short of opening the coalfields of the Donets Basin to corporations, so that the exploitation of the mineral riches of the empire remained hindered for decades by outworn vestiges of the old estate system.

Yet another indication of the tsarist government's interest in reforms to facilitate economic development may be seen in a decree dated May 3, 1873. Nicholas I had banned Old Believer merchants from engaging in certain kinds of trade and industry, in the hope of forcing them to convert to Orthodoxy. Although the adherents of various tendencies of this illegal, fundamentalist offshoot of pre-Petrine Russian Christianity had distinguished themselves as keen entrepreneurs in centuries past, the autocratic regime preferred to persecute the Old Believers no matter what the cost to the economic development of the empire. Now, in 1873, a modicum of religious toleration appeared useful for the sake of progress. This reform

[21] See the various statements in favor of the estate system by prominent Moscow merchants between 1830 and 1865 in Thomas C. Owen, *Capitalism and Politics in Russia: A Social History of the Moscow Merchants* (Cambridge, 1981), chaps. 1–2. Some of the same points are made by Alfred J. Rieber, *Merchants and Entrepreneurs in Imperial Russia* (Chapel Hill, 1982), esp. in chap. 1, "State Paternalism and Social Stagnation," and chap. 3, "The Persistence of Tradition," which correctly traces aspects of the patriarchal merchant attitudes into the twentieth century.

[22] Laverychev, *Krupnaia burzhuaziia*, 37–8, citing I. P. Khlystov, *Don v epokhu kapitalizma, 60-e-seredina 90-kh godov XIX v.* (Rostov-on-Don, 1962), 125–6.

hardly presaged the legalization of the schismatics, however; they received full civil rights only after the revolution of 1905.[23]

The cautious reforming spirit of Reutern had international implications as well. In 1863, the State Council considered the draft charter of a new bank, to be established in London with a basic capital of 2.5 million pounds sterling under the name Anglo-Russian Bank. Although founded under English law, the bank would have operated exclusively in Russia. The State Council viewed with apprehension the precedent that the approval of this charter might set. First, the bank threatened to give "England a new means with which to exert influence on our economic affairs and our public opinion, which is in many respects highly impressionable." Even more dangerous to the autocratic principle was the prospect that Russians might resort in large numbers to incorporating new enterprises under English law, free from the bureaucratic stranglehold that the concession system of 1836 imposed on corporate activities throughout the tsarist empire. In the end, the State Council accepted Reutern's view that the economic benefits to be derived from chartering the Anglo-Russian Bank outweighed the political drawbacks. "Foreign banks," it concluded, "had the great advantage of enriching the country quickly with large amounts of capital, which would take many years to accumulate" from domestic sources. At the same time, the tsarist government, ever jealous of its power, required that each foreign company receive special permission from the Ministry of Finance before being allowed to operate in Russia, in effect extending to foreigners the administrative controls that weighed heavily on domestic corporations. Although the project never came to fruition because the prospective founders abandoned it, the government in 1863 created the mechanism by which foreign companies received permission to operate in Russia from this time to the revolution of 1917.[24]

These episodes indicated that under Reutern's careful stewardship of the imperial finances, the tsarist government gave thoughtful consideration to many economic reforms. At the center of the debate, of course, stood the outmoded law of 1836, which satisfied neither the corporate entrepre-

---

[23] See William L. Blackwell, *The Beginnings of Russian Industrialization, 1800–1860* (Princeton, 1968), chap. 9 and Pavel G. Ryndziunskii, "Staroobriadcheskaia organizatsiia v usloviiakh razvitiia promyshlennogo kapitalizma," *Voprosy istorii religii i ateizma*, vol. 1 (Moscow, 1950), 188–248. The decree of May 3, 1873, which does not appear in the *PSZ*, is cited in *Torgovoe i promyshlennoe delo Riabushinskikh* (Moscow, 1913), 49.

[24] Leonid E. Shepelev, *Aktsionernye kompanii v Rossii* (Leningrad, 1973), 102–5, quotations from 103. See Chapter 5 of the present book, section on ethnic restrictions, for a discussion of minor changes in the 1890s.

neurs nor the bureaucrats. Of all the emperors who ruled between 1825 and 1917, Alexander II seemed the most likely to borrow from Western Europe the latest capitalist institutions because he introduced numerous legal and administrative forms that imitated English, French, and German models. Alexander's economic advisors realized that corporate law constituted a key element of a modern industrial order, and any fair-minded historian must respect their difficult labors over the years to produce a new law appropriate to the burgeoning economy of the 1860s. Intelligent bureaucrats could only be embarrassed to read in the section on corporations in the 1863 edition of the Code of Laws the absurd notation "charters of several joint-stock companies permit exceptions to the general regulations contained in this [2160] and following articles." Shepelev, who quoted this passage, noted that by the early 1870s only twenty-eight of the fifty-nine articles in the law of 1836 "could be considered to have practical significance."[25] In its five-volume report on the need for reforms in the administration of the economy, the Stackelberg Commission (1862–5) recommended a system of local control over the creation and operation of industrial enterprises. It also pointed out that the laws were so poorly adapted to current conditions as to require "the complete transformation of the very system of industrial legislation."[26] The government's effort to reform the corporate law failed miserably, however. The proposals and counterproposals that filled the archive of the Finance Ministry therefore deserve close attention. Although the details of the legislative process might be considered unbearably dull, the reader should be assured that the drama was enlivened by moments of high comedy.

The Butovskii Commission

A sketch of the bureaucratic discussions that lasted almost fifteen years but produced no new reform makes clear the absurdity of the process. Between 1858 and 1874, tsarist policy makers carried on study after study. Their efforts produced a small mountain of paper and two bills (in 1867 and 1872),[27] but no new law. These episodes starkly illuminated the persistence

---

[25] Shepelev, *Kompanii*, 108.
[26] *Trudy Komissii, uchrezhdennoi dlia peresmotra ustavov fabrichnogo i remeslennogo*, 5 parts (St. Petersburg, 1863–5), part 1, iii, quoted in Leonid E. Shepelev, *Tsarizm i burzhuaziia vo vtoroi polovine XIX veka: problemy torgovo-promyshlennoi politiki* (Leningrad, 1981), 94.
[27] Shepelev, alone among legal historians, speaks of the revision of the latter bill as the bill of 1874.

of the dilemma of encouragement and control that the law of 1836 had failed to resolve.

Late in 1858, the tsar approved a full review of the existing law on corporations. By February 1861, a bill one hundred paragraphs long had emerged from the Ministry of Finance, ready for interministerial discussion. Everyone realized that the old law's prohibition on futures contracts and its insistence on named shares had not only failed to prevent speculation but had also constrained corporate development by preventing the free circulation of stocks in domestic and foreign markets. The finance ministry therefore proposed the legalization of futures deals, the purchase of stocks with partial payment, and unnamed shares.

It refused, however, to abandon the most repressive bureaucratic "restraints" (*obuzdaniia*) aimed at curbing fraud: the concession system and its corollary, the requirement that corporate managers obtain governmental permission before making changes in the charter regarding an increase or decrease in the size of basic capital, the issuing of bonds, or the distribution of reserve capital to stockholders. The bill also added a new stipulation to deter speculation by the founders: Each draft charter submitted for the state's approval must be accompanied by a sworn statement that one-fifth of the basic capital had already been raised. In order to make corporate boards of directors more responsive to stockholders, the bill granted to the general assembly certain new powers: to establish the size of the reserve fund and the annual dividends, to elect all of the directors and officers, to change the charter within limits prescribed by law, and to establish an audit commission (*revizionnaia komissiia*) to scrutinize the work of the board. In addition, individual stockholders would be allowed to place issues on the agenda of the general assembly without the board's permission, and the number of votes necessary to decide ordinary questions (those not requiring ministerial approval) would be lowered from 75 to 50 percent.[28]

Between February 1861 and February 1865, various ministries and agencies produced commentaries on this proposal. Although the government also solicited opinions from business organizations, Shepelev found in the Leningrad archive statements from only two: the Riga Exchange Committee and the semibureaucratic Moscow sections of the manufacturing and commercial councils. The first body considered the one-fifth rule an impossible burden on new companies; a more effective curb on spec-

---

[28] Shepelev, *Kompanii*, 98–100.

ulation, it opined, would be a rule that shares be sold only in the region near the company's headquarters. This unique suggestion perhaps expressed the hostility of Baltic Germans toward the many corporations, founded in Petersburg, that carried out their operations in distant provinces, as well as a demonstration of their pride in the relatively advanced economic institutions of Riga. For their part, the Muscovites favored the introduction of preferred shares (*privilegirovannye aktsii*), which would carry a preferential right to dividends, as a way of rekindling the public's interest in corporate investment in the wake of the first postwar fever and bust. The Ministry of Finance rejected the advice from Riga but added the suggestion from Moscow to the bill.[29]

The Ministry of Internal Affairs offered its own ideas on ways to limit speculation: First, no company should be permitted to undertake a project unless the capital necessary for it surpassed the resources of individual entrepreneurs; second, the minimum size of a company's stock capital should be set at 500,000 rubles to discourage the proliferation of small, weak firms; and third, shares must cost at least one hundred rubles, to limit speculation.[30] Although Reutern refused to include these provisions in the bill, these suggestions were important as symptoms of the police mentality, still strong in the tsarist bureaucracy, that viewed with suspicion the workings of the free market.

Despite the urgings of the tsar himself, in November 1865 and October 1866, that the bureaucracy act promptly on this bill, the State Council greeted it in April 1867 with a totally unexpected response, one that sealed its doom. So important did the corporate law now appear to the State Council in light of the recent European reforms that the council insisted on sending the bill to the Ministry of Justice for its considered legal opinion. Count Konstantin I. Palen and his subordinates there displayed so great a concern for the bill that, in addition to general remarks, they offered detailed proposals for revision of fifty-six of its ninety-nine articles. This is not to minimize the cogency of Palen's commentary. Arguing the need to free corporations from excessively strict regulation, he pointed out the benefits that would accrue from a multitude of small companies in the agricultural sector, especially in the grain and wool trades, to the benefit of poor peasants and gentry, traditionally the victims of local profiteers and usurers. Palen therefore proposed a much lower minimum amount for the

[29] Shepelev, *Kompanii*, 101–2.
[30] Shepelev, *Kompanii*, 102.

preliminary investment prior to confirmation (only one-twentieth of basic capital), the introduction of shares to the bearer, and even the right of founders to receive a charter without making all the changes proposed by the ministries during the petitioning process. Nothing if not a bold conceptualizer, Palen proposed sending the bill to all existing corporations for comments and called for a "fundamental revision" of the statutes on full and limited partnerships as well as the law of 1836![31]

Finance Minister Reutern returned the bill to the State Council in November 1869, having indicated his willingness to accept all of Palen's suggestions except the reduction of the initial operating capital from one-fifth to one-twentieth of the total. However, so sweeping had been the revisions made in the previous few years that it is fair to speak of this bill as a substantially new one, all the more so because another round of comments by the State Council and the public lay ahead. In mid-February 1870, the tsar approved the council's proposal to publish the bill and to solicit comments from the public by September 1. According to Shepelev, no significant responses arrived. Perhaps the manufacturers and investors had grown dazed from watching the bureaucratic carousel of drafting, debating, and delay in the previous nine years.[32]

The second major effort to produce a new law began after the deadline passed in September 1870. Certainly there was no scarcity of expertise or new ideas, only of a method for forging a final version acceptable to all the ministries. The new editorial commission met under the chairmanship of Aleksandr I. Butovskii of the Department of Trade and Manufacturing in the Ministry of Finance, an economic expert who had helped to draft the bill of 1861. The commission included the most diverse officials from the Ministries of Internal Affairs, Transportation, Justice, and even Foreign Affairs (the last because the bill contained regulations of foreign companies operating in the Russian Empire). In a rare demonstration of

---

[31] Shepelev, *Kompanii*, 105–6.
[32] Shepelev, *Kompanii*, 107–8. He noted, 108, that the text of the bill appeared in the major newspapers in Petersburg and Moscow on May 20, 1870. In Moscow in the spring of 1980, this writer submitted to the staff of TsGIAM numerous written requests to examine policy statements of the Moscow Exchange Committee (MEC) regarding corporate law, labor law, import tariffs, and railroad freight rates. After the usual delays, the archivists responded with denials that such documents existed in the MEC records (f. 143). The answer remained the same even when such documents were identified precisely by subject and date, cited from the jubilee history of the exchange: Nikolai A. Naidenov, ed., *Moskovskaia birzha, 1839–1889* (Moscow, 1889). Among these documents was a statement regarding railroad freight rates dated October 23, 1870, cited in Naidenov, ed., *Moskovskaia birzha*, 60.

confidence in public representation, Butovskii invited the president of the PEC, Aleksandr G. Zolotarev, to join the deliberations.[33]

One of the members of this commission, the economist Fedor Gustavovich Terner (originally Thörner in German), published in 1871 a survey of corporate law in the European states that included proposals for reform in the Russian laws. Citing the German scholar Schäffle, Terner stressed the importance of the entrepreneur, a factor at least as crucial to economic development as land, labor, and capital.[34] Although numerous scandals had demonstrated that unscrupulous founders could reap huge bonuses from a fledgling company "and then leave the stockholders to the whim of fate," two kinds of regulation existed with which to limit such fraud. Either a government could impose strict regulations on each company in the form of a concession, while granting limited liability to the managers and investors, or the state could exercise indirect control to instill a spirit of prudence among managers of enterprises who handled large amounts of clients' funds – banks, insurance companies, and so on – by stipulating that such managers bear unlimited liability for the debts of the enterprise. Terner favored the latter alternative and regarded the concessionary principle as useful only when a company received "any sort of subsidies, guarantees, or special rights regarding the expropriation or receipt of governmental property for its own use." Otherwise, he argued, state interference in corporate activity only damaged the prospects of economic growth. Once clear legal guidelines were established, the managers of all companies except those that handled capital or received special favors from the state should be allowed to act freely as long as they registered with the appropriate authorities and obeyed the law.[35] He especially endorsed the legalization of unnamed shares, both because they would circulate more easily than named shares, for example, as collateral for bank loans, and because "there is almost no company founded in the past decade that did not reserve this right to itself in its charter as an exception" to the law of 1836.[36]

If these suggestions seem familiar, it is because they closely resembled the program of corporate law reform proposed by Pakhman a decade

---

[33] Shepelev, *Kompanii*, 111. Fourteen commission members are named in TsGIA, f. 20, ed. kh. 1916-a, list 38.
[34] Fedor Gustarovich Terner, *Sravnitel'noe obozrenie aktsionernogo zakonodatel'stva glavneishikh evropeiskikh stran* (St. Petersburg, 1871), 45, citing Albert E. F. Schäffle, *Das gesellschaftliche System der menschenlicher Wirtschaft*, 2nd ed. (Tübingen, 1867).
[35] Terner, *Obozrenie*, 43–4.
[36] Terner, *Obozrenie*, 83.

before. Terner's openness to recent European reforms demonstrated how influential the theoretical notions of Pakhman and other economists had become within the bureaucracy. Indeed, in the twenty-two sessions that followed between November 1871 and April 1872, the Butovskii Commission abandoned the half measures proposed with agonizing slowness by the various ministries in the 1860s. It embraced a conception of corporate law in keeping with laissez-faire economic theories then fashionable in Western and Central Europe. The bill produced by the commission was the first in Russia to advocate the replacement of the concessionary principle by a simple system of administrative registration (*iavochnaia sistema*) of new corporate charters, principles embodied in corporate laws adopted shortly before in England (1862), France (1867), and Prussia (1870).

Butovskii and his advisors hoped that the new system would remove the inevitable implication of state support that accompanied the tsar's signature on a corporate charter, an implication that tended to make investors and creditors incautious despite the lack of any mechanism by which the state could judge the soundness of a particular company. More importantly, they recognized that the existing system encouraged petitioners to bribe officials who facilitated the charter's "passage through various departments of the ministries," as the bill's authors delicately put it. In accordance with the views of Pakhman, Terner, and other economists, the new bill did not entirely abolish the concession system, but limited it to ministerial (not imperial) approval of companies with special privileges from the state as well as potentially fragile entities: insurance companies, brokerage (*komissionnye*) businesses, and banks. All other companies would be considered legally constituted once the first general assembly approved the charter, all shares were sold and at least one-tenth fully paid for, and the corporation was registered at the Ministry of Finance. To combat speculation, carelessness, and fraud, the bill set a minimum share price (100 rubles), a minimum number of stockholders (seven), a down payment for shares of at least 10 percent, and a time limit of two years for full payment.

Especially noteworthy were two unprecedented measures to enhance entrepreneurial freedom. The bill mandated no minimum size of basic capital, and it provided for shares "to the bearer," which would circulate easily on the stock exchange, as long as such shares had been fully paid for (Article 59). Named shares remained obligatory only in companies active in sensitive border regions, whose charters excluded "certain persons" from participation. The commission had in mind enterprises whose activities could be considered quasi-military, such as those operating steamships on the Caspian Sea. (A law of 1869 had banned foreign subjects from owning shares in Caspian Sea shipping companies and had mandated named shares in such enterprises as a means of enforcing this restriction.)[37] Numerous other provisions of the bill, such as the reference to preferred shares, recently proposed by the Moscow Exchange Committee (MEC), demonstrated the commission's solicitude for the rights of corporate entrepreneurs.

However, the interests of stockholders received special emphasis as well. If a company lost more than half its basic capital, it must cease operations and be liquidated so as prevent further reduction of shareholders' equity. The bill also provided several means by which shareholders in the general assembly could defend their interests. For example, owners of only one-tenth of the company's shares could convoke a special meeting of the assembly; anyone owning at least 1 percent of the stock or shares worth 5,000 rubles or more in a company capitalized at 500,000 rubles must be allowed to vote; and no individual could cast more than half of the votes in any one meeting. As well, to form a quorum, holders of at least half the stock must be present to decide major questions (increase of basic capital or liquidation); one-fifth must be present to conduct routine business, such as the election of officers; and the motions must carry by a vote of three-quarters in the former cases and by a majority in the latter. Numerous articles regulated the activities of the board and the audit commission, including a mandatory annual review of the company's books by the latter (article 152).

These proposals, although generally welcome to reform-minded commission members and corporate leaders, came at a cost: Because it laid down detailed rules for all kinds of companies, the bill swelled in size to 194 articles.[38] So complex a set of regulations could hardly be approved by perfunctory hearings within the bureaucracy. Despite the ominous signs of legislative entropy that now loomed ahead – long debates, further revisions, inevitable delays as ministerial views changed in the course of months and years – Reutern saw no alternative to extended discussions of the bill among those who would have been obliged to abide by its

---

[37] Shepelev, *Kompanii*, 113–14; Avgust I. Kaminka, *Aktsionernaia kompaniia: iuridicheskoe issledovanie* (St. Petersburg, 1902), 392; on the Caspian Sea shipping companies, *PSZ* 2–47714, dated November 24, 1869.
[38] Shepelev, *Kompanii*, 112–14; Kaminka, *Kompaniia*, 393.

provisions. In the spirit of *glasnost'*, the Butovskii Commission's bill now became the object of public comment.

Recommendations from business organizations

Upon its provisional approval by the Ministry of Finance on April 6, 1872, the bill was printed in book form in six hundred copies.[39] Having received by October 15 approximately thirty commentaries on the law from newspapers, exchange committees, and other groups, the ministry published the most important of these in an edition of four hundred copies,[40] which was followed soon by a four-hundred-copy edition of commentaries arranged according to the various articles in the bill.[41] The exchange committees in Moscow and Petersburg published their own separate statements in 1872 and 1873, respectively.[42] Other substantial comments that remained unpublished, having arrived after the deadline, included those of the RIS, the Caucasus and Mercury Steamship Company, and the Russian Insurance and Annuity Company.[43] These statements provided an unprecedented view of the entrepreneurs' opinion on corporate law. Although they did not of course contain rhetorical attacks on the principle of autocratic rule, they revealed that business leaders chafed under the law of 1836 and resisted the continuation of bureaucratic control, in even so attenuated a form as that proposed in the Butovskii bill. This point is important because it undermines the common Soviet claim that businessmen enjoyed a comfortable place in the tsarist regime, an assertion all too easily accepted because of the dearth of documentary evidence about the actual views of business leaders in the half century before the revolution of 1905.

As might be expected, business organizations and individual spokesmen

---

[39] Kaczkowski, "Towarzystwa," 109; *Proekt polozheniia ob aktsionernykh obshchestvakh*...(St. Petersburg, 1872).
[40] *Zamechaniia na Proekt polozheniia ob aktsionernykh obshchestvakh, sostavlennyi osoboiu kommissieiu pri Ministerstve finansov*, 2 parts (St. Petersburg, 1872). This compendium consisted of twenty-one comments in one pagination, most of them excerpted from various newspapers and journals.
[41] *Svod zamechanii*...(St. Petersburg, 1872).
[42] Moscow, Birzha, *Zamechaniia na proekt polozheniia ob aktsionernykh obshchestvakh* (Moscow, 1872); St. Petersburg, Birzhevoi komitet, *Zamechaniia S.-Peterburgskogo birzhevogo komiteta i kommissii birzhevogo kupechestva na proekt polozheniia ob aktsionernykh obshchestvakh* (St. Petersburg, 1873). Publishing information on these and other commentaries on the Butovskii bill is given in Shepelev, *Kompanii*, 114.
[43] Shepelev, *Kompanii*, 114.

for corporate law reform welcomed the principle of incorporation by registration, but other aspects of the bill attracted their criticism for perpetuating various administrative controls over economic activity. The hundred-ruble minimum share price appeared too high to the Odessa Section of the Commercial Council, the *Sankt-Peterburgskie vedomosti* (St. Petersburg news), and the iron manufacturer Evgenii I. Ragozin, who favored a minimum price of 50, 25, and 10 rubles, respectively. Most commentators opposed the retention of the concession system for railroads, banks, and insurance companies. Especially infuriating to *Golos* (The voice), Leon M. Rozental', Ragozin, and Privy Councilor Aleksandr K. Girs was article 52. By authorizing the finance minister to annul a company's registration certificate at any time if inaccurate statements were found in the original application, this provision placed a veritable "sword of Damocles" over every corporation registered in the empire. *Torgovyi sbornik* (The commercial reporter), the newspaper of the RIS at that time, opposed the arbitrary power of the registrar to deny a company's application and the lack of an appeal procedure. *Birzhevye vedomosti* (Stock-exchange news) in Petersburg condemned previous bureaucratic "interference and regulation" over companies and explicitly endorsed the freedoms granted by the German law of June 11, 1870. The Riga Exchange Committee confined its critique to minor points, such as the prolix rules governing audit commissions, but only because it valued highly the principle of registration and hoped (in vain) to avoid a long debate that might doom the reform.[44]

An especially penetrating criticism came from the PEC, the elective body of merchants in the most Europeanized city in Russia, apart from the German cities of the Baltic coast. In a detailed commentary on the bill, endorsed as well by a special commission of merchants, the Petersburg leaders praised the Butovskii Commission's efforts "to remove from legislation all tutelage over the public." However, they recommended that this goal be pursued further by amendments allowing each individual to weigh "all the chances for success of an enterprise" and then to risk his or her capital in the stock market without the extensive regulations stipulated by the bill.[45] The merchants' most trenchant objections to the bill stemmed from their disappointment at the government's refusal to embrace the principle of caveat emptor. Article 38 of the bill would have allowed

---

[44] *Zamechaniia* (1872), 131, 5, 125, 15, 87, 124–5, 222 (quoted), 33, 179, 192, 132–3.
[45] *Zamechaniia*, 1873, 2. In quoting the passage about tutelage, Laverychev, *Krupnaia burzhuaziia*, 41, failed to note that the Petersburg merchants were endorsing the Butovskii Commission's own denunciation of bureaucratic tutelage.

investors to nullify their subscription to the shares of a new corporation and withdraw their stock at par value, regardless of the market price of the shares, if they disagreed with any decision taken at the first meeting of the general assembly. This provision, which stood in "direct contradiction" to accepted methods of subscription, would of course have crippled the ability of managers to launch a new venture:

> The best safeguard against inflated [*dutykh*] and groundless [*neosnovatel'nykh*] enterprises lies in the discretion and caution of the public itself, and this can never be achieved as long as anyone has reason to hope, however mistakenly, that the matter will be judged for him by others, that is, in this case by the general assembly of subscribers.

The implicit bias of the merchants toward the power of the founders at the expense of the stockholders became clear in the further demand for a means of limiting "excessive arbitrariness [*proizvol*] on the part of subscribers," an unusual complaint to say the least, in view of the numerous cases of flagrantly arbitrary abuses by founders and managers in the stock-exchange scandals of the previous fifteen years. Curiously enough, the Petersburg commentary also faulted the Butovskii bill for leaving vague some aspects of corporate law, including the form of the founders' contract; the role of noncash investments; methods of making advance deposits, or "earnest money," in the purchase of shares; courses of action open to the founders when the initial subscription failed to raise the necessary amount of capital; and the rights and responsibilities of the founders.[46]

Finally, the attempt of the Butovskii Commission to keep all companies under a single set of regulations struck the Petersburg merchants as unwise. Enormous differences existed between companies that sold shares to the public and those that did not. The restrictions imposed on the former in order to protect the public should not apply to the latter as well. Even the first category contained enterprises so diverse in size and function as to require various sets of rules. The minimum number of founders specified in the bill (seven) was cited as a typical example of the excessive rigidity of the document.[47]

None of these criticisms should be considered as evidence that the merchants of Petersburg, Riga, and Odessa disapproved of the reformist nature of the bill. Indeed, their dissatisfaction is known only because they were eager to comment on a reform that met many of their demands for

---

[46] *Zamechaniia*, 1873, 9–10.
[47] *Zamechaniia*, 1873, 2, 9.

greater entrepreneurial freedom. We have no such candid statement of their views on the repressive law of 1836,[48] but the fact that they criticized as vigorously as they did the far less restrictive bill of 1872 suggests an abhorrence of the outmoded and repressive law, which had been imposed by Nicholas I without any consultation with merchants. By their silence on the issue of registration, for example, the Petersburg merchants appeared to endorse the proposed system of streamlined incorporation.

The abandonment of the Butovskii bill

At this promising juncture, the excruciatingly slow legislative process lurched to a halt. After reviewing the comments of business organizations in thirty-six more sessions, the commission produced yet another revised version in March 1874, which met the approval of the Ministry of Finance. Then this bill – now all of 198 articles long – proceeded to the State Council for final editing. (It is this document that Shepelev called the bill of 1874.) Although the bill contained few changes in its basic orientation, three modifications showed the influence of the irrepressible bureaucratic striving toward pettifogging regimentation and control: a minimum size of basic capital (100,000 rubles), a limit of 50 percent on the number of shares that could be owned by the founders, and specific punishments to be imposed on managers who violated either the general law or the corporate charter.[49] Needless to say, the Petersburg merchants' suggestion that different sets of legislative norms be devised for small and large companies went unheeded.

Then, on the eve of its final approval by the highest authorities, Finance Minister Reutern precipitously abandoned the Butovskii bill. As he explained in a memorandum eight years later (apparently it took that long for the minister of internal affairs to inquire into the matter!), "No further action was taken in view of the state's difficult financial situation and the apprehension that the less difficult procedure for establishing joint-stock companies would result in the undesirable development of small companies."[50] Reutern's allusion to the state's financial woes implied that little capital could be spared to subsidize new corporations, and this may have

---

[48] The jubilee history of the Petersburg Exchange is silent about corporate law except that the title of the *Zamechaniia* (Comments) of 1873 is given erroneously as *Zakliucheniia* (Resolutions). Aleksandr G. Timofeev, *Istoriia S.-Peterburgskoi birzhi, 1703–1903 gg.* (St. Petersburg, 1903), 207, note 1.
[49] Shepelev, *Kompanii*, 115.
[50] Quoted in Shepelev, *Kompanii*, 115.

been a valid point. (Again, the finance minister's intense concern for the state's own interests, apart from those of any particular social group, appeared typical of Russian bureaucratic attitudes.) However, his reference to the dangers allegedly posed by the proliferation of small companies can only be called ludicrous. The very reason cited in 1871 for basing the bill on the new principle of incorporation by registration – to facilitate the creation of a multitude of small companies – served in 1874 as the pretext for abandoning it!

Clearly, Reutern had lost interest in this reform just as it neared fruition after over a decade of painstaking editorial labor. Shepelev pointed out the irony that linked the ill-fated bills of 1867 and 1872–4: They both reached the State Council too late. The bill of 1867 met rejection because by 1870, the concessionary system had passed out of fashion. Likewise, the sponsors of the bill of 1872 had the misfortune of bringing it to the State Council shortly after the panic in the European stock markets in 1873, a destructive financial storm that called into question the wisdom of unfettered corporate development.[51] As Shepelev noted, Reutern could easily have obtained in the State Council an amendment to remove the problem of tiny companies, for example, a provision raising the minimum amount of basic capital to 300,000 or 500,000 rubles, without sacrificing the essence of the bill: the principle of registration of new companies in the absence of prior bureaucratic approval.[52] This, however, he refused to do.

In his perceptive commentary on this episode, the legal scholar Kaminka pointed out the very different consequences of the stock-market crash of 1873 in various countries. In Western Europe and America, governments responded by enacting "a stricter and more detailed normative system," that is, one based on incorporation by registration under a set of firm legislative guidelines, but in Russia, the crisis of 1873 so alarmed the tsarist policy makers that they abandoned the proposed implementation of a stringent version of that system.[53]

Thus, the last opportunity for reform under a moderately enlightened finance minister had slipped away. Under Alexander III and Nicholas II, such an energetic industrializer as Sergei Iu. Witte failed to bring a rational corporate law reform before the State Council, much less to win the

[51] Shepelev, *Kompanii*, 115–16.
[52] Shepelev, *Kompanii*, 115.
[53] Avgust I. Kaminka, "Proekt polozheniia ob aktsionernykh predpriiatiiakh," *Zhurnal ministerstva iustitsii*, 3, no. 1 (Jan. 1897), 128.

The failure of reform, 1860–1874　　　　　　　77

acquiescence of the Ministries of Internal Affairs, War, and Justice. The impetus for reform under Alexander II should not be exaggerated, however. In December 1874, the tsar himself endorsed Reutern's repudiation of the Butovskii bill: New corporate charters should be approved, wrote the emperor, only "with extreme caution," and in August 1877, Reutern's reiteration of this policy of allowing new companies to be formed "only under exceptional circumstances" received imperial endorsement.[54] The essentially negative story of corporate law reform between the Crimean and Russo-Turkish wars underscores the cautious nature of Alexander II and his advisors and the inadmissibility of applying to them the label "liberal." As Kaminka noted sardonically in 1902, the bill of 1872 failed to gain approval precisely because of its "comparative merits"; the registration principle was "apparently still too bold for us," even in the era of the so-called Great Reforms.[55]

For decades thereafter, the irrationalities inherent in the unreformed system continued unabated. Although Professor Ivan T. Tarasov, in his learned treatise on corporate law, introduced numerous distinctions of dubious analytical value,[56] he formulated in cold, logical terms a devastating indictment of incorporation procedures under Reutern. The concession system not only represented an "extreme form of governmental tutelage" (*pravitel'stvennoi opeki*), it coupled bureaucratic arbitrariness (*proizvol*) with extensive graft (*podkup*), "to which founders of joint-stock companies frequently resort, having sufficient material resources for this." Although the introduction of the European registration system without strict safeguards would constitute "a criminal pandering to the worst instincts" of corporate speculation and fraud, the existing Russian practice stood in need of "radical reform," including the abolition of the concession system. The "vagueness, imprecision, and incompleteness" of the law of 1836 led corporate founders to include in new charters many provisions

---

[54] Quoted in Shepelev, *Kompanii*, 116.
[55] Kaminka, *Kompanii*, 393.
[56] In Ivan T. Tarasov, *Uchenie ob aktsionernykh kompaniiakh* (Kiev, 1878), 154 and 183, he distinguished between what he called the *aktsionernaia korporatsiia*, with privileges granted by the state; the *aktsionernaia kompaniia*, without such privileges; and the *aktsionernoe tovarishchestvo*, essentially the French *société en commandite par actions*, which combined the sale of shares to the public with unlimited liability of full partners, an institution nonexistent in Russia. So esoteric were his distinctions between these forms of corporate enterprise and between the so-called Anglo-American and Continental systems that he overlooked the crucial structural and cultural differences between the joint-stock company and the share partnership in Russia. The Slavophiles did not concoct in their imaginations the phenomenon of the overly theoretical Russian intellectual infatuated with European ideas.

that were "completely at variance with the general law." Utter confusion resulted:

> The development of corporations in Russia in recent years has taken place, as it were, outside the legislation in force, or even despite it, because it is difficult to find among the charters of joint-stock companies accepted and confirmed in the past decade a single charter that does not consist entirely of a systematic collection of exceptions [to the law].[57]

We find in the next decade a pathetic footnote to this sorry tale of failed reform under Reutern. In 1883, Minister of Finance Nikolai Kh. Bunge abrogated the temporary ban on the formation of new banks in cities where one already existed on the grounds that the law, passed in May 1872 in order to restrict speculation in bank shares, had caused much economic "stagnation."[58] The State Council welcomed this change and also suggested that Bunge draw up a general corporate law reform, presumably to be modeled on the bill abandoned in 1874. Three years later, in 1886, perhaps in response to a petition from the Moscow merchants requesting free incorporation of new companies, Bunge admitted the need for a new corporate law to replace "the incomplete and outmoded" legislation then in effect. Except for these few well-intentioned words, however, Bunge left no record of any efforts to improve the law.[59] Fifty years had passed since the promulgation of the old corporate law by Kankrin and Bludov. Another fifteen years would elapse before the tsarist government undertook another reform. It too was destined to end in failure.

---

[57] Tarasov, *Uchenie*, 144, 174, 140.

[58] *PSZ* 3–1484, dated April 5, 1883. For a discussion of the law of 1872 and the general problem of state interference in the Russian banking system, see the section on manipulation of the banking system in Chapter 4 of the present study.

[59] Shepelev, *Kompanii*, 120 (quoted). The petition from Moscow in 1886 is mentioned, unfortunately without reference, in Laverychev, *Krupnaia burzhuaziia*, 42. It was not available when requested from the archivists who guard the exchange committee's records in TsGIAM, f. 143.

4

Opeka (Tutelage), 1865–1890

> Industry, progress, education, all sleep; and looking out of the carriage windows at the vast expanse of snow, the mind naturally receives the idea that it is the counterpane of a sleeping nation.
> – George Hume, English machinery salesman, in a letter composed on a train near Kharkov (February 11, 1879)[1]

The Russian verb based on the noun "tutelage" or "wardship" (*opeka*) is *opekat'*, meaning "to have the wardship of," "to watch over," or "to take care of." The frequent use of these words in discussions of Russian economic history (witness the use of the term *opeka* by the scholars Pakhman and Tarasov quoted in the previous chapter) suggests that the notion of bureaucratic wardship over the Russian economy had strong roots in what passed for political culture under the tsars.[2] In the field of corporate history, clear expressions of this attitude can be found as early as the reign of Peter the Great. In his decree urging the establishment of a Russian company to trade with Spain, he declared that the College of Commerce "must look after this innovation as a mother looks after her child growing to maturity." Such encouragement was essential "because everyone knows that our peo-

---

[1] George Hume, *Thirty-five Years in Russia* (London, 1914; reprinted New York, 1971), 196.
[2] As in English, in French the noun "tutelage" (*tutelle*) has no verbal form; the French counterpart of *opekat'* is *prendre sous la tutelle*. German has two nouns (*Vormundschaft* and *Schutz*) and both a short and an extended verbal form (*schützen* and *in Schutz nehmen*), while Polish has a noun, a verb, and an adjective: *opieka, opiekować się,* and *opiekuńczy*. The richness of the Russian and Polish uses of this concept, as in words for "the person who exercises tutelage; guardian" (*opekun'* and *opiekun*, respectively) and "the person over whom tutelage is exercised; ward" (*opekaemyi* in Russian) indicates that the concept is deeply rooted in the culture of these Slavic peoples. To be sure, an English adjective, "tutelary," does appear occasionally, as in examples cited in the *Oxford English Dictionary* from works published as early as 1611 and as late as 1908; but the word appears far less frequently in English than in Russian. See *The Oxford English Dictionary*, vol. 11 (Oxford, 1933; reprinted 1961); Russia, Akademiia nauk, *Slovar' russkogo iazyka v chetyrekh tomakh*, vol. 2 (Moscow, 1958); and Max Vasmer, *Russisches etymologisches Wörterbuch*, 3 vols. (Heidelberg, 1953), vol. 2, 270.

ple do not initiate anything by themselves" (ponezhe vsem izvestno, chto nashi liudi ni vo chto sami ne poidut).[3]

The benefits of the state's tutelage over the merchants remains open to question, however. None of the ministers of finance under the last three tsars had viewed the Russian economy from the perspective of a merchant. Reutern was trained as an economist; Bunge, a professor of economics at the University of Kiev, had no practical experience except service on the board of a bank in that city; and Vyshnegradskii, an expert on the physics of mechanical friction, had served on several corporations more or less as a token bureaucrat, and one susceptible to shady deals at that. Witte, the most prominent of all tsarist ministers of finance, had risen from a position as traffic manager on the Southwestern Railroad (1870–9) to serve as an expert on the Baranov Commission (1876–85). The author of the omnibus railroad freight rate law of 1889, he became minister of transportation in 1892, but he lacked experience in the financial aspects of corporate enterprise. In fact, he was technically ineligible to manage either the Southwestern Railroad or the transport ministry, having taken a university degree in mathematics instead of completing the usual training for a transport engineer (*inzhener putei soobshchenii*) at the Transport Academy.[4]

All these men considered themselves enlightened enough to solicit the

[3] N. N. Firsov, *Russkie torgovo-promyshlennye kompanii v pervuiu polovinu XVIII stoletiia* (Kazan, 1896), 23, quoting *PSZ* 1–4540, dated August 4, 1724. Needless to say, no record of this company's activities has ever been found. Early companies are also the subject of a study by Aleksandr S. Lappo-Danilevskii, "Russkie promyshlennye i torgovye kompanii v pervoi polovine XVIII veka," *Zhurnal ministerstva narodnogo proshveshcheniia*, 320, no. 12 (Dec. 1898), part 2, 306–66 and 321, no. 2 (Feb. 1899), part 2, 371–436. (Lappo-Danilevskii's work appeared separately in an edition unavailable to me: St. Petersburg, 1899.)

[4] On Reutern, Leonid E. Shepelev, *Tsarizm i burzhuaziia vo vtoroi polovine XIX veka: problemy torgovo-promyshlennoi politiki* (Leningrad, 1981), 71–7; and Oliver S. Hayward, "Official Russian Policies Concerning Industrialization during the Finance Ministry of M. Kh. Reutern, 1862–1878," doctoral dissertation, University of Wisconsin, 1973. On S. A. Greig and A. A. Abaza, Shepelev, *Tsarizm*, 77–82. On Bunge, Shepelev, *Tsarizm*, 135–50; Hayward, "Bunge, Nikolai Khristianovich," in *MERSH*, vol. 6, 35–8; and John L. Pesda, "N. K. Bunge and Russian Economic Development, 1881–1886," doctoral dissertation, Kent State University, 1971. On Vyshnegradskii, Shepelev, *Tsarizm*, 150–7 and sources from the section on restrictions on conflict of interest in the present chapter. On Witte, Shepelev, *Tsarizm*, 193–200; Witte's own *Vospominaniia*, 3 vols. (Moscow, 1960), esp. vol. 1, viii, 84, 203–7, 245; and Theodore Von Laue, *Sergei Witte and the Industrialization of Russia* (New York, 1963). Russia, Ministerstvo finansov, *Ministerstvo finansov 1802–1902* (St. Petersburg, 1902), also gives useful portraits of the ministers, for example, on Witte, vol. 2, 323–5. All these men but Witte are the subject of witty sketches by C. Skalkovsky [Konstantin A. Skal'kovskii], *Les ministres des finances de la Russie, 1802–1890*, trans. P. de Nevsky (Paris, 1891), a translation of relevant chapters from Skal'kovskii's *Nashi gosudarstvennye i obshchestvennye deiateli*, 2 vols. (St. Petersburg, 1890), with a chapter on Vyshnegradskii added for the French edition.

views of business leaders in the various regions of the empire, something that their predecessors under Nicholas I had rarely done. However, the fact that the tsarist state remained an autocracy until 1905 meant that the government enjoyed immunity from public accountability. As we shall see, the autocratic impulse persisted even after the establishment of the semiparliamentary State Duma and the reconstitution of the State Council in 1906. The degree to which the Russian state responded to the needs of a qualitatively new and at least potentially influential social stratum – the corporate leadership – was to have important political implications in the entire period between the Crimean War and 1914, whether or not every decade witnessed an open conflict over economic policy between these leaders and the Ministry of Finance.

So diverse were the forms of tsarist tutelage and so many were the economic fields affected by it that a comprehensive discussion of the phenomenon would require a detailed examination of Russian economic institutions. For the purpose of illustrating the problem under Alexander II and Alexander III, it suffices to point out several aspects of tsarist economic policy under the unreformed corporate law: methods of granting new charters of incorporation; measures to limit conflicts of interest in the business world; and supervision of the banking system. The chapter closes with an analysis of the ambivalent thoughts of the eminent chemist Dmitrii I. Mendeleev on the issue of governmental tutelage over corporate enterprise.

Rationalization of the concession system

As Finance Minister Reutern had admitted when he abandoned the corporate law reform in 1874, the benefits of rapid corporate development remained unclear to the tsarist bureaucracy. In his "Financial Testament" of February 1877, he made explicit his misgivings. Periodic episodes of stock-exchange fever he considered a "necessary evil," whose only benefit was to purge the economy of weak, artificially "inflated" (*dutye*) enterprises. His concluding remarks left no doubt that even this enlightened minister shared the traditional bureaucratic mistrust of unfettered competition. Measures must be taken, he warned, to prevent "feverish" speculation in stocks and bonds; no new banks should be allowed, in order that existing ones not suffer undue competition; and joint-stock companies should be approved only when formed on the basis of enterprises already in operation.⁵ The implementation of such a restrictive policy would, of course, have limited the corporate form of enterprise to previously family-owned firms or partnerships, primarily in light industry and trade. Grandiose undertakings such as railroads, steamship lines, or insurance companies would have met a blanket rejection. The preliminary evidence indicates that Reutern's successors did not follow his recommendations. For example, seventeen of the forty-five corporations founded in 1881 launched new enterprises, and the average amount of basic capital of new enterprises headquartered in Petersburg was almost twice that of companies incorporated on the basis of existing enterprises there (1,859,375 versus 1,087,500 rubles).⁶ However, Reutern's warning served as a powerful indication of the bureaucrats' revulsion for the unrestrained speculation that marred the 1860s and 1870s.

What of the process by which new companies received official confirmation? Reutern's refusal in 1874 to support the principle of incorporation by registration left prospective founders at the mercy of arbitrary bureaucrats in the Ministry of Finance and the Committee of Ministers. The unreformed law of 1836 remained in the code, but only twenty-eight of its articles were considered relevant. At the same time, each new corporate charter gained the force of law after it received the imperial signature, even when its provisions conflicted with those in the statute of 1836. Faced with this chaos in the law, founders tended to draft new charters on the model of those recently approved by the state, on the plausible grounds that a charter similar to others would not attract unwelcome scrutiny. As the commission that drafted the law of 1872 noted, this practice of incorporation by imitation meant that "the law on joint-stock companies in the Code of Laws is almost completely ignored. Every charter makes reference to this law, but it is safe to say that it exists only on paper and that at present we essentially have no general law on joint-stock companies."⁷

In their eagerness to repress the evil of speculation, Reutern and his fellow ministers apparently ignored the inevitable results of their failure to implement a rational reform: the spread of graft and corruption. The most elegantly phrased charter could not win bureaucratic approval with-

---

⁵ Quoted from A. N. Kulomzin and V. G. Reitern-Nol'ken, comp., *M. Kh. Reitern: biograficheskii ocherk* (St. Petersburg, 1910), 156–7, by Vladimir Ia. Laverychev, *Krupnaia burzhuaziia v poreformennoi Rossii, 1860–1900 gg.* (Moscow, 1974), 41.

⁶ Data from RUSCORP.

⁷ *Proekt polozheniia* ... (St. Petersburg, 1872), 46, quoted in Leonid E. Shepelev, *Aktsionernye kompanii v Rossii* (Leningrad, 1973), 108.

out the payment of requisite bribes along the way. As Vasilii A. Kokorev wrote to Chizhov after the protracted review of the charter of the Moscow Merchant Bank, "In Petersburg it is difficult to make your case without incurring expenses [*khlopotat' bez izderzhek*]."[8]

Likewise, the Slavophile Aleksandr I. Koshelev, a man who had seen the seedy side of Russian business practices in his liquor concession, chronicled the horrors that he witnessed during a five-month stay in the capital in 1867.

> Bribery, personal funds [created by embezzlement], violations of legal procedure, etc. went to extremes in Petersburg. Everything was possible, but at the same time one could be refused the most just and lawful [request].... The immorality, unscrupulousness, and foolishness of the upper administration surpassed all the swindling and stupidity of the provincial and district bureaucrats.[9]

Koshelev did not name specific agencies where graft exceeded the norm, but other sources suggest that the millions of rubles to be made in corporations, especially railroads, raised the incidence of corruption in the Ministries of Finance and Transportation.

In his memoirs, the Finance Ministry economist Terner explained how the proliferation of bureaucratic complications in the granting of railroad concessions drew into the new companies several types of founders, each with specialized skills. First came the men who drafted the charter in accordance with the law or recent practice. The second group took on "the task of going to the clerical offices on behalf of the enterprise and of managing all the details necessary to obtain the concession." After these individuals had carried out their vaguely described functions, presumably through illegal gifts to the occupants of important desks, the technical experts arrived, men "who actually take the matter into their own hands" as managers of the firm. "Such a division of labor by itself entails no great inconvenience," Terner concluded, but each task required adequate payment. Often the drafters of the charter and those who guided it through the bureaucratic maze received far more compensation than did the managers themselves.[10] This fact suggests the great importance of the first two stages of the incorporation process.

---

[8] Letter dated October 15, 1868, cited by Laverychev, *Krupnaia burzhuaziia*, 41, from Chizhov's archive (GBL-OR, f. 332). Access to this archive was denied to the author in January 1980 on the grounds that he had seen part of it in 1971–2.
[9] Aleksandr I. Koshelev, *Zapiski (1812–1883 gody)* (Berlin, 1884), 191.
[10] Fedor G. Terner [originally Thörner], *Vospominaniia*, ed. M. G. Terner and E. G. Terner, 2 vols. (St. Petersburg, 1910–11), vol. 1, 116–17.

Although Terner did not stress the illegalities that the concession system fostered, other sources left no doubt as to the great potential for corruption that pervaded this system. The economic expert Skal'kovskii recalled that the process of taking a draft charter through "several chanceries and departments gave rise to incredible amounts of graft. One department head earned 2.5 million rubles [in illegal payments] in three years. It was, [however], necessary to know the ins and outs in order to give bribes successfully, for everything was left unclear on purpose." The American railroad contractor Winans used a clever ploy to win the renewal of his concession for the lucrative Petersburg–Moscow line. One sunny day, he visited the appropriate office carrying an umbrella, and when the topic of the weather came up, he wagered 100,000 rubles that rain would fall. "He lost the bet, of course, but received the contract." A highly placed bureaucrat identified by Skal'kovskii as St——v (apparently the corporate figurehead Count Grigorii A. Strogonov) received one million rubles for obtaining the government's approval of a single railroad concession.[11]

Details of the mechanisms of corruption in the late 1860s may be found in various documents of the period, especially the diary of Anatolii N. Kulomzin, a conscientious senior clerk in the chancery of the Committee of Ministers from 1869 onward. Kulomzin's predecessor, I. P. Varpakhovskii, had routinely approved corporate charters without bringing them before the committee and without insisting on adherence to the law. When Varpakhovskii encountered draft charters that bestowed inordinate power on founders and directors, he routinely refrained from criticizing such documents, apparently for a price. Nor had he invented this system. Upon the death of Akinfii P. Sukovkin, the chief clerk (*upravliaiushchii delami*) of the committee from 1853 to 1861, "shares of all sorts of companies whose charters had passed through the committee" were found among his papers, apparently gifts from grateful founders.

[11] Konstantin A. Skal'kovskii, *Vospominaniia molodosti (po moriu zhiteiskomu), 1843–1869* (St. Petersburg, 1906), 259. Skal'kovskii himself developed the skill of taking bribes; for documentation, see Mikhail A. Pavlov, *Vospominaniia metallurga*, 2nd ed. (Moscow, 1945), 149; and the correspondence with the French banker Baer in Skal'kovskii's archive, LOII, f. 202, ed. kh. 21/25, some of which is cited in the only Soviet article devoted to this brilliant and capable, if overly sticky-fingered, official in the Department of Mines: A. A. Fursenko, "Materialy o korruptsii tsarskoi biurokratii (po bumagam K. A. Skal'skovskogo)," in N. E. Nosov and others, eds., *Issledovaniia po otechestvennomu istochnikovedeniiu* (Moscow and Leningrad, 1964), 149–56. The best sources on his career are E. N. Vasil'ev, "Pamiati K. A. Skal'kovskogo," *Gornyi zhurnal*, year 82, 3, no. 8 (Aug. 1906), 252–63; and V. B. Bertenson, *Iz vospominanii o K. A. Skal'kovskom* (St. Petersburg, 1912). A short account in English is Thomas C. Owen, "Skal'kovskii, K. A.," in *MERSH*, vol. 35, 157–60.

The Soviet historian Shepelev credited Kulomzin with the creation of an ingenious scheme to introduce coherence and a modicum of honesty into the concessionary procedure, often against the will of highly placed officials of the Ministry of Finance and members of the Committee of Ministers. Particularly significant were various reforms limiting "the arbitrariness [*proizvol*] of the boards" for the benefit of stockholders, such as the imposition of a maximum number of votes that one person could cast at a general assembly; a mechanism to remove a director before the end of his term, which usually lasted three years; and an increase in the powers of the audit commission. Kulomzin and his immediate superior, Fedor P. Kornilov, implemented these and other changes in a gradual, almost imperceptible fashion with the help of the noted economic expert Konstantin V. Chevkin, who represented the State Council on the committee. After each committee member received a printed copy of the draft charter, Chevkin would summon Kulomzin to his home. There, in secret, the two men edited the draft, adding to the document slight but crucial improvements suggested by Kornilov. Once these changes were adopted by the committee upon Chevkin's insistence, Kulomzin incorporated them into each new draft. "It was necessary to hide the entire procedure carefully from the president [of the committee] and to act in secret. Chevkin made one or two comments on each charter and in this way the charters were gradually improved." The committee also reviewed petitions requesting changes in existing charters. Here, the effort to resist the proposals of corporate managers proved difficult, especially in the case of large and important railroad companies. "In these matters Chevkin was invaluable. With infernal perseverance he upheld every objection and every word, and retreated only in extremity." Kulomzin, who eventually succeeded Kornilov as chief clerk of the committee, maintained high standards of administrative probity well into the 1890s, even when pressed by powerful courtiers to make exceptions to the law.[12]

The brave efforts of Kulomzin, Kornilov, and Chevkin to uphold standards of fairness and rationality constituted only one aspect of the complicated relationship between the tsarist state and large corporations. However successful these men may have been in the Committee of Min-

[12] Leonid E. Shepelev, *Aktsionernye kompanii v Rossii* (Leningrad, 1973), 109–10, quoting from Kulomzin's diary in GBL-OR, f. 178. Shepelev specified that another copy is held in TsGIA, f. 1642. The publication of this copious document, with suitable annotations, would illuminate many aspects of bureaucratic behavior and economic policy in the late tsarist period.

isters, bureaucrats elsewhere eagerly took huge bribes. The Third Section (secret police, 1826–80) in 1876 reported that the talented director of the chancery in the Ministry of Finance, Dmitrii F. Kobeko, was "generally known to take and even extort bribes in the most shameless manner." For his help in arranging lucrative subsidies for steamship and railroad companies, Kobeko received generous payments, including one for 100,000 rubles.[13] After being forced to leave the chancery, Kobeko continued to serve the Finance Ministry as its appointed representative on the boards of ROPIT and the Southwestern Railroad. Several paradoxes marked the man's later career. First, for all his corruption, he served Reutern and Witte as a capable economic expert. Indeed, on Witte's recommendation, Kobeko won appointment to the State Council, where he so distinguished himself by his reformist views that the tsar removed him in 1907 for alleged "liberalism."[14] Finally, as a board member of two large transportation companies, Kobeko probably enjoyed more opportunities for graft than he had found as a bureaucrat.

In Kobeko, we see one of the many ambiguities inherent in capitalist institutions encouraged by a powerful, but traditionally oriented bureaucracy: Talent and dishonesty on occasion went together. Likewise, the most highly trained bureaucrats – the names of Kulomzin, Skal'kovskii, and Witte immediately come to mind – often possessed a better understanding of economic realities, at least in theory, than did corporate leaders themselves, especially those from the poorly educated strata of the merchant estate. The main point is that the very existence of bureaucratic control over every aspect of a corporation's activities prompted managers to pay any price in order to receive governmental permission and financial support, without which their enterprises could not operate in the face of European competition. Outrageously large bribes to government officials were the inevitable result of such circumstances.

Restrictions on conflict of interest

Although the dual problems of conflict of interest and graft within the central bureaucracy owed much to the lack of an adequate corporate law, they also reflected a peculiar feature of Russian cultural history. Unlike the British, French, and German economies, the tsarist system had no sub-

[13] Laverychev, *Krupnaia burzhuaziia*, 48–9.
[14] Witte, *Vospominaniia*, vol. 1, 346–7. Witte attributed Kobeko's removal from the chancery to a scandal that resulted from the financial indiscretions of his spendthrift French mistress.

stantial reserve of educated, honest, and cosmopolitan mercantile and professional men from which to draw the first generation of managers of new corporations. The growth of the problem of bureaucrats in corporations, the government's perception of conflicts of interest in the late 1870s, and the promulgation of a conflict-of-interest law in 1884 all proceeded from that elemental feature of Russian social history.

Why, then, did a pool of talented merchants not exist from which corporate managers could be recruited? Except in the main economic centers of Petersburg, Moscow, Warsaw, Kiev, Odessa, and the Baltic ports, the merchant estate showed little aptitude and less interest in corporate forms of enterprise. In 1873, Babst complained, "Of commercial and industrial men with a comprehensive knowledge and understanding of contemporary forms of trade and of banking in particular, there are almost none in Russia."[15] Even the highly successful textile men of the Moscow region depended on sympathetic intellectuals, like the economist Babst, the art historian Chizhov, and the journalist Ivan S. Aksakov, to launch the first banks in Moscow.[16] Because the management of a commercial bank demanded a special kind of expertise, conflicts of interest often arose in this new field of corporate enterprise. The need for managers with specialized financial skills left the founders of the first Russian banks in the 1860s and 1870s with no choice but to hire a large number of tsarist bureaucrats who possessed the requisite training.

Among the treasury officials who served on banks were one Izosimov, who simultaneously directed the Riazan branch of the State Bank and the Riazan Bank of Trade until his removal from the latter post by Reutern in 1873; one Kul'zhinskii, director of the Taganrog branch of the State Bank in the late 1870s, who simultaneously presided over the board of the Azov-Don Commercial Bank; and the Moscow treasury official (and mayor of the city!) Dmitrii D. Shumakher, president of the board of the Moscow Commercial Loan Bank from its creation in 1870 until its spectacular collapse in October 1875. With special permission of the tsar, Minister of Internal Affairs Petr A. Valuev headed the board of the Petersburg Discount and Loan Bank in 1868. Aleksan-

---

[15] [Ivan K. Babst], "Pis'mo o bankakh, II," *Russkie vedomosti*, 1873, no. 174, quoted in Isaak I. Levin, *Aktsionernye kommercheskie banki v Rossii*, vol. 1 (no more published) (Petrograd, 1917), 231.

[16] Thomas C. Owen, "The Moscow Merchants and the Public Press, 1858–1868," *Jahrbücher für Geschichte Osteuropas*, N.S., 23, no. 1 (Mar. 1975), 28–9; Alfred J. Rieber, *Merchants and Entrepreneurs in Imperial Russia* (Chapel Hill, 1982), 153–65, 192–5; Levin, *Banki*, 178–84.

dr I. Butovskii, director of the Department of Trade and Manufacturing, became the first president of the council of the Volga-Kama Commercial Bank.

Perhaps no one surpassed Evgenii I. Lamanskii in multiple officeholding. The vice-director of the State Bank and its director (1866–81) after the retirement of Baron Stieglitz, Lamanskii occupied numerous banking positions, any one of which would have raised serious questions of conflict of interest: as Butovskii's successor in the presidency of the Volga-Kama Bank council; as an early stockholder of the Moscow Merchant Bank; as president of the council of the Russian Bank for Foreign Trade; as president of the first general assembly of the Siberian Bank of Trade; as initiator of the Petersburg Mutual Credit Society, the first in the empire; and as a member of its board from its creation in 1864 until 1879.[17] One passage from Kulomzin's diary of 1869 is often quoted by Soviet historians to illustrate how the rich and powerful under the tsars engaged in "a bacchanalia of the most impudent bribery and extortion" (as the Soviet historian Pogrebinskii subtly put it in 1954). Kulomzin noted that Lamanskii had a secret interest in many railroad companies whose fate he helped to decide in his capacity as director of the State Bank, the source of special subsidies to large corporations:

Apparently Lamanskii has no money, especially the millions needed for railroads; why [then] is he invited to participate in all the companies? Evidently this is done because of his position as director of the State Bank. In this connection, a most curious episode occurred recently in the Committee [of Ministers]. The charter of a company was introduced for discussion, and I gave a report on it. Prince Gagarin, acting with the tsar's permission, raised the question whether this company should be rejected because five high officials of the Finance Ministry, including Lamanskii, were participants in it. But the committee members scratch one another's backs [*No v komitete ruka ruku moet*], and all were of the opposite opinion.

Lamanskii clearly could not resist the temptation to convert his influence into a source of wealth for himself and his friends. As director of the State Bank and the Petersburg Mutual Credit Society, he provided a generous line of credit to a group of speculators in a railroad company. These men purchased new shares at 80 percent of par value and sold them for double the price five months later. Kulomzin confided to his diary that Lamanskii,

---

[17] Levin, *Banki*, 233–4.

"whom I had always considered a knight of honesty, uses his official position like an absolute huckster."[18]

Kulomzin's diary is only the most vivid source of evidence of abuses of power by aristocrats and gentry who became wealthy in the world of corporate finance by virtue of their important posts in the tsarist bureaucracy. Because this concentration of bureaucratic influence occurred in the very largest companies, precisely those that received subsidies and special waivers from the repressive corporate law, even the most honest individual who occupied high posts simultaneously in the state bureaucracy and large corporations inevitably faced a conflict of interest. A bureaucrat's decision could easily favor the company in which he served as a director, and as a corporate official the same man could command a handsome salary for his specialized knowledge of the bureaucratic machine. Nor did a man's educational and bureaucratic attainments necessarily qualify him for the task of corporate manager. Commercial and industrial education remained the specialty of secondary schools managed as philanthropies by merchants for their own kind. A highly ambitious and talented man from the gentry might enter the world of corporate management and learn enough lore of the business world to lead a successful career. (Chizhov, the former mathematics teacher, art historian, and cultivator of silkworms, was perhaps the best example of a self-taught corporate leader.) Most, however, brought little specialized knowledge to the job and even less business acumen. In many cases, the colorful uniform of a retired privy councilor, general, or admiral added glitter to the company's annual report, but the experience of these men in essentially bureaucratic and military careers provided little of use to the corporation. Their primary function was evidently to facilitate communication between the board and key officials of the various ministries.

Anecdotal evidence must be used with caution, but it is appropriate in this connection because of the lack of solid documentary records illuminating the murky area where legal and ethical standards succumbed to the influence of greed. Several vivid portraits of essentially decorative directors may be cited to make the point. One retired general, Dmitrii A. Benckendorff, simply sat on numerous boards and councils without saying a word. Once, when an important question came to a vote, Benckendorff avoided giving his opinion by placing his handkerchief to his face as if to stop a nosebleed and hurriedly left the room. Several months later, when

---

[18] Quoted from a diary entry of 1869 by A. P. Pogrebinskii, "Stroitel'stvo zheleznykh dorog v poreformennoi Rossii i finansovaia politika tsarizma (60–90-e gody XIX v.)," *Istoricheskie zapiski*, 47 (1954), 156; and Shepelev, *Kompanii*, 130.

another important decision arose, the president of the council, Adolf Rothstein, turned to Benckendorff and said, "Dmitrii Aleksandrovich! It seems to me that your nose is about to begin bleeding." The grateful general left the room without embarrassment and did not return until after the vote had been taken.[19] The author of this story noted that another retired general, "worse than a nonentity, by some miracle became a director on the board of some tiny corporation and after a few years was sitting on the council of first-rate banks and was a director of large enterprises." Although he "had neither money, nor connections [sviazei], nor expertise, nor intelligence... this ignoramus not only sat on his fat bottom but actually managed the business... to the very end of his life." When asked why such a person could win reelection, his fellow directors answered with a shrug, "The devil knows why. People must have gotten used to him."[20]

The facade of a corporation managed by aristocrats and retired officials occasionally hid the worst sort of incompetence and dishonesty. In 1884, a railroad entrepreneur without funds and a well-known count without business experience collaborated in the launching of a company to sell tickets and deliver freight for the major railroads. Lacking sufficient cash and having failed to sell to the public the necessary portion of shares (worth half the company's basic capitalization of 200,000 rubles), they began operations with only 10,000 rubles after securing a fraudulent certificate from a friendly bank official stating that the capital had been raised. The count's many connections brought lucrative contracts with railroad companies, and individuals who contributed money to help keep the scheme afloat received jobs as agents of the company. After three years, however, the "grandiose enterprise" began to falter under its huge expenses. Aware of impending disaster, the agents stole back from the company the money they had invested at the outset. After the count died, a sorry chain of events ensued: The railroads refused to renew their contracts, the board members fled, and the enterprise collapsed. The many merchants who lost from 100 to 1,000 rubles each "simply spat," but some lost their life's savings as a result of this fraud.[21]

It is impossible at this point to specify what proportion of these men

---

[19] Nikolai E. Vrangel', *Vospominaniia (ot krepostnogo prava do bol'shevikov)* (Berlin, 1924), 157–8. In 1899, Benckendorff still sat on the council of the Russian Bank for Foreign Trade. Andrei K. Golubev, ed., *Russkie banki*, 3rd ed. (St. Petersburg, 1899), 321.

[20] Vrangel', *Vospominaniia*, 157.

[21] L. Spiridovich [pseud.], *Dela nashikh aktsionernykh kompanii* (Moscow, 1897), 10–13, quotations from 12, 13.

functioned as merely decorative board members and what brought useful managerial expertise to their new positions. However, it seems clear that the problem of incompetence masked by a mellifluous title diminished over the decades as well-trained graduates of the School of Mines took positions with mining and metallurgical companies and the School of Transport produced several thousand transport engineers to staff the burgeoning railroad network. To be sure, many of these engineers worked primarily for the state. In the large steamship and railroad firms that received state subsidies, the various ministries appointed representatives, generally well-trained engineers or specialists like Kobeko, to supervise the operations of the company. As for the hundreds of bureaucrats and engineers who took posts as managers of a corporation, their professional expertise doubtless improved the functioning of the enterprise. However, the acute shortage of well-trained managers in both the state and the corporations made it necessary for many engineers and bureaucrats to hold positions simultaneously in both realms. Of 1,006 transport engineers active in their profession in 1884, only 462 worked full time for the Ministry of Transportation. Of the 370 men then on leave to work elsewhere, fully 343 were employed by railroad companies, and another 6 "full-time" officials held such positions.[22] Of the 225 officials of the finance ministry who held 251 posts in corporations, mutual credit societies, and other enterprises, 13 were presidents of boards and directors (apparently executive directors), 15 were members of boards, 20 sat on audit commissions, and 20 served as bookkeepers and other technical personnel.[23] Notwithstanding the technical competence of these men, their opportunities for corruption doubtless multiplied.

The intertwining of these positive and negative aspects of the phenomenon in a peculiarly Russian pattern may best be seen in the career of Ivan A. Vyshnegradskii, two of whose acquaintances left vivid descriptions of his activities in the worlds of business and state service before his appointment as acting minister of finance in January 1887 and as minister from January 1888 to August 1892. A highly talented professor of mechanics at the Technological Institute (as even a Stalinist reference work

---

[22] TsGIA, f. 1261, op. 3, ed. kh. 69–1879, l. 119v.
[23] Shepelev, *Kompanii*, 130, citing TsGIA, f. 1261, op. 3, d. 69. Engineers in the state's employ were generally considered to be mediocre in expertise and more prone to graft than engineers in academic posts and in corporations, according to Donald W. Green, "Industrialization and the Engineering Ascendancy: A Comparative Study of American and Russian Engineering Elites, 1870–1920," doctoral dissertation, University of California, Berkeley, 1972, 234.

admitted with nationalistic pride typical of Soviet historical writing during the Cold War),[24] Vyshnegradskii also earned a substantial ancillary income. Witte recalled:

I did not doubt that when Vyshnegradskii was engaged in private business affairs, was in private companies, and was practically an agent of Bloch and various other wheeler-dealers, he did many improper [*nekorrektnye*] things. Of course they were not illegal, but they were things that a person in his position – a privy councilor, a professor, etc. – and in general a more or less respected person, should not have done. Thus Vyshnegradskii, by serving in private companies, accumulated a rather large fortune for himself.

Vyshnegradskii insisted, for example, on receiving a 500,000-franc "commission" from the Paris banker Rothschild for helping to arrange a loan to the tsarist government. Although Vyshnegradskii then turned the money over to the Russian banker Gosk'e, whom Rothschild had excluded from the consortium and from whom Vyshnegradskii had secured a private loan, the whole matter appeared unethical to Rothschild and to Adolf Rothstein, who transmitted the unusual request to Paris, as well as to the tsar himself, whom Witte informed of the episode in 1892.[25]

Whatever the man's predilections for graft, no one doubted his extraordinary managerial ability. Here the phenomenon of conflict of interest stands in its clearest form, since in the absence of a substantial corps of qualified managers from the merchant estate and other professional groups, large corporations had no choice but to turn to capable bureaucrats. In his memoirs, a manager who served alongside Vyshnegradskii on the board of the Petersburg Water Company in the mid-1870s testified to the professor's organizational skill. By his "fanatical striving to put the matter on a firm foundation" and by his "inexhaustible dedication to work" (*trudoliubie*), Vyshnegradskii became indispensable to the company, all the more so because his fellow board members proved either too old or too busy with other commitments to ensure the success of the company. As Vyshnegradskii's ability to reduce unnecessary expenses became generally known, he gained "a solid position in the stock-exchange world." While still a professor at the Technical Institute he was earning over thirty thousand rubles a year, and by the time of his appointment to the Finance Ministry he had amassed a fortune of 2 or 3 million rubles. Vitmer at-

---

[24] *Bol'shaia sovetskaia entsiklopediia*, 2nd ed., vol. 9 (1951), 541–2, praised Vyshnegradskii as an expert mechanical engineer, devoted only one sentence to his career in the Finance Ministry, and did not mention graft.
[25] Witte, *Vospominaniia*, vol. 1, 277 (quoted), 293–4.

tributed this successful career to "the utter lack of talented people" in the Petersburg business world.[26] Besides the water company, Vyshnegradskii served on the boards of the Southwestern and Rybinsk-Bologoe railroads.[27]

Vitmer's memoirs are the source of a statement by Vyshnegradskii that Soviet historians readily quote to show the man's greed and cynicism, but the context of the remark shows it to be not entirely shameful. Vitmer recalled complimenting the professor on his scrupulous attention to detail in reducing the operating costs of the water company.

> I once said to him: "Ivan Alekseevich, what if people behaved toward the state treasury with the same attention and honesty with which you look after the interests of our stockholders?" "Well, old man," he answered, "the state treasury was created in order for people to rob it. Who doesn't steal from it?"

The professor's coarse remark reminded Vitmer of allegations that Vyshnegradskii had left his post in the artillery department "not entirely pure, but had amassed a nice little fortune [*poriadochnyi kapitalets*] that formed the kernel of his later enrichment." For his part, Vitmer considered such stories as "just rumors." It is clear from the context of the remark that Vyshnegradskii was expressing the general attitude of Russians toward the state treasury, not only his own view. Moreover, as manager of the water company, he apparently never behaved unethically.[28]

Nor did Vyshnegradskii gain a reputation as a grafter in his exalted position as minister of finance. To be sure, he comported himself like a nouveau riche; Vitmer noted that despite the elegance of his large home, where he gave two grand balls a year, Vyshnegradskii "still wiped the lip of a new bottle of wine with his palm." At the same time, however, he seems not to have behaved according to the cynical precept that he had uttered a decade earlier. A thrifty and careful bureaucrat, "he watched over every kopeck in the state treasury," even to the point of pedantry, and did not enrich himself at its expense, "I am convinced."[29] Witte explained that after accumulating a sizable fortune in the business world, Vyshnegradskii behaved honestly as a tsarist minister because "all his staff observed his every move, his every action."[30]

---

[26] Aleksandr N. Vitmer, "Otryvochnye vospominaniia," *Istoricheskii vestnik*, year 32, 125 (Sep. 1911), 862–5.
[27] Russia, Ministerstvo finansov, *Ministerstvo finansov 1802–1902*, vol. 2, 11.
[28] Vitmer, "Vospominaniia," 864–5. In a typical Soviet quotation of this remark, Laverychev, *Krupnaia burzhuaziia*, 49, followed it with the sentimental observation that it was the workers who bore the financial burden of wholesale graft.
[29] Vitmer, "Vospominaniia," 869–70.
[30] Witte, *Vospominaniia*, vol. 1, 277.

The question of conflicts of interest involving bureaucrats who served in corporations underwent serious scrutiny by the State Council in 1884 during consideration of a bill aimed at limiting the most flagrant abuses. The council's historical review of this matter, which traced the emergence of the problem back to the first major episode of stock-exchange fever in the late 1850s, employed a unique Russian word, *sovmestitel'stvo*, to describe the phenomenon of holding both a bureaucratic and a corporation position. Although the word literally meant "the simultaneous holding of more than one position" (*mesto*), it carried the implication of impropriety. (Analogous words existed for "the person simultaneously holding several offices," *sovmestitel'*, and the verb denoting his action, *sovmestitel'stvovat'*.) The report defended the practice on the grounds of a shortage of qualified managerial personnel in the rapidly expanding Russian corporate economy: "Due to the lack of persons in the industrial world with the necessary special knowledge, it proved desirable to draw on specialists in finance and technology who were in the imperial service." The report went so far as to make a virtue of necessity: "The inclusion in industrial companies of educated persons who held a position in the state service seemed the strongest guarantee of the proper conduct of such affairs." The government itself appointed certain experts from the ministries to the boards of some companies that received state financial aid and had strategic significance. From the 1860s onward, this report continued, multiple officeholding became especially common, largely because the emancipation impelled landowners (including bureaucrats) to seek remunerative posts in industry. In 1868, acting on the advice of Reutern, the tsar imposed limits on the participation of important bureaucrats serving in railroad companies, but other sectors of the economy remained exempt from this restriction.[31]

As Samuil A. Greig, the finance minister, noted in 1879, "There are cases when a commercial or industrial enterprise requires persons who have a high degree of knowledge and enjoy special regard in public opinion, although still in government service in a high office." Ever the faithful functionary who deferred to the whim of the autocrat, Greig preferred to allow *sovmestitel'stvo* to be practiced at the discretion of the tsar. The finance minister advocated an unconditional ban on the practice only when a man might join the board of a company "dependent," as for subsidies and other favors, on the agency in which the bureaucrat himself worked.[32] However,

---

[31] Shepelev, *Kompanii*, 129, citing a report in TsGIA, f. 1162.
[32] TsGIA, f. 1261, op. 3, ed. kh. 69–1879, ll. 18–18v. (quoted).

as another report made clear, such conflicts of interest were explicitly prohibited by the Code of Laws of 1876 (vol. 3, article 529). Article 485 of the Criminal Code specified harsh punishments: exile to Siberia with deprivation of all property or assignment to a corrective labor unit. Yet the tsar himself had authorized so many exemptions to this law on the grounds of economic expediency that in essence the law prescribed "no restrictions whatever," despite the "very undesirable consequences" that flowed from the presence of "the very large contingent" of bureaucrats in companies engaged in business relations with the officials' own agencies.[33]

The idea of placing strict limits on multiple officeholding was broached by Konstantin N. Pos'et, the efficiency-minded minister of transportation, in a memorandum to the tsar in April 1879, apparently because this ministry, which had extensive dealings as a customer of many firms, often confronted conflicts of interest. In May, Alexander II solicited opinions and proposals from other agencies. Views differed. The ministers of internal affairs, justice, and the navy, supported by Mikhail S. Kakhanov, clerk of the Committee of Ministers, considered it harmful to the state's financial interests and called for a ban. Greig, Minister of State Domains Valuev, and State Secretary Egor A. Peretts considered the practice "a useful and even unavoidable consequence of the shortage in Russia of experienced and trustworthy leaders of joint-stock companies." If banned, it would surely continue illegally. Furthermore, property rights would be abridged, namely the right of governmental officials to dispose of capital that they had invested in companies.[34]

Delayed by the assassination of Alexander II in March 1881, the impetus for reform resumed three years later, presumably because Alexander III and his advisors saw no indication that the abuses were declining of their own accord. After a review of reports submitted by various agencies,[35] the Committee of Ministers sought to ban officials from founding any company except those that processed agricultural products or mined minerals on land owned by such individuals. As for service on corporate boards, the committee found the practice useful only for those few companies that received direct governmental support. A total ban in other cases would be impossible, but it was necessary to prevent the highest officials from participating in corporations. The ban affected individuals in the three highest bureaucratic ranks and in several other important posts

[33] TsGIA, f. 1261, op. 3, ed. kh. 69–1879, l. 82r., 106r.–107v.
[34] Shepelev's paraphrase, *Kompanii*, 131.
[35] TsGIA, f. 1162.

(*nachal'stvennye dolzhnosti*). With the exception of owners of land where natural resources would be exploited by the company in question, officials needed special permission to act as founder or manager of a company. The right to own shares of course remained unaffected. Nor was permission necessary to participate in general assemblies or on audit commissions, and no limitations were imposed on individuals who set up and managed mutual credit societies, which did not produce profits. Shortly after the tsar signed this bill into law (December 3, 1884), the Committee of Ministers issued a supplemental list of posts whose occupants were banned from corporate positions.[36]

Although complaints continued to be heard after 1884 about the shortage of qualified managers, the law apparently had little effect on the practice of multiple officeholding. In Shepelev's words, it simply flourished "in a different form," either by the installation of close friends of high officials on corporate boards or by the replacement of "parallel multiple officeholding" by a "consecutive" form of the same practice. After retirement, former government officials gravitated to important positions in large companies and banks, where they could draw substantial salaries because of both their expert knowledge of state agencies and, "what was more important, their ties with the state apparatus,"[37] presumably their acquaintance with officials still in state service. A self-congratulatory review of economic legislation under Alexander III issued by the Ministry of Finance praised the law of 1884 on the grounds that by ending numerous abuses it protected "the state's properties" from the threat of widespread graft. It had a "humane side" as well, in that it allowed lower bureaucrats to continue to supplement their modest salaries by working for companies as long as these officials informed their superiors of their multiple positions.[38]

The extent of the practice prior to 1884 and the effects of the law after its promulgation remain to be ascertained by a thorough study of the careers of important bureaucrats and corporate managers. At this point it is sufficient to note that the tsar and his advisors addressed the conflict-of-interest problem primarily out of a concern for the state's own interests: the reduction of the drain of state wealth that resulted from institutionalized dishonesty and the maintenance of the good honor and impartiality of its highest officials. Moreover, the government used a typically formalistic

---

[36] *PSZ* 3–2559; supplement dated June 14, 1885, *PSZ* 3–3065 (list at end of vol., 164–3).
[37] Shepelev, *Kompanii*, 133.
[38] N. E. Volkov, *Ocherk zakonodatel'noi deiatel'nosti v tsarstvovanii Imperatora Aleksandra III, 1881–1894 gg.* (St. Petersburg, 1910), 210.

and tutelary method of implementing the restrictions of 1884–5, in that the rules imposed extremely strict guidelines, to which the tsar could make as many exceptions as he pleased. Whatever the real impact of the rules against multiple officeholding, both the problem and the attempts to solve it in the 1880s were significant because they bore unmistakable traces of the institutional framework of Russian capitalism: the shortage of qualified personnel; the awesome power of the state in defining individual career options, whatever the costs to the cause of economic development; and the bureaucracy's readiness to exercise tutelage over its most capable subordinates in pursuit of the appearance of probity and impartiality. In a similar vein, the Ministry of Finance sought to buttress the credit system by inserting into the charters of all new banks from 1883 onward a clause that banned *sovmestitel'stvo* in banks; no director of a bank could hold a similar position in another financial institution.[39]

Manipulation of the banking system

Regulation of conflicts of interest in banking constituted only one aspect of a larger pattern of the state's regimentation of the financial system. As usual, the bureaucrats defended their interference on the grounds that entrepreneurs lacked sufficient caution and abused the new forms of corporate power. Whatever the validity of these reproaches, the familiar patterns of governmental tutelage asserted themselves in the financial sector. Particularly evident were two facets: the continued dependence of banking companies on the enormous economic power of the state for their very survival and the repressive solicitude of Finance Ministers Reutern and Bunge as they alternated between widely varying policies, including a ban on new banks in the 1870s and minutely detailed regulations in the 1880s.

It is no exaggeration to assert that the State Bank dominated the entire banking system in the Russian Empire under the last three tsars. The autocratic state had of course long exercised absolute control over fiscal and monetary policy, and from at least the time of Catherine II had used the credit system in ways that hindered rather than promoted the emergence of private banks.[40] The persistence of the high degree of state control was

---

[39] Rudolf Claus, *Das russische Bankwesen* (Leipzig, 1908), 108, summarizes the provisions of *PSZ* 3–1484, dated April 5, 1883. Other aspects of the law are discussed in the section on manipulation of the banking system of this chapter.
[40] Klaus Heller, *Die Geld- und Kreditpolitik des russisches Reiches in der Zeit der Assignaten (1768–1839/43)* (Wiesbaden, 1983), esp. chap. 2 on Catherine's policies.

especially significant because it set Russia apart from the major European countries, where the leading banks had weaker ties to the government. The creation of the State Bank on June 1, 1860, predated the flurry of joint-stock bank incorporation in the decade between 1863 and 1872. The largest commercial bank in the empire, it steadily increased its basic capital from 15 million rubles in 1860 to 20 million in 1869 and 25 million a decade later, so that it competed directly with privately owned banks in the discounting of bills of exchange and in issuing loans backed by collateral such as commodities in customs houses or special warehouses, state and corporate securities, and mortgage notes.[41]

To their credit, the early directors of the State Bank, Baron Aleksandr L. Stieglitz and Evgenii I. Lamanskii, consciously limited the degree of competition that their institution posed to private banks. It enjoyed no special rights but, like other banks, was prohibited by law and its own charter from discounting bills of exchange due more than six months after the date of issue, and it could not grant long-term loans to corporations.[42] To the merchants, perhaps more reassuring than these restrictions was the right of local exchange committees to elect several of their members to the discount committees of the bank's branch offices in major cities. These men presumably set the bank's discount rate on bills of exchange (in effect, an interest rate on short-term commercial loans) a notch higher than the rate charged by their own banks, so as to avoid losing all their business to the State Bank.[43] The banks, especially those in St. Petersburg, in turn willingly served the state's own interests when called upon to do so. In response to a confidential request of the minister of finance, several banks restricted the granting of new loans so as to dampen the speculative fever that swept the stock market in 1866.[44]

Clearly the State Bank remained the dominant force in the Russian credit system at least until the granting of a new charter in 1894 and probably well into the twentieth century. In 1868, only three joint-stock banks and five mutual credit societies (*obshchestva vzaimnogo kredita*) existed in the empire. The rapid increase in the number of private banks from 1868 to the panic of 1873 failed to weaken the State Bank's power. In 1875, the "high point" of the private banking system, the State Bank still

---

[41] Iosif F. Gindin, *Gosudarstvennyi bank i ekonomicheskaia politika tsarskogo pravitel'stva (1861–1892 gody)* (Moscow, 1960), 84.
[42] Gindin, *Bank*, 116.
[43] Between 1877 and 1881, the elective principle was abolished everywhere except in Moscow: Gindin, *Bank*, 332.
[44] Gindin, *Bank*, 359.

had 750 million rubles in commercial deposits, while the total value of deposits and current accounts in all private banks stood at 525 million rubles.⁴⁵ Iosif F. Gindin, the leading Soviet historian of the tsarist financial system, attributed this imbalance to the long-standing Russian tradition of state-controlled banking; the occasional failure of a private bank, which made bureaucrats fearful of a major expansion of the banking system; and the shortage of available capital from 1875 onward, as the state treasury and landlords increased their demand for cash. He concluded that although joint-stock banks appeared to be independent from the state, in reality they remained completely subordinate to the minister of finance for their very existence. Only the finance ministers' changing conceptions of the needs of the Russian financial system could explain the marked variations in the pace of bank development: the rapid proliferation of banks in 1863–73; strict limitations in 1873–83; and renewed growth from 1883 onward.⁴⁶

As director of the State Bank, Lamanskii impressed the organizers of the Nizhnii Novgorod Fair in 1867 with his willingness to speak informally with merchants in a spirit of "sympathy based on mutual respect and accommodation of the interests of each with the interests of the state," as did statesmen "in England and Belgium," in the words of a conservative journalist.⁴⁷ A dozen years later, Lamanskii announced to the MEC, "I consider it my duty to inform the committee that the State Bank is now, as before, vigilantly attentive to the needs of commerce and remains devoted to its duty to promote the revival of industrial activity by providing credit."⁴⁸

Such bland generalities masked the essential nature of state aid to the banks. Two forms of tutelary action recurred: illegal loans to banks and other corporations in financial difficulty and the arbitrary selection of banks to be saved or abandoned in the occasional panics that swept through the Russian economy in the late nineteenth century. To be sure, Lamanskii's active sponsorship of corporate development by the tsarist bureaucracy could be considered legitimate in view of the shortage of qualified managers in Russia. Even Gindin accepted this pretext.⁴⁹ However, the intertwining of the fate of private companies with the fortunes of individual bureaucrats

---

⁴⁵ Gindin, *Bank*, 351.
⁴⁶ Gindin, *Bank*, 352–3.
⁴⁷ Prince V. P. Meshcherskii, *Ocherki nyneshnei obshchestvennoi zhizni v Rossii*, 2 vols. (St. Petersburg, 1868–70), vol. 1, 353.
⁴⁸ Laverychev, *Krupnaia burzhuaziia*, 34, quoting the minutes of a meeting of July 26, 1879, in the exchange committee archive, TsGAM, f. 143.
⁴⁹ Gindin, *Bank*, 359.

brought with it several unfortunate circumstances. Bureaucrats found it difficult to resist the temptation to approve companies of doubtful merit in which they had a personal interest, as Kulomzin saw in the Committee of Ministers. More serious than these episodes of conflict of interest were the problems of illegal state aid to corporations in temporary financial difficulty. Gindin's history of the State Bank chronicles dozens of cases in which the bank granted loans simply to rescue enterprises considered by Lamanskii and his advisors to be important to the economic development of the empire. There "irregular loans" (*neustavnye ssudy*, literally "loans granted contrary to the charter" of the State Bank) became so common that they must be viewed as an integral feature of tsarist economic policy under Alexander II and Alexander III. Called by the bureaucrats "special loans and expenditures" (*ssudy i zatraty na osobykh osnovaniiakh*),[50] they constituted a form of governmental aid to private industry as financially important as it was illegal. The result was a typically Russian swamp of administrative arbitrariness, where the extraordinary became routine; the government repeatedly violated its own laws; and bureaucrats found it possible to justify both legal and illegal actions, by law in the former case and by expediency and precedent in the latter.[51]

Gindin stressed the essential continuity between illegal loans from the state treasury prior to 1860 and the State Bank's irregular loans, which began in the late 1860s. In 1867, on the eve of the dissolution of the Russian-American Company, the State Bank loaned the enterprise 205,000 rubles on an unsecured bill of exchange (*solo-veksel'*, that is, one that lacked the signature of a second guarantor). Two years later, the first individual received such special treatment. An eight-year loan of 650,000 rubles, secured by real estate, went to Prince Lopukhin, a prominent landlord and producer of beet sugar, wine, and beer in Kiev Province. In 1871, the Miliutin trading firm received 300,000 rubles, secured only by a *solo-veksel'*, to maintain its thirty steamships and five hundred smaller vessels on the Empress Mariia canal system. Large loans to railroads and industrial corporations followed in 1873.[52] However, the bureaucracy's solicitude for the agricultural pursuits of the Russian gentry limited the scope of

---

[50] Gindin, *Bank*, 128.
[51] Gindin, *Bank*, 131, cited cases of special state credits to producers of coarse woolen cloth (*sukno*) for army uniforms in the period from 1798 to 1825.
[52] Gindin, *Bank*, 142. His list of favored capitalists rescued by irregular State Bank loans reads like a "Who's Who" of Russian economic life in the next two decades. See, for example, the Moscow manufacturers of cement, textiles, chemicals, glass, and woolen cloth who enjoyed special treatment between 1875 and 1892: Gindin, *Bank*, 324–6.

state financing for commerce, industry, and finance. Gindin calculated that the State Bank's irregular loans from 1869 through 1882 totaled 77.3 million rubles, of which 9 went to beet sugar, 5.8 to mining and metallurgy, and 2.6 to other enterprises owned predominantly by the gentry.[53] Laverychev noted in these figures a clear policy of granting loans for periods of three to five years to corporations in which "courtiers and highly placed bureaucrats" had a direct or indirect interest.[54] Gindin saw more than greed in this bias toward agriculture. The state itself depended on rising grain exports to offset adverse effects on the empire's balance of payments caused by the downward trend in the exchange rate (*kurs*) of the ruble.[55] However, he also recognized that despite the government's aim of "accelerating the economic development of the country," the financing of gentry and aristocratic landlords by the State Bank (not to mention the Gentry Land Bank, founded in 1885) diverted "resources from the crediting of trade and industry."[56] Even when large companies gained financial aid, they succumbed to increased governmental control over their activities. Certainly many manufacturers and bankers welcomed illegal infusions of capital into their failing enterprises in times of distress, but the tutelage inherent in the distribution of such favors clearly hindered the expansion of the capitalist system as a whole.

Irregular loans to prominent banks were most common, of course, in Petersburg. The Volga-Kama Bank, founded there in 1870 by prominent merchants (Mikhail and Aleksei M. Polezhaev and Ivan A. Vargunin) with the support of industrialists in Moscow (Exchange President Timofei S. Morozov and Kuz'ma T. Soldatenkov) and in Rybinsk (Exchange President Ivan A. Miliutin), escaped financial disaster in 1875 and 1879 thanks to Lamanskii's irregular loans.[57] However, Gindin's account shows that even the most conservative bankers in Moscow could not survive without such aid. In 1877, three banks in that city, including Nikolai A. Naidenov's Bank of Trade, as well as the Volga-Kama Bank, found themselves in difficulty as a result of their loan of 1.4 million rubles to a mismanaged rail plant owned by Nikolai I. Putilov in Petersburg. Only the granting of an

---

[53] Gindin, *Bank*, 128, 136–53.
[54] Laverychev, *Krupnaia burzhuaziia*, 40.
[55] Gindin, *Bank*, 399.
[56] Gindin, *Bank*, 398; Iosif F. Gindin, "Neustavnye ssudy Gosudarstvennogo banka i ekonomicheskaia politika tsarskogo pravitel'stva," *Istoricheskie zapiski*, 35 (1950), 88, cited in Laverychev, *Krupnaia burzhuaziia*, 38.
[57] Gindin, *Bank*, 370. Founders are listed in the bank's charter: *PSZ* 2–48058, dated February 24, 1870.

irregular loan by the State Bank to Putilov saved the Moscow banks.[58] Fifteen years later, when depositors withdrew their funds from the Bank of Trade as a result of rumors of the insolvency of a major debtor, the Babkin woolen textile company, the minister of finance took "extreme measures to support the bank." A ten-year irregular loan of 900,000 rubles at 6 percent interest saved both the Babkins and Naidenov's bank.[59] Gindin concluded that a fully ramified network of private banks had developed in the Moscow region to provide the short-term credit needs of the textile industry there, but that "direct governmental financial support" proved necessary to strengthen this network whenever periodic downturns in the business cycle created "general financial difficulties" in Moscow.[60]

These episodes of financial rescue by the state had indirect political consequences of enormous significance. Naidenov occupied the most prominent position in the Moscow merchant world, the presidency of the MEC, from 1877 to his death in 1905. Well known for both his prudent financial policies and his absolute devotion to the tsarist autocracy,[61] Naidenov typified the enterprising textile manufacturers of the Moscow region, men who devoted their considerable entrepreneurial abilities to meeting the challenge of European competition, but whose efforts would have failed without state aid in the form of import tariffs and occasional financial largess. Naidenov's conservatism owed much to cultural and religious influences, but the economic dependence of his bank on the good will of the tsarist ministers undoubtedly reinforced his feelings of awe and devotion toward the autocrat.

The crucial nature of state intervention on behalf of private banks became clear to all in the panic that swept the entire Russian financial system in 1875. To save various banks in Moscow that he knew to be well managed, Reutern advanced a total of 25 million rubles. However, he refused to grant a special 4-million-ruble credit to the Moscow Commercial Loan Bank, on the grounds that its foreign department had, without the knowledge or permission of the bank's council, lost up to 7 million rubles in insufficiently secured loans to the Berlin banker Bethel Henry Strousberg.

---

[58] Rieber, *Merchants*, 194, citing Gindin's book on the State Bank and numerous documents in the archive of Fedor V. Chizhov in GBL-OR, f. 332.
[59] Gindin, *Bank*, 327, quotation from a document in the finance ministry archive.
[60] Gindin, *Bank*, 322.
[61] Thomas C. Owen, *Capitalism and Politics in Russia: A Social History of the Moscow Merchants, 1855–1905* (Cambridge, 1981), 97–8, 142–3, 151, 168–71, 185–7. For essential information on his banking activities and political views, see his turgidly written, but revealing memoirs: *Vospominaniia o vidennom, slyshannom i ispytannom*, 2 vols. (Moscow, 1903–5; reprinted Newtonville, Mass., 1976).

The failure of Strousberg's bank caused the collapse of the Commercial Loan Bank in October 1875.[62] As he explained in a confidential memorandum to Lamanskii dated October 11, 1875, Reutern had no desire to refuse well-founded requests for temporary financial assistance. He authorized Lamanskii to act "in all cases where a joint-stock bank or an important banking firm turns to the State Bank with a request for help." Aid should be given "if a thorough examination of the matter reveals that the difficulty is only temporary and the petitioner of aid can provide full security for the loan from the State Bank."[63] Reutern clearly had the power to rescue any Russian bank, but he used discretion in this case, in effect punishing the Commercial Loan Bank for its violation of banking regulations. (Note his attention to "full security": Always the state sought to protect its own financial interests.) In favoring Naidenov and his fellows over the improvident lenders at the Commercial Loan Bank, Reutern did not act capriciously. The fact remains, however, that he chose to break the law. When he authorized Lamanskii to distribute temporary credits to banks in need, Reutern followed the old tradition of tutelary intervention by the state.

The prerevolutionary economic expert Levin concluded his richly detailed account of the bank crisis of 1875 with a vivid portrait of the man who stood at the center of the storm. Particularly striking was the peculiar combination of enormous power, calm judgment, and pretensions to omniscience that characterized the most capable of the tsarist ministers:

The Ministry of Finance bore on its shoulders the entire burden of the crash. It was flooded with complaints from depositors, explanations from the management of the failed bank, petitions from other banks and representative organizations, and information from the press about the spread of the crisis to new firms and institutions. Reutern himself probed every question, personally considered everything, and spread calm everywhere, but did not, however, spend a single kopek from the treasury. He personally took part in the discussion of the attorney's fee, and on each occasion he authorized the expenditure of funds for the liquidation commission. In a word, he demonstrated, as we have seen, a comprehensive, statesman-like understanding of the necessity to calm the money market, and he never ceased being the thrifty and zealous master of the smallest details.[64]

Here is a perfect portrait of the bureaucrat exercising in an emergency the kind of governmental tutelage that would justify, at least in his mind, the retention of enormous power in less troubled times.

[62] Gindin, *Bank*, 369. Levin, *Banki*, 213–25, provided a vivid account of this sad episode.
[63] Quoted from the Credit Chancery archive by Levin, *Banki*, 215.
[64] Levin, *Banki*, 230–1.

A bank crisis in Kiev in 1876 likewise illustrated the importance of central control in occasional emergencies. Nikolai N. Flige (1876–1943; Fliege in German) recalled the drama that followed his father's election as vice-director of the Kiev Private Bank in 1876. The elder Flige soon found to his horror that the bank had at its disposal only 900,000 rubles of its nominal 1.5 million rubles of basic capital. He reported the anomaly to his uncle, Nikolai Kh. Bunge, director of the Kiev branch of the State Bank and professor of economics at Kiev University. Bunge immediately telegraphed to Petersburg a request for "unlimited credits," arguing that the crash of this bank would endanger "the economic life of the southwestern region." (Kiev was the center of the Russian beet-sugar industry.) "The credit was approved." Then began the delicate operation to save the bank from panic.

Flige knew that a refusal to open the bank after the Christmas holiday "would be tantamount to suicide." Having already invested in the bank his own assets and those of his wife in order to demonstrate his personal commitment to solvency, he saw to it that the panicked depositors who crowded into the lobby received their securities (mainly lottery tickets) and cash, now covered by the credit line from Lamanskii. Although the price of the bank's stock fell from three hundred to thirty-three rubles, the crisis ended on the third day as the reassured customers returned to deposit what they had recently withdrawn. Members of the bank's board bravely pledged to donate sufficient cash to cover half the losses caused by mismanagement prior to the crisis. After "many months," Flige restored order to the bank's books so that seven years later, the price of its stock again stood at three hundred rubles.[65] The steadfast defense of financial probity by the Lutheran Germans Bunge and Flige no doubt contributed to the successful outcome of this crisis, but the main point is that without an emergency illegal loan from Petersburg, the Kiev Private Bank would have failed. Tutelage in defiance of the law again appeared justified.

True, the few banks in the empire that were managed by men fully versed in the latest European business techniques, as in Warsaw, Lodz, and Riga, rarely if ever needed rescue. The Riga Commercial Bank, founded by German and English merchants in that old Hanseatic city with seven other German firms in Petersburg, Moscow, Berlin, Königsberg, and Hamburg, as well as the Kronenberg firm in Warsaw, grew steadily

---

[65] Memoir, unnumbered chapter, file 3, pp. 2–4, Flige collection, BAREEHC. Flige erroneously named Baron Stieglitz as the director of the State Bank during this episode.

over the decades, paying dividends in every year (up to 14 percent in 1898) except 1901, during the sharp depression of 1900–3.[66] Nonetheless, the financial difficulties of the mid-1870s – the crash of the Commercial Loan Bank and the stresses occasioned by the Russo-Turkish War – drove at least seven banks into liquidation, not only small ones like the Industrial Bank in Moscow and the Commercial Bank in Kostroma but also the Kronstadt Commercial and the Reval Commercial banks, both founded by men with impressive German surnames.[67] It was apparently criminally lax mismanagement by the board that drove the Libau Commercial Bank into liquidation in April 1882.[68] These failures, like the crises in Moscow and Kiev in the 1870s, underlined the persistent fact: Vigorous, even arbitrary tutelage by Lamanskii in Petersburg appeared necessary to keep the Russian banking system intact.

What of the laws that Reutern and Bunge implemented in this period to govern the operation of the financial network? Here, in somewhat less dramatic but no less significant ways, the principle of tutelage also asserted itself. Until the early 1870s, Reutern allowed the proliferation of banks, notably in ports where joint-stock banks had not previously existed: Odessa, Nikolaev, and Taganrog in the south and Libau, Riga, and Kronstadt in the north. The rapid pace of proliferation may be seen in Table 4.1. (It traces the development of joint-stock banks only, not the many municipal, mutual-credit, and agricultural institutions that also sprang up in this period.)

As early as 1869, Reutern expressed misgivings. He feared that the unregulated proliferation of lending institutions, whether joint-stock banks or those operated by municipalities and zemstvos, might weaken the entire financial system. Preferable to a cyclical pattern of rapid proliferation and periodic collapse of banks would be a slow expansion of the credit network under the cautious eye of the finance minister. Reutern's abandonment of the corporate law reform in 1874, discussed in Chapter 3, formed part of an overall policy of careful tutelage, one that led him to implement two reforms in the credit system at that time.

Until the 1870s, the essence of the corporate law of 1836 – the concession system of incorporation in the form of a separate law – had never met a serious challenge. We have seen how a rational alternative to this system,

---

[66] Eugen von Stieda, *Das livländische Bankwesen in Vergangenheit und Gegenwart* (Leipzig, 1909), 323, 368. This work stands as a model of banking history.
[67] Levin, *Banki*, 244–5.
[68] Levin, *Banki*, 250–1.

Table 4.1. *Banks in the Russian Empire, 1864–1900*

Year	New banks chartered	Year	New banks chartered	Year	New banks chartered	Year	New banks chartered
—	—	1871	12	1881	1	1891	0
—	—	1872	9	1882	0	1892	1
—	—	1873	12	1883	1	1893	0
1864	1	1874	0	1884	0	1894	0
1865	0	1875	0	1885	0	1895	1
1866	1	1876	0	1886	1	1896	1
1867	0	1877	0	1887	1	1897	2
1868	2	1878	0	1888	0	1898	2
1869	3	1879	1	1889	3	1899	2
1870	5 (6)	1880	0 (33)	1890	1 (34)	1900	0 (39)

Source: RUSCORP database. Numbers in parentheses indicate banks existing in those years from Komitet s″ezdov predstavitelei aktsionernykh kommercheskikh bankov, *Russkie aktsionernye kommercheskie banki v 1916 g.* (St. Petersburg, 1916), 71.

in the form of a comprehensive corporate law coupled with registration of new companies, failed adoption in 1874. Another, less drastic modification of the concession principle appealed to Reutern, one that entailed less red tape while allowing his ministry to retain more control over the founding of new companies than would have been the case had the reform bills of 1872 or 1874 become law. He sought to implement a simpler concession policy, to be operated by his own ministry, in order to put an end to the obvious absurdity of a separate imperial law for each of a dozen identical companies. The debate over the wisdom of such a departure from the traditional concessionary system began over the procedure for licensing a series of seemingly minor warehouse companies. By 1872, it had led to important changes in the way that banks of moderate size received their charters. The system implemented by Reutern was destined to last until 1917.

Reutern began groping toward a less complicated system of incorporation in 1869, when he sent to the Committee of Ministers the draft charter of a small warehouse company in Orel, called Podspor'e (Assistance), accompanied by a memorandum stating that the charters of ten such companies were also under consideration in his ministry. Reutern requested permission to approve the charters himself, following the tsar's confirmation of the Assistance Company. The finance minister paid special attention to these warehouse companies because they functioned as sources of short-term credit. Merchants who deposited their goods in a warehouse received documents called "warrants" (*varranty*), which certified the acceptance of the goods for storage or shipment by the company. In November 1869, warehouse companies had received the right to give loans to merchants who wished to use such warrants as collateral. (This legalization of the use of commodities as collateral for loans lengthened the list of approved types of collateral, which included corporate stocks from 1848 onward.) Reutern cited a precedent for his request to confirm the ten additional charters without the tsar's signature. On July 29, 1868, he had been empowered to give routine approval to the charters of small, nonprofit public banks (*obshchestvennye banki*), and on March 21, 1869, he received the same power over savings and loan institutions (*ssudo-sberegatel'nye kassy*). Just as these small credit institutions in dozens of district and provincial cities all operated under a standard charter, so, Reutern argued, the ten warehouse companies, whose charters were "literally identical" to one another, should be allowed to go into operation without the bureaucratic complications of the usual confirmation process.

After protracted discussions within the State Council, including Reutern's rejection in 1870 of a "model charter" (*normal'nye ustav*) for all future warehouse companies on the grounds that it might prove too inflexible, the Department of State Economy finally approved both the charter of the Assistance Company and a broad mandate giving the finance minister the power to confirm charters "of other similar companies" without the tsar's approval. After the State Council endorsed this reform, the tsar confirmed it on June 4, 1871. Between August 4 and December 10, 1871, no fewer than eight warehouse companies, with names like Success, Abundance, Benefit, and Confidence, received Reutern's approval. In the same spirit, the tsar granted to the finance minister the right to confirm charters of new banks established by zemstvos, whose charters were modeled on those of the Kherson and Kharkov Land Banks (established in 1864 and 1871, respectively) and whose modest profits were earmarked for public-works projects and credits to the peasantry.[69]

The precedent established by the laws of May and June 1871 opened

---

[69] The reform of June 4, 1871, forms part of the preface to the charter of the Assistance Company: *PSZ* 2-49703. On the additional warehouse companies, see the chronological list of laws at the end of the *PSZ* volume for 1871. The law on zemstvo banks is in *PSZ* 2-49609, dated May 17, 1871. Quotations from Shepelev, *Kompanii*, 116–18.

the way for a major change in the procedure for incorporating new joint-stock banks. A law dated May 31, 1872,[70] granted to the finance minister the "temporary" authority to confirm the charter of any new bank with less than 5 million rubles, "as long as these charters represent no deviation from charters of similar [*odnorodnykh*] institutions already confirmed by the tsar." The obvious benefit of this relaxation of the law of 1836 consisted in the reduction of bureaucratic formalities facing entrepreneurs. The charters of new banks of moderate size would issue from the Ministry of Finance, without passing through the State Council and the office of the tsar.

Paradoxically, however, the immediate result of this reform was the opposite of what might have been expected. Having witnessed the stock-exchange fever of the late 1860s, Reutern feared that an excessively rapid expansion of the credit network might weaken the banks that already existed. Accordingly, he readily endorsed a proposal by the Department of State Economy that henceforth, no new banks should be established in Petersburg, Moscow, or any other city where a bank or mutual credit society already operated. This restriction became part of the law of May 31, 1872. (With characteristic absurdity, the law forbade such banks without "special permission," as if the concession system did not exist.) Likewise, no more than two land banks would be allowed to operate in a single province. The law also imposed several additional restrictions on banks so as to reduce the dangers of panic and collapse. Clauses were added to existing charters, and required in new ones, that prohibited banks from organizing corporations and participating in subscriptions to their securities. Indeed, banks were not allowed "to purchase any securities not in circulation on the stock exchange." New structural restrictions were added to reduce speculation in bank stocks: No bank could operate with less than 500,000 rubles of basic capital, and the price of a share must be set at 250 rubles or more.[71]

Reutern's cautious policy appeared rational in the immediate aftermath of the law's promulgation. Of the twelve banks approved in 1873, six (in Kozlov, Rybinsk, Berdichev, Kerch, Kherson, and Kursk) failed to raise the minimum capital required by their charters.[72] The Moscow Industrial Bank closed its doors in 1877 after six years of essentially unprofitable

---

[70] *PSZ* 2–50915; Shepelev misnumbered it 50913.
[71] *PSZ* 2–50913; further documentation in Levin, *Banki*, esp. 199.
[72] Levin, *Banki*, 212.

operation. Between 1872 and 1882, a dozen banks reduced the size of their basic capital, six of them by 50 percent or more.[73]

Yet the absolute ban allowed so little flexibility that occasional protests arose against the ministry's heavy-handed tutelage over the banking system. The law of May 31, 1872, froze the number of banks in major cities at six in Petersburg, five in Moscow, two each in Riga and Warsaw, and one each in such major commercial centers as Odessa, Kiev, Kharkov, Nizhnii Novgorod, Tiflis, Taganrog, Rostov-on-Don, and Kishinev. In 1873, Professor Ivan K. Babst of Moscow University, a well-known spokesman for the Moscow merchants, argued for greater entrepreneurial freedom. "Concern over the question whether a bank is needed in a given locality would [best] be left, it seems, to the good judgment and calculations of those individuals who risk the establishment of a new bank and contribute their funds to the business." His criticism that the law had been drafted and implemented with excessive haste echoed the views of many bankers who complained that they had not been consulted. Above all, a model charter (*normal'nyi ustav*) should be drawn up to reduce the red tape encountered in establishing a new corporation. Babst apparently voiced no objection against the various restrictions as to the size and activities of banks, but he proposed the adoption of a model charter as a first step toward incorporation by registration.[74]

As we have seen, Reutern turned his back on this idea in 1874. The warehouse and bank reforms of 1871–2 must therefore be regarded as obstacles to further innovation rather than as an accommodation to the needs of modern industrial development. For banks as well as other corporations, the tsarist government retained the concession system, in that the prior permission of the finance minister was necessary before any new credit institution could be created. Reutern's policy of cautious tutelage caused great disappointment among Russian business leaders who had endorsed the registration principle.

More than a decade later, in 1883, Finance Minister Bunge abrogated Reutern's restrictive policy in favor of a new set of guidelines for the establishment of joint-stock banks. To ensure solidity, various minima were prescribed: No fewer than five founders were required; half of the

---

[73] Details in Levin, *Banki*, 198.
[74] Statistics from RUSCORP. Levin, *Banki*, 211–12, quoting Babst's anonymous "Pis'mo o bankakh," *Russkie vedomosti*, 1873, no. 169. On Babst's role as a spokeman for the Moscow merchants, for example, at the first congress of the Association of Banks (*S"ezd predstavitelei aktsionernykh kommercheskikh bankov*) in 1872, see Levin, *Banki*, 240–1; and Rieber, *Merchants*, 191–5.

basic capital must be collected during subscription, the remainder within the next six months; the bank's obligations must not exceed five times its combined basic and reserve capital and ten times the amount of its basic capital plus its current account at the State Bank; and half of a bank's annual profits must be placed in the reserve capital fund until it reached one-third of the basic capital, so that in an unprofitable year dividends of up to 8 percent could still be paid to stockholders. No board member or employee could receive credit from his own bank in the form of bills of exchange or serve simultaneously on the board of another bank. To protect the interests of stockholders, no person could cast more than 110 votes at a general assembly meeting, and a one-third vote representing at least one-fifth of the basic capital was sufficient to call for a governmental audit of the bank's records, at the bank's expense.[75]

An official account of economic policy under Alexander III saw nothing negative in this law but proclaimed proudly that it "inaugurated the government's supervision [*nadzor*] over the activities of private banks." It commended a similarly restrictive law on insurance companies, under which the Ministry of Finance enjoyed the right to conduct special audits "when necessary." The law also prescribed in detail the procedures for the elaboration of "tables of mortality, the size of discount percentages, and formulas for computing premium reserves."[76]

Although Reutern constrained the growth of the banking system and Bunge encouraged the creation of new banks, both men adhered to essentially paternalistic policies. Neither minister can be considered somehow "antibusiness." Reutern icily ignored the pleas of Professor Babst and the PEC in the early 1870s for abolition of the concession system, but he acted with energy and skill to save endangered banks in times of financial crisis. In different ways, both Reutern and Bunge sought to aid the development of a sound credit system. Inaction by the government would have allowed Russian banks to collapse, and everyone knew it. Notwithstanding the demands of bankers for registration, it seemed preferable to both men to exercise careful stewardship over the nascent credit system. The point where such well-meaning tutelage became uninformed and arbitrary repression of creative market forces remained unclear, both then and now. In any case, the old tsarist system of extreme centraliza-

---

[75] *PSZ* 3–1484, dated April 5, 1883, paraphrased in Levin, *Banki*, 253–4; and Claus, *Bankwesen*, 107–8.
[76] Volkov, *Ocherk*, 209, 243, citing a law dated June 6, 1894.

tion persisted for decades thereafter in the financial sector of the Russian economy.

Professor Mendeleev's dilemma

To conclude this discussion of the tsarist regime's policy of tutelage over corporations, it is useful to inquire into the attitudes of the merchants as they labored under the solicitude of the bureaucratic machine. Unfortunately for the historian, they proved reluctant to criticize the economic policies of the tsarist regime except within carefully defined limits, as at the commercial-industrial congresses of 1870 and 1882. For Moscow, we have cited the articulate statements of Professor Babst and Fedor V. Chizhov. The voluminous publications of the various sectoral and regional industrial organizations throughout the empire remain to be examined in detail. At this point, the views of entrepreneurs in heavy industry in its formative period, the 1880s and 1890s, can best be discerned in the writings of one of the most energetic and articulate spokesmen for the cause of Russian industrialization: the renowned chemist Dmitrii I. Mendeleev (1834–1907).

Besides advocating the rather simple program of generally higher import tariffs to provide protection for Russian industry, Mendeleev brought to the debate over economic policy numerous creative ideas. Particularly important for an understanding of corporate law is his ambivalent attitude toward the phenomenon of bureaucratic tutelage, expressed in an article published in 1884. Mendeleev began by advancing the optimistic notion that governmental tutelage, accompanied by the traditional forms of aid – interest-free loans, huge bonuses for companies that processed foreign raw materials instead of purchasing finished goods, and grants of land – were neither necessary nor appropriate as industry reached maturity. Private investment, he asserted, could invigorate Russian industry, and adequate capital already existed for this purpose. Of the finished goods currently imported, worth a total of 500 million rubles, fully 300 million rubles' worth could be supplied a decade hence by Russian factories processing Russian raw materials.

As the rapid expansion of the beet-sugar industry in the Ukraine had shown, modern productive techniques raised levels of "education and morality." "The plant represents to blind people only the exploitation of labor by capital; they do not see the creative power" of industrial enterprises. Like the professional judiciary and universal military service, modern industry would create a new, positive spirit and drive out the old attitudes of passivity and fatalism that had long prevented independent activity among the masses. As new careers in the business world opened up, sterile "classic bureaucratic" attitudes would melt away, and the weak figures typified in Russian literature – lazy Oblomovs, ineffectual Rudins, "and their moral offspring" – would gradually disappear. Mendeleev recognized that high profits of at least 12 percent per annum would be necessary to attract sufficient amounts of capital into industry, but under good management "a whole mass" of Russian companies could achieve annual profit rates of 50 percent. To be sure, a major improvement in the capabilities of the manufacturers themselves was needed. "Therefore the matter will not depend on profits [alone]. It is a matter of initiative, knowledge, persistence, constancy of labor, and general honesty in managerial practice."[77]

Witte recalled that Mendeleev's many articles and pamphlets on behalf of industry prompted "vicious slander" to the effect that he had sold his pen to the capitalists.[78] In fact, Mendeleev did have close friends in business circles. This is clear from a recently published chronicle of his public activities and from the photographs showing him surrounded by oil men in Baku, on display in his former office, now a museum at Leningrad State University. (With characteristic Soviet delicacy, the captions to these photographs identify Mendeleev's millionaire acquaintances as "specialists" in petroleum production.) However, as his mildly critical appeal for "general honesty" in the business world indicated, the great scientist's efforts to promote Russian economic development, especially in petroleum and heavy industry, derived less from his attraction to wealth, whether as an investor or as a paid publicist for industrial interests, than from his faith in applied technology and his patriotic devotion to Russian economic development.[79]

Ironically, despite his optimistic vision of a dynamic Russian industry freed from the heavy hand of bureaucratic authority, Mendeleev continued to see the state as the motive force behind the destruction of outworn, precapitalist notions. Tutelage, in other words, he saw as both inevitable

---

[77] Dmitrii I. Mendeleev, "O vozbuzhdenii promyshlennogo razvitiia v Rossii," *Vestnik promyshlennosti* (Feb. 1884), 10–11, 13.
[78] Witte, *Vospominaniia*, vol. 1, 150.
[79] Roman B. Dobrotin and others, *Letopis' zhizni i deiatel'nosti D. I. Mendeleeva* (Leningrad, 1984). On his campaign for industrial development, two useful studies in the form of doctoral dissertations are Beverly S. Almgren, "Mendeleev: The Third Service," Brown University, 1968; and Francis M. Stackenwalt, "The Thought and Work of Dmitrii Ivanovich Mendeleev on the Industrialization of Russia, 1867–1907," University of Illinois, 1976.

and necessary if exercised in a sufficiently enlightened manner. Private capital existed in abundance, but only the state could direct it into productive channels by providing cheap long-term credit to large corporations. Mendeleev also justified state intervention with historical and biological metaphors. In the life of both a state and an individual,

> instincts, so to speak, predominate at first, and [only] later, in maturity, does consciousness [exert control]. Therefore the maturing historical organism requires a conscious attitude toward its development if it does not wish to see abnormalities, diseases, and accidents. "Maybe" [*Avos'* – a colloquial word expressing ignorance and fatalism] is not suitable in this case.

Progress depended on the leading role of the tsarist state: "the impending swift, inevitable, and sweeping industrial development of Russia will proceed from the Tsar and through Him." Mendeleev could conceive of no alternative to the state's "initiative, which has grown and developed historically in every possible way, but also and especially because a conscious understanding of the general interest is to be expected more from the few than from the mass."[80]

This dubious Westernizing notion – that the autocratic state since Peter the Great had successfully implanted European institutions in Russia – led the chemist into a logical contradiction. On the one hand, levels of technical expertise and business ethics remained so low among Russian manufacturers that the state must exert firm leadership to break the bonds of inertia and ignorance. On the other hand, the state itself could not be trusted to foster the dynamism that industry needed for success in the fatal struggle against Europe. We have already noted the energy with which such enlightened officials as Reutern, Bunge, and the young Witte imposed omnibus regulations by autocratic fiat. Mendeleev himself admitted the prevalence of antiindustrial attitudes within the government and bemoaned the refusal of the bureaucracy to allow the creation of elective

---

[80] Mendeleev, "O vozbuzhdenii," 6–7. This article appeared in a Soviet version in Mendeleev's collected works and a volume of economic essays: *Sochineniia*, 25 vols. (Moscow, 1934–54), vol. 20, 74–93; and *Problemy ekonomicheskogo razvitiia Rossii* (Moscow, 1960), 173–88. The Soviet editors restored several passages deleted by the tsarist censor. At one point, Mendeleev demanded a ministry of trade and industry and dismissed the various consultative agencies created by the regime, such as the Council of Trade and Manufacturing, as "powerless, deaf, and narrowly bureaucratic": *Problemy*, 181. Curiously, however, the same Soviet editors inserted ellipses after the words "will proceed" and elsewhere in order to remove Mendeleev's pro-tsarist rhetoric! Such selective censorship by both the tsarist and Soviet regimes illustrated the hostility of both forms of Russian autocracy toward the spontaneous development of capitalist institutions.

chambers of commerce and consultative organizations.[81] Russian "industry does not have its own banner;... it is just taxed." A ministry of industry was needed to coordinate the multitudes of "laws, fees, taxes, rules, etc." that applied to corporate enterprise. No bureaucrat would tell a peasant what crops to plant. "But if on my land I decide to build a forge with a lathe to repair my neighbors' machines, or a plant to make smoke-black, oh, what ordeals must be endured, how many plans to be presented, certificates of permission to be obtained and accounts given."

While calling for "requisite freedom" (*dolzhnoi svobody*) for entrepreneurs, so that "the urgent needs of a multitude of plants and factories can be comprehended,"[82] Mendeleev also admitted the inevitability of continued tutelage by the state. His speech at the Commercial-Industrial Congress of 1882 praising the regime of Alexander III for having provided Russian industry with "a welcome rain of measures" (*zhelannyi dozhd' meropriiatii*) conducive to Russian industrial development has been widely quoted by Marxist historians, who generally argue that manufacturers willingly accepted "the old-fashioned forms of state organization and methods of bureaucratic tutelage."[83] Although the evidence presented in this study shows that Russian manufacturers by no means submitted graciously to

[81] On the periodic, but futile demands by merchants for such organizations and for a ministry of trade and industry responsive to them, see Owen, *Capitalism and Politics*, 108–11; G. M. Gorfein, "Iz istorii obrazovanii Ministerstva torgovli i promyshlennosti," in S. N. Valk, ed., *Ocherki po istorii ekonomiki i klassovykh otnoshenii v Rossii kontsa XIX–nachala XX v.* (Moscow, 1964), 161–79. The Menshevik historian Pavel A. Berlin, *Russkaia burzhuaziia v staroe i novoe vremia*, 2nd ed. (Moscow, 1925), 214–15, characteristically exaggerated the importance of the Council of Trade and Manufacturing and its regional affiliates (created by *PSZ* 2-50957, dated June 7, 1872), the shortcomings of which are discussed in Owen, *Capitalism and Politics*, 68, 111–14.

[82] Mendeleev, "O vozbuzhdenii," 9–10; in *Problemy*, 183. One passage deleted by the tsarist censor is particularly relevant. Mendeleev stressed that a new agency could be expected to foster industrial development "only on one condition, which is absolutely essential, given the nature [*po sushchestvu*] of industrial affairs, namely that it must combine on the one hand representatives of the entire country, in the form of the tsar's ministers and advisors, and on the other hand representatives of the people from the zemstvos and municipalities." Only in this way could tsarist ministers in Petersburg receive accurate and detailed information from the provinces (182). This body of state and elected representatives, meeting regularly, should be empowered to submit to the tsar drafts of laws for the improvement of industry (183). Max Weber himself could not have stated better the essential importance of accurate information in a capitalist system or the profound incompatibility between autocratic and capitalist modes of behavior shown by the tsarist government's refusal not only to create the body of experts urged by Mendeleev, but even to allow the publication of the proposal itself.

[83] [Osip] A. Ermanskii [né Kogan], "Krupnaia burzhuaziia do 1905 goda," in Lev Martov, P. Maslov, and A. Potresov, eds., *Obshchestvennoe dvizhenie v Rossii v nachale XX veka*, 4 vols. (St. Petersburg, 1909–14; reprinted The Hague, 1968), vol. 1, 326; Ermanskii quoted Mendeleev's famous phrase from vol. 1 of the stenographic report of the 1882 congress.

the most absurd tsarist regulations, Mendeleev's tendency to refer favorably to the initiatives of the Ministry of Finance demonstrates how difficult it was to break free of the smothering protection of the all-powerful state. The great chemist found it essential both to criticize governmental tutelage and to invoke it for further industrial progress. From the horns of this dilemma he offered no escape.

5

Proizvol (Arbitrary acts), 1880–1905

> As St. Petersburg directs everything within this great Empire, so every thing must wait until St. Petersburg directs. A grain elevator cannot be built at Odessa, nor can a newspaper be published in Tashkent, without [its founders'] first receiving permission from St. Petersburg.
> – Thomas E. Heehan, United States consul in Odessa (1890)[1]

Arbitrary action by the Russian bureaucracy in defiance of the wishes of the population has constituted one of the great themes of Russian history, from the brutalities of Ivan the Terrible and the repressive punishments of Nicholas I to the totalitarian excesses of Stalin and the elitist rule of the post-Khrushchev oligarchy, practitioners of what James H. Billington once called "arteriosclerotic dacha despotism."[2] Aleksandr Solzhenitsyn, in his futile appeal to the Soviet leaders for the repudiation of Marxist ideology, admitted the strength of the autocratic political tradition in Russia and the population's concomitant lack of experience in self-government. However, he made what he considered a crucial distinction between well-intentioned, competent authoritarian rule and narrow-minded arbitrariness:

Everything depends on *what kind* of authoritarian system we shall have in the future. What is unbearable is not authoritarian rule itself but the ideological lies that are crammed down our throats every day. What is unbearable is not so much authoritarian rule but arbitrariness and lawlessness [*proizvol i bezzakonie*], the utter lawlessness that prevails when in every region, province, or field of

---

[1] George S. Queen, *The United States and the Material Advance in Russia, 1881–1906* (New York, 1976), 54, note 66, quoting United States, *Consular Report*, no. 116 (Washington, 1890), 111.
[2] James H. Billington, "Soviet Attitudes and Values: Prospects for the Future," in "The U.S.S.R. and the Sources of Soviet Policy," Kennan Institute for Advanced Russian Studies, Occasional Paper no. 34 (1978), 105–11, quotation from 106.

activity one boss, often ignorant and cruel, runs everything according to his will alone.³

Although tsarist bureaucrats and Soviet historians occasionally applied the word *proizvol* to the activities of capitalists, such as price fixing by cartels in the reign of Nicholas II,⁴ the word best fits the economic policies of the tsarist regime itself, even under its most enlightened ruler, Alexander II, and its most vigorous proponents of industrial development, Finance Ministers Vyshnegradskii and Witte. In theory, if not always in practice, it is possible to distinguish between two kinds of arbitrary action by tsarist bureaucrats. On the one hand, the government reserved to itself the right to violate its own laws; even the Code of Laws itself stated this contradictory principle. As Count Aleksandr Kh. Benckendorff is reported to have quipped, "Laws are written for subordinates, not for those in authority."⁵ It was in this spirit that Reutern intervened to rescue favored banks in the financial crises of the 1870s, as discussed in the previous chapter. On the other hand, even when the state observed its own laws, it drafted and implemented them with so little regard for the opinions of its subjects that tsarist legislation often appeared as arbitrary and inconsistent as the most blatantly illegal actions of individual bureaucrats.

Like Reutern and Bunge before them, Vyshnegradskii and Witte maintained strict tutelage over capitalist institutions considered too weak or corruptible to flourish without constant state supervision. From the perspective of corporate managers, however, such actions appeared capricious and harmful. Four aspects of corporate law in the decades before the revolution of 1905 showed clearly the routine nature of arbitrary legislation. The tsarist bureaucracy imposed unprecedented restrictions on landownership by corporations in which foreigners, Jews, and Poles participated as managers and stockholders; it maintained inconsistent and unpredictable policies toward cartels; and it failed to adopt the modest program of corporate law reform elaborated by the Tsitovich Commission (1897–8). Finally, a law regulating the procedures for general assembly

---

³ Aleksandr Solzhenitsyn, *Pis'mo vozhdiam Sovetskogo soiuza* (Paris, 1974), 45.
⁴ T. D. Krupina, "K voprosu o vzaimootnosheniiakh tsarskogo pravitel'stva s monopoliiami," *Istoricheskie zapiski*, 57 (1956), 144–76.
⁵ Russia, *Svod zakonov rossiiskoi imperii, izdanie 1857 goda* (St. Petersburg, 1857), vol. 1, part 1, article 1 declared, "The Emperor of Russia is an autocrat and unlimited monarch," with references to *PSZ* 1–3006 of March 30, 1716; *PSZ* 1–5509 of Feb. 28, 1730; and *PSZ* 1–17906 of April 5, 1797. Benckendorff's comment, "*Zakony pishutsia dlia podchinennykh, a ne dlia nachal'nikov*," is cited in Konstantin A. Skal'kovskii, *Malen'kaia khrestomatiia dlia*

meetings, promulgated in 1901, addressed only minor aspects of the problem of corporate law reform.

Restrictions on foreigners, Jews, and Poles

Especially arbitrary from the standpoint of corporate managers were the various laws that limited the rights of foreign subjects and of non-Russians in the tsarist empire to participate in corporations in various parts of the country. A series of statutes passed in the late nineteenth century to protect ethnic Russian landowners in the western provinces from the economic influence of foreigners, Jews, and Poles exerted an indirect, but powerful effect on corporations.

In the interest of economic growth, foreign capital and expertise, crucial elements in Russian economic development in previous centuries, could hardly have been excluded in the reign of Alexander III. As Reutern noted in 1863,

if only with the help of [foreign] loans the plant owner maintains the operation of his plant, the trader increases the volume of his trade, and the landowner improves his farm, then no matter how large the portion by which their benefits are reduced to pay the [foreign] bank, the aid that they receive will clearly enrich the country with new production and will also increase the revenues of the [state] treasury.[6]

A quarter-century later, Vyshnegradskii expressed similar sentiments in favor of attracting foreign capital. Although in theory it would have been preferable for Russians to develop their own resources and retain the profits generated by such economic activity, "the relative insufficiency of capital" made it necessary to invite foreigners to make major capital investments in Russia. "In view of the weak development in Russia of private enterprise and the timidity [*nereshitel'nost'*] with which native capitalists approach new enterprises that have not yet become firmly implanted and therefore carry an inevitable risk and do not promise a sure receipt of profits," it was necessary to encourage foreign companies to develop Russian resources, improve the technical level of industrial activity, and teach these techniques to Russian workers. Without the foreign contribution to domestic

---

[6] Leonid E. Shepelev, *Aktsionernye kompanii v Rossii* (Leningrad, 1973), 104, quoting from TsGIA, f. 1152 (Department of State Economy).

industrial development, the empire would be obliged to import foreign manufactured goods at a serious cost to the country's balance of payments.⁷

Because the Ministry of Finance considered it essential to attract foreign capital investments for the sake of industrial development, it resisted pressures from the Committee of Ministers to restrict foreign participation in Russian corporations. In the end, however, xenophobia triumphed over economic rationality, especially when the possibility arose that control of strategically sensitive enterprises might slip out of Russian hands. To meet this threat, the bureaucrats did not set down a clear policy, but relied primarily on the concession system to scrutinize each new charter and make adjustments that seemed fitting in each case. The result was a crude policy of sorts, but one elaborated in tiny increments in the form of arbitrary restrictions on various forms of foreign economic activity.

The first exclusion affected shipping companies on the Caspian Sea. A law dated November 24, 1869, banned foreigners from owning stock in enterprises, including trading firms, engaged in shipping there. To enforce this restriction it mandated that all shares be named.⁸ Because every corporate charter required directors to own a certain number of shares while in office, this stipulation automatically excluded foreigners from managerial positions as well. In the reign of Alexander III, this restriction gradually made its way into charters of railroad, insurance, mining, and other companies. A law of March 14, 1887, which denied to foreign subjects the right to own or lease rural land in Russian Poland, in eight of the nine provinces of "western Russia," and in Bessarabia, Courland, and Livonia, extended this prohibition to foreign corporations as well (article 6). To ensure that no foreigners participated in Russian corporations operating in these areas, charters confirmed by the tsarist government from August 1887 onward required that if the company owned or leased rural land in these areas, no citizen of a foreign country would be allowed to own stock, and all shares must be named. In December 1888, foreigners and foreign-owned companies were allowed to continue mining ore and coal on their own lands in the Kingdom of Poland, but without the right to acquire additional land or to expand to that of neighbors, even with the consent of the latter.⁹ A decree of January 23, 1885, limited Siberian gold mining

---

⁷ Shepelev, *Kompanii*, 127–8, quoting a speech given in October 1888.
⁸ *PSZ* 2–47714.
⁹ *PSZ* 3–4286. The nine western provinces are named in the law of December 10, 1865; the law of March 14, 1887 did not mention Mogilev. The first charter to bear the restrictive clause was *PSZ* 3–4674, dated August 7, 1887 (*SURP*, 1887, no. 725). Restrictions on mining in tsarist Poland are listed in *PSZ* 3–5664, dated December 24, 1888.

and metallurgy to Russian subjects.[10] From 1892 onward, petroleum companies in which foreigners owned stock could acquire land only with the special permission of the Ministry of State Domains.[11]

The impulse to ban foreigners from such strategically sensitive sectors as maritime transportation and mining proved especially troublesome when the object of bureaucratic arbitrariness was not a domestically chartered enterprise but a corporation headquartered abroad. Conventions granting equal protection of the law to companies from foreign countries were concluded with France (1863), Belgium and Germany (1865), Italy (1866), Austria (1867), England (before 1874), Greece (1887), and several other European powers. In 1878, the Ministry of Foreign Affairs agreed to consider foreign companies in Russia as juridical persons, but if they were to operate in the Russian Empire, they still needed to obtain special governmental permission and to observe any legal restrictions that might apply. For example, a law of 1871 established strict rules for insurance companies.

By 1887, foreign companies operated under a set of ten conditions that opened the way to the most arbitrary treatment by tsarist ministers, including the requirement to establish a special agency in Russia, publish annual reports, refrain from corporate mergers without governmental permission, pay a fee to the State Bank, and submit to Russian law for the settlement of any legal disputes. Especially onerous was the provision that a foreign company must cease operations entirely whenever the tsarist government withdrew its permission; in such a case, the Russian officials could act "without any explanations of the reasons" for the ultimate action.[12]

Vyshnegradskii also insisted that foreign companies already operating in the empire be brought under these quintessentially arbitrary conditions. The objections of the Ministry of Foreign Affairs to this change failed to overcome the determination of the ministers of finance, justice, and internal affairs. However, with the unerring instinct of an arbitrary bureaucrat, Vyshnegradskii reserved to himself the right to grant friendly exemptions from the laws on foreigners. For example, he often omitted from the conditions that governed the activities of each foreign company the clause that allowed the Russian government to terminate their operations without

---

[10] Bachschi Ischchanian, *Die ausländischen Elemente in der russischen Volkswirtschaft* (Berlin, 1913), 106.
[11] Shepelev, *Kompanii*, 125.
[12] Shepelev, *Kompanii*, 125–6.

explanation. On December 3, 1898, Witte cancelled this stipulation entirely. As the chancery of the Committee of Ministers admitted, "It created a very negative impression in foreign industrial and commercial circles, fostering doubt as to the firmness of the regulations that defined the position of foreign companies in Russia." By the turn of the century, therefore, foreign companies enjoyed in some respects "more favorable conditions" than did domestically chartered corporations. As the report of the chancery observed, some Russian subjects actually established companies abroad and registered them as foreign enterprises because the bureaucratic procedures were "easier and faster" despite the complications inherent in such a roundabout maneuver.[13]

Witte, no less than his predecessors, refused to surrender his arbitrary power, whether in a repressive or conciliatory manner. A vivid example of his use of intimidation appears in the memoirs of a prominent British merchant in Petersburg, James Whishaw, who managed the Russian affairs of numerous London businessmen. Whishaw earned a sizable income leasing land for petroleum drilling operations carried out in Baku by English companies. Since he had taken Russian citizenship, the onerous restrictions on foreigners, especially the need to obtain permission from the Ministry of State Domains, did not apply to him. At this point, however, Witte saw fit to remind Whishaw of the awful power of the tsarist state.

I am not shy, and I am afraid I am not very diffident, but I frankly confess that I never saw Witte without feeling afraid of him. [Witte announced:] "You are an Englishman, but for purposes of business you have become a Russian subject. I know everything you are doing. I know also that you are within the law, but you are doing acts that must be put a stop to. I am, however, going to help you, for I wish to milk the English cow." I had wit enough to say in my execrable Russian that the cow was plentifully supplied with milk. He then told me that all the companies owning land held by me must be legalized in Russia, and the land transferred from my name to them, not to the English companies but to holding companies in Russia, that is to say that every company in England must also have their [sic] company in Russia, and that I would be the responsible agent. He told

[13] Shepelev, *Kompanii*, 125–8, quoting a chancery report. Witte's change of policy apparently took the form of the deletion of the offending clause from conditions that governed foreign companies' operations in Russia. The provision does not appear in several such documents issued on December 3, 1898 (*PSZ* 3–16144 and others). An American scholar dated the change somewhat later, asserting that "until 1899 the statutes of all foreign corporations stipulated that they could be dissolved at any time. To increase investor confidence foreign companies were required only to abide by Russian laws after April 1899." John P. McKay, *Pioneers for Profit: Foreign Entrepreneurship and Russian Industrialization, 1885–1913* (Chicago, 1970), 284, citing an undated report in the French Finance Ministry archive.

me how this was to be done, and he guaranteed that every company I brought forward, provided it satisfied the conditions imposed by a council of Ministers in Russia, would receive Imperial sanction. It followed then that all the English companies for whom I had been acting, finally received sanction to act in Russia, each company having its board of directors, but the responsibility rested on me as the responsible agent."[14]

True to his word, Witte abided by the terms of this oral agreement. The main point, however, is that he forced British businessmen to relinquish some of their rights in order to bring the companies represented by Whishaw under the domestic concession system.

Even more arbitrary were the laws designed to strengthen the economic position of ethnic Russians against encroachments by Jews and Poles. The rationale for these regulations lay in ethnic discrimination, not the protection of the national interest against a perceived threat from abroad. In the quintessential bureaucratese of a memorandum promulgated by the Ministry of Finance in 1899, it was necessary "to protect the ownership of land in specific localities and in certain fields of industry from the encroachment [*vtorzhenie*] of undesirable elements."[15] Two extremely repressive decrees enacted during the era of the so-called Great Reforms – the laws of July 10, 1864,[16] and December 10, 1865[17] – prohibited Jews and Poles from acquiring rural land in selected areas. The former applied to Vilna and Kiev regions (*general-gubernatorstva*, literally the two groups of provinces supervised by the governors-general headquartered in these cities), the latter to the nine western provinces: Vilna, Kovno, Grodno, Minsk, Mogilev, Vitebsk, Podolia, Volynia, and Kiev. In order to prevent any evasion of these restrictions by Poles or Jews who might acquire land indirectly through control of a corporation, the state included in the charters of various companies founded from 1872 onward an explicit ban on ownership of land in excess of 200 desiatinas (approximately 540 acres) in the southwest region. A law of December 27, 1884,[18] required such restrictions in the charters of all companies active in this geographical area, and in 1892, all leases of land there were limited to twelve years. Such

---

[14] James Whishaw, *Memoirs of James Whishaw*, ed. Maxwell S. Leigh (London, 1935), 109–10.
[15] Shepelev, *Kompanii*, 122, citing a memorandum in TsGIA, f. 560, dated March 29, 1899. For a comprehensive discussion of the tsarist government's policies toward Jews, see Hans Rogger, *Jewish Policies and Right-Wing Politics in Imperial Russia* (Berkeley, 1986), esp. chap. 5: "Government, Jews, Peasants, and Land After the Liberation of the Serfs."
[16] *PSZ* 2–41039.
[17] *PSZ* 2–42759.
[18] *PSZ* 3–2633, article 3.

companies could issue unnamed shares, but any exemption from these restrictions required, conversely, the issuing of named shares, a change that generally depressed their value by restricting ownership to ethnic Russian subjects of the tsar. That same year, Jews (along with parish priests, convicted felons, and Mining Department employees) were denied the right of eminent domain in the mining of iron, zinc, lead, and coal in the Kingdom of Poland.[19]

A law of May 22, 1880, deprived Jews of the right to live on, obtain, or lease land in the Don Military Region. Two years later, the infamous "May Laws" not only extended this prohibition to all areas except cities of the Jewish Pale, but also broadened it to include a ban on management and disposal by Jews of real estate in these areas.[20] In order to prevent any evasion of these restrictions by corporations, a decree of 1892 required that all new corporate charters forbid Jewish employees from managing the enterprise's real estate.

These restrictions on corporations formed part of the campaign by the Russian state to reduce the economic and cultural influence of the Jewish population outside the Pale of Settlement. Typical were decrees that established quotas in 1887 to limit Jewish access to high schools and universities; banned Jews from appointive and elective posts in municipal government; and excluded "Jewish employees from railroads and steamship lines, and even from certain institutions, such as hospitals (although partly supported by Jews)." In 1889, Jewish residents were forced out of Rostov-on-Don and Taganrog; between 1888 and 1890, numerous Jewish workers were transported from St. Petersburg; and at Passover in 1892, approximately fourteen thousand Jewish artisans were summarily banished from Moscow "without selling their property or paying or collecting debts." Similar incidents occurred in Tula, Novgorod, Kaluga, Riazan, Riga, Libau, and Ialta. In 1899, even fully registered Jewish merchants were barred from participation in elections of guild officers.[21]

Even as this ethnic persecution intensified, however, the traditional system of social categorization by "estates" (*sosloviia*) continued to decay, as shown by the tax law of June 8, 1898, which "finally repudiated the estate principle in commerce and industry."[22] The right to engage in trade and

[19] *PSZ* 3–8545, dated April 28, 1892.
[20] *PSZ* 2–60970; *PSZ* 3–834, dated May 3, 1882; Shepelev, *Kompanii*, 123–4.
[21] "Russia," *The Jewish Encyclopedia*, 12 vols. (New York, 1906), vol. 10, 526, 527 (quoted); "Moscow," *The Jewish Encyclopedia*, vol. 9, 41.
[22] G. Vol'tke, *Pravo torgovli i promyshlennosti v Rossii v istoricheskom razvitii*, 2nd ed. (St. Petersburg, 1905), 30. The main episodes in the complex history of corporate taxation in

industry now belonged to anyone who purchased the requisite certificate, that is, this document no longer carried with it any estate privileges. Factory owners and traders who wished to retain their membership in the merchant estate continued to purchase the annual guild certificate as well as certificates allowing manufacturing or wholesale or retail trade, but holders of the latter documents were under no obligation to join a merchant guild. This change ended the awkward system, inaugurated in 1865, under which individuals who engaged in business activities belonged to two estates at the same time, for example, the gentry and the merchants.

For managers, this weakening of the estate structure merely confirmed the status of the corporation, implied in the law of 1865, as an institution separate from the merchant guilds. Under the law of 1898, corporations continued to purchase business certificates, but none of the managers, as individuals, was under any legal constraint to enroll in a merchant guild. Because the tax system opened the business world to persons traditionally barred from membership in the merchant guilds, it implicitly weakened the barriers against Jews. The bureaucracy moved promptly to limit access to the new certificates. On November 24, 1898, the Ministry of Finance decreed that bankrupts, exiled persons, and other individuals who had been prohibited by law from engaging in trade and commerce would, if caught, lose their certificates and forfeit the payment. Jews who lived out-

---

the Russian Empire include the introduction of a supplementary 3 percent tax on profits in 1885, modified in 1898 and 1906 in a progressive direction. An excellent general study before the advent of Witte is I. Ia. Rudchenko, *Istoricheskii ocherk oblozheniia torgovli i promyslov v Rossii* (St. Petersburg, 1893). Later accounts, not examined by me, are N. G. Ovchinnikov, *Ocherk novogo Polozheniia o gosudarstvennom promyslovom naloge* (Ekaterinburg, 1898); and Aleksandr M. Nedoshivin, *Promyslovoe oblozhenie predpriiatii, obiazannykh publichnoiu otchetnost'iu* (St. Petersburg, 1907). The debates preceding the 3 percent corporate tax law of January 15, 1885 are analyzed in light of archival documents by Nina I. Anan'ich, "K istorii podatnykh reform 1880-kh godov," *Istoriia SSSR*, 1979, no. 1 (Jan.–Feb.), 159–73. The views of Moscow manufacturers are described in G. F. Semeniuk, "Moskovskaia tekstil'naia burzhuaziia i vopros o promyslovom naloge v 90-kh godakh XIX veka," *Uchenye zapiski Moskovskogo oblastnogo pedagogicheskogo instituta im. N. K. Krupskoi*, 127, series "Istoriia SSSR," vyp. 7 (1963), 141–74. A general survey, with separate chapters on the reform of 1885 and on legislative initiatives of the 1890–1910 period as well as a copious bibliography, is Linda Jean Bowman, "The Business Tax in Imperial Russia, 1775–1917," doctoral dissertation, University of California, Los Angeles, 1982.

The role of these tax laws in distorting nominal capital figures of corporations is discussed in Fred V. Carstensen, "Foreign Participation in Russian Economic Life: Notes on British Enterprise, 1865–1914," in Gregory Guroff and Fred Carstensen, eds., *Entrepreneurship in Imperial Russia and the Soviet Union* (Princeton, 1983), 144–5. He also noted that the Singer Company increased its basic capital from 5 million to 50 million rubles between 1897 and 1913 in order to reduce the ratio between basic capital and taxable profits: Carstensen, *American Enterprise in Foreign Markets: Studies of Singer and International Harvester in Imperial Russia* (Chapel Hill, 1984), 91–5.

side the Pale of Settlement fell under even more stringent controls in that they had to produce a statement from the police testifying to their right to reside and engage in business before they would be allowed to purchase a certificate.[23] This system obviously left room for bribery of the police.[24] It also created a strong incentive for Jews to conceal their personal involvement in a commercial or industrial enterprise by setting up a corporation as the entity that would purchase the annual business certificate.

Not surprisingly, just as the bureaucracy had extended to corporations the restrictions on landowning promulgated in the 1880s, so it moved to limit the liberal implications of the tax law of 1898. Paradoxically, therefore, the relaxation of the estate restrictions in the business tax law promoted, as an indirect consequence, a further tightening of the ethnic regulations on the corporation. For example, in order to limit the circulation of shares of beet-sugar companies, which for reasons of climate tended to operate in the Right-Bank Ukraine within the Pale of Settlement, Witte at the end of the century ordered a bill to be drafted that would have set a minimum share price of 1,000 rubles and required that all shares be named and that their purchase by Jews or foreigners be forbidden.[25]

Clearly, the Russian government feared the spread of Jewish economic influence more than it did that of foreigners. As the historian Vol'tke pointed out, non-Jewish foreign citizens enjoyed greater economic freedom in the Russian Empire than did Jewish citizens in their own land:

The retention of restrictions on the activity of Russian Jews in trade and industry, when almost complete freedom in these fields is granted throughout the empire to all other ethnic minorities [*inorodtsev*] and to foreigners from all over the world, remains at present a strange and incomprehensible anomaly. In no [other] country is there a law that grants to a foreigner any kind of advantage over that country's citizen, who is required to meet all his obligations, including the shedding of blood as a soldier, and who leaves his earnings in his own native land, not [taking them] abroad.[26]

It was hardly any consolation that foreign Jews faced even more stringent limitations on their economic activities, including the necessity of receiving

---

[23] *SURP*, 1898, no. 150, law no. 2023; not in *PSZ*.
[24] Vol'tke, *Pravo*, 39–41.
[25] Vladimir Ia. Laverychev, *Gosudarstvo i monopolii v dorevoliutsionnoi Rossii* (Moscow, 1982), 105–6, citing TsGIA, f. 575, op. 1, d. 269, noted that the Council of Ministers debated this measure in 1900; whether it passed is not clear.
[26] Vol'tke, *Pravo*, 47.

the permission of the Ministries of Foreign Affairs, Finance, and Internal Affairs before purchasing a business certificate.[27]

Restrictions on Poles proceeded from the same motives as those on foreigners and Jews. Relatively less severe, they reflected the bureaucrats' somewhat reduced level of concern. The laws of Alexander II that prohibited Jews from owning rural land in the Vilna and Kiev governor-generalships (July 10, 1864) and in the nine western provinces (December 10, 1865) applied also to Poles. Likewise, under the law of December 27, 1884, Poles as well as Jews were prevented from evading these statutes through corporate landowning, as companies that issued shares to the bearer - those that might be purchased by Poles or Jews - could not own rural land in these areas in excess of 200 desiatinas. The rationale for these regulations was the allegation that Polish landlords, although only a tiny percentage of the 10 million persons in the western region, prevented the Russian, Ukrainian, and Belorussian peasantry from gaining economic influence commensurate with their numbers. In 1869, the State Bank issued its first irregular loan to a landlord in Kiev, Prince Lopukhin (see the section on manipulation of the banking system in Chapter 4). The bureaucrats felt that the prince deserved a special eight-year loan of 650,000 rubles for the maintenance of his beet-sugar plant, winery, and brewery because it was necessary to "promote the government's goal of strengthening the Russian element in this region."[28]

Although the economic data that alarmed the bureaucrats have yet to be examined by historians in an effort to determine the cogency of the arguments in favor of restrictive legislation against foreigners, Jews, and Poles, there can be no doubt as to the perception of an alien threat. This pessimistic outlook may never have been phrased explicitly, but its ominous implications were clear: Left to their own devices in a fair competition, Russian peasants and landlords could not win the economic battle with Germans, Jews, and Poles. The reasons for the inability of Russians to hold their own in the free market remain obscure, but the amorphous concept of "culture" may be invoked as a partial explanation. Levels of literacy in the Russian village remained far below those of Western and Central Europe; peasants had received scarcely any exposure to modern

---

[27] Other limitations pertained to the size of the enterprise; for example, a foreign Jew could operate a steamship company in Russia only if it were large enough to generate a basic business tax of at least five hundred rubles per year. Vol'tke, *Pravo*, 43–44.
[28] Iosif F. Gindin, *Gosudarstvennyi bank i ekonomicheskaia politika tsarskogo pravitel'stva (1861–1892 gody)* (Moscow, 1960), 142, citing TsGIA, f. 583.

commercial practices, and entrepreneurial habits remained relatively weakly developed even among the lower strata of Russian merchants. At the same time, the condescending attitude of enterprising Poles, Jews, and Baltic Germans directed toward Russians was hardly justified. Despite the ethnic stereotypes, certain groups of Russians, notably the persecuted Old Believers and non-Orthodox sects in the southeast borderlands of the empire, showed an impressive aptitude for commercial agriculture and the grain trade. Rather, the state's own policies over the previous centuries appear to have stifled the impetus toward entrepreneurial behavior among ethnic Russians. The complexities of the problem are too manifold to be resolved here, but the cultural passivity of the Russian peasantry served to justify the arbitrary legislation of the tsarist government in the 1880s. Seen from the perspective of the late twentieth century, the blatantly repressive ethnic policies of the Russian bureaucracy appear morally repugnant. For their part, the tsar and his advisors perceived their decrees as a form of generous defensive action of their weak Russian brothers against the predations of historic enemies.

Whatever the moral and political overtones of the debate, one fact seems clear enough: The cumulative effect of the restrictions on the ownership, leasing, and management of land by non-Russians in the western and southern borderlands seriously hindered the development of corporate enterprise in the most populous regions of the empire. One Jewish historian contrasted the highly developed commerce in the Pale of Settlement to the primitive practices prevalent in the Volga and Ural regions, where grain traders lacked the "initiative, enterprise, and skill" of Jewish merchants. He also argued that by imposing ethnic restrictions on Jewish merchants, the tsarist government was actually harming the interests of the Russian landlords and peasantry by preventing full access to domestic and international markets.[29] It was apparently this concern that led the merchants of Kiev in 1893 to resist state-imposed quotas for Jews in the exchange, or at least to defend the current one-third maximum for non-Christian members.[30]

The tangle of irrationalities in the arbitrary corporate law can be appreciated by a glance at their effect on two particularly sensitive areas of

---

[29] Iosif M. Bikerman [Joseph Bickermann], *Cherta evreiskoi osedlosti* (St. Petersburg, 1911), 58–77, quotation from 76. Without citing statistics, he declared that the expulsion of Jewish merchants from Kiev in 1835 and from Moscow in 1892 only enriched the cities to which these merchants moved: Berdichev and Lodz, respectively.

[30] *Dvadtsatiletie Kievskoi birzhi* (Kiev, 1895), 122.

the empire, Turkestan and the Transcaucasus. Archival and anecdotal evidence combine to give a vivid picture of the legal fetters that prevented corporations from taking full advantage of economic opportunities on the frontiers of the empire.

Acting on a request from the Ministry of War, the State Council outlawed landowning in the Turkestan region (*krai*) by corporations in which Jews and foreigners participated. A decree promulgated in November 1893 stipulated that corporations could purchase real estate in this region only if their charters restricted the ownership of stock to Christian Russian subjects, to non-Christian natives of Turkestan, or to natives of the Central Asian states immediately bordering the area. Moreover, in each case the corporation was required to submit a petition for permission to purchase land, via the governor-general of Turkestan, to the minister of war, who had the power to reject the request or to grant it upon the approval of the minister of finance. Three powerful officials thus enjoyed the arbitrary right to refuse a corporation's petition for landowning.[31] Shepelev noted that because the bureaucracy neglected to make this measure retroactive, its implementation increased "the chaos in the legal situation of companies that were [otherwise] completely similar" in structure and legal standing.[32]

Several years later, apparently in an effort to relax these restrictions, the minister of war endorsed a new formula: If a corporate charter did not explicitly bar foreigners, non-Russians, and non-Christians (except natives of Turkestan and neighboring regions), the enterprise could acquire real estate, but only with the permission of the Committee of Ministers and the tsar himself.[33] By allowing Jews and foreigners indirect ownership of land in the sensitive area, the government appeared to be accommodating the principle of cosmopolitan entrepreneurship. However, the need for permission of the ministerial committee and the tsar further strengthened the contrary principle of arbitrary action by making exceptions to the law of November 1893 contingent upon bureaucratic whim.

The effects of these regulations on individual corporations appear predictably negative. Vladimir Ia. Laverychev, one of the few Soviet scholars to recognize the existence of policy conflicts between the tsarist regime and the corporate elite and to document his assertions with a modicum of

---

[31] *PSZ* 3–10102, dated November 29, 1893.
[32] Shepelev, *Kompanii*, 124. This remark applied also to the discriminatory laws of the 1880s regarding foreign stockholders of companies active in the western provinces.
[33] V. Maksimov, *O tovarishchestvakh*, 2nd ed. (Moscow, 1911), 67–8, citing *PSZ* 3–14121, dated May 19, 1897.

archival evidence, provided useful information on precisely this point. He cited the case of a large and productive textile company headquartered in Lodz, whose owners, the Poznański family, petitioned for permission to acquire land for cotton-ginning plants in Turkestan, the source of much of the raw cotton used in Russian and Polish mills. Final approval of this request came only after a lengthy correspondence between the Ministries of War and Finance and the Turkestan governor-general, who looked with favor on the creation by the Poznańskis of a new company, called Khlopok (Cotton), in which several Petersburg manufacturers participated. Referring to the provisions of the statutes of 1893 and 1897, Laverychev wrote with typical understatement, "Such restrictions undoubtedly hindered the development of industry and trade." (He neglected to mention that the Poznańskis were Jewish.) The Emile Zündel cotton-textile company, founded by the heirs of an Alsatian pioneer in the development of the Moscow textile industry in the 1840s, requested permission to buy a plot of land in Turkestan in 1898 and received it two years later. Although this delay constituted a clear hardship, it contrasted favorably with the bureaucracy's treatment of other Moscow companies. For example, the Prokhorovs, of whose Russian peasant pedigree and devotion to the Romanov dynasty there was not the slightest doubt, likewise requested permission in 1898 to obtain land in Turkestan, but the Ministry of War refused.[34]

The economic impact of such perverse complexities in the law can easily be imagined. Strict regulations limited freedom of entrepreneurial action; complicated procedural requirements caused delays of many months, so that even a positive answer from Petersburg might be of little use if it came too late for application in a rapidly changing economic situation; and refusal by a tsarist minister or the emperor himself left no recourse at all. The inherent irrationality of the arbitrary process was highlighted by the fact that a Jew like Poznański might receive a favor, while a native Russian son like Prokhorov might not. Perhaps the greatest irony was that the minister of finance and many other officials saw their actions as useful to the national interest. They failed to see that, even as they took vigorous action to promote economic activity by individuals and institutions they regarded as trustworthy, the very structure of the tsarist legal system, and especially the ever-present recourse to arbitrary action implicit in the

---

[34] Vladimir Ia. Laverychev, *Krupnaia burzhuaziia v poreformennoi Rossii, 1861–1900 gg.* (Moscow, 1974), 59 (quoted), 60, citing, among other sources, documents in the military history archive (Tsentral'nyi gosudarstvennyi voenno-istoricheskii arkhiv) in Leningrad, f. 400.

system of permission for landowning by corporations, constituted a major, if invisible, hindrance to corporate capitalist activity.

A splendid example of the distrust and fear with which traditional bureaucrats regarded the most reputable corporations was recorded in the memoirs of Baron Nikolai E. Wrangel. An official turned businessman, he left a remarkable portrait of a governor-general who appeared incapable of understanding the needs of modern capitalist corporations. In 1899, Wrangel helped to found an electric power company in the Caucasus. With the aid of a loan from the International Bank, headquartered in Petersburg, the entrepreneurs drew up the corporate charter and offered 7 million rubles' worth of stock to leading petroleum producers and managers of electricity companies. Witte showed enthusiasm for the new venture, but the charter also required the signature of the autocratic governor-general of the Caucasus region, Prince Grigorii S. Golitsyn. To the dismay of the entrepreneurs, this "crazy petty tyrant [*malyi samodur*], with whom it was difficult to deal," delayed giving his permission. Wrangel then resolved to broach the matter in conversation with the prince during the winter social season in Petersburg. (The two men were personally acquainted because Wrangel's brother and nephew had both married Golitsynas.) He did do reluctantly, however, because even the prince's brother avoided raising the issue: "'Whenever I discuss petroleum with him, he flies into a rage.'"

To Wrangel's surprise, Prince Golitsyn appeared to favor the idea because he recognized that electrical power lines posed less of a fire hazard than steam engines in the oil fields. He also seemed pleased that the shares had already been subscribed. However, his mood changed abruptly when he learned the identity of the potential stockholders. Although Wrangel had avoided mentioning the electric companies, such as the Siemens and Halske enterprises, of which he was vice-president, Golitsyn lost his temper when Wrangel mentioned the role of the International Bank and the fact that some of the stockholders' names were as yet unknown to the founders:

"What do you mean, unknown? Does that mean that they could fall into the hands of Jews and foreigners? I won't agree to that. I will not permit shares to the bearer. How the foreigners are fleecing Russia!"
"The minister of finance has already allowed them."
"Witte is a Mason and has been bought by foreigners."
"Perhaps, Prince, you have not read his speech in Moscow. He declared that

Russia cannot do without foreign capital. He of course would not have said this if the tsar refused to allow foreign capital [into the country]."

This appeal to imperial arbitrariness in the service of modern industry failed to moderate the princely tantrum:

"What do you mean, the tsar! He doesn't know what he wants and dances to Witte's tune. He's a milksop [*Triapka*]!"
"Of course," I said, "you, Prince, as an adjutant general know the tsar's character better than I do."
Golitsyn had become angry. "I won't allow it; I won't, I absolutely will not allow it!"

Although the tsar eventually approved the corporate charter, which showed two Russians (Nikolai E. Wrangel and Viktor F. Golubev) as the founders,[35] Prince Golitsyn's intransigence provides an instructive example of the rationale for the restrictive corporate legislation of the tsarist regime and its arbitrary implementation of that legislation.

Wrangel correctly noted that Golitsyn's hatred of foreigners and Jews in Russian corporations formed part of a larger antipathy toward non-Orthodox and non-Russian populations. For example, Golitsyn arbitrarily persecuted the peaceful and thrifty religious sectarians, notably the Dukhobors, Stundists, and Molokane, who had fled to the Caucasus to escape the repressive policies of the tsarist government in the central provinces. Golitsyn also turned Azerbaijanis against Armenians:

"Divide and rule" was his motto, but by introducing into the ethnically variegated Caucasus region the vicious Russification practiced by other military governors in Poland, Finland, and the Baltic provinces, he only exacerbated the tensions between the natives and the imperial rulers and laid the foundation for the breakup of the empire during World War I and the subsequent revolutionary upheaval.[36]

Wrangel's frustration with the tempestuous tyrant of the Caucasus throws into sharp relief the clash between capitalist rationality and tsarist arbitrariness in the late imperial period. The cosmopolitan Wrangel transcended the xenophobia that prevailed among the military and bu-

---

[35] The charter of the "Transcaucasus Electric Power Company" (Elektricheskaia sila) for the generation of electricity in the Caucasus region, confirmed by the tsar on June 11, 1899, is *PSZ* 3-17167; the text appears in *SURP*, 1899, no. 1128. No restrictions on ownership of land were specified. The prohibition on ownership of land where such right was denied to foreigners and Jews (a routine clause in charters issued in this period) implied that non-Russians and non-Christians were allowed to participate in this company.

[36] Baron Nikolai E. Vrangel', *Vospominaniia (ot krepostnogo prava do bol'shevikov)* (Berlin, 1924), 158–9 (quoted); 180, on Siemens and Halske; 132–3, on persecution of sectarians.

reaucratic elite of the imperial administration and evinced a thoroughly tolerant attitude toward ethnic diversity, seeing it as a necessary feature of modern industrial civilization. In contrast, the narrow-minded Golitsyn continued to react to the complexities of economic development with the outworn reflexes of a Russian general: "*kvas* patriotism" (a visceral hatred of all things foreign), reliance on drill-field discipline, and ethnic prejudice. Wrangel's vivid portrait of Prince Golitsyn shows perfectly that the reluctance of the tsarist regime to relax its grip on the laws regulating corporate enterprise represented just one aspect of the traditional conflict between the unreformed and unreformable modality of centralized, arbitrary rule and the imperatives of capitalist economic development.

Ambivalence toward cartels

The arbitrary policies of the tsarist regime affected with special severity the most advanced and highly centralized corporations in the empire. Toward the end of the century, Russian corporate leaders, like their counterparts in Germany, began to establish price-fixing arrangements ranging from temporary and unstable agreements among producers, called "rings" or "corners" in the United States, to more solid aggregations such as "pools," "cartels," or "syndicates" (*sindikaty*) and fully integrated enterprises, called "trusts" (*tresty*) in a single field or "concerns" (*kontserny*) in several sectors.[37] (Strictly speaking, a syndicate functioned as the exclusive

---

[37] For a concise review of the terminology applied to such institutions, see G. Tsyperovich, *Sindikaty i tresty v Rossii*, 2nd ed. (Moscow, 1919), 13–18; and Valerii I. Bovykin and G. R. Naumova, "Istochniki po istorii monopolii i finansovogo kapitala," in I. D. Koval'chenko, ed., *Massovye istochniki po sotsial'no-ekonomicheskoi istorii Rossii perioda kapitalisma* (Moscow, 1979), 120–60, which includes a useful survey of source materials. The Soviet historical literature on this phenomenon is immense, primarily because Lenin, Trotskii, and Bukharin interpreted the growth of such institutions as proof of the inevitable centralization of economic power, which a revolutionary proletarian government could simply appropriate for allegedly democratic purposes. Soviet scholars continue to place this notion at the center of their studies of "finance capital," "monopoly capitalism," and "state-monopoly capitalism" in tsarist Russia. See, for example, A. P. Pogrebinskii, "Spornye voprosy izucheniia gosudarstvenno-monopolisticheskogo kapitalizma v dorevoliutsionnoi Rossii," in A. L. Sidorov, ed., *Ob osobennostiakh imperializma v Rossii* (Moscow, 1963), 124–48, esp. 128–31; and the well-documented works of Vasilii I. Bovykin: *Zarozhdenie finansovogo kapitala v Rossii* (Moscow, 1967); and *Formirovanie finansovogo kapitala v Rossii (konets XIX– 1908 g.* (Moscow, 1984). Despite the efforts of Soviet historians to show the maturity of syndicates, their influence in the Russian economy appeared less than complete on the eve of World War I and even in 1917. For a valiant Soviet effort to fit the facts into the Leninist model, see the impressive collection of archival and other documentation in A. L. Sidorov, ed., *Dokumenty po istorii monopolisticheskogo kapitalizma* (Moscow, 1959), vol. 6 of the series *Materialy po istorii SSSR*.

A less tendentious treatment by a prominent economist, who, unlike Lenin, had studied

sales agency for all enterprises united in a cartel.³⁸ Although *kartel'* existed in Russian, the term *sindikat* predominated in the economic literature, despite the alternative use of *sindikat* for a group of banks that undertook to subscribe the stock offering of a new corporation.)

From the perspective of corporate law, the most important feature of these "entrepreneurial combinations" (*predprinimatel'skie ob"edineniia*) or "unions" (*soiuzy*), as they were also called at the time, was the fact that they stood condemned by tsarist legislation. Article 913 of the Russian Criminal Code forbade any agreements in restraint of trade in food and other products of mass consumption. Article 1180 mandated jail terms of from four to eight months for anyone who initiated an artificial increase of prices on food and other goods or a decrease of prices aimed at destroying competition; penalties increased to incarceration for from sixteen to twenty-four months if a shortage actually occurred.³⁹ These statutes were meant to avert episodes of social unrest that might arise if merchants, during a wheat shortage, held back supplies in an effort to force prices to panic levels. Read literally, however, these statutes forbade any price-fixing agreements among industrialists or producers of coal, petroleum, and other mass-consumption goods.

During the depression at the turn of the century, leaders of the largest mining and metallurgical companies created two of the most prominent syndicates: Prodameta (1902) for the sale of iron and iron products, and Produgol' (1904) for the sale of coal. As an expert in the iron industry later explained, some sort of price coordination was essential to prevent

---

the problem in detail, is Richard T. Ely, *Monopolies and Trusts* (New York, 1900). He stressed that "monopoly means something more than business on a large scale" (144), and he explicitly questioned the ability of any organization to act as a "complete monopoly" without controlling 75 to 80 percent of the market for a given product (15, 76). Finally, Ely (142) repudiated the Marxian tenet, expressed by socialists such as Paul de Rousiers in *Les industries monopolisées aux Etats-Unis* (Paris, 1898), that monopolies necessarily presaged the triumph of socialism. (Tsyperovich, *Sindikaty*, 180, quoted Rousiers's allegation that "if industrial evolution in fact leads to monopoly, then clearly it also leads to the formation of a universal socialist order.") A statement of this concept in English is "State-Monopoly Capitalism," *Great Soviet Encyclopedia*, vol. 7, 675–9, esp. 678–9. By the 1960s, the most sophisticated American Marxists had abandoned the Leninist teleology, as in Paul A. Baran and Paul M. Sweezy, *Monopoly Capital: An Essay on the American Economic and Social Order* (New York, 1966), 363: "The answer of traditional Marxist orthodoxy – that the industrial proletariat must eventually rise in revolution against its capitalist oppressors – no longer carries conviction."

³⁸ Robert A. Brady, *Business as a System of Power* (New York, 1943), 211, note 67.
³⁹ E. S. Lur'e, *Predprinimatel'skie sindikaty po russkomu pravu* (St. Petersburg, 1914), 44–5. Lur'e also noted some inconsistencies among the Criminal Code, the Civil Code, and Senate decisions regarding the validity of contracts that established artificial price levels. Articles 913 and 1180 are quoted verbatim in Tsyperovich, *Sindikaty*, 130–1.

ruinous damage to huge enterprises when overproduction or insufficient demand drove prices below production costs: "It is possible to avoid all this only by having constant control over the market, and this is possible only by means of a corresponding concentration of every given sector of industry... Our metallurgical industry had no choice but to adopt this policy of industrial agreements."[40] A Soviet scholar recently listed forty-nine syndicates that came into existence between 1898 and 1908, including ten in 1908 alone.[41]

Despite the formal illegality of price-fixing arrangements, such combinations in restraint of trade received support from the government itself. As early as the 1880s, the proliferation of beet-sugar plants threatened to drive the price of sugar so low as to make continued production unprofitable for all. In response to declining prices, sugar producers established in 1887, with Bunge's approval, the first major cartel in Russia. Called from 1897 onward the Russian Society of Sugar Producers (Vserossiiskoe obshchestvo sakharozavodchikov; RSSP), this organization functioned not only as a business organization or "trade association" (in current American terminology) but also as a cartel. In 1888, it included 78 percent of Russian sugar producers and in 1893, 91 percent. In November 1895, the tsar confirmed a system whereby the Committee of Ministers, advised by the minister of finance, set the amount of sugar needed for domestic consumption, the amount of sugar to be kept in reserve, and the minimum and maximum prices to be allowed in the domestic market. The guidelines specified the amount of sugar that each plant would be allowed to sell in Russia, on the basis of its output in previous years. The surplus was exported, at greatly reduced prices, to maintain the domestic price at levels high enough to generate a moderate profit for producers and substantial excise tax revenues for the government.[42]

---

[40] Ipolit Glivits [Hypolit Gliwic], *Zheleznaia promyshlennost' v Rossii* (St. Petersburg, 1911), 132. Gliwic, one of many talented Polish engineers in the metal industry of "South Russia," as Ukraine was then called, served as Prodameta's director in the Kingdom of Poland. He eventually became a delegate to the League of Nations, a professor at the Warsaw Free University, and briefly minister of industry in the independent Polish government. He committed suicide in April 1943 upon his arrest by the Nazi police in Warsaw. *Polski Słownik Biograficzny*, vol. 8 (1959), 74–5; *Wielka Encyklopedia Powszechna PWN*, 13 vols. (Warsaw, 1962–70), vol. 4, 265.

[41] Bovykin, *Formirovanie*, 235.

[42] I. M. Gol'dshtein, ed. and trans., *Zakonodatel'stva raznykh gosudarstv o sindikatakh i trestakh* (St. Petersburg, 1910), 94–6. Percentages from Tsyperovich, *Sindikaty*, 31. The complicated history of sugar production norms can be traced in Count Andrei A. Bobrinskoi, *K voprosu o znachenii sakharnoi normirovki* (Kiev, 1908); M. Ia. Gefter, "Iz istorii monopolisticheskogo kapitalizma v Rossii: sakharnyi sindikat," *Istoricheskie zapiski*, 38 (1951),

The cordial relationship between the sugar cartel and the tsarist government may be explained partly by the fact that the organization's leadership included some of the most wealthy and influential aristocrats of the Right-Bank Ukraine, notably Andrei A. Bobrinskii, brother of Aleksei, the minister of agriculture from July to November 1916. However, most syndicates, including Prodameta and Produgol', took the form of a joint-stock company and were led not by relatives and friends of courtiers but by engineers and technicians, many of English, French, Belgian, German, Polish, or Ukrainian extraction. Whether the cartels and syndicates in heavy industry owed their influence to the machinations of European diplomats and bankers eager to reduce the Russian Empire to the status of a semicolony is a question debated by Stalinist historians without a satisfactory resolution.[43] In any case, one observer noted in 1910 that despite articles 913 and 1180, "the number of syndicates in Russia is growing rapidly" and that "the government itself has been obliged to help entrepreneurs, directly or indirectly, to establish syndicates."[44]

What of the contention that syndicates fixed prices "in secret" and "acted in the guise of joint-stock companies, hiding their monopolistic essence behind this mask" so as to do their nefarious work safe from public or governmental scrutiny? The charter of Produgol' stated clearly the purpose of the company: to sell mineral fuel of the Donets Basin.[45] It strains credulity to assert that the tsarist bureaucracy, which itself approved this and all other charters, could have remained ignorant of such obvious combinations.

Indeed, the regime found pragmatic arguments to legitimize its permissive policy. As Minister of Trade and Industry Ivan P. Shipov announced in 1910, "In general it must be recognized that syndicates cause much harm but often bring no less benefit. Therefore no special protection should be given to syndicates or to their creation, but at the same time neither should we establish artificial restrictions on them." To the MEC,

---

104–53; and Laverychev, *Gosudarstvo*, 101–17, a concise account by a seasoned Soviet historian of the "monopolies." See also Roger Munting, "The State and the Beet Sugar Industry in Russia before 1914," in Bill Albert and Adrian Graves, eds., *Crisis and Change in the International Sugar Economy, 1860–1914* (Norwich, England, 1984), 21–9.

[43] A fair-minded account stressing the contribution of French expertise to Russian mining and metallurgy is McKay, *Pioneers*. His chapters 8 and 13 address the issue of economic imperialism with references to relevant Soviet accounts.

[44] Gol'dshtein, *Zakonodatel'stva*, 93–4.

[45] M. P. Viatkin, ed., *Monopolii v metallurgicheskoi promyshlennosti Rossii, 1900–1917: Dokumenty i materialy* (Moscow, 1963), 7, note 10 (quoted). The Produgol' charter is *PSZ* 3-24520, dated May 11, 1904; the text is in *SURP*, 1904, no. 510.

which called for decisive state action to prevent the creation of a metallurgical trust, he cautioned, "You have indicated that a black cloud is looming, but I do not know what the cloud is bringing. It may bring a hailstorm or a beneficial shower, or possibly both at the same time."[46]

Such equivocation had several advantages for the government's point of view. First, by permitting the syndicates to maintain stability in prices, the government derived a measure of reassurance against the dangers of sudden depression, with the concomitant threats of massive unemployment and social unrest. Although Soviet historians delight in pointing out the "monopoly profits" reaped by businessmen and tsarist bureaucrats who cooperated in such ventures,[47] the huge corporations that went beyond free enterprise to protect their own security were simply acting rationally in the absence of a central planning mechanism.[48] Tsarist policy makers evidently allowed mildly excessive profits for the sake of price stability.

Second, the law could be invoked upon occasion to prevent syndicates from growing excessively strong. Writing in 1917, the jurist Avgust I. Kaminka admitted that no corporation was ever punished under these statutes; the Senate, acting as the highest appellate court, never issued any clarifications. A suit against Produgol' "perished in the innermost recesses of the judicial chanceries." However, even as this policy constituted "an indirect acknowledgment" of the legality of syndicates, the disparity between the laws against price fixing and the government's toleration of the practice left open the possibility that a prosecutor "might seize a random victim [*vyrvet sluchainuiu zhertvu*] and submit it to punishment with the full severity of the law."[49] Syndicates had no defense against prosecution because they remained illegal under articles 913 and 1180.

Finally, it suited the government's purpose to keep the syndicates in a precarious legal position. As large, complex, and highly visible institutions in the Russian economy, syndicates attracted periodic outbursts of public

---

[46] Quoted without reference in Tsyperovich, *Sindikaty*, 126–7.
[47] Krupina, "K voprosu," 154–61, discussed high profits, bribes, and kickbacks.
[48] On the role of business organizations in creating a system of managed prices in the United States in the 1920s, to the detriment of free enterprise, see Joseph H. Foth, *Trade Associations: Their Service to Industry* (New York, 1930); and Guy Alchon, *The Invisible Hand of Planning: Capitalism, Social Science and the State in the 1920s* (Princeton, 1985).
[49] Maksimov, *O tovarishchestvakh*, 57; and A. I. Kaminka, *Osnovy predprinimatel'skogo prava* (Petrograd, 1917), 298–304, quotations from 300, 303, 304. Krupina, "K voprosu," devoted special attention to the tsarist government's refusal to use articles 913 and 1180 against Prodameta and other major syndicates. However, her case is weakened by her reiteration of the preposterous Stalinist assertion of the "subordination of the state apparatus to the monopolies" (173). She herself noted (145) that the courts used these articles to nullify restrictive agreements, for example regarding the sale of sugar in Kiev (1895), of glue in Warsaw (1903), and of bricks in Petersburg (1909).

anger.⁵⁰ The government gained political advantage from its role as an allegedly impartial arbiter between the opposing forces of syndicates and consumers.

The last major initiative by the bureaucracy in this regard illustrated this curious ambivalence. In 1913, the Ministry of Trade and Industry drafted a bill, never passed, to legalize syndicates, but with such stringent requirements – including state inspection of corporate files and the threat of civil suits for abuses of monopoly power – that the regulations would have constituted a ban on syndicate activities. To the end, the state preferred to rely on its own massive economic and administrative power to discipline the syndicates through changes in tariff duties, railroad freight rates, governmental stockpiling of crucial materials to be released onto the market during shortages, confiscation of excess profits, and even expropriation of the offending enterprise.⁵¹ Meanwhile, the tsarist courts played a similar role. As a mining engineer later recalled in emigration, the coal syndicate lost its ability to enforce price-fixing contracts among its members when, in 1913, a district judge in Petersburg upheld article 1180 of the Criminal Code, which declared such contracts null and void.⁵²

Whether or not this legal limbo was calculated to induce political circumspection in the business leadership is not clear. Perhaps the tsarist policy makers lacked the sophistication to devise such a perverse policy, and in any case, the vagueness of the law might just as easily have engendered frustration as fear. Whatever the government's intentions, the point is established: The law on corporate pricing agreements remained in need of reform, and the ministers of Nicholas II refused to act.

The Tsitovich Commission and its failure

By the late 1890s, Witte saw the need to address the untidiness of the corporate law and to curb the various abuses that persisted in spite of the

---

[50] The campaign against Prodameta in the State Duma, led by Aleksandr I. Guchkov and P. V. Kamenskii, is discussed in Gol'dshtein, *Zakonodatel'stva*, 98; and M. Ia. Gefter, "Bor'ba vokrug sozdaniia metallurgicheskogo tresta v Rossii v nachale XX v.," *Istoricheskie zapiski*, 47 (1954), 128–48. Tsyperovich, *Sindikaty*, 108–37, related several antisyndicate campaigns by the state and the zemstvos in 1908–17.
[51] V. S. Diakin in Diakin and others, eds., *Krizis samoderzhaviia v Rossii, 1895–1917* (Leningrad, 1984), 439–40.
[52] A. I. Fenin, "Ekonomicheskoe razvitie i polozhenie Rossii do mirovoi voiny," HIA, ms. in Box 13, Petr B. Struve papers, 85–6. Struve accepted this article for publication in the journal *Vozrozhdenie* (Paris) in April 1926 (notation on original draft, Box 12), but whether it appeared in that publication, now a bibliographical rarity, is not clear.

severity of regulations inherited from the past. Although his attempt to reform the law ended in as ignominious a failure as Reutern's a quarter-century before, the tale is worth telling as a case study in tsarist anticapitalist prejudices.

Of the illegalities in the corporate business world there is no lack of evidence. We have already cited (in the section on conflict of interest in Chapter 4) the case of the freight dispatching company, founded in 1884 with the aid of a false declaration from a bank, that collapsed when its own agents embezzled its funds. Although the charter had been scrutinized by the Committee of Ministers and the Finance Ministry received annual balance sheets, the concession system did not prevent unscrupulous directors of such companies from practicing fraud on investors, creditors, the public, and the state. Managers had little to fear from lawsuits brought by stockholders in such cases. In one textile company, the Great Iaroslavl Manufacturing Company, the directors, supported by a majority of stockholders, abused the rights of the minority by understating the value of the corporate stock and by refusing to allow the sale of the minority's shares to outsiders after a nominal waiting period. Because the courts refused to hear the case, the minority found no legal recourse.

The strict regulations of the government proved useless when managers, stockholders, and audit commission members all conspired to falsify the financial situation of a corporation. A company founded in 1893 continued operations with the benefit of loans from banks based on inflated statements of the enterprise's assets. Although the law required a company to begin liquidation whenever its assets fell below 40 percent of the nominal basic capital amount, all the individuals involved in this company kept the problem secret. When the company finally declared bankruptcy, creditors learned to their dismay that they would collect little more than 25 kopecks on the ruble. The legal expert Spiridovich stressed that many such undercapitalized companies operated in the Russian Empire.[53]

A speculative fever swept the capitals in the fall of 1893. Instead of being confined, as in 1869, to the Hotel Demuth in Petersburg and, in Moscow, the Chizhov Court and the apartment of a Georgian princess, it enveloped all the big hotels, as crowds of people who owned interest-bearing securities sold them to buy dividend-paying stocks whose values were soaring.[54] A law dated June 8, 1893, had removed all restrictions

---

[53] L. Spiridovich [a pseudonym], *Dela nashikh aktsionernykh kompanii* (Moscow, 1897), 10–23, described these three episodes in detail.

[54] I. I. Levin, "Rost Petrogradskoi fondovoi birzhi," *Bankovaia entsiklopediia*, 2 vols. (Kiev, 1916), vol. 2, 223–6.

against futures dealings in stocks, defined as any purchase of stock in the absence of cash (*nalichnye den'gi*) and with delivery at a certain time in the future (*na izvestnyi srok*). It remained a crime, however, to use this mechanism solely for speculative purposes, that is, to contract for a sale at a higher price without actually transferring the stocks to the purchaser at the time the agreement was made. A companion decree set clear limits on deals concluded without a broker, mandated the audit of brokers' records by the Finance Ministry, and entitled the ministry to deprive a broker of his certification if he violated existing regulations.[55] In the words of one careful historian,

> there was a good deal of destabilizing speculation in Russian shares, as knowing operators pyramided their original gains with more purchases at ever higher prices. They gambled that they could push overpriced shares still higher. This tactic of course made stock prices vulnerable to rapid cumulative declines, especially since margins of less than 25 percent were common.[56]

Several ingenious mechanisms not foreseen by tsarist legislators fueled the speculative fever. In 1893–5, brokers who quoted prices in the stock exchange bulletin set deliberately vague figures, for example, 350–370 rubles for a given stock, so as to buy at the lower price and sell to the public at the higher one without fearing accusations of fraud. Insiders were careful to sell packets of only 25 to 50 shares to the public, lest stockholders obtain sufficient stock to exercise control over the board of directors. Brokers also profited from rapid fluctuations in the prices of stocks, buying at the trough and selling at the peak. None of these devices broke any laws, but they allowed insiders to reap handsome profits at the expense of the public and contributed to the speculative mania by exaggerating price fluctuations. In an effort to dampen the fever, Witte reduced the supply of borrowed money used in speculation by prohibiting corporate founders from using their new stock as collateral for bank loans before the first annual report

---

[55] *PSZ* 3–9741 implicitly legalized time deals on stocks and bonds by forbidding such deals on gold currency (*valiuta*) and securities reckoned in gold, solely for the purpose of realizing a speculative profit. *PSZ* 3–9742, dated June 8, 1893, on brokers.

[56] McKay, *Pioneers*, 223. Deals on time (*na srok*) played a special role in this fever to the detriment of investors who were unskilled in the finer points of corporate finance. Many purchasers of stock concluded time deals *in blanco* (*blankovaia sdelka*), that is, by an agreement in which the buyer, without first having purchased a stock, agreed to sell at a high price in the future, hoping to buy it in the meantime at a low price. Because the future price bore no relation to the stockholder's ability to pay for the shares at the time he was to buy them, the wildest figures flew about in the market, limited only by "the interest of the seller *in blanco* himself [*sobstvennogo interesa blankista*]." V. Biriukovich, "Birzha i publika," section "Khronika," *Vestnik Evropy*, 176, year 30, vol. 6 (Nov. 1895), 337–65, esp. 343 (quoted). On the role of banks in supplying poorly secured loans for this speculative mania, see Levin, *Banki*, 269–70.

had been issued. This restriction had apparently little positive effect.[57] Sharp decreases in stock prices beginning in August 1895 and the saturation of the market resulting from several hundred incorporations contributed to the severity of the depression of 1900–3, in which dozens of major corporations went bankrupt.[58]

This episode of stock-exchange fever demonstrated the need for a major revision of the tsarist corporate law. With much fanfare, the government announced on November 11, 1894, the establishment of a commission, chaired by Actual State Councilor Petr P. Tsitovich, to draft a comprehensive reform. This panel of experts began work in March 1897 and produced a bill a year later, on March 28, 1898. True to form, however, the tsar and his advisors failed to enact the recommendations of the commission.

The Tsitovich Commission could hardly have included a more illustrious or better qualified array of experts from the bureaucracy and the business world. Among the fourteen officials were representatives of the Ministries of Justice, Internal Affairs, Transportation, and Agriculture. Three economic specialists contributed their expertise: Vladimir I. Kovalevskii, head of the Department of Trade and Manufacturing in Witte's Ministry of Finance; Ivan P. Shipov, the future minister of trade and industry; and Aleksandr I. Vyshnegradskii, son of the late finance minister and a leading banker in his own right. The exchange committees of Petersburg, Moscow, Kiev, Kharkov, Odessa, Warsaw, Nizhnii Novgorod, Rostov-on-Don, Riga, and Libau sent representatives, as did major banks, the Southwestern Railroad, and even the Finance Ministry's publications: *Vestnik finansov* (Financial herald) and *Torgovo-promyshlennaia gazeta* (Commercial and industrial gazette).[59]

Like Reutern's board of experts a quarter-century before, the Tsitovich Commission sought to introduce the principle of incorporation by registration. Proof of the popularity of this reform could be seen at the Commercial-Industrial Congress of 1896. D. Iu. Rozenblium of the Warsaw Exchange Committee called for the registration system because it

---

[57] Shepelev, *Kompanii*, 160–1, 163.
[58] Shepelev, *Kompanii*, 149–52. An episode of unethical stock selling for personal profit by gold company executives, which even Witte refused to prosecute for fear of inciting a further decline in the stock market, was related in Vrangel', *Vospominaniia*, 155–7.
[59] *Zhurnal zasedanii vysochaishe uchrezhdennoi kommisii po peresmotru deistvuiushchikh zakonopolozhenii o birzhakh i aktsionernykh kompaniiakh* (St. Petersburg, 1896), 1–3. A slightly different list of participants appeared in the printed bill in TsGIA, f. 20, op. 3, delo 2306, and in Shepelev, *Kompanii*, 168.

would entail less initial expenditures for petitions and thus make incorporation easier, to the benefit of small enterprises that could not afford to petition under the existing concessionary system. Borrowing creatively the biological rhetoric of the reactionary and anti-Semitic right, Rozenblium warned against the influx of "alien" (*chuzhie*) foreign corporations, whose greater economic efficiency and lower unit costs threatened to transform Russian companies into "parasites" of the giants, "injecting infection into the healthy organism of economic life!" The solution to this danger he saw in a decentralized system of small savings banks authorized to invest in local companies and, of course, in a simplified procedure for the creation of such small corporations by registration under appropriate administrative supervision.[60]

Just how permissive a corporate law could become at the end of the century was clear in the United States, where, in the words of one economic expert, a particularly lax law passed by the Delaware legislature served to "remove all effective control over private corporations." Under these regulations, only three founders were needed to launch a new company; "it may conduct business anywhere in the world"; the minimum capital stock could be as low as $2,000, only one-half of which must be subscribed at the outset; only one director need reside in Delaware; the charter could be changed easily; a company could own stock in other corporations, so as to create amalgamations with effective monopoly influence; and information about the finances of a company could be denied to the state on the grounds of business secrecy.[61] No Russian business leader, much less a bureaucrat, proposed such a radical dismantling of controls over corporations in the empire, in which American economists like Ely saw the potential for great mischief making by unscrupulous corporate directors. At the same time, however, the Tsitovich Commission strove to introduce a substantial reform. In November 1896, it solicited comments on its draft from exchange committees and other commercial-industrial organizations. During the first discussion of the bill by the commission and business representatives, on March 6, 1897, Witte himself delivered a powerful indictment of the existing jumble of regulations. In the Russian empire, corporate law, "one might say, does not exist at all."

[60] D. Iu. Rozenblium, "O melkikh aktsionernykh predpriiatiiakh," *Trudy vysochaishe utverzhdennogo vserossiiskogo torgovo-promyshlennogo s"ezda 1896 g. v Nizhnem-Novgorode*, 8 vols. (St. Petersburg, 1897), vol. 3, part 6, 47–9 (quotations from 48).
[61] Ely, *Monopolies*, 268; on 276–8 he quoted a brochure describing the recently enacted Delaware law.

He advised against imposing a set of excessively detailed rules on corporations. A concise law, although imperfect, would be preferable; "excessive strictness would bring harm, not good."[62]

Although exchange committees did not make detailed editorial comments on the draft, a group of Petersburg manufacturers submitted a memorandum in May 1897 urging a reduction of bureaucratic tutelage over corporate enterprise. In a typical statement by Russian business leaders in the period from 1861 to 1905, the manufacturers endorsed the registration system of incorporation because of its "simplicity and speed," supported registration by local authorities instead of the Ministry of Finance in order to avoid overcentralization, and suggested that any penalties for abuses of the new law be relegated to the criminal code so as to keep the civil law as uncomplicated as possible.[63]

With these suggestions in mind, the conferees met in eighteen sessions. Editorial work in 1897 reduced the original draft from 204 articles to a more manageable, but still weighty 142. Further editing of the bill, performed in January 1898 by a select group of experts – two each from the Finance and Justice ministries, three bankers, and Professor Tsitovich himself – resulted in a draft 128 articles long. The final version, in 124 articles, emerged on June 8 from discussions between the Finance Ministry and other agencies.

It appeared by mid-1898 that the Tsitovich Commission had done its job well. The bill replaced the outmoded concession system with the long-awaited principle of incorporation by registration. However, the old habit of bureaucratic arbitrariness did not entirely disappear. Railroads, insurance companies, and banks would still require preliminary confirmation by the tsarist bureaucracy, as proposed in 1872. Furthermore, special permission was needed before founders could establish a company smaller than the norm, issue low-priced shares, or float bonds. In defiance of the Petersburg manufacturers, the commission followed the precedent of 1872 by proposing the creation of a central registrar of corporations in the Department of Trade and Manufacturing in the Ministry of Finance. In order to ensure financial soundness, the bill set minima for capitalization (150,000 rubles) and the price of shares (150 rubles). In a rare concession

---

[62] Quoted from *Vestnik finansov, promyshlennosti i torgovli*, 1898, no. 24, 663–4, in Shepelev, *Kompanii*, 169.

[63] Quoted in Shepelev, *Kompanii*, 168–9. The *Rigaer Börsenblatt* (Riga exchange news) and *Rigaer Handelsblatt* (Riga commercial news) carried reports on the commission's work, according to *Rigaer Handels-Archiv*, vol. 25, no. 1 (Mar. 1898), 201.

to the principle of laissez-faire, the bill provided that these amounts could be increased later simply by informing the ministry. Both named and unnamed shares, as well as common and preferred stock, received official recognition. Equally refreshing was the right of each stockholder to participate in the company's affairs to the extent of his ownership of stock. The bill sought to safeguard the interests of stockholders further by prescribing strict controls over the activities of founders, managers, and members of the eventual liquidation commission. A judicial audit of the company's books could be initiated by the owners of only one-tenth of the stock. Especially strict was the stipulation that at least one-quarter of the basic capital be raised through the sale of stock and placed in the State Bank before a company could be registered, with a time limit of three years for full sale of the initial stock offering. Public subscription in the stock of a new company before its creation through the registration process thereby would have become illegal. Other provisions sought to ensure the fair distribution of earnings to stockholders and to prevent the artificial inflation of dividend payments, a detriment to the enterprise in the long run.[64]

Several business organizations commented on this bill between late 1898 and early 1900. Although the Exchange Committees of Riga and Odessa applauded the proposed abolition of the concession system, the manufacturers of Petersburg complained that the required deposit of one-quarter or more of the basic capital in the State Bank before registration of the charter "would hinder even more the already difficult process of attracting capital" and, paradoxically, place the fate of new enterprises in the hands of professional founders tied to the huge banks.[65]

One expert on corporate law also awarded the commission low marks for the incomplete nature of its reform bill. In its desire to prevent the concentration of corporate power in the hands of a tiny number of wheeler-dealers, the Tsitovich Commission had drafted such debilitating restrictions that if enacted, they might well have slowed the pace of corporate development. Although he applauded the decision to abandon the unwieldy concession system, a change that promised to eliminate both the bureaucratic complexities and exorbitant fees charged by intermediaries, Kaminka opposed the idea of a national registry (*torgovaia zapis'*) for cor-

[64] Shepelev, *Kompanii*, 172, citing *Vestnik finansov, promyshlennosti i torgovli*, 1898, no. 24, 663–8.
[65] Quoted from TsGIA, f. 150, in Shepelev, *Kompanii*, 175; on Odessa and Riga, Shepelev, *Kompanii*, 176.

porations. Such centralization would scarcely represent any improvement over the existing muddle. Rather, he favored regional registration offices on the grounds that officials in Petersburg had no interest in corporations founded in Warsaw and that the charters registered at such offices could be consulted at will by anyone who cared to do so. He also opposed giving local authorities the power to refuse to register a corporate charter and criticized the lack of any appeal process. As long as the founders complied with all provisions of the law, Kaminka argued, no bureaucrat should be given arbitrary power to prohibit the formation of a new company.[66]

Having reviewed the work of the Tsitovich Commission and the criticisms of business organizations and a legal scholar, we must address a vexing problem of logic before moving on to examine the fate of the bill itself. Our account of bureaucratic tutelage and arbitrariness has carried the implication that the cause of efficiency and economic progress would have been served by a careful dismantling of the concession system and the abrogation of various restrictions barring foreigners, Jews, and Poles from positions of responsibility in corporations active throughout the empire. At the same time, however, it is impossible to deny the pervasive problems of dishonesty, speculative greed, and crudeness that afflicted many of the most prominent business leaders in Russia. The question arises: In view of the fact that strict regulation had not prevented illegalities on the stock market and within companies in the decades since 1836, how could a reformed system giving the state less control, through registration instead of concession, have been expected to cure these problems, which were essentially cultural, not legalistic, and which reflected the low level of honesty, the shortage of competent managers, and other hallmarks of Russian economic backwardness? The answer would seem to lie in the gradual improvement in the culture of capitalism, the eradication of artificial restrictions on talented foreigners, Jews, and Poles (on the assumption that they would have brought a more "Europeanized" standard of business behavior to Russia), and the encouragement of entrepreneurship within honest channels. But all this represented a long-term solution. In the short run, the relaxation of bureaucratic restrictions might well have contributed to an increase in corporate fraud.

At the same time, it seems clear that centuries of tutelage and arbitrary

---

[66] A. I. Kaminka, "Proekt polozheniia ob aktsionernykh predpriiatiiakh," *Zhurnal ministerstva iustitsii*, 3, no. 1 (Jan. 1897), 129, 131 (quoted), 132. He scorned the commission's attempt to substitute a new, overly legalistic term – "joint-stock enterprise" (*aktsionernoe predpriiatie*) – for the various names already applied to Russian companies (129).

rule had failed to raise standards of ethical conduct. Indeed, the government's ultimate refusal to embrace even the Tsitovich Commission's limited proposals meant that it relinquished whatever right it ever had to stand as the guardian of honesty and efficiency. By choosing to reject reform, the Russian government helped to perpetuate the servility and dishonesty engendered by the existing system, whatever the complexities and short-term logical incongruities of pursuing progress through relaxed controls in the context of cultural backwardness.

We shall never know whether the reforms elaborated by the Tsitovich Commission would have raised or lowered standards of corporate conduct in either the short or the long term, for the very idea of changing the law of 1836 began to encounter bureaucratic resistance in 1898. Witte himself showed no eagerness to press for passage, but contented himself with the publication of the bill and an account of the commission's work.[67] Shepelev perceived in this action Witte's concern over the recent proliferation of corporations under the existing concession system, as well as the growing unpopularity, especially among xenophobic gentry and merchants, of the influx of foreign capital into Russian industry, a trend identified with Witte personally.[68] Serious complications arose when the Ministry of Justice put forth its own, rather different, scheme in 1899 as part of its general revision of the Civil Code (begun early in the reign of Alexander III, in 1882!). The fact that this effort had not been coordinated with the heroic labors of the Tsitovich Commission, despite the service of the jurist E. E. Pirvits on both commissions, testifies to the compartmentalization and confusion that reigned within the bureaucracy under Nicholas II.

Instead of adopting the registration system, the keystone of Tsitovich's work, Pirvits and his advisors envisaged a decentralized form of incorporation by concession. The approval of the State Council and the tsar would be required if the founders of a new corporation sought exemptions from the law of 1836 or the right of eminent domain over the property of others; all foreign companies also needed the tsar's permission. The minister of finance or other appropriate minister would be empowered to confirm the charters of mining, metallurgical, and machinery companies capitalized at a million rubles or more, while the Board for Zemstvo and Municipal Affairs and the governor in each province would be authorized to confirm the charters of all others. The minimum size of basic capital

---

[67] Shepelev, *Kompanii*, 172, citing *Vestnik finansov, promyshlennosti i torgovli*, 1898, no. 24, 663–78.
[68] Shepelev, *Kompanii*, 172–3.

was set at 150,000 rubles; shares must be priced at 150 rubles or more, except that small companies capitalized at less than 200,000 rubles could issue shares costing as little as 50 rubles. Installment purchases were allowed, with a time limit of two years for full payment. Although the maintenance of the concession system appeared reactionary in light of the proposals of the Tsitovich Commission (to say nothing of Reutern's bill of 1872), the Justice Ministry made an important concession to liberality by mandating that, as long as the tsar's dispensation for an exception to the laws of eminent domain was not required, neither the ministers nor the local authorities could refuse to confirm a properly drafted charter. Disagreements among ministries were to be resolved in the Committee of Ministers.[69] However, the utter absurdity of a concession system that lacked a mechanism for refusal appears to have gone undetected in the rarefied legal minds of Pirvits and his fellow jurists.

Few business organizations submitted comments on the justice ministry's draft, but the exchange committees of Riga and Warsaw criticized it for failing to introduce incorporation by registration.[70] Given the strong evidence of antipathy toward capitalist industry on the part of both bureaucrats and the gentry who controlled most provincial zemstvo boards, one can only surmise that the prospect of placing the fate of corporations in the hands of these agrarians filled industrialists with horror.[71]

[69] Shepelev, *Kompanii*, 173–5, paraphrasing a document in TsGIA, f. 1276; and the text of the justice ministry bill, printed in "Zhurnal zasedanii podkommisii iuridicheskogo obshchestva, obrazovannoi dlia obsuzhedniia proekta postanovlenii ob aktsionernykh tovarishchestvakh," *Russkoe ekonomicheskoe obozrenie*, 4, no. 2 (Feb. 1900), 42–66. This article also contained the commentary of Professor Lev I. Petrazhitskii, the bankers I. F. Doss and Iakov I. Utin, and five other academic and governmental experts who discussed the bill in nine sessions from November 1899 to January 1900. Except for Utin and the lawyer G. B. Sliozberg, who favored concessions for railroads and insurance companies, the subcommission endorsed Senator A. A. Gerke's call for incorporation by registration at local courts, with no grounds for rejection except an improperly phrased charter and with an appeal procedure through the court system to the Governing Senate, the tsarist supreme court (2–3).

[70] Shepelev, *Kompanii*, 175.

[71] The mutual antipathy between zemstvo leaders and the commercial-industrial elite is generally slighted by Soviet historians, who portray the gentry and the manufacturers as parts of an allegedly unified "ruling class." On the hostility that separated zemstvo men from merchants in the Moscow region in the late nineteenth century, see Thomas C. Owen, *Capitalism and Politics in Russia: A Social History of the Moscow Merchants* (Cambridge, 1981), chap. 4. Numerous complaints of metallurgical entrepreneurs in Ukraine against zemstvo taxes appeared in the publications of the South Russian Coal and Iron Association (SRCIA), e.g. Sovet s"ezdov gornopromyshlennikov iuga Rossii, *Zemstvo i gornaia promyshlennost'* (Kharkov, 1908); and N. F. fon-Ditmar's short but spirited pamphlet, *Nezakonnost' zemskogo oblozheniia zemel' s mineral'nymi bogatstvami* (Kharkov, 1908), reprinted from the SRCIA's weekly newspaper, *Gorno-zavodskii listok*, 1908, no. 35. The AIT likewise castigated zemstvo taxation of the coal and iron industries as "the most fantastic,

Having lost momentum during 1899, the Tsitovich bill met its doom at the end of that year. Witte saw fit to call yet another conference of merchants' and bankers' representatives in November 1899. On December 4, this group made clear its misgivings about the bill. Whether they found it too restrictive or excessively lax is not known, the journals of the conference having been lost. In any case, the point is a minor one.[72] As in 1874, the decision to abandon the comprehensive reform of corporate law came not from the manufacturers, whose role was limited to providing respectful petitions to the bureaucrats, nor directly from the agrarian foes of industrial capitalism in the Ministries of Internal Affairs

---

lacking the least guarantee of any kind of justice or equality." V. Arandarenko, "Korennyi nedug v oblozhenii promyshlennosti," *Promyshlennost' i torgovlia*, 3, no. 1 (Jan. 15, 1910), 78–81, quotation from 79. An evenhanded commentary by an economist who served both the SRCIA and the Soviet regime is Petr I. Fomin, *Gornaia i gornozavodskaia promyshlennost' Iuga Rossii*, 2 vols. (Kharkov, 1915–16), vol. 2, 137.

[72] Alone among the merchants in the empire, the conservative leaders of the MEC in the heart of the central textile region raised their voices against the principle of incorporation by registration. In a memorandum to Witte dated December 11, 1899, the MEC warned that the introduction of the new system would lead the great banks to launch a multitude of "small companies with inexpensive, unnamed shares." Whether the merchants' opposition to the liberalization of the corporate law stemmed from their apprehension over the specter of a stranglehold exercised by the great Petersburg banks – *Finanzkapital* in the immortal title of Rudolf Hilferding's treatise (Vienna, 1910) – or from their fear of competition from new companies in the mass market is not clear from the brief quotation of this memorandum in a recent Soviet article: Iu. A. Petrov, "Moskovskie banki i promyshlennost' k nachalu XX v.," in I. M. Pushkareva and others, eds., *Samoderzhavie i krupnyi kapital v kontse XIX–nachale XX v.: sbornik statei* (Moscow, 1982), 124, citing the exchange committee archive, TsGIAM, f. 143, op. 1. Shepelev, *Kompanii*, 176, noted that the MEC submitted a statement in February 1900 but did not describe its contents. In any case, the opposition to the registration system by the most influential organization of Russian manufacturers in the Witte era adds one more nail to the coffin of the notion of a united "rising bourgeoisie" in Russia prior to 1905. The Moscow manufacturers of course suffered as much as anyone from the red tape that pervaded the concession system. Not surprisingly, there are scattered references to petitions for reform before the Tsitovich Commission began its work, for example, in April 1886 and in October 1892: Laverychev, *Krupnaia burzhuaziia*, 42 (no reference given); and Nikolai K. Krestovnikov, *Semeinaia khronika Krestovnikovykh i rodstvennykh im familii (Pis'ma i vospominaniia)*, 3 vols. (Moscow, 1903–4), vol. 3, 96, 90, citing a letter by a representative of the Moscow Section of the RIS dated October 23, 1892. No one from the MSRIS participated in the Tsitovich Commission. The two most prominent men from the Moscow Exchange Committee on that commission, Nikolai A. Naidenov and Grigorii A. Krestovnikov, were well known for their economic and political conservatism and could hardly have been expected to lead a campaign to emancipate industry from ministerial tutelage for what they perceived (in their memorandum of December 11, 1899) as the benefit of the large Petersburg banks. The third representative of the MEC on the commission, Konrad K. Bansa (Banza in Russian) of the Wogau firm, studiously avoided political issues, as did most Englishmen, Frenchmen, and Germans among the merchant elite in Russia. He spoke well before the commission, but only to explain the procedure by which the MEC quoted prices of corporate stock. *Zhurnal kommissii*, 92, 135.

and Justice, but from an economic expert in the Ministry of Finance itself.

On December 1, 1899, the director of the Department of Trade and Manufacturing, V. I. Kovalevskii, submitted to Witte a memorandum arguing that the registration system of incorporation would endanger economic development if introduced in the existing political climate. (He did not explain why he had failed to raise this objection as a prominent member of the Tsitovich Commission.) The main difficulty lay in

> the multitude of restrictive decrees regarding the rights of separate categories of individuals to engage in agriculture, various kinds of industrial activities, and so forth. The great majority of joint-stock companies (approximately 70 percent of their total) are founded at the present time in areas where restrictive laws are in force. In violation of the literal sense of these laws, [companies] are allowed to issue shares to the bearer and to admit into participation as minority members in the administration of [corporate] enterprises individuals who are altogether prohibited by these regulations from owning real estate in these localities and from engaging in the industrial activities practiced by the companies.

If the registration system were adopted,

> no deviations from these laws would be possible, so that all companies active in the borderlands would be required to issue named shares, which could not be transferred to foreigners, Jews, and other proscribed individuals. Persons in these categories would also be barred from managerial positions.

From all this, Kovalevskii drew the inevitable conclusion. Witte would be well advised to abandon the reform drawn up by the Tsitovich Commission in order to retain control over the pace of corporate development, and especially to continue the smoothly functioning procedures by which the minister of finance routinely violated the law by granting various exceptions to the ethnic restrictions on corporate industrial activity in the borderlands.[73] In the tangled jurisdictional thickets of the late tsarist bureaucracy, Witte could resort to various administrative actions in order to attract foreign capital and allow Europeans and Jewish subjects of the tsar into economic fields barred to them by law.[74] Arbitrary action now stood

---

[73] Shepelev, *Kompanii*, 177–80, 185.

[74] In 1896, Witte had convinced the Committee of Ministers to adopt purely administrative guidelines that relaxed the prohibition against the ownership by foreigners of shares in companies with real estate holdings outside urban areas of the western provinces (those named in the decree of March 14, 1887). Similar restrictions were relaxed with regard to the ownership by Jews of shares of companies operating in the Pale of Settlement. Having permitted the ownership of shares in sensitive companies to non-Christians and non-

on the side of ethnic toleration and economic progress, while rational reform of an outmoded law posed the danger of inhibiting the vigorous expansion of corporate enterprise.

Kovalevskii tactfully refrained from naming the obvious way out of the dilemma: both to implement the registration system and to abrogate the various ethnic and citizenship restrictions, of which Witte had complained in memoranda to the tsar in 1895 and to A. N. Kulomzin in 1899. Kovalevskii and Witte both knew that Nicholas II and his ministers would hardly have approved such a dual reform, especially since several energetic journalists, notably Sergei F. Sharapov and Il'ia F. Cion (Tsion in Russian), in 1898 branded as a form of treason to Mother Russia Witte's gold standard and his policy of attracting foreign investment capital.[75] Caught between domestic opposition to foreign capital and the desire of enlightened industrialists for a rational reform of the corporate law, Witte found it expedient to retain the existing concession system, which for all its clumsiness and irrationality gave him the power to circumvent the most repressive provisions of the laws against Jews, foreigners, and Poles.

He acted quietly, however, so as not to alarm the Europeans. In early December 1899, precisely at the moment when he decided to abandon the Tsitovich bill, Witte reassured foreign investors, in a statement to the Russian and European press signed by the tsar, that the reform of the outmoded corporate law was proceeding smoothly and would soon reach completion.[76]

Kovalevskii and Witte never abandoned their hope of winning some sort of permanent relaxation of the restrictions on foreigners and Jews.

Russians, the committee moved to retain the exclusionary principle by erecting barriers along a second line of defense: policy-making positions in such companies. Jews and foreigners were welcome to invest in Russian corporations but would be prevented from exercising control. To this end, the Committee of Ministers ruled that managerial positions – director, alternate (*kandidat*), executive director, and manager of real estate holdings – must remain closed to foreigners in the western provinces, to Jews in the Pale, and to both categories of individuals in the areas where residence and the ownership of real estate was denied to them (the Don Military Region, the Caucasus, Turkestan, the steppes, and the Amur and Maritime regions in the Far East) and in fields of industry from which foreigners and Jews were excluded by law. However, Witte won an important concession with regard to these managerial posts, namely that foreigners and Jews could occupy less than half the managerial positions in such companies, a restriction that, the finance ministry conceded in 1906, could not be enforced. Shepelev, *Kompanii*, 181–2. Witte's successful efforts to maintain these relaxed regulations in the Committee of Ministers in the form of a law to this effect, approved by the tsar on June 19, 1899, is described in Shepelev, *Kompanii*, 183–5.

[75] Shepelev, *Kompanii*, 182–3, gave a good account of the journalistic campaign of Sharapov and others, which led even Nicholas II to express opposition to foreign capital investments.
[76] Shepelev, *Kompanii*, 178.

Between 1899 and 1902, they drafted several bills that would have given the finance minister extensive powers to confirm corporate charters under a streamlined concession system. They based their appeals on the fact that such discretion in the hands of the finance minister would reduce harmful delays in the confirmation procedure. The most that they won, however, was a law (dated June 8, 1899) requiring each ministry to comment on a draft charter within one month.[77] As Witte himself ruefully admitted, comprehensive reform was out of the question:

> A registration system would indeed facilitate the work of the central institutions, but a decision on this matter has not yet been made. The question also arises whether it is altogether proper for us to introduce the registration system. I for one suggest that its introduction in Russia is impossible. In order to do this, it would be necessary to abolish by law all the restrictions that now exist on the right to engage in commercial and industrial activity.[78]

The law of 1901

Only one reform of the corporate law succeeded in passing through the bureaucratic labyrinth during Witte's tenure as minister of finance. This law, dated December 21, 1901, dealt narrowly with the activities of general assemblies and audit commissions.[79] It was designed to eliminate two major causes of the recent stock-exchange fever: the concentration of power in the hands of owners of large blocks of shares, who pushed their own resolutions through general assembly meetings with the aid of figureheads (*podstavnye liudi*); and the spread of multiple officeholding (*sovmestitel'stvo*)

---

[77] Shepelev, *Kompanii*, 188–90. The ingenious Kovalevskii drafted a bill in 1900 that would have authorized the Ministry of Finance temporarily to confirm new corporations whose statutes conformed to a "model charter" (*normal'nyi ustav*), without special privileges. Under its provisions, the finance minister (with the agreement of the ministers of war, internal affairs, and agriculture, but without the approval of the full Council of Ministers) could have granted routine confirmation to companies that issued unnamed shares and owned up to 200 desiatinas of land in areas closed to foreigners and Jews. This attempt to evade existing restrictions met defeat in late 1901 at the hands of the ministers of war, agriculture and state domains, justice, and internal affairs. Shepelev, *Kompanii*, 194–201. Shepelev's account of the drafts and counterdrafts of the various ministries and the Committee of Ministers in the Witte era constitutes a superb narrative of this highly complex drama. It is all the more useful for its inclusion of extensive quotations from archival documents.

[78] Speech before the State Council, September 6, 1899, quoted in Shepelev, *Kompanii*, 191.

[79] *PSZ* 3–20874. It also appears in *SURP*, 1901, no. 124 (Dec. 24, 1901), item no. 2500. Gustav Sodoffsky, "Die Entwicklung der Aktiengesellschaften in Russland und die Bestimmungen vom 21. Dezember (a. St.) 1901," *Jahrbücher für Nationalökonomie und Statistik*, 3rd series, 26 (1903), 54–81, reviewed the provisions of this law and also recapitulated some official statistics of corporate development.

by a small number of directors who sat on the boards of numerous banks and corporations and tended to defend the interests of the banks rather than the companies.[80] It became law after discussions with representatives of leading corporations and banks and the usual interministerial discussions between August and December 1901.

The statute contained several reforms favorable to the interests of stockholders. All stockholders who wished to attend the general assembly must be allowed to do so as long as they informed the company of their intention at least a week in advance (part I, articles 1–5), and the presiding officer at the meeting must be elected by the stockholders from their midst (article 6). The owners of at least one-fifth of the total stock, or their proxies (instead of one-half, as previously specified by law), must be present to constitute a quorum, and at least one-half (reduced from three-quarters) of the stock must be represented if major changes, such as an increase or decrease of basic capital or liquidation of the enterprise, appeared on the agenda (articles 7, 12). Although secret ballots were required during the election of officers, an open vote on all other questions became mandatory whenever requested by one voter (article 9). The board was required to hold a general assembly within one month whenever owners of one-twentieth of the total stock so requested for a specific purpose (article 11). An audit commission, to be composed of five stockholders not on the board of directors or in any other position in the corporation, must verify the company's records and property inventories at least one month before the annual general assembly (articles 14–15). After serving as a director or manager, a stockholder must wait two years before becoming eligible for election to the audit commission (articles 14–16). A group of stockholders representing one-fifth or more of the votes at a general assembly had the right to elect one of their number to the commission. No stockholder could cast more than one-fifth of the votes in the general assembly or represent more than one-tenth of the total shares in the enterprise. (Recently confirmed charters had set the maximum at one-tenth of the votes, but this limit was easily evaded by the use of figureheads, who voted as instructed by the real owners of large blocks of stocks.)[81]

Perhaps the most ambitious section of this law was the last, which required that the executive director (*direktor-rasporiaditel'*) of a bank resign,

---

[80] Shepelev, *Kompanii*, 201–2. One representative of the finance ministry characterized such control as "the tyranny over all of Russian industry by 40 to 50 men." Quoted in Shepelev, *Kompanii*, 208.
[81] Shepelev, *Kompanii*, 203.

within three years, from corresponding positions that he held in other corporations (part V). This provision was obviously aimed at slowing the tendency toward industrial concentration, by which bankers from the 1890s onward had gained control of large corporations. Especially in St. Petersburg, such men had even taken the initiative in launching new companies, often showing little concern for the strength of the enterprise after collecting handsome fees for selling the initial share offering to the public.[82] The effectiveness of this measure doubtlessly remained limited, however, because interlocking directorates could easily be arranged by placing one of the bank's several directors, rather than the executive director, on a corporate board.[83]

Part II of the law, which mandated changes in existing charters, likewise exerted a less sweeping effect than it appeared to do. The preamble stated that the law applied to all joint-stock companies, including banks, and to all share partnerships as well. (Part I exempted railroad companies, while part III noted that insurance companies came under a similar law dated June 15, 1901.) However, the law contained a huge loophole: the exemption of all share partnerships the shares of which were not quoted on the stock exchange. As noted in Chapter 1, large companies, the moderately priced shares (*aktsii*) of which circulated on the exchange, tended to be called joint-stock companies, whereas share partnerships had often existed formerly as family-owned firms and issued a limited number of expensive shares (*pai*) to a small circle of relatives and friends, who often served as managers themselves. The structure of such "purely family enterprises," argued Witte in introducing this exception, made the abuse of power by managers virtually impossible. Moreover, the formal requirements of the law regarding public notice of general assemblies clearly would have been inappropriate. At the same time, the few share partnerships whose stocks appeared on the exchange, for example, the Nobel Brothers Petroleum Company, came under the provisions of the law.[84]

[82] A conference chaired by Kovalevskii declared in 1901 that the control of banks over companies constituted "an undoubted evil," and that the banks' role in financing new stock issues was "even more dangerous." Quoted in Shepelev, *Kompanii*, 208. The exchange committees of Moscow, Warsaw, Odessa, and Kiev defended multiple officeholding as a necessary consequence of the shortage of capable bankers and managers, a view held until mid-1901 by Witte himself. Shepelev, *Kompanii*, 208–9, 206.

[83] A careful account of interlocking directorates among major banks and iron and coal mining, petroleum, metallurgical, electrical, and cement companies in 1914 is V. I. Bovykin and K. F. Shatsillo, "Lichnye unii v tiazheloi promyshlennosti Rossii nakanune pervoi mirovoi voiny," *Vestnik Moskovskogo universiteta*, series *Istoriia*, 1962, no. 1 (Jan.), 55–73. The article contains useful schematic diagrams.

[84] Quotation from Shepelev, *Kompanii*, 215. A hybrid in its structure, the Nobel Company

In this regard, the legislators failed to address two forms of managerial abuse unique to the share partnership. First, as Spiridovich noted, the female stockholders in family-owned companies could hardly have been expected to exercise their nominal rights against their fathers, brothers, and husbands, especially in the strongly patriarchal families of ethnic Russians characteristic of the central industrial region. The concepts of formal checks and balances in such an intimate setting constituted "nothing but a comedy, necessary to no one at all, worth nothing, and leading nowhere. How, really, will a sister or wife take a resolution and demand an accounting from her brother or husband?"[85] The extension of the law of 1901 to such enterprises probably would not have helped to solve the problem of male arbitrariness, but neither did the exemption. Second, some crafty entrepreneurs had begun in the 1890s to establish new companies under the name "share partnership" precisely because these words carried the connotation of solidity and good management, as in the case of the Nobel Company. The shares of many of these companies circulated on the exchange without being officially quoted in the regular reports, so that the law of December 1901 posed no barrier to the victimization of the public by the unscrupulous managers of such enterprises.[86] Thus, stockholders in the majority of share partnerships had no recourse except the formal provisions of the charter.

Moreover, as the Ministry of Finance admitted fifteen years later, the law of 1901 did not achieve its primary purpose because it brought about little improvement in the internal government of large corporations. The interests of small stockholders continued to suffer at the hands of powerful insiders and their compliant underlings. Although often numerous, the small stockholders could hardly challenge the rule of the few, who as owners of large blocks of shares, dominated both the general assemblies

---

began operations with 600 shares (*pai*) priced at 5,000 rubles each in 1879. On November 25, 1883 (*PSZ* 3–1857; *SURP*, 1884, no. 8), it received authorization to issue additional stock in the form of 20,000 shares (*aktsii*) with a par value of 250 rubles, and the charter was amended to read both *paishchiki* and *aktsionery* for "stockholders." To the end the company was called a *tovarishchestvo na paiakh*, not an *aktsionernoe obshchestvo*.

[85] Spiridovich, *Dela*, 30–1. Pavel A. Buryshkin, *Moskva kupecheskaia* (New York, 1954), 58–9, recalled that some of the largest textile corporations in the Moscow region remained in the same family for generations and that any encroachment by outsiders met with fierce, even illegal, resistance. At the turn of the century, his father purchased some shares in the Nikol'skoe cotton firm, owned by the heirs of Savva V. Morozov, but the managers refused to deliver the shares even after ordered to do so by a judge. Buryshkin received his shares only years later, after several Morozovs had died.

[86] Shepelev, *Kompanii*, 216.

and the audit commissions.[87] A final comic touch may be found in the law's preface, which stated that the tsarist government issued it as a temporary measure in anticipation of a general law on corporations. As usual, the "temporary" regulations remained in force to the end. The bureaucrats failed to implement the reforms drafted by the Tsitovich Commission and to frame another bill before the onset of World War I.

[87] Shepelev, *Kompanii*, 216. Curiously enough, the banker Iakov I. Utin complained that some individuals who owned only a few shares disrupted general assemblies or gained significant concessions from important stockholders by threatening to cause a scene. Utin proposed limiting admission to owners of a significant block of shares. Article 12 allowed smallholders to participate, but only if they chose a proxy to represent their shares in common.

6

Bezobrazie (Outrage), 1905–1914

> The smooth, peaceful course of political life; the protection of property and individual interests against arbitrary [*proizvol'nye*] violations; stable laws [*tverdoe pravo*]; legality [*zakonnost'*]; and extensive education in the country – all these are as essential to industry as air. Therefore, gentlemen, the immediate interests of Russian industry coincide with the sacred strivings of all Russian society, which must realize that the vigorous development of commerce and industry in our country will inevitably introduce healthy principles into the entire atmosphere of state and public life.
> – Aleksandr I. Konovalov, in a speech at the centennial celebration of his family's textile firm (September 1912)[1]

The period between the revolution of 1905 and the outbreak of World War I in July 1914 witnessed a welter of confusing portents of political change, both positive and negative. Relaxed censorship, increased religious freedoms, the installation of a semiparliamentary regime, and rising urban literacy rates have provided optimists with a certain factual support for their contention that Russian society was well on the road to adopting the hallmarks of West European culture and shedding the legacy of the tsars: autocratic rule, mass illiteracy, and the debilitating coarseness of life among peasants and workers. Critics of this optimistic assessment point, however, to the tsarist government's refusal to accord full legislative power to the State Duma and State Council, the persistence of a ministry responsible to the tsar, and the failure of liberals to pass a land reform that might have forestalled the peasant revolution of 1917.[2]

In the realm of economic development, prewar trends were likewise mixed. On the one hand, corporations flourished as never before. According

---

[1] Aleksandr I. Konovalov (quoted without reference), in Pavel A. Berlin, *Russkaia burzhuaziia v staroe i novoe vremia*, 2nd ed. (Moscow, 1925), 295; the identical passage, apparently drawn from Berlin's book, appears in Pavel A. Buryshkin, *Moskva kupecheskaia* (New York, 1954), 305.
[2] Aspects of the historiographical debate are considered in Chapter 8.

155

to one estimate, the number of incorporations reached 318 in 1899, and after falling sharply in the depression of 1900–3, attained the unprecedented figure of 399 in 1913, for a total of over 2,000 companies in the 1902–14 period, all in spite of the delays inherent in the concession system.[3] However, if we employ the issue of corporate law reform as a symptom of bureaucratic attitudes toward the corporation in general and to foreign, Jewish, and Polish entrepreneurs in particular, then the verdict of the historical record becomes negative indeed. Only in a few isolated instances did the tsar and his advisors allow minor relaxations of the repressive system inherited from the nineteenth century. Paradoxically, the very confusion that prevailed in the system of granting new corporate charters under the concession system gave manufacturers their most important means of evading the restrictions imposed by Alexander II and Alexander III. The efforts of the Timashev Conference to rationalize the corporate law in 1911 encountered the same stubborn opposition from the Ministries of Agriculture, Law, Internal Affairs, and War that had doomed Witte's plans for reform. When, in 1913 and 1914, clear legal norms finally emerged from the bureaucratic maze, they proved so inimical to the very foundations of capitalist enterprise that the normally soft-spoken representatives of corporate interests, from the Association of Industry and Trade (AIT) to the French ambassador himself, complained loudly and bitterly of the regime's insensitivity to the requirements of modern economic life.

The need for reform

As noted in the preceding chapter, Witte often succumbed to the traditional temptations of ministerial arbitrariness. However, he ridiculed the many restrictions that the tsarist government imposed on foreign, Jewish, and Polish participation in corporations in the outmoded spirit of xenophobic nationalism. What angered Witte was not so much the principle of legislative restrictions on corporations (although he tried, with little success, to relax or evade such restrictions) as the zeal with which over-

---

[3] Leonid E. Shepelev, *Aktsionernye kompanii v Rossii* (Leningrad, 1973), 135, 225, citing two sets of annual figures for 1893–1901 and for 1901–14 (foreign companies but not railroads included in the latter period). Peter I. Lyashchenko [Petr I. Liashchenko], *History of the National Economy of Russia to the 1917 Revolution*, trans. L. M. Herman (New York, 1949), 655, 661, 713, differentiates between foreign and domestic companies founded from 1899 (325 and 69, respectively) to 1913 (343 and 29). Totals of domestically chartered corporations from RUSCORP are slightly larger: 331 in 1899 and 357 in 1913.

cautious bureaucrats endeavored to impose their primal ethnic prejudices on modern capitalist enterprise.

Witte related a debate in the Council of Ministers (as the Committee of Ministers was renamed in October 1905) over a proposal by a group of businessmen, led by Count Józef A. Potocki, to establish a company to build a railroad line from the Shepetovka station of the Southwestern Railroad to Kamenets-Podol'skii, a distance of 224 versts, via Starokonstantinovka and Proskurov (now Khmel'nitskii). Because of his Polish heritage, Potocki appeared to Prime Minister Petr A. Stolypin and other officials as undeserving of the privilege. Particularly vociferous was Sergei V. Rukhlov (minister of transportation, 1909–15), a supporter of the reactionary Union of the Russian People. The Council of Ministers resolved to approve the company with state financial backing of its bonds, but only if the charter limited the participation of "non-Russian" managers and technical personnel. Shortly thereafter, Potocki visited the minister and at dinner that evening described the conversation to Witte.

"What a strange minister of transportation you have. Today I visited him and discussed the charter of the Shepetovka–Proskurov Railroad Company. It turned out that he intended not only to limit participation by persons of non-Russian origin, as the Council of Ministers decreed, but to exclude them completely because he considered their participation to be politically dangerous in that region. I asked him, 'Your Excellency, how well do you know that region? You are apparently judging it on the basis of incorrect reports.' The minister answered, 'No, I myself served there, as the assistant warden of the Letichev prison.' I permitted myself," concluded Count Potocki, "to observe respectfully that His Excellency apparently was acquainted only with the clients of the institution in which he had served, and not with the population of the region as a whole."

That Stolypin and Rukhlov viewed as little better than a common criminal the eminent Count Potocki – a graduate of the Lwow University School of Law, the son of a provincial governor in Lwow province, the husband of a Princess Radziwiłł, a former member of the Lwow provincial assembly, and a wealthy landowner who had voluntarily taken Russian citizenship in 1887 – demonstrated the dimensions of the Russians' arrogance toward the ethnic minorities.[4]

The tsar eventually approved the company's charter, but it contained clauses that testified to Rukhlov's xenophobic bias. Of the five directors and

---

[4] Sergei Iu. Witte, *Vospominaniia*, 3 vols. (Moscow, 1960), vol. 3, 215–16; on Józef Potocki (b. 1862), Witte, vol. 3, 213, and P. N. Shchegolev, ed., *Padenie tsarskogo rezhima*, 7 vols. (Leningrad, 1925–7), vol. 7, 399; on Rukhlov's support of the Union of the Russian People, Michael T. Florinsky, *The End of the the Russian Empire* (New York, 1961), 140.

five alternates on the board, only one of each could be non-Russian subjects. Moreover, the minister of transport could dictate which positions on the board and in the company's local offices must be filled by Russian subjects. These provisions did not adversely affect Potocki or other Polish-surnamed subjects of the tsar, but like all railroad charters approved from at least 1901 onward, this one contained a clause that threatened the worst sort of arbitrary bureaucratic interference: The minister of transportation, with the approval of the finance minister, could remove any director from the board without cause.[5]

With bitter sarcasm, Witte blamed Stolypin for perpetuating the outmoded ethnic bias against capitalists from minority nationalities.

Stolypin placed primary emphasis on the peculiar principle of Russian nationalism. According to this ideal, in order to be a loyal subject of the tsar and a true son of the motherland, the mighty Russian Empire, one must have a name ending in "ov," belong to the Orthodox Church, and have been born in central Russia. (Of course, if a patriot could show proof that he had at least maimed, if not killed, several peaceable Jews, so much the better.)

Likewise, Witte viewed the dismissal of Poles and Jews from government service as a "tribute to a senseless political tendency." He noted that a capable Russian stationmaster in Odessa named Kotel'skii was forced to resign because some considered him a Pole.[6]

Under Kankrin, Reutern, and Vyshnegradskii, the industrialists voiced few complaints against such high-handed administrative actions. Merchant leaders often lacked the literary and rhetorical skills necessary to defend their interests. They tended to endure bureaucratic tyranny for the sake of aid that only the state could give: tariff protection, commercial credit, and purchases of industrial goods. By the turn of the century, however, education among the Russian corporate leadership had reached impressive levels; the various sectoral and regional organizations of industrialists were led by mining engineers and other holders of technical degrees. Even in the Moscow region, where in mid-century the merchant leadership had included illiterate millionaires proud of their peasant traditions, a new generation led by university graduates defended the principle of economic rationality against the indignities of the bureaucratic state.[7] The growing

---

[5] *SURP*, 1910, no. 820, dated June 21, 1910, art. 33.
[6] Witte, *Vospominaniia*, vol. 1, 144, and vol. 3, 215–16.
[7] A well-documented discussion of education among the Moscow merchants before 1905 is Jo Ann S. Ruckman, *The Moscow Business Elite: A Social and Cultural Portrait of Two Generations, 1840–1905* (De Kalb, Ill., 1984), esp. 159–61. For vivid accounts of bureaucratic

sophistication of the industrial elite found expression in debates over both economic and political policies.

For example, various business organizations voiced dissatisfaction with ethnic restrictions. Upon its creation in 1902, the Consultative Board of Gold and Platinum Producers petitioned the government for better transport facilities in Siberia, free ports at the mouths of Siberian rivers, reform of the business tax, and "a change in the system of founding corporations." This organization felt ethnic restrictions with particular severity because its members operated in regions closed to Jewish residence and because its leaders included three Jews: Leopold F. Grauman (president), S. I. Littauer (vice-president), and Baron A. G. Gintsburg.[8]

By 1905, the formerly apolitical technocrats of the mining and metallurgical industry could no longer ignore tsarist incompetence and repression. In an urgent report to Witte in April 1905, the Consultative Board of Iron Producers complained that the wave of labor violence then sweeping the empire resulted from the lack of peaceful avenues of protest. Among the changes considered essential were equality before the law and freedom of speech, press, and association (for manufacturers as well as workers!).[9] Although hardly an issue of major political importance, the reform of the corporate law appeared fully consistent with the other features of a free society.

Representatives of the coal, iron, timber, sugar, petroleum, and textile industries, meeting in Moscow on July 4–6, 1905, petitioned for a legislature elected by secret, equal, and universal (but not direct) suffrage; the decentralization of government; the abolition of communal agriculture; the introduction of state-funded health, old-age, and accident insurance for workers; a progressive income tax; and universal public education. Among the clearly self-serving petitions were "a tariff policy devoted to the optimum defense and development of the people's labor," the creation of a ministry of trade and industry, and the legalization of chambers of

---

insensitivity to the needs of the woolen textile industry, see the memoirs of a university-educated liberal merchant, Sergei I. Chetverikov, *Bezvozvratno ushedshaia Rossiia: neskol'ko stranits iz knigi moei zhizni* (Berlin, n.d. [1920s]).

[8] On the establishment of the Gold and Platinum Board (*Postoiannaia soveshchatel'naia kontora zoloto- i platinopromyshlennikov*), I. G. Mosina, *Formirovanie burzhuazii v politicheskuiu silu v Sibiri* (Tomsk, 1978), 48. Board members are named in the organization's newspaper, *Zoloto i platina* [Gold and Platinum], year 4, no. 1 (Jan. 1, 1907). An informative account of business organizations in Siberia is A. A. Govorkov, I. G. Mosina, and G. Kh. Rabinovich, "'Predstavitel'nye' organizatsii burzhuazii v Sibiri (konets XIX v.–1914 g.)," *Voprosy istorii Sibiri*, 6 (Tomsk, 1972), 26–40.

[9] *Gorno-zavodskii listok*, 18, no. 15–16 (Apr. 9–16, 1905), 7637–7.

commerce empowered to issue mandatory regulations over local trade. As the iron producers had done in April, the assembly also demanded the establishment of the registration system of incorporation.[10] In December 1905, an editorial in the newspaper of the South Russian Coal and Iron Association (SRCIA) denounced the brutal "repressions by administrative fiat" of unrest in Poland and in the Russian villages. "Industrialists are men of order, enemies of extreme theories."[11] From Moscow to Baku, manufacturers condemned the destructive violence of both the socialists and the tsarist government and called for "a fundamental and real – not superficial – reorganization of the governmental system."[12]

Even the apolitical mining engineer Nikolai S. Avdakov, president of the SRCIA and later of the AIT, presided over a commission that called, politely but firmly, for the transformation of the outmoded Mining Code (*Gornyi ustav*) and the agencies that administered it. Tsarist legislation on mining contained 1,280 articles, plus "supplements, changes, instructions, rules, clarifications, and commentaries in such abundance that it is difficult to make sense of it and wide scope is left to discretion." At least three proposals for the reorganization of the Department of Mines were advanced by business organizations between 1907 and 1910. Needless to say, no revision occurred under Nicholas II, and even the Ministry of Trade and Industry (created in October 1905), presumably the industrialists' closest ally in the governmental bureaucracy, brusquely rejected all such plans. Various legal obstacles prevented mining entrepreneurs from invoking the principle of eminent domain on the lands of others, especially gentry and Cossacks. A law of June 2, 1887, allowed unrestricted mining on private and state lands except in Cossack military regions, but only in an area up to one square verst.[13]

The bureaucracy remained adamant on these and other issues, however. After Witte's dismissal from the Ministry of Finance, the government

---

[10] TsGIA, f. 150, op. 1, ed. kh. 265, ll. 18–23, 3, 3 verso (quoted), a clipping of an article reviewing the events of July 4–6 in *Torgovo-promyshlennaia gazeta*, October 24, 1905.
[11] *Gorno-zavodskii listok*, 18, no. 48–9 (Nov. 26–Dec. 3, 1905), quotations from 8235, 8236.
[12] Lead editorial, dated January 1, *Neftianoe delo* (Baku), 8, no. 1–2 (Feb. 25, 1906), 11.
[13] Nikolai S. Avdakov, *O zhelatel'nom preobrazovanii Gornogo vedomstva v sviazi s interesami gornoi i gornozavodskoi promyshlennosti* (St. Petersburg, 1907), 7 (quoted). On the plans for reorganization, G. M. Gorfein, "Osnovnye istochniki po istorii vysshikh tsentral'nykh uchrezhdenii XIX–nachala XX v.," in Glavnoe arkhivnoe upravlenie, *Nekotorye voprosy izucheniia istoricheskikh dokumentov XIX–nachala XX v.* (Leningrad, 1967), 73–110, esp. 87–8. On the Cossack lands, Vladimir Ia. Laverychev, *Krupnaia burzhuaziia v poreformennoi Rossii (1861–1900 gg.)* (Moscow, 1974), 44–5; N. E. Volkov, *Ocherk zakonodatel'noi deiatel'nosti v tsarstvovanii Imperatora Aleksandra III, 1881–1894 gg.* (St. Petersburg, 1910), 155–7.

abandoned his policy of weakening the restrictions on Jewish and foreign participation in Russian corporations. On May 10, 1903, the tsar signed into law a measure limiting the right of Jews to own and use rural land, not only within the Pale of Settlement but also outside it. As a result of this law, new corporations that issued shares to the bearer were forbidden to hire Jews as managers of rural real estate anywhere in the empire. From 1910 onward, few companies received an exemption to this law.[14] As a Polish legal expert wrote in 1908, "The legislation on joint-stock companies in Russia is truly in a sad state."[15]

The Timashev Conference

Pressure for yet another review of the tsarist corporate law grew in the wake of the revolution of 1905. The issue of incorporation by registration figured prominently among the concerns of the first national business organization in the Russian Empire: the Association of Industry and Trade, founded in 1906. In a typically forthright statement, the AIT endorsed the principle of registration because it promised "the elimination of red tape, arbitrariness, and centralization." However, corporations must also be granted "the full plenitude of rights [*vsiu polnotu prav*], regardless of the composition of their participants, or at least a definite minimum of rights," without which registration alone "would be a step backward." This position remained unchanged throughout the various discussions in the period after 1906.[16]

Writing in the AIT's biweekly *Promyshlennost' i torgovlia* (Industry and trade) in 1910, Iu. K. Grinval'd placed the tsarist government's failure to reform its laws in an international perspective. He stressed that those governments most willing to tolerate entrepreneurial freedom enjoyed greater economic growth than those that did not. For example, the German corporate law contained few restrictions, such as a minimum of five founders for a new company. Unfortunately, the Tsitovich Commission had

---

[14] *PSZ* 3-22932, dated May 10, 1903; Shepelev, *Kompanii*, 219.
[15] "W smutnym zaiste stanie znajdue się w Rosyi prawodawstwo akcyjne." Józef Kaczkowski, "Towarzystwa akcyjne w państwie rosyjskiem: Studyum prawno-ekonomiczne," *Ekonomista*, 8 (1908), no. 1, 103.
[16] Shepelev, *Kompanii*, 267 (quoted), 268, citing a statement dated December 11, 1911. In its published statement, the AIT deleted the words "red tape" and "arbitrariness." V. Ivanovich, ed., *Rossiiskie partii, soiuzy i ligi: sbornik programm, ustavov i spravochnykh svedenii* (St. Petersburg, 1906), 68, noted that in its statement of political and economic principles in 1906, the Moscow Bureau (*biuro*) of the AIT called for the replacement of the concession system by registration.

refused to endorse several of the best features of the German law, among them the lack of restrictions on the amount of stock that the founders were permitted to distribute among themselves. More attractive, Grinval'd wrote, was the French law of 1867, which, although it required the sale of all stocks before a company could begin operations, placed a far lower minimum price on shares (25 francs for companies capitalized at below 200,000 francs and 100 francs for larger ones, compared to the German minimum of 200 marks for corporations with state subsidies and 1,000 marks for others) and freed founders from personal liability. Best of all appeared to be the British law, which set no minimum for capitalization or share prices and did not require the complete sale of stock before operations began. Proof of the British law's effectiveness in promoting entrepreneurial activity lay in the statistics for 1906: 40,995 joint-stock companies with a total capitalization of 2 billion pounds sterling.[17]

This enthusiasm for fundamental reform briefly touched the tsarist bureaucracy itself. Vasilii I. Timiriazev, the first director of the Ministry of Trade and Industry (October 1905–February 1906), favored giving Jews the right to own stock in corporations active in areas and industries denied to Jews as individuals. Although the Council of Ministers rejected this proposal in January 1906, the following month the tsar approved a law that allowed corporations with Jewish directors, alternates, or executive directors to acquire land where individual Jews were barred from agricultural activity. In 1910, this restriction was amended to allow Jews to manage the real estate of such companies in all parts of the empire except those specifically closed to Jews.[18] Timiriazev's successor (February–May 1906), the economist Mikhail M. Fedorov, went even farther. In perhaps the most liberal statement ever issued by one of Nicholas's ministers, Fedorov declared that the October Manifesto of 1905, which promised a modicum of civil liberties and political representation to the population, had as its logical corollary the introduction of the registration system of incorporation and the abolition of the ban on Jewish corporate enterprise: "The state's tutelage and supervision over the course of industry are incompatible with the concept of a state based on the rule of law [*pravovoe gosudarstvo*]."[19]

---

[17] Iu. K. Grinval'd, "Uchrezhdenie aktsionernykh obshchestv v Germanii," *Promyshlennost' i torgovlia*, 3, no. 3 (Feb. 1, 1910), 165–8; "Uchrezhdenie . . . vo Frantsii," *Promyshlennost' i torgovlia*, no. 6 (Mar. 15, 1910), 379–82; "Uchrezhdenie . . . v Soedinennom Korolestve," *Promyshlennost' i torgovlia*, no. 11 (June 1, 1910), 722–6.

[18] Shepelev, *Kompanii*, 253.

[19] Shepelev, *Kompanii*, 255 (quoted), 256–7. *Neftianoe delo*, 8, no. 24 (Dec. 31, 1906), 1504,

Even in the State Duma, where gentry, peasant, and worker representatives expressed strongly anticapitalist attitudes, especially against cartels, thirty-three members called for a registration system of incorporation in 1910. In response, the tsar appointed, for the last time, an interagency conference to discuss the reform of the corporate law. Chaired by Minister of Trade and Industry Sergei I. Timashev, this conference of 80 men included representatives from the Ministries of Finance, Justice, Internal Affairs, Agriculture, and Transportation and prominent bankers and industrialists as well as members of the State Duma and State Council elected by commercial and industrial organizations. Like the commissions that had produced the bills of 1874 and 1899, the Timashev Conference worked diligently (in four sessions in December 1911 and January 1912) to prepare a comprehensive reform of the corporate law. Like them – need it be said? – the conference drafted a bill unacceptable to a majority of the ministers and to the tsar himself.[20]

Timashev, whose commitment to reform seemed genuine, framed a moderate set of standards for new corporations: 100,000 rubles of basic capital and a minimum share price of 100 rubles for most companies, and only 50,000 and 50 rubles respectively for small companies active in a limited geographical area. Although shares priced at 100 rubles and less were to be made out by name and fully paid for in advance of operations, the bill also allowed shares to the bearer as well as common and preferred stock. To protect stockholders from fraud by the founders, the bill mandated a minimum of between five and seven founders, who must purchase at least one share each and together own at least 10 percent of the total. No increase in basic capital was to be allowed until the first issue had been entirely paid for; and no decrease was to be made within six months of the day of founding, and then only after three public notices. All these guidelines rested on the centerpiece of the reform: the abolition of the concession system in favor of incorporation by registration.[21]

As might have been expected, several ministers opposed the principle

---

paraphrased with obvious approval a reform program submitted by the Ministry of Trade and Industry to the Council of Ministers. Among the reforms was a modern labor law (including freedom to organize unions and to strike), expansion of elective business organizations, vocational education, and – especially noteworthy for our purposes – incorporation by registration.

[20] Shepelev, *Kompanii*, 261–4, 268–9.

[21] TsGIA, f. 23, op. 14, delo 205, ll. 51–2 (hereafter, Timashev Conference), pages 84–5 of a printed proposal: "Predpolozheniia o zhelatel'nykh izmeneniiakh v deistvuiushchem zakonodatel'stve o torgovo-promyshlennykh aktsionernykh kompaniiakh." Shepelev, *Kompanii*, 264–79, deftly summarizes the debates in the Timashev Conference.

of registration as a threat to the foundations of the tsarist empire. K. A. Strol'man of the Ministry of Internal Affairs criticized registration precisely because it would permit "the evasion of a whole series of statutes limiting the acquisition of nonurban real estate by certain categories of individuals." In the course of the initial debate, Timashev won support for registration from representatives of the Ministries of Finance, Transportation, Justice, and even Internal Affairs when he vowed that the new system would entail no weakening of the discriminatory laws on corporate and individual landholding. Experts from the Main Administration of Land Tenure in the Ministry of Agriculture and State Domains and from the comptroller's office inclined toward a dual system – concessions for corporations facing restrictions because of real estate holdings or mining operations, and free registration for others. This attempted compromise proved unsatisfactory, however, to both the reactionaries and the proponents of reform.[22]

Far more interesting, in light of the insistent demands for registration expressed by prominent business leaders from the 1860s to the end of the century, were the ingenious arguments in favor of the existing concession system put forth by bankers and manufacturers in the Timashev Conference. Iakov I. Utin, representing the Petersburg Discount and Loan Bank, considered the concession system to be better for large corporations precisely because it allowed exceptions to the restrictive laws on rural property ownership. Likewise, P. S. Chistiakov, speaking for the producers of iron, gold, and platinum, pointed out the impossibility of establishing a large metallurgical company in the Ural Mountains without exemptions from the laws limiting corporate ownership of land. (He obviously referred to companies that issued unnamed shares.) Although A. A. Pomerantsev of the Gold and Platinum Board favored the proliferation of small companies under a modern registration system, he too defended the concession system for large enterprises in view of "the repression of our restrictive laws."[23] One of the twelve business representatives in the State Council, the Warsaw banker Stanisław M. Rotwand, warned that the standardization of existing regulations "would not benefit the development of corporations because a large proportion of enterprises belong to the category that needs to enjoy [special] favors in that regard." Another spokesman of industrial interests in the State Council, former minister Vasilii I. Timiriazev, put

---

[22] Shepelev, *Kompanii*, 270 (quoted), 271.
[23] Timashev Conference, ll. 124–5.

the matter more bluntly: as long as ethnic and citizenship restrictions remained in force "it would be difficult to see in the registration system any significant advantages over the concession system."[24]

Two leaders of the AIT eloquently expressed the manufacturers' misgivings. Władysław Żukowski noted that "all previous attempts to reform the corporate law were ruined by a whole series of restrictions on the civil rights of joint-stock companies." He called for a clarification of the major point in the debate: whether, under a registration system, corporations would or would not be subject, as "juridical persons," to the same restrictions that affected individuals. If so, the introduction of registration "could destroy all the benefits" of that liberal principle because large firms, which issued unnamed shares, would no longer be able to obtain the various exceptions that had been routinely granted under the concession system.

Likewise, S. S. Novoselov observed that the AIT could not endorse the new registration system unequivocally because no one had yet specified "what bundle [*komplekt*] of civil rights joint-stock companies would enjoy" in the areas of ownership of real estate and business activities. If the law differentiated between the company's rights and those of separate individuals who participated in it, then one could only welcome a registration system because it would simplify the establishment of new corporations without imposing onerous restrictions. The matter would be "completely different," however, if a corporation were to be prohibited from enjoying civil rights on its own behalf whenever certain individuals became its stockholders or managers. Under the laws barring Jews and foreigners from acquiring large tracts of land, from engaging in the mining of iron and gold, and from the production of petroleum, only two kinds of corporations could be established by registration. Those that owned significant amounts of land would be required to issue named shares exclusively to non-Polish Christian subjects of the tsar and to elect Christians as managers. On the other hand, any company that issued unnamed shares would be allowed to own real estate only in cities within the Jewish Pale and, if engaged in mining or petroleum production, would be required to exclude Jews from the board of directors. (Among the many business

---

[24] Quotations in Shepelev, *Kompanii*, 270 (Rotwand) and Timashev Conference, l. 131 (Timiriazev). Other speakers at the session of December 9, 1911 included representatives of the SRCIA, the MEC, the Riga Exchange Committee, and one Glazberg of the Russo-Asian Bank. Timiriazev eventually endorsed the dual system proposed by the Main Administration of Land Tenure. Timashev Conference, ll. 131–6; Shepelev, *Kompanii*, 271.

organizations represented at the conference, only the Nizhnii Novgorod Exchange Committee endorsed corporate registration under the existing laws. The anomaly may be explained by the fact that few large corporations had their headquarters in this Volga market town; moreover, ethnic Russian merchants in the provinces traditionally revered the tsar and, to put it charitably, showed indifference to the plight of the Jews.)[25]

Timashev continued to press for reform after his conference disbanded in January 1912. In late June, he submitted to the Council of Ministers a new bill based on the concession system, with exemptions from restrictive laws, coupled with a registration procedure for small companies, some of which would also have received exemptions. Each company formed by registration would be limited to ownership of 200 desiatinas of land; those in need of more real estate would require a concession. Unnamed shares were permitted, but companies with real estate must hire land managers who were permitted by law to own land in that region. Companies affected by the law of March 14, 1887, which governed land ownership by foreigners in the Polish and western provinces, must have Russian subjects as executive directors and in a majority of directors' posts. These rules merely recapitulated provisions of the charters approved in recent years by the Council of Ministers, which, in Timashev's proposal, would retain the authority to grant other exceptions as well.[26]

By drafting a bill that did little more than recapitulate the untidy system already in existence, Timashev offered to the commercial-industrial elite of the empire a reform that lacked any substance. In June, the Petersburg Society of Mill and Factory Owners (PSMFO) warned that a registration system would entail "new constraints and restrictions, exactly the opposite of the case in other countries." It proposed instead the simplification of the concession system (including confirmation of ordinary charters by the minister of trade and industry, not the tsar) rather than its abolition.[27]

A joint statement by the PSMFO, the PEC, and its subsidiary Securities Exchange vigorously criticized several aspects of the bill. No minimum capitalization should be required, and shares in small companies should be priced as inexpensively as 25 rubles. Suits against the management by stockholders should be allowed only when initiated by owners of at least

---

[25] Timashev Conference, l. 127 (Żukowski), ll. 127–8 (Novoselov), ll. 131–2 (Nizhnii Novgorod merchants).
[26] Shepelev, *Kompanii*, 272–3.
[27] PSMFO memorandum of June 20, 1912, to the Minister of Trade and Industry, quoted in Shepelev, *Kompanii*, 275–6; annual report of the PSMFO for 1912 (dated Mar. 12, 1913), TsGIA, f. 150, op. 1, ed. kh. 58, l. 85 v. (quoted).

one-fifth of the basic capital, on the grounds that frivolous legal actions would drive down share prices and entail large legal expenses. Article 19 required each stockholder to receive at least one vote at the general assembly, but that no person enjoy more than one-third of the total; the petitioners advocated the apportionment of voting strength solely on the basis of stock ownership, with unlimited voting by proxies. Article 22 held the management collectively responsible for the lawful operation of the corporation and prohibited directors from holding analogous positions in other companies. The Petersburg businessmen sought to release a director from responsibility for a given decision if he had voted against it or not favored it, and proposed that the prohibition on multiple officeholding be limited to credit institutions, as mandated by the law of 1883. This point received special emphasis:

Very often, joint-stock enterprises can be formed only with the participation of certain individuals who are already members of the board of [existing] joint-stock institutions. In Russia there is by no means a surplus of industrial leaders [*promyshlennye deiateli*]. Moreover, in our country shares are generally not distributed among the masses of small capitalists, but are more or less concentrated in large blocks among a small number of people. This is explained by the historical development of Russian joint-stock businesses, [in particular] by the transition from personally owned enterprises to so-called family-owned joint-stock (share) partnerships. Thus in our country very often one and the same capitalist invests large amounts in several joint-stock enterprises on the condition, which is completely understandable, that he participate in the management of these enterprises.

Finally, article 26 of the bill allowed liquidation to begin when favored by owners of one-twentieth of the capital stock; the businessmen proposed raising this figure to one-fifth in the interest of institutional stability.[28]

The Petersburg organizations thus strove to minimize the restrictions on managerial discretion and to reduce the power of small stockholders both in the general assembly and in the courts. However self-serving this defense of founders and managers, whose probity the bureaucrats had good reason to doubt, the industrialists rested their defense of multiple officeholding on a solid historical foundation. Had the Timashev Conference succeeded in destroying the concentration of corporate power in the hands of a small number of wheeler-dealers, the pace of corporate development might well have slowed significantly.

[28] Obshchestvo zavodchikov i fabrikantov, S.-Peterburgskii birzhevoi komitet, and Sovet fondovogo otdela S.-Peterburgskoi birzhi, *Proekt izmenenii v deistvuiushchem zakonodatel'stve o torgovo-promyshlennykh aktsionernykh kompaniiakh* (St. Petersburg, n.d.), 8, 16–18, 22 (quoted), 24.

The proposals of the Petersburg businessmen went unheeded, as usual, by the minister of trade and industry, who defended his bill as the only one capable of winning approval in the Council of Ministers. An ominous sign was the fact that the justice ministry, having recently completed its own review of the corporate law, expressed concern that incorporation by registration appeared too lax; in any case, not all companies should be allowed 200 desiatinas of land as a matter of course.[29]

At this point the AIT added its voice to the growing chorus of opposition to registration:

> The fundamental idea of the corporate form [of economic organization] consists in the easy circulation of shares in the company, so that the enterprise is able to attract capital from the public at large. Named shares in joint-stock companies are an aberration. They were created in our country for purely artificial reasons, namely the possibility of evading restrictive decrees [imposed on Jews and foreigners] and the lack of any other form of partnership with limited liability for participants except that of the joint-stock company.

In view of the disappointing work of the Timashev Conference, the AIT endorsed the legalization of limited-liability partnerships (the German *Gesellschaft mit beschränkter Haftung*) for enterprises not in need of exemptions from the restrictive laws, so that small companies could offer limited liability to investors and be formed with a minimum of bureaucratic formalities. Corporations would continue to exist under the unreformed law of 1836, which was tempered by a host of ministerial exemptions. Registration without such exceptions "would have an extremely pernicious effect on the further development of corporations and would cause significant harm to our industry and trade."[30] This stance reflected the AIT's realization that no hope existed for the attainment of its maximum program, enunciated by Zukowski and Novoselov in December 1911.

However, the refusal of the tsarist government to abandon its ethnic and citizenship restrictions on corporations moved two manufacturers to issue angry denunciations. These statements had, of course, little effect on the direction of policy in St. Petersburg, but they were significant as indications of the frustration felt by leading businessmen. The silk and iron producer Jules Goujon (Iulii P. Guzhon), a native of Moscow who, as a descendant of Alsatian textile experts, held both French and Russian citizenship, angrily denounced the regime's anti-Semitic legislation as a

---

[29] Shepelev, *Kompanii*, 278–9.
[30] Shepelev, *Kompanii*, 277–8, quoting a memorandum to the Council of Ministers and the Ministry of Trade and Industry, dated July 4, 1912.

fatal obstacle to modern industrial development. The denial to "six million Jews of the most elementary human and civil and economic rights" and the arbitrary enforcement of the anti-Jewish laws "are bringing the Jewish masses to ruin" and causing harm to "the business interests of the entire country." He urged immediate reforms, including the abolition of the Pale of Settlement, "in the direction of alleviating the Jews' general situation and equalizing their commercial and travel rights with those of the native population." Unlike other ethnic minorities and foreigners in Russia, the Jews – "almost one-third of the commercial-industrial population, and economically the most active and energetic group" – lacked the right of unrestricted travel within their own country. "The right of all people to settle freely anywhere they choose is universally recognized in all civilized and semicivilized countries of the world."[31]

Shortly thereafter, Aleksandr I. Konovalov, owner of one of the most advanced cotton-textile mills in the Moscow region, criticized the economic irrationalities of the concession system. In a bold speech to the State Duma in 1913, he complained that prospective founders of new companies waited three to four months for the approval of up to six agencies in Petersburg. The Russian economy needed "emancipation [*raskreposhchenie*] from these fetters, which shackle the formation and growth of joint-stock enterprises." The time had come, he declared, to replace "the arbitrariness of the administrative authorities with the creation of firm norms of legality [*tverdye normy zakona*], equal for all" and to eliminate "red tape and tutelage" from the administration of corporate enterprise. Corporate law reform must include both the creation of a simplified registration system and the simultaneous abolition of all prohibitions on corporate enterprise and property ownership previously imposed on "specific categories of the population," meaning Jews and other ethnic minorities.[32]

---

[31] Letter from the Moscow Association of Manufacturers to the AIT in Petersburg, dated Oct. 28, 1912. Goujon wrote the letter in the form of a petition from the AIT to Prime Minister Kokovtsov, but the AIT apparently declined to submit the statement to the minister. Goujon's letter is "the only statement in the Association's archive which expresses moral indignation as well as economic objections to the restrictions on Jews." Carl A. Goldberg, "The Association of Industry and Trade, 1906–1917: The Successes and Failures of Russia's Organized Businessmen," doctoral dissertation, University of Michigan, 1974, 356–7. Goldberg, 357–9, translated the entire letter from a copy in the AIT archive, TsGIA, f. 32 (translation slightly modified).

[32] Shepelev, *Kompanii*, 286, quoting *Promyshlennost' i torgovlia*, the organ of the AIT, 1913, no. 13 (July 1), 5–7. In an earlier article on tsarist corporate law, Shepelev included different, but no less outspoken excerpts from this report of Konovalov's speech. Leonid E. Shepelev, "Tsarizm i aktsionernoe uchrezhditel'stvo v 1870–1910-kh godakh," in N.

Nor did the criticism of governmental highhandedness emanate exclusively from Moscow. In its memorandum of June 20, 1912, the PSMFO had denounced the veto power over all new corporate charters enjoyed from 1905 by the Ministry of Internal Affairs. Under a decree issued in 1905, the ministry was empowered to certify "the trustworthiness and property status" of each prospective corporate founder.[33] A formula better designed to permit bureaucratic arbitrariness could scarcely be imagined.

The complaints voiced by Goujon, Konovalov, and the PSMFO, although based on the principle of modern capitalist rationality, contained a certain element of exaggeration. Certainly the Timashev Conference had failed to devise a satisfactory reform, but the system of exemptions that Witte had devised in the previous century remained intact. Citing documents in the archive of the Ministry of Trade and Industry, Shepelev wrote that the preliminary approval given to each new charter by the bureaucrats in the Corporate Section (Aktsionernoe otdelenie) of the Commerce Division (Otdel torgovli) generally encountered no resistance in the Council of Ministers. Even the AIT admitted in 1914 that the section's administrative action was notable for "the lack of special constraints in the confirmation of corporate charters." In other words, the Corporate Section routinely granted numerous exceptions to the law, for example, giving approval to companies with capitalizations of 100,000 rubles or less and with stocks priced at 100 rubles or less. From the beginning of 1910 to the end of 1913, 112 companies, or 10 percent of all newly formed corporations, received the right to purchase stock in other companies, an operation prohibited by law.[34]

This latter phenomenon worried a former head of the Corporate Section, N. S. Dobrovol'skii. He convinced Finance Minister Vladimir N. Kokovtsov that unrestrained mutual purchases of stock by several corporations, coupled with mutual exchanges of directors, could easily lead to the creation of what Dobrovol'skii called an "organic monopoly" not subject to the kind of state supervision that existed over Produgol' and other well-known syndicates. Even more troublesome to the bureaucrats was the possibility that by acquiring stock in other enterprises, a company might evade the numerous restrictions on land ownership and industrial activity. In June 1914, Count Ilarion I. Vorontsov-Dashkov, viceroy of

E. Nosov and others, eds., *Problemy krest'ianskogo zemlevladeniia i vnutrennei politiki Rossii: dooktiabr'skii period* (Leningrad, 1972), 306.

[33] Quoted in Shepelev, *Kompanii*, 276.
[34] Shepelev, *Kompanii*, 281 (quoted), 282.

the Caucasus, pointed with alarm to several petroleum companies that evaded the laws regulating corporate ownership of land by acquiring stock in existing companies that enjoyed the right to operate in the restricted lands. Whether, as Shepelev asserted, these evasions of the corporate law accounted for the lack of energy with which the Ministry of Trade and Industry pursued the reform of the law, or whether the ministry simply recognized the futility of attempting a further reform in the face of resistance from other ministries, remains an open question. In any case, the failure to introduce a registration system in 1911–12 coincided with the proliferation of exemptions to the restrictive laws.[35] Under the outmoded concession system, therefore, new corporations received numerous privileges in defiance of the law.

The reactionary counteroffensive

Perhaps emboldened by the failure of Timashev's initiatives for reform, bureaucrats in the Ministries of Agriculture and of Internal Affairs who opposed the exceptions routinely granted by the Ministry of Trade and Industry began in 1912 to demand strict enforcement of the law. They sought to extend to every existing corporation the various restrictions imposed on "the Jew, the foreigner, and the person of Polish extraction," as the AIT put it in July 1912. To this end, they launched a frontal assault on the several thousand corporate charters issued in the previous decades. No matter that each charter had, in the words of the jurist, "the force of law."

In April 1913, even as Timashev endeavored to salvage the registration system, Aleksandr A. Rittikh, vice-director of the Main Administration of Land Tenure in the Ministry of Agriculture and State Domains, reported to the Council of Ministers alarming statistics of large-scale purchases of rural land by corporations. During the last stock-exchange boom (apparently 1895–1900), Rittikh stated, corporations had earned speculative profits from the purchase and sale of land, presumably at the expense of the long-suffering Russian peasant. Moreover, in an unspecified number of cases, Jews had used the corporate form of enterprise to evade the prohibitions against ownership of rural land.[36] In fact, as noted by the foremost historian of Jewish entrepreneurship in Russia, Arcadius Kahan,

[35] Shepelev, *Kompanii*, 283 (quoted), 284.
[36] Shepelev, "Tsarizm," 304.

many Jews incorporated their businesses not only to attract investment capital and to work with non-Jews in finance, commerce, and industry, but also "to avoid some of the more blatant forms of discrimination that operated against individual or family firms, but not against corporations."[37] Neither the Ministry of Agriculture nor Kahan cited statistics to show the extent of this practice, and its very illegality makes any such effort difficult, but the fact that at least some Jews used incorporation to evade the law seems clear enough.

Eager to stamp out such illegalities, the Council of Ministers adopted a proposal that exceeded all rational limits. Pending a definitive resolution of the problem, the council refused to consider any corporate charters that provided for land ownership, on the grounds that "large-scale ownership of land by corporations represents a serious danger and in the final analysis causes more harm than benefit to the state."[38] On June 28, 1913, the council decreed a return to the rules in force prior to 1906: The right to acquire real estate in areas prohibited to Jews would be granted only to companies that issued named shares and in which more than half the directors' positions and all executive directorships and real estate positions were held by Christians.[39] In the face of this reactionary campaign, Minister of Trade and Industry Timashev abandoned his moderate plan for a dual system of incorporation.

The discriminatory laws against Jews in corporations appeared to be aimed specifically at the beet-sugar industry of Ukraine. According to one Jewish scholar, a quarter of all sugar refineries in the southwestern provinces were already under Jewish control in 1872, and by 1910 the proportion exceeded one-third (182 of 518) of the sugar companies in the southwest and Bessarabia. Whereas most landlords who produced sugar from their own beets used traditional methods, Jews tended to apply the latest technology in this industrial application of organic chemistry.[40] The Brodskii family of Kiev, which began producing beet sugar in the 1840s, acquired

---

[37] Arcadius Kahan, "Notes on Jewish Entrepreneurship in Russia," in Gregory Guroff and Fred V. Carstensen, eds., *Entrepreneurship in Imperial Russia and the Soviet Union* (Princeton, 1983), 123. Kahan cited no sources.

[38] M. Ia. Gefter, "Tsarizm i zakonodatel'noe 'regulirovanie' deiatel'nosti sindikatov i trestov v Rossii nakanune pervoi mirovoi voiny," *Istoricheskie zapiski*, 54 (1955), 188, note 2, quoting from TsGIA, f. 1276.

[39] Shepelev, *Kompanii*, 279–80; Shepelev, "Tsarizm," 305–6.

[40] I. M. Dijur, "Jews in the Russian Economy," in Jacob Frumkin, Gregor Aronson, and Alexis Goldenweiser, eds., *Russian Jewry (1860–1917)* (New York, 1966), 129. Dijur specified the percentage in 1910 as 31.5, obviously an error for 35.1 (182 divided by 518). He supplied no reference, but presumably relied on official publications.

nine plants by the 1880s and seventeen by 1912, as well as various other enterprises in banking, flour milling, brewing, distilling, and timber production.[41] The impact of the ruling of 1913 appears limited, however, in that it merely obliged Jewish sugar producers in the Pale of Settlement to move their plants from rural areas to nearby cities, where Jews were allowed to own real estate. The technologies used in the production of coarse granulated sugar (*pesochnyi sakhar*) in the villages were less complex than those employed in plants that made refined sugar (*rafinad*), and the profit margins in the former fell short of those in the latter, to the benefit of urban Jewish sugar refiners.

Having tasted victory in the struggle to evict Jewish corporations from the countryside, the reactionary bureaucrats now turned to an all-out attack on corporate landholding, whatever the ethnicity or citizenship of the stockholders and managers. Just as alarming as Jewish landholding appeared the fact that in 1912, as the SRCIA admitted, sixty-one coal mining corporations in Ukraine owned or leased 150,500 desiatinas of land, or 2,467 on the average, more than all but the wealthiest landlords there.[42] Aleksandr V. Krivoshein, director of the Main Administration of Land Tenure, shepherded through the Council of Ministers a law, dated April 18, 1914, that restricted all corporations in the entire empire to only two hundred desiatinas, the maximum allowed to Jewish and foreign corporations in the Pale and the western provinces. Only with the permission of three agencies – the Ministries of Trade and Industry and of Internal Affairs, plus the land tenure administration headed by Krivoshein – could a corporation henceforth acquire more than two hundred desiatinas anywhere in the empire. If the land lay in particularly sensitive areas (apparently the Caucasus and Turkestan, according to precedent), the minister of war must also give his approval. Of course, Jews were banned entirely from managerial posts in companies that received permission to own large tracts of land for industrial purposes, such as mining and petroleum drilling. Even if a company purchased land simply to erect buildings on it, Jews could not comprise more than half the board of directors.[43]

---

[41] *Bol'shaia sovetskaia entsiklopediia*, 3d ed., vol. 4, 42.
[42] Gefter, "Tsarizm," 189, note 1. Either the SRCIA or Gefter miscalculated the average as being 2,470 desiatinas.
[43] Shepelev, *Kompanii*, 280. Shepelev, "Tsarizm," 311, noted that this law never appeared in print, not even in the *SURP*, which continued to the end of 1917. M. Ia. Gefter, a Soviet historian of Jewish extraction, described this law in his article published in 1955, but he tactfully avoided mentioning the word "Jews," the very crux of the law! Gefter, "Tsarizm," 188.

The alacrity with which the Council of Ministers and the tsar approved these restrictions stood in sharp contrast to the maddeningly slow process of study, discussion, and eventual inaction that marked the history of corporate law reform in the previous decades. This unhappy episode showed the resilience and determination of the enemies of corporate capitalism in the inner circles of Nicholas's government. Until its abrogation by the tsar three months later, this law stood as a monument to agrarian reaction at the end of the imperial period.

The law constituted, moreover, only part of the general assault on the rights of Jewish subjects of the tsar. Charges of ritual murder in Kiev were raised in March 1911, when Mendel Beilis went on trial for the death of a Christian boy who, it turned out, had been killed by a gang of criminals. The world-famous trial ended in Beilis's acquittal in September 1913.[44] Also in March 1911, the Permanent Council of Gentry Societies resolved to endorse the exclusion of Jews not only from the army but also from the teaching profession and from legislative, administrative, and judicial posts in the tsarist government. Jewish youth were to be segregated from Russians in the schools.[45] Later that year, Nikolai E. Markov II, leader of the Union of the Russian People and a member of the Council of the United Nobility, demanded the expulsion of all Jews from the empire. In 1912, the government banned Jewish merchants from the great fairs in Siberia and Nizhnii Novgorod, and prohibited first-guild Jewish merchants from leasing rural land in the Pale of Settlement. The police raided the exchange in Samara, and in Kiev they curtailed the economic activities of Jews. Non-Jewish merchants complained in vain that trade and industry would collapse under such repression, but the tsarist ministers did not cease their campaign. Shortly after Kokovtsov's forced resignation as prime minister and minister of finance on January 30, 1912, his successor in the latter position, Petr L. Bark, issued an attack on international financiers (a thinly veiled allusion to Jewish bankers), to which the reactionary *Novoe vremia* (New times) responded with a jubilant welcome of a "new era" that would witness an end to "the liberal-cosmopolitan

---

[44] Louis Greenberg, *The Jews in Russia*, 2 vols. (New Haven, 1944–51), vol. 2, 88–93. A richly detailed account of the entire episode is Maurice Samuel, *Blood Accusation: The Strange History of the Beilis Case* (New York, 1966).

[45] Aron Ia. Avrekh, *Stolypin i tret'ia duma* (Moscow, 1968), 37, note 40, citing a document in the Central State Archive of the October Revolution (Tsentral'nyi gosudarstvennyi arkhiv oktiabr'skoi revoliutsii) in Moscow, f. 584.

domination by the chancery" and to the alleged power of Jewish banks in the Russian economy.[46]

In an uncharacteristically charitable analysis of these repressive measures, a recent Soviet work stressed that Rittikh, the chief architect of the law of April 1914, did not oppose private capital in principle and considered Krivoshein's measure to be compatible with modern corporate development. Indeed, although Rittikh blamed mining companies for causing artificial increases in the price of agricultural land, he sought to prevent damage to Russian industry by exempting mining companies from the two-hundred-desiatina limit. (According to this account, such an exclusion was written into the law and therefore did not depend on a waiver from the various governmental agencies.) Moreover, the two-hundred-desiatina maximum could be increased for any company that made a strong enough case to the Ministries of Trade and Industry and of Internal Affairs and the land tenure administration (as well the Ministry of War in certain borderlands). The rules against Jewish landholding were not at all new, but merely extended existing regulations against Jewish directors and real estate managers in mining companies. Finally, the provisions of the law could be evaded by the old recourse of hiring Russians to act as "front men."[47]

The failure of the tsarist government to publish the law of April 18 makes it difficult to weigh these claims, but the most detailed account, that of Shepelev, leaves little doubt that Bark, Krivoshein, Rittikh, and the tsar pursued their anticorporate legislative agenda with vigor and enthu-

[46] Heinz-Dietrich Löwe, *Anti-Semitismus und reaktionäre Utopie: Russischer Konservatismus im Kampf gegen dem Wandel von Staat und Gesellschaft, 1890–1917* (Hamburg, 1978), 140, 141 (quoted).
[47] Valentin S. Diakin and others, eds., *Krizis samoderzhaviia, 1895–1917 gg.* (Leningrad, 1984), 444–5. Whether this curiously defensive account of the repressive law of April 18, 1914 represents a welcome trend toward impartiality on the part of cosmopolitan Leningrad historians in an era of relaxed international tensions or a frank acquiescence in the brutal treatment of Jews by the tsarist regime is a question best left to future students of Soviet social science. On the whole, however, this volume provides a well-researched and even-handed treatment of major political and economic trends in the last tsarist period. The section on corporate law, written by Valentin S. Diakin, draws on Shepelev's fine monograph and documents in TsGIA. Diakin argues cogently that the tsarist regime tolerated the growth of syndicates because it considered them economically useful, "not out of a principled defense of the interests of capital" (438, quotation from 442). He also uses a refreshingly apt terminology in arguing that the acrimonious debate over the issue of corporate landholding pitted "bureaucratic red tape and arbitrariness" (*biurokraticheskaia volokita i proizvol*, 442) in most of the ministries against the principle of legal protection for Jews and foreigners in corporate enterprise, as represented none too successfully by the Ministries of Finance and of Trade and Industry.

siasm. To be sure, the Council of Ministers explained the measure as one intended "to facilitate the influx of capital to joint-stock companies" and thereby stimulate economic development. To this end, Jews would not be prohibited from investing in corporations that owned rural land, only from holding managerial positions in them. All the same, Shepelev did not refer to any exemption for mining companies; nor did he indicate that the law affected only new companies, with no retroactive effect,[48] as some contemporaries claimed.

The law of April 18, 1914, had several major consequences. First, it signaled to everyone concerned – manufacturers and landlords, Jews and anti-Semites, citizens of the tsar and foreigners – that the regime stood ready to attack the corporation at its most vulnerable pressure point: exemptions from the restrictive law of 1836. Having refused in 1911–13 to implement a registration system, which would at least have allowed prompt incorporation, the tsarist government now sought to impose, apparently even on existing companies, the most stifling features of the registration system, without granting the positive aspects of such a reform. Nicholas II and his ministers, not content to enforce the restrictions imposed by Alexander III, showed their utter disregard for corporate enterprise as they pursued an almost medieval vision of agrarian Russian life.

Second, it provoked the largest outpouring of protest ever made by the Russian corporate elite. The regime's contempt for the rule of law, its reactionary striving to buttress the economic position of the gentry and peasantry, and its fundamental hostility to modern corporations and banks could no longer be tolerated.

In early May, referring specifically to a repressive corporate law reform prepared in the Ministry of Justice, the AIT denounced the bureaucrats' incessant efforts to keep the operations of corporations "under the tutelage of the government."[49] Even Diakin, who described Rittikh's regulations in the most favorable light, admitted that the industrial spokesmen displayed in 1914 more anger than they had in the past to similarly obtuse measures. At the eighth congress of the AIT in May 1914, Pavel P. Riabushinskii complained that manufacturers must go to Petersburg "bowing humbly [*na poklon*], as to the khan's headquarters" (a reference to the

---

[48] Shepelev, "Tsarizm," 311.
[49] Shepelev, *Kompanii*, 286 (quoted), 287, citing an anonymous article by "D" in *Promyshlennost' i torgovlia*, 1914, no. 9 (May 1), 459–62.

Mongol overlords of medieval Muscovy). Hearty applause greeted his veiled endorsement of a political revolution: "Our country will outlive [*sumeet perezhit'*] its little government." At the same meeting, Jules Goujon hinted that a sharp decrease in foreign capital investment might occur as a result of the law of April 18 and the government's prosecution of syndicates: "If trade and industry remain under the yoke [*pod gnetom*, another reference to the myth of Mongol barbarity] of the police or the police idea, then nothing more can be done." The conservative president of the MEC, Grigorii A. Krestovnikov, long a supporter of autocracy against the liberal minority of Moscow manufacturers, was stunned into redundancy: "This measure is so inconceivable that I refuse to believe that it has occurred."[50]

Count Andrei A. Bobrinskii of the RSSP branded the law of April 18 "a serious constraint on the sugar industry." His telegram elicited from the Council of Ministers two curious arguments: The new law would not affect the rights of existing companies (*ne zatragivaet prav sushchestvuiushchikh uzhe kompanii*); and it would scarcely harm the sugar industry at all, "since this law in no way prohibits joint-stock companies from acquiring landed property *in unlimited amounts*, but only requires that such acquisition depend on the actual need for land,"[51] such need to be determined, presumably, by arbitrary bureaucrats. Avdakov, who led a delegation of AIT leaders to speak with Prime Minister Goremykin in June, received essentially the same assurances. The government simply sought to prevent corporations from amassing unnecessarily large landed estates. Besides, "in certain cases exceptions can be made; with regard to some companies such exceptions have already been made since the regulations were issued."[52] The AIT refused to accept such vague assurances. It demanded that the restrictions not have retroactive effect (this point was apparently unclear even to those who had read the text of the regulations) and insisted

---

[50] Diakin, ed., *Krizis*, 445 (quoted), 446. Gefter, "Tsarizm," 189, portrayed Goujon as a "bourgeois monarchist" who humbly petitioned the tsar for a redress of grievances. Krestovnikov's remark, quoted on 189, note 2, was cited by Gefter from an interview in *Russkie vedomosti*, cited in *Neftianoe delo*, 1914, no. 10, 29. Krestovnikov's consternation owed much to the fact that he was closely related to Krivoshein by marriage, as both men's wives were daughters of the prominent Moscow merchant Timofei S. Morozov (1823–89).

[51] Gefter, "Tsarizm," 192, note 4, quoting a document in TsGIA, f. 1276; italics in original.

[52] Gefter, "Tsarizm," 191–2, citing TsGIA, f. 32. Shepelev, "Tsarizm," 313–14, cited an AIT telegram to Goremykin dated June 21; he also related a visit by Avdakov, Zukowski, and Maydell to Timashev on June 24, as well as Goremykin's meetings with sugar, metal, and lumber producers.

on a change in the law itself. Piecemeal exceptions to the law now appeared unacceptable.[53]

Even more angry was the reaction of Europeans. The predominant role of French investors in south Russian mining and metallurgy made them sensitive to any threatened diminution of the rights of corporations in that area. Senator Paul Doumer, himself a major investor in Produgol', warned the tsarist Foreign Minister Sazonov that the agitation among French businessmen caused by the tsarist government's threat to prosecute Produgol' "could have the most unfortunate consequences." The security of French investments in Russia, he noted ominously, "has been compromised by savage measures [*zhestokie mery*], which no one can justify."[54] With particular reference to the law of April 18, the London *Times* joined the chorus of complaints about tsarist insensitivity to the needs of modern capitalist institutions. To Kokovtsov, an English businessman coldly stated that all the favors bestowed on foreigners by the tsarist government could not induce him to remain active in the Caucasus because "we lack one condition in your country that we cannot do without: *You have no judges of the English type.*"[55]

In their efforts to roll back the law of April 18, 1914, the AIT and other business organizations found few political allies except the government of France. Although the State Duma had helped to initiate the ultimately unsuccessful movement for a registration system of incorporation when it proposed such a reform in 1910, in general, Russian businessmen looked upon the parties represented in the lower chamber of the legislature as excessively doctrinaire, led by intellectuals ignorant of the benefits of capitalist industry.[56] For their part, duma members representing the landlords, peasants, and workers often expressed antipathy toward corporations in general and syndicates in particular. Numerous regulations that favored Russian industrialists, such as the requirement that municipalities, zemstvos, and other organizations purchase Russian rather than

---

[53] Vladimir Ia. Laverychev, *Gosudarstvo i monopolii v dorevoliutsionnoi Rossii* (Moscow, 1982), 90, 187, citing *Neftianoe delo*, 1914, no. 13, cols. 43–5.
[54] Gefter, "Tsarizm," 190, note 5, quoting a document in the foreign ministry archive.
[55] Gefter, "Tsarizm," 190; italics in original. The Englishman's statement about independent judges, quoted from *Rech'* (May 3, 1914), struck Gefter as amusingly supercilious, but there is no reason to doubt the sincerity of the remark or the importance of an impartial judiciary to the functioning of a modern capitalist economy, whether in England or on the edge of Asia.
[56] Berlin, *Burzhuaziia*, 270–5, gives useful details from the period of the Third and Fourth State Dumas: 1907–17.

foreign manufactured goods, intensified this resentment.⁵⁷ For its part, the Russian Cotton Association criticized as "unacceptable" the State Duma's bills of 1913 and 1914 on the abatement of air and water pollution because they made no allowances for the heavy smoke that inevitably accompanied the production of bricks, porcelain, and metals and because they contained standards for water purity in industrial regions that the manufacturers considered unrealistic.⁵⁸ The AIT ridiculed the anticapitalist proclivities of the intelligentsia and peasantry: "The atmosphere in the duma regarding economic questions was an interesting combination of intelligentsia antagonism toward all productive activity, plus a big dose [*s gustoi struei*] of peasant hostility toward all forms of economic behavior except walking behind a plow."⁵⁹

The businessmen won a victory of sorts when Goremykin secured the tsar's agreement to rescind the law of April 18. The prime minister informed the monarch on July 15, 1914, that the law "had greatly constrained corporate activity in the country." Abrogation of the law would also serve to improve diplomatic relations with France as the danger of war with Germany increased. The Council of Ministers would retain, as before, discretionary power over the right of corporations to own land. The tsar approved the action on the following day.⁶⁰

Although the tsar and his advisors appeared to reinstate the policy in effect before April 18, 1914, in fact, Jews found themselves under somewhat more onerous restrictions than before. Goremykin's report specified that companies not be limited to owning a certain amount of land and that Jews be allowed to constitute only a minority on the board of directors

---

⁵⁷ A circular of the naval ministry dated August 15, 1902, which required all Russian ships to purchase domestically produced equipment, is cited with scorn by the U.S. consul in Petersburg: By keeping out foreign merchandise of high quality, "this ordinance destroys one of the greatest incentives in Russia to productive development." Consul W. R. Holloway to Assistant Secretary of State David J. Hill, National Archives Microfilm Publications, Microcopy no. 81, "Despatches from United States Consuls in St. Petersburg, 1803–1906," roll 18, vol. 23, message no. 269, dated Sep. 19, 1902. On agitation in the State Duma against flour and metal cartels, Sovet s"ezdov predstavitelei promyshlennosti i torgovli, *Promyshlennost' i torgovlia v zakonodatel'nykh uchrezhdeniiakh, 1907–1912 gg.* (St. Petersburg, 1912), 474–5; and Mikhail Ia. Gefter, "Bor'ba vokrug sozdaniia metallurgicheskogo tresta v Rossii v nachale XIX v.," *Istoricheskie zapiski*, 47 (1954), 124–48.
⁵⁸ Obshchestvo khlopchatobumazhnykh fabrikantov, *Otchet za 1913–1915 gg.* (Moscow, 1915), 33–41. Goldberg, "Association," chap. 9, gives the best extant discussion of the vexing issue of industrial pollution, never resolved by the tsarist regime.
⁵⁹ Berlin, *Burzhuaziia*, 270–1, quoting the preface to the AIT's review of the Third Duma, *Promyshlennost'... 1907–1912 gg.*, xiii.
⁶⁰ Gefter, "Tsarizm," 192–6.

while being barred completely from executive directorships and control of corporate real estate. As Shepelev noted, none of the guidelines followed by the Council of Ministers from 1906 through 1913 had set restrictions on the activities of Jews as corporate managers or executive directors.[61]

The tsar's signature in July did nothing, of course, to streamline the old concession system. In a speech to the State Council in 1914, the eminent economist Ivan Kh. Ozerov bemoaned delays of from six months to a year in the granting of a corporate charter. Each ministry scrutinized applications so closely that the backlog in the Ministry of Internal Affairs approached three hundred (primarily because of restrictions on Jews in mining enterprises), and the Ministry of Finance pondered almost fifty proposals for new railroad lines. In an effort to circumvent tsarist red tape, Russians resorted to incorporation "in Berlin, in France, or in England," where the registration procedure could be "completed in several days."[62] Even in India, native entrepreneurs under the British Raj during the last four decades of Queen Victoria's reign enjoyed more freedom than the tsarist government granted to its own subjects on the eve of the Great War.[63]

[61] Shepelev, "Tsarizm," 315.
[62] Ivan Ozeroff [Ivan Kh. Ozerov], *Problèmes économiques et financiers de la Russie moderne* (Lausanne, 1916), 126 (quoted), 128–9, 134. Ozerov did not indicate how many Russian entrepreneurs founded such nominally foreign companies. He listed the outmoded corporate law as one of several reasons for Russian economic backwardness (21). Boris V. Anan'ich, "The Economic Policy of the Tsarist Government and Enterprise in Russia from the End of the Nineteenth Century through the Beginning of the Twentieth Century," in Gregory Guroff and Fred V. Carstensen, eds., *Entrepreneurship in Imperial Russia and the Soviet Union* (Princeton, 1983), 138, quoted a memorandum from Ozerov to Minister of Finance Bark in September 1914 complaining of delays of six to nine months in the approval of corporate charters by the Russian bureaucracy.
[63] The Indian Companies Act of 1850 allowed incorporation by registration, and the act of 1857 extended limited liability to all corporations except banks and insurance companies. Radhe S. Rungta, *The Rise of Business Corporations in India, 1851–1900* (Cambridge, 1970), 41, 46–7. To be sure, as the secretary of commerce and industry in India, quoted by Rungta, 215, stated in 1913, "English Company Law when imported into this country requires modifications if it is to deal with conditions which do not exist in England."

7

Tupik (Dead end), 1914–1917

> Merchants and industrialists know that business can be done only when firm foundations of social life exist, when there is confidence in the future, and when firm laws [*tverdyi zakon*] reign, not arbitrariness. Under the old regime, the most prominent representatives of the commercial-industrial class were opponents of the tsarist system because that system exemplified, above all, the rule of arbitrariness and coercion, the lack of legality and of rational control over the expenditure of state resources, and hindrances to personal initiative and independent action; for freedom is the foremost condition of the development of industry.
> – Petrograd Commercial-Industrial Union (1917)[1]

The enormous strains of the war appear to have exerted two rather different effects on tsarist corporate policy. On the one hand, the government eagerly dismantled German and Austrian corporations in the Russian Empire, sometimes to the detriment of the war effort. On the other hand, some officials, notably Minister of Trade and Industry Vsevolod N. Shakhovskoi, endeavored to relax prewar restrictions on corporations so as to facilitate wartime production. However, close examination of his efforts reveals them to have been ineffectual. When the tsarist regime collapsed in February 1917, its corporate law consisted of a confused tangle of inconsistent regulations, including "temporary" statutes that had remained in effect for decades. Although the electoral statement quoted in the epigraph exaggerates the political opposition of the commercial-industrial elite in the prewar period, exasperation increased rapidly from the beginning of World War I to the February revolution.

In power for barely eight months, from February to October 1917, the

---

[1] Petrogradskii torgovo-promyshlennyi soiuz, *Zadachi torgovo-promyshlennogo klassa v uchreditel'nom sobranii* (n.p. [Petrograd], n.d. [1917]), 16–17. According to the endpaper of this publication, members of the Petrograd Commercial-Industrial Union included at least eighteen business organizations, both local (the stock and commodity exchanges) and national (AIT, organizations of flour millers, small industrialists, and others).

Provisional Government wrestled with all the political and social issues that had accumulated in the previous half century. Although it failed, in the wartime emergency, to satisfy the demands of workers and peasants, its reform of the outmoded corporate legislation of the tsarist regime demonstrated how easily the old concessionary system could be abolished by a government responsive to the needs of modern capitalism.

Our survey of the history of Russian corporate law would not be complete without a brief commentary on the wild shifts in policy under the Soviet government. The Bolshevik seizure of power in October 1917, the nationalization of banks in December and of all large factories the following June, and the catastrophe of the Russian Civil War (1918–20) reduced corporations to legal nonentities. The brief accommodation between capitalism and the Soviet regime during the period of the New Economic Policy (NEP) provided, however, a fascinating case of coexistence on the basis of legal structures that bore a strong resemblance to those of the imperial government. The Five-Year Plans obliterated private property in the means of production, but the early years of the Gorbachev period (1985–9) witnessed yet another episode of grudging toleration of corporate capitalism by the Soviet regime.

Half measures during the wartime emergency

The final years of the tsarist period provided ample opportunities for the government to display its principled indifference to the logic of modern capitalism, foreign and domestic. A decree dated February 2, 1915 (promulgated under article 87 of the Fundamental Laws of 1906, that is, prior to approval by the legislature), deprived Austrian, Hungarian, German, and Turkish subjects of the rights to own rural land in the Russian Empire and to serve as directors or employees in any corporation that owned land in Russia.[2] This measure might have had a strategic rationale, but excessive and compulsive xenophobia led the government to adopt other, clearly irrational policies toward corporations owned by enemy subjects. Among these were the decrees of May 10 and July 1, 1915, which required, respectively, the liquidation of any trading firm or corporation in which citizens of the German Empire held predominant interest.

---

[2] *Sbornik deistvuiushchikh postanovlenii, izdannykh v poriadke stat'i 87 osnovnykh gosudarstvennykh zakonov: dopolnenie k Sbornika, izdannomu v 1913 godu* (Petrograd, 1915), 277–85, article 2 on corporations and 4 on rural landownership.

Because Germany had been the most important trading partner of the Russian Empire before 1914, the economic effects of these decrees proved devastating to the economy. Even more importantly, however, they demonstrated that the tsarist government resisted the notion of the corporation as a juridical person. In 1916, Sergei P. Nikonov, a member of the law faculty of Petrograd University, stressed that the tsarist government had consistently failed to distinguish between the corporation and the stockholders who owned the enterprise. Nikonov, who preferred to view the corporation as a distinct legal entity separate from its stockholders and managers, criticized the bureaucracy for its decrees, issued in 1915 and 1916, that abolished corporations in Russia simply because they were owned by German subjects. Such laws proceeded from the erroneous assumption that the company represented the "personification" of its owners rather than a juridical person whose existence and perquisites were defined by its charter.[3]

The sorry effects of this crude policy on the Russian economy can be seen from the well-documented case of one enterprise. The trading firm of Wogau and Company fell under the provisions of the decrees of May and July 1915 because 4 million of the 12 million rubles' worth of capital owned by the partners in this limited partnership (*tovarishchestvo na vere*) belonged to German subjects and because the firm's partners held key positions in twenty major Russian companies. The firm, a pioneer in the development of banking, insurance, copper, iron, cement, and other corporations in Russia, paid the ultimate price for its enterprising activities in the previous decades. The companies that it had fostered suffered as well. Thus, the state took control of the Anchor Insurance Company and forced Wogau and Company to sell its shares in the International Bank, the Petrograd Discount and Loan Bank, the Russo-Asian Bank, the Kol'chugin Copper Company, and many other companies. The British ambassador and the tsarist minister of foreign affairs protested vainly on behalf of one of the firm's five partners, a British subject named Schumacher, as did the minister of trade and industry on behalf of the firm itself. The ministers of war, internal affairs, and justice even sought to close the Anchor and Kol'chugin companies. The government finally decided to appoint its own representatives, endowed with veto power, to the boards of various corporations – Kol'chugin, Anchor, Beloretsk Iron, Moscow

---

[3] Sergei P. Nikonov, *Iuridicheskaia priroda torgovykh i promyshlennykh predpriiatii po russkomu pravu* (Petrograd, 1917), 89.

Electrolytic, and numerous textile companies – in which the Wogau clan had played a major financial or managerial role. Most of the twenty companies were either abolished or suspended by government order.

In desperation, the company published a pamphlet detailing the history of the firm and its many contributions to Russian economic development. None of the full partners owed allegiance to the German emperor, and Schumacher was the subject of an allied power. Although the partners Mauritz Marc and his son Hugo had, it is true, taken Russian citizenship as late as November 1914, they and a third partner, Rudolf Hermann, had received St. Vladimir and St. Anna medals for their outstanding business activities.[4] This pamphlet apparently enlightened no one but historians in later decades, for the government liquidated Wogau and Company on September 10, 1916. It did not act in defiance of the public mood. A large mob burned the firm's office in the Anchor Insurance Company building on Lubianka Square in the heart of the Moscow commercial district. The archive of this unique enterprise also perished in the flames.[5]

The arbitrary and shortsighted policy of the Russian government contrasted sharply with the British government's acceptance of the wartime naturalization of George von Chauvin, the talented director of the firm of Siemens Brothers in England from 1899 onward. Although trade with Germany was of course outlawed once the war began, Chauvin simply renounced his German citizenship in November 1914 and dropped the particle from his name. He continued to serve his company and, through it, the British electrical industry until his retirement in 1925.[6]

The failure of the tsarist government to devise a consistent policy toward corporations before the war meant that various unsatisfactory palliatives had to be devised once the emergency engulfed the country. Confusion reigned in the regulations regarding corporate bond issues. Ten years of

---

[4] Erik Amburger, "Das Haus Wogau & Co. in Moskau und der Wogau-Konzern, 1840–1917," in Amburger, *Fremde und Einheimische in Wirtschafts- und Kulturleben des neuzeitlichen Russland: Ausgewählte Aufsätze*, ed. Klaus Zernack (Wiesbaden, 1982), 78–82; Iosif F. Gindin and K. N. Tarnovskii, eds., "Istoriia monopolii Vogau (torgovogo doma 'Vogau i Ko')," in A. L. Sidorov, ed., *Dokumenty po istorii monopolisticheskogo kapitalizma v Rossii* (Moscow, 1959), vol. 6 of *Materialy po istorii SSSR*, 641–738; listed are the many prominent companies, tied to the Wogau firm, that were liquidated, suspended, or subordinated to government control in 1915 and 1916 (677–97).

[5] The pamphlet was reprinted in Gindin and Tarnovskii, "Istoriia," 697–737. Amburger, "Haus," 79, blamed the governor-general of Moscow, Prince Iusupov, for instigating the mob; protests from allied and neutral powers led to the prince's resignation.

[6] J. D. Scott, *Siemens Brothers, 1858–1958: An Essay in the History of Industry* (London, 1958), 73, 82, 92.

work on a reform of corporate bonds ended in failure in 1915. Business groups (the AIT, PSMFO, PEC, MEC, and the Association of Trade and Agriculture) proposed allowing companies to issue bonds equal in value to three-fourths of their equipment, such as ships and machinery, and without a waiting period. The bureaucrats held to traditional guidelines: Only real estate could be considered in fixing the value of assets with which a corporation backed its bonds, and most corporate charters limited the amount of any future bond issue to one-half of the share capital. (The strict limits on corporate landholding and the widespread practice of leasing rather than purchasing land, as in the Ukrainian coal fields, made these rules doubly repressive.) Fearing that the capital market might be swamped with securities of dubious value, policy makers insisted that a company obtain the state's permission prior to any bond offering. The Ministry of Trade and Industry proposed yet another device to protect the interests of bondholders: that they be allowed to elect representatives to the annual general assembly of stockholders. As usual, no law resulted from these discussions, but the disagreements between businessmen and bureaucrats showed the depths of differences in both perception and policy among the two groups. For example, the Petersburg businessmen, who opposed various restrictions in the bill, commented caustically on the proposal for special ministerial permission prior to each new bond issue. Not only in Western Europe but in Hungary as well, corporations were permitted to offer bonds to the public under a general statute. By this means "the element of arbitrariness is ruled out as being completely incompatible [*nesovmestnyi*] with the very concept of law."[7]

Besides regulations governing corporate taxation, which remained mired in confusion to the very end,[8] the perennial question of incorporation by

[7] Leonid E. Shepelev, *Aktsionernye kompanii v Rossii* (Leningrad, 1973), 288–93; quotation from Obshchestvo zavodchikov i fabrikantov, "Proekt pravil otnositel'no vypuska obligatsii torgovo-promyshlennymi aktsionernymi obshchestvami (tovarishchestvami na paiakh)" (St. Petersburg, 1912), 2. This pamphlet was a joint statement of the PSMFO, the PEC, and the Council of the Stock Exchange (*sovet fondovogo otdela*) within the Petersburg Exchange (*birzha*).

[8] It is possible here only to hint at the many vexing facets of this complicated question. On the impact of the corporate income tax schedule issued on January 2, 1906 (*PSZ* 3–27178), see Fred V. Carstensen, *American Enterprise in Foreign Markets: Studies of Singer and International Harvester in Imperial Russia* (Chapel Hill, 1984), 91–5. On the marked increase in corporate tax revenues in ensuing years, see "Promyshlennost' i nalogi," *Gorno-zavodskoe delo*, 18, no. 10 (March 12, 1910), 344, which paraphrased a speech by V. I. Massal'skii at an economic banquet hosted by the liberal Moscow textile manufacturer Pavel P. Riabushinskii. A protest by the PSMFO against various limitations on corporate salaries (implemented in 1898 to prevent managers from granting themselves excessive bonuses so as to reduce the nominal profits of the enterprise, thereby diminishing its tax burden)

concession or registration came under discussion once again in the emergency brought on by the war. Here, as often in the decades since 1836, the clash of opinions proved both sharp and inconclusive. In the fall of 1915, Prince Shakhovskoi's ministry began work on a bill to facilitate the incorporation of new enterprises, to be implemented as an emergency measure under article 87 of the Fundamental Laws. Shakhovskoi's plan, which he saw as a major step toward a simplified concession system to be established after the war, centered on a "model charter" (*normal'nyi ustav*). Any company would receive prompt confirmation of its charter by the Ministry of Trade and Industry if it met certain guidelines: a minimum capital of 75,000 rubles (in contrast to the current 100,000); a minimum stock price of 100 rubles; the sale of one-quarter of the shares in the first six months and of the total within two years; and future increases in basic capital that reflected growth in the reserve capital of the company. A basic capitalization of 600,000 rubles or more would have entitled a company to petition the minister of trade and industry for permission to issue bonds. Five percent of the annual net profit was to have gone into the reserve capital fund until it equaled one-third of the basic capital. Up to one-third of the stock could be represented by one person at the general assembly, in contrast to the one-tenth maximum in most charters. Permission of the minister of trade and industry would be necessary if a corporation sought to purchase land where it was denied to foreigners and Jews, and in such a corporation, non-Jews and Russian citizens must occupy the posts of executive director, mining supervisor, and real estate manager and a majority of the seats on the board. Within these guidelines, the minister would also have been empowered to grant changes to an existing charter. If a charter contained provisions that went beyond these limits, it must be approved by the Council of Ministers (but not the tsar).[9]

In his memoirs, Prince Shakhovskoi claimed that his corporate reform bill of May 1916 contained no restrictions on Jews in corporate positions: "I defended my position with the argument that often the non-Jews elected

---

is in TsGIA, f. 150, op. 1, ed. khr. 58, l. 84 recto. This law is also discussed by Józef Kaczkowski, "Towarzystwa akcyjne w państwie rosyjskiem: Studyum prawno-ekonomiczne," *Ekonomista*, 8 (1908), no. 1, 98. Linda J. Bowman, "The Business Tax in Imperial Russia, 1775–1917," doctoral dissertation, University of California, Los Angeles, 1982, stressed the "regressive" nature of business taxes even after 1905 and the "drastically increased tax rates" imposed during World War I. Following Carstensen and others, she noted the distortions that resulted from tax evasion: "The size of capital invested in corporations consequently had more to do with taxation than with actual investment patterns" (288, 302, 289).

[9] Shepelev, *Kompanii*, 317–19.

to these posts were simply front men [*podstavnye litsa*], while the Jews ran the business. I insisted that the persons serving in such posts should be elected, and that I saw no basis for the restrictions." Ever loyal to his monarch, he noted proudly that the tsar upheld the opinion of the minority, which supported Shakhovskoi.[10] In 1875, such a reform would have opened the way to a modern corporate economy unencumbered by ethnic restrictions. Four decades later, the change represented only a tiny step toward the relaxation of the bureaucratic stranglehold. Certainly in wartime, this measure, by itself, would have done little to invigorate the economy or to change the commercial and industrial leaders' opinion that the tsarist regime was incompetent to win the war.

Nor can Shakhovskoi be considered a consistent defender of economic rationality as the industrialists perceived the concept. Shortly after his appointment in February 1915 as minister of trade and industry in place of the more experienced Sergei I. Timashev (1909–15), Shakhovskoi fell into a shouting match with the south Russian coal producers over the reasons for the wartime fuel shortage. The coal men blamed the inadequate capacity of the railroads, while the new minister pointed to diminishing production, "which he ascribed to labor shortages caused not by military conscription but by low wages and poor living conditions at the mines." This "major confrontation" pushed the industrial leadership into an open political clash with the bureaucracy at the Ninth AIT Congress in May 1915.[11]

Although Shakhovskoi failed to implement his concession reform bill, he did succeed in relaxing restrictions on corporate landholding for those companies whose properties in the western provinces had fallen into enemy hands, were threatened with capture, or carried out war production. A resolution of the Council of Ministers, approved by the tsar on April 5, 1916, gave the minister of trade and industry temporary wartime authority to grant land to companies evacuated from the war zone, in spite of existing real estate restrictions, as long as the land was necessary for the operations of the enterprise and the minister informed the council on each occasion.

[10] Vsevolod N. Shakhovskoi, *"Sic transit gloria mundi" (Tak prokhodit mirskaia slava), 1893–1917 gg.* (Paris, 1952), 178. Leonid E. Shepelev, "Aktsionernoe zakonodatel'stvo vremennogo pravitel'stva," in N. E. Nosov and others, eds., *Issledovaniia po sotsial'no-politicheskoi istorii Rossii* (Leningrad, 1971), 372, noted that Shakhovskoi sought to implement Witte's unsuccessful plan for a model charter in 1901. Whether or not the bill became law, it did not appear in the *SURP* for 1916.

[11] Ruth Amende Roosa, "Russian Industrialists during World War I: The Interaction of Economics and Politics," in Guroff and Carstensen, eds., *Entrepreneurship*, 167 (quoted); on the resulting leftward political drift, 168–75.

On May 13, 1916, the tsar authorized Prince Shakhovskoi to allow emergency acquisition of up to fifty desiatinas (135 acres) of land by companies evacuated from the war zone, in danger of capture by the enemy, or engaged in war production, without a general assembly meeting. However, board members became personally liable for reimbursing stockholders if such an action resulted in a loss to the company. Another decree, issued the same day, gave Shakhovskoi similar wartime powers over all companies supplying the army and navy, but it set a two-year time limit and banned any relocation to the Don Military Region and the Amur Region. On October 18, 1916, the first decree of May 13 was amended to allow Shakhovskoi to grant permission for the use of corporate property as collateral for government loans, without general assembly approval, subject to directors' liability for any losses.[12] These reforms, enacted as temporary measures, owed their existence to the war emergency. Business leaders found little to praise in them.

In May 1916, forty-six members of the State Duma called for a liberal registration system, with no restrictions on land ownership or function and low minima (twenty thousand rubles of capitalization and a par share value of twenty-five rubles!). At this time, Aleksandr I. Vyshnegradskii delivered a strongly worded call for corporate law reform on behalf of the Russian Banking Association, in which he served as president. He warned that the influx of European capital necessary to rebuild the shattered Russian economy after the war would be

> significantly hampered if the Russian government were to adhere to its policy of religious and national restrictions in the field of corporate law. The banks venture to express the opinion that without liberal reforms [in this regard] our industry will scarcely justify the hopes placed upon it for its emancipation from foreign dependence and the creation of new sources of national wealth.[13]

A year later, the bankers renewed their attack on the arbitrary nature of laws affecting corporations.

> A large portion of legislative norms have as their goal the limitation, by some means [or another], of banking activities or their supervision under the vigilant

---

[12] *SURP*, 1916, part 1, nos. 730, 1009, 1204, and 2324. The last decree, in typical bureaucratic jargon, consisted of one sentence fifteen lines long. Shepelev, *Kompanii*, 320, noted that the second decree of May 13 passed despite the opposition of Assistant Minister of Internal Affairs Nikolai V. Pleve, who had warned in January that such a relaxation of the real estate laws affecting corporations "would significantly nullify the government's efforts, over many years, to protect the common Russian people [*massa russkogo naroda*] from the harmful influence of the Jews."

[13] Shepelev, *Kompanii*, 322–3; Vyshnegradskii quoted on 322.

eyes of government agents. And when, under the pressures of the requirements of life, a law is needed to expand the banks' sphere of action or to modify the basis of some banking operations, the legislator constantly resorts to the system of administrative permission from the Ministry of Finance, which is based only on its subjective discretion.

In light of European corporate law, "the limitations placed on banking activities by our tradition of charters [*nashi ustavnye traditsii*] do not at all correspond to the present demands of economic life."[14] To the very end, the tsarist bureaucracy ignored such calls for a rational corporate law.

The aftermath: corporate legislation of the Provisional Government and the Soviet regime

The story of the tsarist bureaucracy's intransigence ended, of course, with the fall of the government in February 1917. Privately owned corporations continued to flourish in Russia until the Bolshevik coup in October of that year, but they barely coexisted with nominally "socialist" institutions under the NEP (1921–8). In view of the autocratic nature of both the tsarist and Soviet governments, it should come as no surprise that the latter allowed the capitalist corporation scarcely more scope than had the former.

On March 10, only a few days after the tsar's abdication, the Provisional Government announced its intention to reform the corporate law. Less than a month later, Minister of Trade and Industry Aleksandr I. Konovalov produced a law that corresponded to his ideal of entrepreneurial freedom, long denied to him and his fellow manufacturers in the past. The new statute abolished all religious, ethnic, and citizenship restrictions on corporate officers, staff, and stockholders, except for citizens of countries then at war with Russia. Konovalov also promulgated simplified regulations for incorporation and for changing the charters of companies already in existence. So liberal were the new minima – a basic capital of twenty

[14] Quoted in Leonid E. Shepelev, "Arkhivnye fondy aktsionernykh kommercheskikh bankov," *Problemy istochnikovedeniia*, 7 (1959), 76; and Vladimir Ia. Laverychev, "K voprosu o vmeshatel'stve tsarizma v ekonomicheskuiu zhizn' Rossii v nachale XX v.," in I. M. Pushkareva and others, eds., *Samoderzhavie i krupnyi kapital v Rossii v kontse XIX–nachale XX v.: sbornik statei* (Moscow, 1982), 89. Shepelev and Laverychev quoted different passages from the same document: Komitet s"ezdov predstavitelei aktsionernykh kommercheskikh bankov, *O zhelatel'nykh izmeneniiakh v postanovke aktsionernogo bankovogo dela v Rossii* (Petrograd, 1917), but Shepelev cited the archive in which the pamphlet is held: TsGIA, f. 1553, op. 1, d. 20.

thousand rubles and a par share value of twenty-five rubles – and so few were the formalities of incorporation with the permission of Konovalov's ministry that the AIT joyfully announced on April 1 that the Russian state had essentially implemented the long-awaited system of incorporation by registration (*iavochnaia sistema*).

Konovalov, an outspoken critic of the tsarist corporate law in the previous decade, took this opportunity to disparage once more "the restrictions by which the old regime stifled individual development [*dushil proiavlenie lichnosti*].'"[15] He laid special emphasis on the failure of the tsarist government "to draw up a more or less coherent program of mining legislation," echoing the criticism of the Ural metal producers, who in 1910 had called the Metallurgy Council (sovet po gornopromyshlennym delam) "a superfluous agency that even causes harm."[16] For its part, the RSSP printed with apparent approval the decree of March 10, which asserted that the "complicated procedure" imposed by the tsarist government had "severely hindered the development of Russian trade and industry" in general.[17]

European observers likewise greeted the reform with enthusiasm. As a Frenchman with close ties to Russian industry observed, Konovalov's abolition of the old "leading-strings" (*lisières*) on Russian industry reduced to "several days or at the most several weeks" the period between the application for a corporate charter and the beginning of business operations. In similar terms, an Englishman castigated the old tsarist system as "a remnant of barbarity."[18]

The areas of the tsarist empire that acquired independence in the wake of the war and revolution also adopted modern forms of corporate legislation. The government of independent Poland inaugurated in February 1919 the limited-liability partnership modeled on the German GmbH in areas formerly under Austrian and Russian rule, and that same month a registry of corporate enterprises began to function in Lodz.[19]

[15] Shepelev, "Zakonodatel'stvo," 370, 373, 378 (quoted).
[16] Laverychev, "K voprosu," 91–2, quoting from TsGIA, f. 48 and 37.
[17] *Vestnik sakharnoi promyshlennosti*, 18, no. 12 (Mar. 19/Apr. 1, 1917), 224.
[18] Raoul Labry, *L'industrie russe et la révolution* (Paris, 1919), 79; William H. Beable, *Commercial Russia* (New York, 1919), 90.
[19] Francis Bauer Czarnomski, ed., *The Polish Handbook, 1925* (London, 1925), 337; on Lodz, Bolesław Pełka, "Organizacja i historia łódzkiej giełdy pieniężnej i jej akta," *Archeion*, 46 (1967), 164, note 18. By the mid-1920s, the codification of the Polish civil law had not yet reached completion, owing largely to the problem of revising five separate legal systems used on Polish soil before 1918, from the Austrian civil code of 1811 to what Czarnomski, 335, called "the primitive Russian Civil Law." In areas previously under Russian control, a presidential decree dated June 25, 1924, set minimum corporate capitalization at 100,000

Dead end, 1914–1917   191

The Baltic republics did the same. In Latvia, for example, corporate laws issued on April 25 and 26, 1925, abolished tsarist charters and created a normative system with a minimum of 100,000 Lats for commercial and industrial companies and 5 million Lats for banks. Latvian citizenship was required of a third of the managers of industrial corporations and of two-thirds in others. In the mid-1930s, however, the authoritarian regime of Karlis Ulmanis inaugurated a policy of "state capitalism," under which at least three-quarters of the shares in joint-stock companies were owned by the Latvian Credit Bank and various state agencies. The sources of this policy apparently lay in both the tsarist bureaucratic tradition and Ulmanis's admiration for Italian fascism.[20]

During the civil war that followed the Bolshevik seizure of power, V. Popov, the acting minister of trade and industry in the Don Military Region, blamed the tsarist regime for hindering industrial development and for promoting the growth of Bolshevism through its toleration of "unjustified repression" of the workers. To prevent new companies in the Cossack lands from enjoying too much entrepreneurial freedom, however, Popov announced a procedure for the incorporation of new companies through the familiar method of special permission.[21]

Especially striking was the element of continuity in autocratic policies represented by both the tsarist and Soviet treatment of corporations. In the tumult of revolution and civil war, the Supreme Economic Council (VSNKh) outlawed the creation of new corporations, but under the NEP the Soviet government adopted policies reminiscent of those of the tsarist regime. In keeping with its relaxed control of small-scale agriculture, trade, and industry, the government on April 10, 1923, issued a decree that allowed corporations to operate within certain financial limits. As under the tsars, however, special permission was required for the creation of each new corporation.[22] Soviet legislators reiterated the traditional dis-

---

zlotys (250,000 for insurance companies, 1 to 2.5 million for banks depending on location, and 5 million for mortgage banks) and the minimum share price at 10 zlotys (100 in banks); shares could be named or made out to the bearer. In areas previously under Austrian and Russian control, each charter required confirmation by the Ministries of Finance and of Trade and Industry. Czarnomski, ed., *Polish Handbook*, 336–7.

[20] Percy Meyer, *Latvia's Economic Life* (Riga, 1925), 127–8. On the 1930s, Nicholas Balabkins and Arnolds Aizsilnieks, *Entrepreneur in a Small Country: A Case Study Against the Background of the Latvian Economy, 1919–1940* (Hicksville, N.Y., 1975), 71–74, 82.

[21] Bol'shoi krug, *Materialy*, August 1918, "Kratkie svedeniia po otdelu torgovli i promyshlennosti," 1–4, 17; quotation from 4.

[22] On the council's ban on new corporations, issued April 18, 1918, see V. Z. Drobizhev, "Bor'ba russkoi burzhuazii protiv natsionalizatsii promyshlennosti v 1917–1920 gg.," *Istoricheskie zapiski*, 68 (1961), 32. The reversal of this policy five years later was announced

tinctions between firms of varying degrees of complexity: the simple partnership (with oral contracts!) for enterprises owning less than five hundred rubles of capital; the full partnership without limited liability; and the limited partnership with limited liability for investors only. They added the "partnership with limited liability," modeled on the German GmbH.[23] However, when dealing with the large corporation, they seemed as bewildered as their tsarist predecessors.

The Soviet statutes (articles 322–366 of the Civil Code) might well have been drafted by Timashev himself. Both *aktsionernye obshchestva* and *paevye tovarishchestva* existed without the slightest structural or juridical differences between them; investors enjoyed limited liability; small companies were formed through a process of routine confirmation by the VSNKh, but permission of the Council of Labor and Defense was necessary if capitalization exceeded 1 million rubles, and the Council of People's Commissars must approve any corporate charter that deviated from existing laws; capitalization and share price minima were set at 100,000 and 100 rubles, respectively, except for pawnshops and other small enterprises; the People's Commissariat of Finance approved the charters of small banks under a normative system; and all new charters were published in the Collection of Statutes and Decrees of the Workers' and Peasants' Government. Unlike the tsarist law, of course, the Soviet statutes lacked ethnic restrictions, but both systems recognized cartels and trusts. Under the NEP, the VSNKh held discretionary power to authorize the creation of "syndicates and other commercial-industrial combinations."[24]

Confusion about the appropriate role of the capitalist corporation in a nominally socialist society continued to the very end of the NEP. Part of the problem can be attributed to the extreme centralization inherent in the Soviet mode of rule. In addition, basic conceptual problems inherited from the tsarist period remained to be solved. How could the point at which a corporation began to exist be defined without excessive restriction or laxness? Were corporate charters to be considered laws, and if so, how could exceptions from the general law be implemented?

At the second conference of legal experts in state industry (*iuriskonsul'ty*

in *Sobranie uzakonenii i rasporiazhenii rabochego i krest'ianskogo pravitel'stva SSSR*, 1923, issue 29, no. 336. On the Kremlin's economic policy during the early years of NEP, see Alan Ball, "Lenin and the Question of Private Trade in Soviet Russia," *Slavic Review*, 43, no. 3 (Fall 1984), 399–412.

[23] Iosif [Leont'evich] Braude, *Aktsionernye obshchestva i tovarishchestva v torgovle i promyshlennosti*, 2nd ed. (Moscow, 1926), 46, 52, 60, 68, 318–19.

[24] Braude, *Obshchestva*, 7–43, paraphrasing the Civil Code of the USSR; quotation from 35.

gospromyshlennosti), held in Moscow in 1927, the legal expert L. A. Landau stressed the contradiction inherent in the issuing of corporate charters that carried the force of law:

> Whenever we have a concession system [*razreshitel'naia sistema*], in which every charter is considered a special law, it is absolutely essential to adapt this charter and the norms of this charter to the needs of a particular case. We [often] have a special law that revokes the general law, and therefore we now have charters that are completely at variance with the general statutes.

Landau favored a further centralization of the concession system instead of the confirmation of new charters by people's commissariats in the various republics, a practice that would only have fostered the proliferation of charters with provisions contrary to the general law.[25] Even more unsettling were the practices described by one Bakhshisaraitsev. Because the law left unclear the criteria for the legal existence of a company, some new enterprises began operations prior to being certified by the state; a few did so before their charters had been written! Another expert, A. M. Gintsburg, concluded that no "general industrial code of laws" (*obshche-promyshlennyi kodeks*) existed, "and it will probably be a very, very long time before it does."[26]

The main speaker at the conference, L. A. Vinogradov, looked hopefully to the day when "joint-stock companies would be drawn into a single governmental system of administration over the national economy." However, he observed ruefully that although German jurists were already expressing interest in a new Anglo-American idea – increasing the power of the board of directors for the sake of economic efficiency, with a corresponding decline in the power of the general assembly – "here we are clinging to the old school, that of the late nineteenth century." It was still impossible for the VSNKh to influence a given enterprise through regional economic councils, an exercise he likened to gesticulating before "a funhouse mirror" (*krivoe zerkalo*). With regret he reported that some cooperatives joined together into a corporation solely to take advantage of tax laws, with the result that they fostered "capitalist, antisocialist forms, which are alien to us. We wish to protect cooperation from the loss of its social significance." It is true that a decree of the Council of People's Commissars, dated February 15, 1927, ordered trusts, as well as companies

---

[25] L. A. Landau, commenting on the speech by L. A. Vinogradov in A. Shneerov, ed., *Voprosy promyshlennogo prava* (Moscow, 1928), 115.
[26] Bakhshitsaraitsev, commenting on the speech by Vinogradov, in Shneerov, ed., *Voprosy*, 117. Quotation from a speech on trusts by A. M. Gintsburg, 19.

with minority state ownership, to reduce their administrative expenses to 15 percent of the total through structural simplification, personnel reductions, decreases in wages, and other measures, but the implementation of such a sweeping change appeared problematic, given the chronic confusion regarding the right of various agencies to control certain enterprises.[27]

In an eerie way, Vinogradov's complaints suggested that the Soviet government found the dynamism of the capitalist corporation no less threatening than had the tsarist regime, although for very different ideological reasons. In the following decade, this same aversion became clear in Germany at the opposite end of the conventional ideological spectrum. A Nazi jurist stressed the incompatibility of Hitler's regime with the principles of European corporate law; his blueprint for regimenting the corporation closely resembled that of the tsarist regime and of the Soviet government in the 1920s. The main "reforms" proposed by this expert included the reduction of anonymity in the corporation through stable stockholder groups, increased personal responsibility of managers, requirements to issue named shares in large denominations, the extension of liability to stockholders, and the authority of the state to veto appointments to boards and audit committees and to prevent a company from being liquidated by its stockholders. All these proposals conflicted fundamentally with the essential nature of the modern corporation.[28]

Nor did the solution to the problem of excessive bureaucratic control in the Soviet Union lie in centralized planning after the abandonment of the NEP.[29] Perhaps it was Stalin himself who best deserved the infamous label of "wrecker" for imposing wholesale irrationalities on the Soviet economy, to say nothing of the waste of human resources occasioned by the purges. As one English salesman who worked in Russia from 1900 to 1931 recalled:

In the sense of a settled policy, there is no Plan. The uncertainty about everything in Russia, always great since the Revolution, has become increased a thousandfold since 1928, when the Plan was inaugurated. Everything is topsy-turvy, and the

---

[27] "Doklad L. A. Vinogradova," in Shneerov, ed., *Voprosy*, 103, 104 (quoted), 105 (quoted), 106, 121 (quoted).
[28] Paul Fischer, *Die Aktiengesellschaft in der nationalsozialistischen Wirtschaft: Ein Beitrag zur Reform des Gesellschaftsrechts* (Munich, 1936), in the series Schriften der Akademie für Deutsches Recht, 61–82 and 140.
[29] The irrationalities of the NEP and the First Five-Year Plan are vividly described in the memoirs of Vladimir N. Ipatieff [Ipat'ev], *The Life of a Chemist: Memoirs, 1867–1930*, trans. Vladimir Haensel and Mrs. Ralph H. Lusher (Stanford, 1946).

Dead end, 1914–1917   195

quick changes of policy have become bewildering.... The only constant is the lack of funds, and the pickpocket methods employed [by the state] to obtain them."[30]

The attitudes of Soviet managers in this system, according to one careful study, mirrored those of the capitalists under the tsarist regime. Economic rationality had its own imperatives, but so powerful were the bureaucratic constraints that no political opposition appeared possible, whether by the "bourgeois specialists" hired in the 1920s, the "red directors" who perished obediently in Stalin's purge, or their successors in the technocracy. "At almost every step, the technicians have bowed to the dictates of the ruling elite, and, in those cases where they have proved somewhat recalcitrant, their resistance has ultimately been futile."[31] These words form a fitting epitaph for Goujon, Konovalov, and Żukowski in their vain struggle for a modern corporate law under the tsarist ministers Timashev and Shakhovskoi.

The phenomenon of inefficient planning impervious to the rationalizing impulses of the managerial elite did not fade during the three decades following the death of Stalin. As Joseph S. Berliner observed, referring to the most recent period of Soviet economic history, "It is nevertheless surprising that with all the resources devoted to technological advance, so few genuinely new innovations can be credited to the USSR, particularly in the postwar period when the Soviets began to draw abreast of the world technology in a growing number of fields."[32] Like

---

[30] John Wynne Hird, *Under Czar and Soviet: My Thirty Years in Russia* (London, 1932), 177. One economic historian has spoken of the "economic dislocations of the early thirties" that Stalin found it necessary to blame on others. Gregory Guroff, "The Red-Expert Debate: Continuities in the State-Entrepreneur Tension," in Guroff and Carstensen, eds., *Entrepreneurship*, 222. Granick noted that Weber's ideal type of a rational bureaucracy had nothing in common with Stalin's party-state, characterized by chaotic managerial methods, rapid changes in production priorities, and "arbitrary" interventions by the Communist Party apparatus (to say nothing of the NKVD) at every level of the industrial pyramid, in defiance of formal bureaucratic rules: David Granick, *Management of the Industrial Firm in the USSR: A Study in Soviet Economic Planning* (New York, 1954), 262–8, quotation from 267. Apparently oblivious to these crucial cultural and institutional factors, Walt W. Rostow, *The Stages of Economic Growth* (Cambridge, 1962), 93, stated that "Russian economic development over the past century is remarkably similar to that of the United States, with a lag of about thirty-five years in the level of industrial output and a lag of a half-century in *per capita* output in industry." Even in his discussion of the differences between the United States and the Soviet Union (98–100), Rostow failed to mention the economic irrationalities of the Stalin era.
[31] Jeremy R. Azrael, *Managerial Power and Soviet Politics* (Cambridge, Mass., 1966), 173. He distinguished four phases in Soviet managerial history, those of the "bourgeois specialists," "red directors," "red specialists" after the Great Purge, and "the new managerial elite."
[32] Joseph S. Berliner, "Entrepreneurship in the Soviet Period: An Overview," in Guroff and Carstensen, eds., *Entrepreneurship*, 199–200. The many problems facing Soviet research institutes specifically charged with economic innovation are discussed in a well-

the tsarist regime, the Soviet government refused to relax its economic restrictions out of fear that the inherent dynamism of independent enterprises would cause unwanted economic and social consequences. It too paid a staggering price in the underdevelopment of its industrial capacity.

It remains to be seen whether the legalization of corporations in the guise of cooperatives and associations by the Gorbachev regime will lead to a new and more successful accommodation between the Russian autocracy and capitalism. Strong echoes of the tsarist legislation of 1836 and the decrees of the early Soviet government under the NEP may be perceived in Gorbachev's reforms. Whether or not his advisors consciously modeled their reforms on the tsarist corporate law, they have quite understandably gravitated toward the concessionary system. Hallowed by centuries of existence before 1928, that system permitted the autocracy to hold a monopoly of political power while allowing a limited amount of autonomy to capitalist energies.

Still, as under the tsarist regime, the accommodation now taking shape under the Gorbachev regime is based on an imperfect legal foundation. For example, the laws allowing joint ventures between Soviet and foreign enterprises – Resolutions 48 and 49, passed on January 13, 1987 – suffer from what Ninel' Voznesenskaia of the Institute of State and Law has called a "legal vacuum":

> It was our institute's proposal that laws be worked up and adopted like the joint-stock legislation that exists in all countries today. Unfortunately, we somehow manage to do without it: a situation fraught with serious conflicts. . . . The joint-stock legislation that exists in capitalist, socialist, and developing countries . . . makes it easier for [joint enterprises] to be set up and also serves as an effective form of control by the government. When joint enterprises are registered, the concerned government organ would be able to check up on how their regulations and agreements might affect our legislation. How can this comparison be made if no such legislation exists? . . . Unfortunately, the USSR is one of the few countries where this approach has been completely ignored. So the situation must be resolved.[33]

documented essay in the same volume by Paul Cocks, "Organizing for Technological Innovation in the 1980s," 306–46.

[33] Interview in Nikolai Zaborin, "Trade Links: What the Law Says," *Moscow News*, July 1988, 14 (modified translation). Even the reform authorizing the establishment of small cooperative enterprises through local registration, instead of the granting of a charter by the Moscow government, has entangled hopeful entrepreneurs in monumental coils of red tape, to judge by delays encountered by the prospective founders of a kitchen-appliance workshop in Rostov-on-Don in early 1989: two months for police permission and ten months for the acquisition of a seal. Robert Cullen, "Letter from Rostov-on-Don," *The*

Again, the lack of adequate legislation has been recognized by experts as a hindrance to rational economic development, but the introduction of firm legal norms necessarily threatens the unlimited power of the autocratic state. Will the Gorbachev regime soon resolve the dilemma that confounded the tsarist bureaucracy for more than a century?

New Yorker, June 12, 1989, 107. In tsarist charters, the seal (*pechat'*) of a corporation was optional.

8

Autocracy, corporate law, and the dilemma of cultural delay

> Someday the future historian of our era will note its curious feature: In small clashes over trifling issues he will discover the slow but relentless action of the powerful currents of history.
>
> – Petr B. Struve (1897)[1]

The main theme of the history of Russian corporate law – the survival of the restrictive features of the legislation of 1836 into the era of railroads, steel mills, and electricity – provides an instructive reminder of the essential continuity of tsarist policy toward capitalist institutions. Created to protect investors from unscrupulous manipulators of corporate stock prices, the law of 1836 established a procedure for incorporation that placed the fate of each new company in the hands of the bureaucracy. Neither Reutern, Witte, nor Timashev abandoned this cumbersome device in favor of the registration system (*iavochnaia sistema*), which predominated in Europe, the United States, and even Japan by the end of the nineteenth century.

An equally important theme is that piecemeal changes in the law of 1836, such as the recognition of unnamed corporate shares by the 1860s and the legalization of futures deals in 1893, did not signify increased liberalization. The ministers of Alexander III and Nicholas II in fact imposed on corporate officials and employees ever greater restrictions – on residence, landownership, and economic activity – that had no foundations except premodern ethnic, religious, and national prejudices.

An intriguing paradox resulted from the incessant conflict between the reformers who pressed for registration and the defenders of the old order: Witte and Timashev, although positively disposed to the creation of new corporations by registration, found it prudent to abandon their plans for

---

[1] Petr B. Struve, "Tekushchie voprosy vnutrennei zhizni," *Novoe slovo*, no. 9 (June 1897), part 2, 190.

reform in order to keep the complicated system of exceptions to the law intact under their benevolent, if arbitrary, ministerial dispensation. The outmoded and untidy concession system allowed slightly more freedom of entrepreneurship than would have been possible under a registration system because the regime refused to abandon its system of discrimination against minorities that the ministers of agriculture, internal affairs, and justice considered dangerous. The demands of economists and business leaders for a thorough reform based on both incorporation by registration and freedom from discrimination repeatedly met a firm rebuff in the last half century of the tsarist period.

Every episode in the history of the Russian corporate law showed the incompatibility between the autocratic political system and the modern corporation. This finding should be hardly surprising to students of the tsarist bureaucracy; but some scholars of Russian economic history have taken too literally the government's own pronouncements of its commitment to economic development. Several thousand corporations certainly flourished under the tsarist regime, and great quantities of foreign capital invested by shrewd European and American financiers fostered the creation of mines and factories in the Russian Empire. However, the dominant impression is one of conflict between two modes of behavior. In Weberian terms, what we have called the "military-autocratic" impulse, toward centralization of power exercised by men of predominantly military backgrounds, clashed with "rational-capitalist" methods, according to which corporate managers sought to respond quickly to shifts in the marketplace with a minimum of interference and delay at the hands of tsarist bureaucrats. If Witte and other ministers of finance recognized that their policies thwarted economic development by wasting valuable entrepreneurial talent, they failed to convince their fellow ministers of the great costs implicit in the concession system. Some of the most enlightened ministers, such as Reutern and Bunge, apparently remained oblivious to the inherent shortcomings of the policy.

The eminent jurist Lev I. Petrazhitskii (Leon Petrażycki in his native Polish) considered scandalous the routine confirmation of corporate charters in the form of separate laws that violated key provisions of the law of 1836.

The chronic disregard for the general law ... contradicts the very essence of that most precious principle of every cultured state, namely the principle of a state based on law [*pravovoe gosudarstvo* – a direct translation of the German *Rechtsstaat*], that most important of fundamental laws of every cultured state, according to which it is administered on the firm foundation of the laws.[2]

Petrazhitskii placed his finger on the crucial defect of the corporate law and, by extension, the entire Russian legal system. To the degree that bureaucratic arbitrariness (*proizvol*) afflicted the economic realm, it hindered the fullest possible development of the Russian economy and prevented the tsarist empire from joining the ranks of what he called the "cultured states" of Europe and North America, where constitutions set limits on executive power. As the *New York Times* editorialized at the beginning of the revolution of 1905, "The industrial regime and the autocratic regime are among Nature's incompatibles."[3]

Alexander Gerschenkron neatly caught the essence of the paradox when he argued that the tsarist regime, in its efforts to foster "westernization" – intensive development to meet the economic, diplomatic, and military challenges posed by European powers – actually deepened the "orientalization" of society. Russian rulers from Peter the Great to Stalin vigorously imported European techniques, imposed them on an essentially passive society in an arbitrary and repressive manner, and met the extraordinary expenses of such ambitious campaigns by squeezing the population to the limits of financial exhaustion. "To the extent that the peasantry was reduced to serfdom in order to force it to bear the cost of economic progress, westernization of the economy seemed to be inseparably connected withits 'orientalization.'"[4] Such a system left no room for the principle of private property enjoyed by citizens of European states. (Whether the essentially pejorative term "orientalization" overstates the repressive nature of statecraft in Turkey, Persia, India, China, and Japan remains a question to be settled by specialists in the history of capitalist institutions in those exotic lands.) In light of the legal history of Europe, his insight supports the

---

[2] Lev I. Petrazhitskii, *Aktsionernaia kompaniia* (St. Petersburg, 1898), 3–4.
[3] George S. Queen, *The United States and the Material Advance in Russia, 1881–1906* (New York, 1976), 54, note 66, citing the *New York Times*, January 24, 1905.
[4] Alexander Gerschenkron, "The Early Phases of Industrialization in Russia and Their Relationship to the Historical Study of Economic Growth," in Barry E. Supple, ed., *The Experience of Economic Growth: Case Studies in Economic History* (New York, 1963), 426–44, quotation from 431. Some support for the concept of an "oriental" economic policy may be found in the history of the Mughal rulers of India, who favored traditional handicrafts and by their haphazard fiscal policies blocked the emergence of large-scale commerce and manufacturing. "There was no capitalist direction as still happens in the case of industries not organized on [the] European pattern." Industrial towns were simply large provincial capitals, not urban centers that grew up around a dynamic industry. S. S. Kulshreshtha, *The Development of Trade and Industry under the Mughals (1526 to 1707 A.D.)* (Allahabad, 1964), 209–11, 196 (quoted), 197.

contention of the present study: that corporations developed more in spite of the tsarist law than because of it.

Unfortunately, when he examined the reign of Nicholas II, whose policies, to be sure, proved less barbaric than those of Peter the Great and Stalin, the tone of Gerschenkron's analysis shifted too far in a positive direction. His memorable theoretical assertion – that the tsarist government's railroad projects, gold standard, and infusions of foreign capital functioned as a "substitute" for the weak domestic market – gave excessive credit to Witte, whose failure to reform the outmoded corporate law has been stressed in the present study. Likewise, Gerschenkron overlooked the persistence of anticapitalist policies when he wrote that the revolution of 1905 marked the end of massive bureaucratic involvement in the economy and the beginning of control by the largest banks, on the German model: "After 1907 none of the 'traditional' features seem to be clearly discernible in the process of continuing industrial growth."[5]

Witte's biographer, Theodore Von Laue, likewise paid insufficient attention to the negative aspects of the minister's program for industrial development. To be sure, he grasped the contradiction between Witte's bureaucratic methods and the need of the modern corporation for firm legal norms:

Rather than let Russian capitalists make their own mistakes and learn by themselves, he predetermined the nature of their experiments by his policy of rapid industrialization. In short, at the very moment when the Minister of Finance began to exhort the Russian *kupechestvo* [merchants] to modernize their ways, he interfered with their spontaneity. He steered the economic development of Russia into an alien channel, substituting state activity for private initiative.... But in doing so he crippled the sense of independence and dynamic initiative which is such an essential ingredient of Western urban-industrial society ... The freedoms of the Western model were incompatible with government initiative in the Russian tradition.

However, Von Laue's main theme was the dubious and unsubstantiated notion that Witte's system represented "a gigantic wager on the capitalists. No wonder the Ministry [of Finance] tried its best to strengthen their position.... That Witte's policy rapidly bore fruit may be gathered from

---

[5] On "substitution," Alexander Gerschenkron, "Russia: Patterns and Problems of Economic Development, 1861–1958," in his *Economic Backwardness in Historical Perspective* (Cambridge, Mass., 1966), 126; on the resemblance of the large Petersburg banks after 1905 to their counterparts in Germany, Gerschenkron, "Economic Backwardness in Historical Perspective," in the same volume, 22, and "Russia," 135–6, quotation from "Early Phases," 434.

the increased rate of domestic capital accumulation in the first decade of the twentieth century."⁶ Thus, despite the admirable explication of the various innovations that secured for Witte a prominent place in the history of the tsarist bureaucracy, the focus on his intentions obscured the debilitating impact of his piecemeal reforms on Russian corporations.

Moreover, Von Laue's characterization of arbitrary state action as "alien" implied the existence of a modern legal system in Russia, one that would have allowed corporate entrepreneurship to flourish had Witte curbed his impatience and allowed Russian merchants to follow the road of Western capitalist development. Witte's methods certainly were alien to businessmen trained in London, Paris, and Berlin; but to Russian merchants they appeared all too familiar, part of a tradition of autocratic rule that stretched back at least to Ivan the Terrible. The misleading image of the state as a catalyst of rational industrial development unfortunately dominated Von Laue's treatment of the Soviet period as well.⁷

Foreigners who experienced tsarist policies at first hand clearly perceived this clash between the autocratic and capitalist modes of behavior. In 1919, the French businessman Raoul Labry, who had supervised the publications of the Russo-French Trade Bureau before the war, ended his criticism of Bolshevik economic policies with a no less scathing attack on the tsarist system of corporate law:

The laws of the old regime entangled our industry in a web of fetters that sapped its strength. For example, the tax system was distressingly unstable. Besides such obligations as the maintenance of a [factory] police force mandated by the state, each of our enterprises bore a tax levied by the zemstvos in accordance with their whims. The mining law, which granted all mineral rights to the owners of the surface land, hindered the development of coal mines. It was impossible to draw up a long-term plan for mining because of the short leases and our ignorance of new conditions that would be demanded by the landowners, who were always ready to raise the cost of the lease infinitely at every renewal. All our companies were at the mercy of the often numerous owners of the land where we had coal mines. Moreover, we lost control of our capital most often because of clauses in our charters required by the law. For example, they specified that the number of Russian directors [on a corporate board] always be greater than that of foreigners; that Russian engineers be the sole recognized intermediaries between companies

⁶ Theodore H. Von Laue, *Sergei Witte and the Industrialization of Russia* (New York, 1963), 304, 300.
⁷ Theodore H. Von Laue, *Why Lenin? Why Stalin?* (London, 1966). For a general critique of Gerschenkron and Von Laue, see Arcadius Kahan, *Russian Economic History: The Nineteenth Century*, ed. Roger Weiss (Chicago, 1989), chap. 2, originally published in 1967, to which is appended Kahan's review of Von Laue's book on Witte.

and the Russian directors; and that at the general assemblies a stockholder could represent only one other stockholder who was unable to attend.[8]

What is most striking about the history of tsarist economic policy in general and of corporate law in particular is that it demonstrated the inability of tsarist bureaucrats to accept or even acknowledge the axioms of modern capitalist culture. In his magisterial study of the legal systems of Germany and Russia from 1600 to 1900, Marc Raeff put this phenomenon in wider geographical and chronological perspective. He noted the care with which German legislators adapted existing guilds and institutions of local government to the exigencies of the rational "well-ordered police state" (*Polizeistaat*). By establishing legal systems that fostered "administrative, moral, and cultural uniformity" without, however, stifling the "innovative energy" of individual citizens, German rulers "paved the way for the withdrawal of the political establishment from many areas of social and economic life" in the more liberal era following the French Revolution and thus laid the institutional foundations for "dynamic modernization." As one German scholar explained the process, "Renewal is selective tradition" (*Erneuerung ist selektive Tradition*).

The Russian political system followed a much different evolutionary path. Peter I regimented his subjects in the interest of war, appealing to abstract natural law, without regard for the wishes of merchants, artisans, and peasants, whom he correctly suspected of an unwillingness to sacrifice themselves and their meager fortunes to the state. His "dynamic, interventionist, and coercive state assumed the task of initiating and directing the productive concerns of society." Although Raeff did not touch on the issue of corporate law, he stressed the deleterious economic impact of the emperor's autocratic policies. Peter and his successors made private economic "activities dependent on state needs and service, thereby weakening and even destroying long-range productive capacities." Oppressive censorship and the ban on representative institutions prevented any single social group or coalition of forces from challenging the autocracy. "The state remained in command and retained the initiative until the end of the nineteenth century, for there was no comprehensive, structured society to deter or to challenge it."[9] Raeff's analysis helps to explain why the

---

[8] Raoul Labry, *L'industrie russe et la révolution* (Paris, 1919), 256; on his position in the *Chambre de commerce russo-française*, 92.
[9] Marc Raeff, *The Well-Ordered Police State: Social and Institutional Change through Law in the Germanies and Russia* (New Haven, 1983), quotations from 171, 109, 107, 103, 206, 213, 250.

corporate proponents of economic rationality, ethnic toleration, and legal reform in the reign of Nicholas II proved too weak to prevail. They faced the enormous task of reversing the fearsome institutional momentum of autocracy, which had been constantly renewed and strengthened in the two centuries following Peter's assumption of the imperial title. The campaign by reactionary agrarians against the legal rights of the corporation in 1914 can best be understood as the final episode in the long history of arbitrary management of the economy.

As an American diplomat reported to Washington at the time of Witte's greatest influence, "Here private initiative does not exist... The regulations of trade and commerce are exceedingly... minute... and [have] the effect of retarding industrial intelligence and enterprise."[10] The tsarist bureaucrats who energetically resisted the rule of law, enforced anti-Semitic regulations, and sought special privileges for the gentry in the spirit of arbitrary rule inherited from the past might well have proclaimed, "Reaction is also selective tradition"!

Precisely how seriously these policies damaged the cause of industrial development in Russia is impossible to measure. The mathematical model has not yet been invented that could specify the economic cost of this form of autocratic repression. Contemporary observers believed that the economic impact was considerable. Both intuition and the historical reality of the post-tsarist period support this hypothesis. Although all the ministers of finance considered themselves patrons of economic growth, they tended to pursue this goal by the most primitive means: decrees, arbitrary punishments, and exceptions to the law granted to petitioners after long delays. Chambers of commerce remained illegal to the end of the tsarist regime despite vociferous demands from major business organizations.[11] Witte once refused to pay postal fees owed by the tsarist government to a Belgian company that managed sleeping cars and restaurants on the Siberian railroad. The minister's arrogance and contempt for the law impelled the Belgian agent to flee Petersburg, "vowing never again to return

---

[10] Queen, *United States*, 54, note 54, quoting State Department Archives, Russia, LI, Despatches 645, Breckenridge to Sherman, November 3, 1897, 54 (Queen's ellipses).

[11] Carl A. Goldberg, "The Association of Industry and Trade, 1906–1917: The Successes and Failures of Russia's Organized Businessmen," doctoral dissertation, University of Michigan, 1974, 413–31. The leadership of liberal Moscow textile manufacturers such as Pavel P. Riabushinskii in the unsuccessful campaign for elective chambers of commerce is discussed in James L. West, "The Rjabušinskij Circle: Industrialists in Search of a Bourgeoisie, 1909–1914," *Jahrbücher für Geschichte Osteuropas*, N.S., 32, no. 3 (Sep. 1984), 358–77. Riabushinskii's press published a fine historical review of the campaign: Moscow, Birzha, Birzhevoi komitet, *O vvedenii torgovo-promyshlennykh palat v Rossii* (Moscow, 1911).

to this country of savages." Likewise, Witte proved incapable of respecting market mechanisms in the all-important petroleum industry. In 1913, Kokovtsov took pride in his efforts to promote what he called "our labor and especially industrial initiative," but he resolutely refused to weaken the state's hold over the faltering railroad network, a major source of discontent among Russian industrialists who found it difficult to compete with state-owned enterprises and suffered from the inefficiencies of the transportation system.[12]

The sorry state of the railroads was symptomatic of the government's general failure to address the needs of the industrial economy. Most of the major lines had passed from corporations into the hands of the state in the reign of Alexander III, but in subsequent decades the Transportation Ministry failed to maintain the vigorous expansion of the system that industrialists considered necessary. Władysław Żukowski of the AIT complained of "the chronic shortage of railroad cars, the snail-like movement of trains, uncertainty in connections, and the systematic misunderstanding of industrial and commercial interests."[13] On the eve of World War I, the railroads barely met the needs of the peacetime economy. During the grain shipping season, in fact, insufficient capacity forced coal and iron producers to ration space in rail cars. In vain the AIT warned of industrial stagnation if the tsarist government continued to neglect the transportation infrastructure:

In recent years the government has shown something of a vacillating attitude toward railroad construction and toward the strengthening of existing routes in order to bring them up to a level consistent with the needs of the country. Not only the government but also the State Duma have taken a stand that tends to slow the country's economic growth.

The Great War demonstrated the high cost of a decade of neglect. After three years of war, the system essentially collapsed, causing the economic

[12] John P. McKay, *Pioneers for Profit: Foreign Entrepreneurship and Russian Industrialization, 1885–1913* (Chicago, 1970), 278, quoting the memoirs of the French ambassador to Russia, Maurice Bompard (1937). John P. McKay, "Baku Oil and Transcaucasian Pipelines, 1883–1981: A Study in Tsarist Economic Policy," *Slavic Review*, 43, no. 4 (Winter 1984), 603–23. Vladimir N. Kokovtsov, *Iz moego proshlogo: vospominaniia 1903–1911 gg.*, 2 vols. (Paris, 1933), vol. 2, 367. On the complaints of the AIT, the best analysis is Ruth A. Roosa, "Russian Industrialists and 'State Socialism,' 1906–1917," *Soviet Studies*, 23, no. 3 (Jan. 1972), 395–417.
[13] Władysław Żukowski, quoted without reference in Zofia Daszyńska-Golińska, "Die wirtschaftliche und politische Lage Polens bei Ausbruch des Krieges," *Archiv für Sozialwissenschaft und Sozialpolitik*, 40, no. 3 (*Krieg und Wirtschaft*, 3), 1915, 714. See also his cogent critique of the Russian government's financial exploitation of the Polish provinces: Władysław Żukowski, "Polish Economic Policy," *Russian Review*, 3, no. 1 (1914), 159–66.

crisis that confounded the Provisional Government and opened the way for the Bolshevik seizure of power. If the performance of the Russian economy during the wartime emergency can be considered a fair test of the tsarist regime's policies in the preceding decades, then the verdict of failure is clear.[14]

How can we explain this extraordinary tenacity? What image of themselves and their society did bureaucrats rely upon for courage in the battle against modernity? At this point, it is only fair to exercise toleration and openmindedness in giving the tsarist bureaucracy its due. Even in its most perverse actions, however grossly tainted by ignorance, arbitrariness, inefficiency, and corruption, the imperial government operated like an awesome machine. Not only the visionary statesmen of Alexander I and the "enlightened bureaucrats" of Alexander II but also the most venal clerks played their essential roles. For centuries the bureaucracy held together the largest country in the world, squeezed enormous revenues from a poor population, fielded a huge army, and maintained its cruel but effective rule.[15] The most eloquent defender of autocracy, Konstantin P. Pobe-

[14] AIT policy statements in 1913 and 1914, cited from the archive of the Council of Ministers by Leonid E. Shepelev, *Tsarizm i burzhuaziia v 1904–1914 gg.: problemy torgovo-promyshlennoi politiki* (Leningrad, 1987), 224–8, quotation from 228; on shortcomings of the state-managed rail system, 220–4. The unsuccessful efforts of the SRCIA to solve the problem of inadequate railroad capacity are discussed in P. I. Fomin, *Kratkii ocherk istorii s"ezdov gornopromyshlennikov Iuga Rossii* (Kharkov, 1908), chap. 16 (on railroad construction) and chap. 19 (on the allocation of freight cars among mining companies). Well informed Russians and foreigners unanimously blamed the imperial government for failing to promote the rational expansion of the railroad network and linked the state's recalcitrance to the collapse of the economy in World War I. See, for example, E[vgenii] V. Korsh, *Dvadtsat' let na zheleznykh dorogakh (1889–1908 gg.): vospominaniia o zheleznodorozhnoi sluzhbe* (St. Petersburg, 1910), esp. 183–7; and Labry, *L'industrie russe*, 122. In 1914, the Russian railroad system ranked sixteenth of twenty in Europe in terms of track length per capita and twentieth in terms of track length per unit of territory, and the government's policy of extracting maximum revenues from its own lines while spending as little as possible on the construction of new ones in 1904–14 led to disaster during the war: Obshchii s"ezd predstavitelei Russkoi promyshlennosti i torgovli (Paris, May 17, 1921), untitled collection of articles, no. 22, A. A. Abragamson and V. N. Nagrodskii, "Zheleznodorozhnyi transport v Rossii v proshedshem, nastoiashchem i budushchem," 1, 17. Annual figures for new railroad construction, 1866–1914, appear in Sergei A. Pervushin, *Khoziaistvennaia kon"iunktura: vvedenie v izuchenie russkogo narodnogo khoziaistva za polveka* (Moscow, 1925), 157 (col. 15).

[15] Concrete evidence of the skill and energy of the bureaucracy can be seen in every volume of the *PSZ*, though it remains unclear how well the commands issued in St. Petersburg were implemented in far-off villages. Supplies for the various military units in the era of Peter the Great were specified in elaborate detail. The annual salaries of field marshals (12,000 rubles) can be compared to those of men in all other ranks, down to pharmacists, postmasters, tailors, and coachmen (the last received 6 rubles). Each cavalry regiment was allotted sixty carts, twenty drums, and ten oboes every three years. *PSZ* 1–2319, dated February 19, 1711. Catherine II likewise issued marvelously detailed decrees. Her

donostsev, foresaw the breakup of the empire along ethnic lines once central power collapsed (as indeed occurred during the civil war of 1918–20). He would have been the first to admit that the military-autocratic mode of government practiced by the tsar and his ministers was ultimately incompatible with the rational-legal norms of economic and political behavior proposed by economists and business leaders, but for the sake of his reactionary ideal, he refused to consider any concessions to constitutionalism, democracy, or the principle of equality before the law.[16] The Bolsheviks in turn created their own peculiar version of the autocratic state to maintain territorial unity.

The fact that the most capable tsarist ministers had received good educations and served the state with selfless devotion gave them a certain justification for despising the merchants, many of whom had a well-deserved reputation for dishonesty, ignorance, and incompetence. The speculative fever that swept the exchanges in the mid-1890s and various scandals in the corporate world in the ensuing depression (including the spectacular bankruptcies of the railroad and iron magnate Savva I. Mamontov and the financier and coal producer Aleksei K. Alchevskii) testified to the woefully low standards of business ethics in Russia.[17]

Two years before he became minister of finance, Nikolai Kh. Bunge listed the various means by which corporate directors harmed the interests of stockholders: winning "a quick profit by transforming an unsuccessful private business into a corporate one"; the overvaluation of a company's property at its creation; poor management; and the issuing of nonexistent profits, in the form of dividends, from the corporation's basic capital. These

---

instructions to surveyors fixing the boundaries of Mogilev and Polotsk provinces were so specific that just the chapter headings filled three full columns in the index: *PSZ* 1–15654, dated January 30, 1783. In the economic realm, Catherine did not shrink from issuing a decree allowing free trade in rhubarb within the empire and abroad: *PSZ* 1–15169. No less meticulous were the instructions issued in the reign of Nicholas I. For example, just the appendix to vol. 15 of the second series of the *PSZ* (1840), all of 1,476 pages long, filled forty-nine microfiche.

[16] Konstantin P. Pobedonostsev, *Reflections of a Russian Statesman*, trans. Robert C. Long (Ann Arbor, 1965), esp. chap. 3: "The Falsehood of Democracy." Max Weber, *General Economic History*, trans. Frank H. Knight (New York, 1927), 276–8; his classic essay on modes of political behavior is Max Weber, "Politics as a Vocation," in *From Max Weber*, ed. Hans Gerth and C. Wright Mills, trans. H. H. Gerth (New York, 1958), 82.

[17] Stuart R. Grover, "Savva Mamontov and the Mamontov Circle, 1870–1905: Art Patronage and the Rise of Nationalism in Russian Art," doctoral dissertation, University of Wisconsin, 1971; V. D. Belov, *A. K. Alchevskii* (Moscow, 1903), and M. Ia. Gertsenshtein, *Khar'kovskii krakh* (St. Petersburg, 1903) on Alchevskii. A competent review of these and other bankruptcies at the turn of the century is Valerii I. Bovykin, *Formirovanie finansovogo kapitala v Rossii: konets XIX v.–1908 g.* (Moscow, 1984), 128–36.

accusations may have been true enough. Still, Bunge's proposed cure for these ills – yet another flood of restrictive legislation – remained within the old tsarist tradition of attempted reform by governmental fiat, a solution inherently ineffective in a modern market economy. Saddest of all is the fact that Bunge himself overlooked the ability of new laws to correct what was essentially a cultural problem, one of insufficient business training among the Russian merchants. His program, intended to stop the flow of "material aid" to failing companies, had as its centerpiece "the establishment of a better system [*poriadok*], through the promulgation of laws for the contemporary development of the national economy," a field in which Russia, he correctly observed, stood more than a century behind West European countries. However noble Bunge's goal might have been, his call for yet more new laws betrayed the classic myopia of the Russian bureaucrat. Child labor laws could hardly have averted the emergence of a socialist movement, as he hoped; and it was ludicrous to assert, as he did, that up-to-date laws pertaining to bills of exchange, bankruptcy, and corporations would suffice to raise the moral level of the mercantile population and thereby "create in our country enterprises that are strong by virtue of sound management and strict accountability exercised by investors."[18]

Moreover, the common stereotypes of the high-minded bureaucrat and the crassly dishonest merchant misrepresented the variety of cultural traditions in the Russian empire. To be sure, many Russian merchants did not comprehend the principle of enlightened self-interest. The Singer Company found that Germans, Jews, and foreigners proved more adept than Russians in the management of its network of sales offices.[19] With some exaggeration, Professor Ozerov castigated all Russian merchants for refusing to adopt modern ways: "Our population and our country have neither the industrial spirit nor the industrial character." Workers who displayed extra effort found their wages reduced by stingy factory owners; and merchants failed to study the domestic market, leaving the way open

---

[18] Memorandum of Nikolai Kh. Bunge, dated September 20, 1880, reprinted in A. P. Pogrebinskii, ed., "Finansovaia politika tsarizma v 70–80-kh godakh XIX v.," *Istoricheskii arkhiv*, 6, no. 2 (Mar.–Apr., 1960), 134, 136.

[19] Fred V. Carstensen, *American Enterprise in Foreign Markets: Studies of Singer and International Harvester in Imperial Russia* (Chapel Hill, 1984), 79–81. He noted (81) that Singer's reliance on foreigners and ethnic minorities, a policy not followed in the company's European operations, "developed not out of choice but out of necessity and reflected the difficulties of finding people with sufficient commercial experience and ability in Russia. It suggests that cultural values, including attitudes toward work and career patterns, may be an important factor in understanding both recruitment and entrepreneurship patterns."

to foreigners to show what "splendid results" could be achieved by a rational sales network.[20] Gregory Freeze recently noted the importance of the traditional estate mentality (*soslovnost'*), even in the early twentieth century, as a crucial barrier to political change under the old regime, a factor "utterly antithetical to the creation of a modern civil society, which is a *sine qua non* for a democratic order."[21]

However, Ozerov placed primary blame on the tsarist bureaucracy. Change could come only through a relaxation of the repressive apparatus.

> The old regime [this before February 1917!], with all its restrictions and prohibitions, hindered and discouraged all initiative by making success depend on the authorization of the governing officials. It annihilated all energies, smothered all humane feelings within the masses, and although industrial energies abounded in Russia they remained unexploited and of no benefit to anyone, like our forests and mineral wealth.... [The tsarist regime] does not allow a free field of activity to individuals; it imposes restrictions and hindrances. Without an ukaz a Russian does not dare do anything. This ukaz is so discouraging that it incapacitates him. ... [Bureaucrats] employ all their energies, all their intellectual efforts in creating hindrances, obstacles, and restrictions.[22]

Ozerov's incisive comment about the duality of the bureaucratic ukaz – motivating and debilitating at the same time – showed the enormity of the vicious circle that blighted the economic life of the tsarist empire.

His somber characterization of the problem, like that of Mendeelev more than three decades before, raised the issue of the time that would have been necessary to cultivate a vigorous entrepreneurial culture among the Russian merchants and peasantry in the hypothetical absence of the repressive, anticapitalist policies pursued by the bureaucracy. One observer of the sorry spectacle of stock-exchange abuses in Russia warned that a long wait might be necessary. First must come a relaxation of oppressive laws to allow the entrepreneurial spirit to flourish. Of prime importance in this regard was a simplified system of incorporation, coupled with a ban on special certificates that allowed founders to obtain shares without payment. Paradoxically, however, such a major shift to European norms might well have provided opportunities for increased abuses by

---

[20] Ivan Ozeroff [Ozerov], *Problèmes économiques et financiers de la Russie moderne* (Lausanne, 1916), 24–8, quotations from 25, 26.
[21] Gregory Freeze, "The *Soslovie* (Estate) Paradigm and Russian Social History," *American Historical Review*, 91, no. 1 (Feb. 1986), 35. For a richly detailed example of such antidemocratic attitudes among merchants, see the memoirs of the president of the MEC from 1876 to 1905, Nikolai A. Naidenov, *Vospominaniia o vidennom, slyshannom i ispytannom*, 2 vols. (Moscow, 1903–5; reprinted Newtonville, Mass., 1976).
[22] Ozeroff, *Problèmes*, 45–6.

Russian wheeler-dealers in the short run: "It suffices to mention that the operations on the English and French exchanges, which in many ways are [our] models, were created in the course of the centuries and were improved gradually under the influence of life itself, not legislative measures."[23] So much for the alleged "advantages of backwardness" in the cultural realm.

This, then, was the problem that may be called "the dilemma of cultural delay." On the one hand, by its repressive economic legislation, the tsarist government no doubt prevented some abuses by corporate managers and their favored cronies, but at a cost of dampening entrepreneurial abilities among the population at large. On the other hand, to introduce the latest word in European corporate law, as Reutern almost did in the early 1870s, would have risked an increase in abuses because of the shortage of qualified and trustworthy corporate directors in the empire. (The word "businessman" is hardly applicable to the railroad magnates and bankers who rode the speculative wave to riches in the decades after the Crimean War.)

It is impossible to say how much "delay" would have been necessary before Russian merchants, freed from the dead hand of bureaucratic tutelage, would have learned relevant European business techniques and risen into positions of authority, displacing the many capable foreigners who managed corporations successfully. In his study of the foreign contribution to Russian industry, John P. McKay perceived a marked trend toward "entrepreneurial self-sufficiency" in the last years of the tsarist regime.[24] For every competent Russian manager, however, we can infer the existence of hundreds of bearded merchants in the provinces who clung to their abaci and pursued the old goal of maximum profit through minimum honesty.

What is certain is that the bureaucracy refused to make the gamble or even to consider it. The most enlightened ministers, including Reutern, Bunge, and Witte, all preferred the old way: rigid laws tempered by arbitrary exceptions for favored petitioners. Capable business leaders were emerging in the major economic centers of the empire in the reign of Alexander II, for example, Leopold Kronenberg in Warsaw, Fedor V. Chizhov in Moscow, Leon Rozental' and the Nobels in Petersburg, and dozens of sturdy German merchants in Riga.[25] These men stood ready to

---

[23] M. Pozner, "Spekuliatsiia i birzhevaia reforma," *Russkoe ekonomicheskoe obozrenie*, 2, no. 4 (Apr. 1898), 99, and no. 3 (Mar. 1898), 69 (quoted).

[24] McKay, *Pioneers*, 368.

[25] On Kronenberg, Ryszard Kołodziejczyk, *Portret warszawskiego millionera* (Warsaw, 1968);

Autocracy, corporate law, and cultural delay

transcend the dishonest maneuverings that had enriched Nikolai N. Sushchov and other former bureaucrats in an unreformed system. The most propitious moment for the abolition of the outmoded concessionary system came and passed in the early 1870s. Paradoxically, it was Reutern, the enlightened finance minister in the era of the Great Reforms, who bore the heaviest responsibility for the failure of corporate law reform in the nineteenth century.

Baron Wrangel, a rare aristocrat who made himself into a corporate director, clearly saw the logical connection between tsarist repression and economic backwardness.

Like a stupid nanny who fears that a child might fall and hurt himself, our myopic and unfeeling bureaucracy refused for two centuries to release the Russian people from leading strings, and thus kept Russians from even trying to move independently. But [the economic successes of] Rostov and the Kuban [on the southern frontier] have shown that Russians can accomplish far more if left to themselves than with the harmful help of ignorant tutors. The fact that our bureaucracy had a special skill in extinguishing any living flame was well known to all except, of course, to the bureaucrats themselves, who never even suspected it.[26]

Indeed, Wrangel suggested that entrepreneurial talent abounded in Russia and would bring about an economic miracle if allowed to flourish. In the terminology used here, the "delay" would have been relatively short. Russians could quickly adopt the best of European corporate techniques if allowed to do so. Therefore the "dilemma" could best be solved by a major reform of the corporate law.

Wrangel took as his example the remarkable career of a liberal Russian landowner, Petr A. Dement'ev, of Tver. Seeking an outlet for his entrepreneurial abilities, Dement'ev left Russia and arrived in America with no possessions whatsoever. In the course of several decades he became a wealthy businessman, founded a port in Florida (which he named St. Petersburg after the imperial Russian capital), and built railroads and

---

on Chizhov, Arkadii Cherokov, *Fedor Vasil'evich Chizhov i ego sviazi s N. V. Gogolem: biograficheskii ocherk po povodu 25-i godovshchiny smerti ego* (Moscow, 1902) and the journal edited by Chizhov and the economist Ivan K. Babst: *Vestnik promyshlennosti* (Herald of industry, 1858–61); Leon Rozental', *Ocherk deiatel'nosti russkikh aktsionernykh obshchestv v techenii 1862 i 1863 gg.* (St. Petersburg, 1865), is a perceptive account by a Petersburg banker; on the Nobels, Robert W. Tolf, *The Russian Rockefellers: The Saga of the Nobel Family and the Russian Oil Industry* (Stanford, 1976); on Riga, G. D. Hernmarck, *Erinnerungen aus dem öffentlichen Leben eines Rigaschen Kaufmanns, 1849 bis 1869* (Berlin, 1899), and Anders Henriksson, *The Tsar's Loyal Germans . . . 1855–1905* (Boulder, Colo., 1983), which lists all corporations operating in Riga in the early twentieth century.
[26] Nikolai E. Vrangel', *Vospominaniia (ot krepostnogo prava do bol'shevikov)* (Berlin, 1924), 133.

mined gold in California. He attracted the attention of the educated Russian public by his essays in the journal *Russkaia mysl'* (Russian thought), entitled "Letters from America." Here was a quintessentially robust entrepreneur from the interior of Russia, vigorous and well educated, to be sure, but still a representative of the social estate that is often portrayed as lacking the ability to adapt to the requirements of modern capitalism: the doomed gentry of Chekhov's unforgettable *Cherry Orchard*.

What is most remarkable about Dement'ev's business career is not that he succeeded in America – millions of immigrants with less education and talent did the same – but that he had an opportunity to return to Russia and apply his abilities there. Near the port city of Poti on the Black Sea stood a large but unexploited tract of timberland owned by the Ministry of Agriculture and State Domains. Dement'ev sought a concession to begin logging operations, build a sawmill, and supply Poti with much-needed lumber. However, knowing all too well the debilitating effects of tsarist tutelage and arbitrary action, he attached to his offer a single condition: He must be allowed full freedom to manage the concession, and no official of the ministry would be permitted to set foot in the forest as long as the concession remained in effect. Aleksei S. Ermolov, the minister, found this condition unacceptable, and so the forest remained idle for years thereafter.[27]

Anecdotal evidence such as this hardly constitutes a proof of Wrangel's generalization about the deleterious effects of tsarist policies and the economic benefits that would have resulted from major reforms. However, in this case, experimentation is out of the question, and the tools for a statistically valid test do not exist. The story of Dement'ev must therefore stand as an important contribution to the discussion of the "dilemma of cultural delay." It illustrates how the unbridled power of the ministers contributed to the persistence of Russian economic backwardness.

Our use of the term "delay" implies that the gap between Russian and European capitalist practices could have been narrowed or closed in the course of time. Even if the gap remained permanent, Russian institutions would have followed, at a distance, the same course earlier traveled in Europe. Nikolai S. Avdakov, president of the AIT, announced to a del-

---

[27] Vrangel', *Vospominaniia*, 134. Hans Rogger, "America in the Russian Mind – Or Russian Discoveries of America," *Pacific Historical Review*, 47, no. 1 (Feb. 1978), 40–1, gives useful details of Dement'ev's career in America, where he used the name Demens. Professor Samuel H. Baron kindly brought this article to my attention. Dement'ev used the pseudonym Tverskoi, after his native town, in his articles in *Russkaia mysl'*, for example, vol. 31 (1910), no. 1, 81–93; 31 (1910), no. 6, 91–104; and 32 (1911), no. 4, 34–45.

egation of English businessmen that "England will always be a model [*obraz*] for us, worthy of imitation in its concern for the national economy."²⁸ This unilinear concept appealed especially to Russian liberals, who preferred to see the tsarist regime as doomed to the fate of the Bourbon dynasty in France. On the eve of the revolution of 1905, the historian Pavel N. Miliukov declared, with the optimism characteristic of that era, that "no legal and moral tradition of autocracy can be found to exist either in institutions or in minds; and so nothing is opposed to its overthrow except the mere fact of its being there, in full possession of power." He even spoke of the "laws of political biology" that were allegedly leading Russia along the path to constitutionalism.²⁹

The problem with this notion is that the importation of a European practice into the Russian context, where such practice had not matured of its own accord, rarely succeeded in duplicating the European effect in the new environment. The railroad companies that proliferated in the 1860s received such irrational subsidies from the state that it eventually felt obliged to acquire them. Large fortunes of course were made in Europe and America by wheeler-dealers in the railroads, but out of that experience emerged what Alfred D. Chandler has called the first examples of "big business," the organizational model for the twentieth-century corporation in all sectors.³⁰ To cite another example, fraud against stockholders by directors and their hired front men persisted well into the present century in Russia, largely because neither the state's repressive laws nor the prevailing standards of corporate honesty provided an effective check on such practices. In Great Britain, however, already by 1860, the accountants themselves had devised standards of probity that they extended to all members of their professional organization, so that corporate managers found it difficult to falsify the financial condition of large enterprises.³¹ The utter lack of an accounting profession in Russia at that time ruled out the possibility of such a solution to corporate dishonesty.

In the long term, such cultural peculiarities exerted a strong influence

---

²⁸ Nikolai S. Avdakov, quoted in *Torgovo-promyshlennyi iug* (Odessa), no. 4 (Feb. 1, 1912), col. 86.
²⁹ Paul Miliukov, *Russia and its Crisis* (New York, 1962), 401.
³⁰ Alfred D. Chandler, *The Visible Hand: The Managerial Revolution in American Business* (Cambridge, Mass., 1977).
³¹ British auditors "enforced their standards by the sanction of refusing an unqualified audit report to those accounts which fell short of them. Indeed, it was accountants who led the way in raising standards of reporting financial data by companies to their shareholders." Legislation ratified these standards in 1918. G. A. Lee, *Modern Financial Accounting*, 3rd ed. (Walton-on-Thames, 1981), 8.

on the political history of the Russian Empire. In the eighteenth century, the great iron manufacturers of the Urals had no need for the corporate form of enterprise because their contracts with the state, to whom they delivered their finished goods, specified their advantages in great detail. Socially and ideologically, these men did not consider themselves a "bourgeoisie" or "middle class," but rose as quickly as possible into the privileged estate – the gentry – in a process that the leading Soviet historian of the subject has called "the gentrification of the bourgeoisie."[32]

This striving by successful manufacturers for aristocratic status is a familiar enough pattern in history, from the Fuggers in sixteenth-century Germany to the family of Kenneth Clark in twentieth-century England. One cultural historian has pointed to the influence of aristocratic traditions of agrarian life and nonscientific education as a major reason for the failure of British industry to maintain its position of world leadership after 1870: "As capitalists became landed gentlemen, JPs, and men of breeding, the radical ideal of active capital was submerged in the conservative ideal of passive property, and the urge to enterprise faded beneath the preference for stability."[33] In Russia under Nicholas II, however, this problem appeared in a far more acute form. The British manufacturers who imbibed aristocratic culture had demonstrated their technological and managerial prowess at the Crystal Palace Exhibition in 1851. Even in Bismarck's Germany, industrialists enjoyed far greater influence, as junior partners of the Junker agrarians in the famous "marriage of iron and rye" sealed by the tariff agreement of 1879, than did Russian producers of textiles and machinery.[34]

This focus on the corporation as the object of regimentation by a government incapable of appreciating the need for legal reform helps to il-

[32] N. I. Pavlenko, *Istoriia metallurgii v Rossii XVIII veka: zavody i zavodovladel'tsy* (Moscow, 1962); Hugh D. Hudson, Jr., *The Rise of the Demidov Family and the Russian Iron Industry in the Eighteenth Century* (Newtonville, Mass., 1986), esp. chap. 8: "The Fourth Generation and Entrepreneurial Decline."

[33] Martin J. Wiener, *English Culture and the Decline of the Industrial Spirit, 1850–1980* (Cambridge, 1981), 14. For econometric arguments that tend to exonerate the British capitalists for the "entrepreneurial failure" alleged by earlier historians, see Donald N. McCloskey, *Enterprise and Trade in Victorian Britain: Essays in Historical Economics* (London, 1981), esp. part 2. Explanations that stress economic factors, particularly the persistence of small businesses and rigid market structures at a time when German, American, and Japanese manufacturers were developing the vertically integrated giant enterprise, are presented in Bernard Elbaum and William Lazonick, eds., *The Decline of the British Economy* (Oxford, 1986).

[34] Richard J. Evans, ed., *Society and Politics in Wilhelmine Germany* (London, 1978); H. A. Winkler, *Liberalismus und Antiliberalismus: Studien zur politischen Sozialgeschichte des 19. und 20. Jahrhunderts* (Göttingen, 1979).

luminate one of the grand themes of Russian history: the resilience of firmly implanted autocratic political institutions in the face of challenges from European ideas and institutions. The corporation is only one of many cultural artifacts that emerged in Europe, came to Russia, and, because of its essential incompatibility with the nature of autocracy, lost much of its dynamism and became subordinate to bureaucratic control after transplantation to Russian soil. Examples of this pattern abound in intellectual history; one need only compare the careers of Voltaire and Radishchev in the age of Enlightenment, of Comte and Chernyshevskii in the positivist movement, and of Bebel and Trotskii among the Marxists to see what a sad end befell the partisans of a European idea in the autocratic context of Russian politics. The story of Russian corporate law in large measure reiterated this pattern. By making clear the methods by which the tsarist state regimented the most powerful economic institution in the modern world, the history of the corporation in Russia therefore transcends the narrow realm of economics. As the focus of the conflicting perceptions and interests of bureaucrats and businessmen, it can best be understood, in the largest sense, as an aspect of Russian cultural history.[35]

Future studies of tsarist economic policy, the role of business organizations, and the activities of prominent business leaders in the Russian Empire will add useful insights to the major debates over the fate of the empire. Two features of that complicated story have been emphasized in the present study: the inability of the tsarist regime to accommodate the inherent dynamism of the modern corporation by a relaxation of legal norms, despite insistent calls by business leaders for such reform from the 1860s onward; and the lack of a sustained political opposition movement among business leaders frustrated by tsarist inaction and incompetence. Observers who explained the lack of a vigorous, antiautocratic bourgeoisie by alleging favoritism toward big capitalists failed to perceive the phenomenon of systemic conflict between autocratic and capitalist modes of behavior. On the other hand, historians who have interpreted the dispute over the corporate regulations of April 18, 1914, as a sign of

---

[35] One historian of corporate law in the United States, Britain, Germany, and Russia at the turn of the century concluded, "While the internal similarities of the managerial revolution stimulated regulatory convergence, underlying and persistent national differences continued to shape each nation's policy toward policy and national life." For example, Theodore Roosevelt's attack on the trusts contrasted markedly with the "compulsory cartel" in Germany. Morton Keller, "Public Policy and Large Enterprise: Comparative Historical Perspective," in Norbert Horn and Jürgen Kocka, eds., *Recht und Entwicklung der Grossunternehmen im 19. und frühen 20. Jahrhundert* (Göttingen, 1979), 524.

216   *The corporation under Russian law*

capitalists' political disenchantment with tsarism have failed to see the weakness of the liberal tendency within the small, culturally diverse, and geographically dispersed commercial-industrial elite.[36]

These interim conclusions provide additional evidence for the current debate over the alternatives open to Russian society as it entered the maelstrom of the Great War. An influential school of thought maintains that the Russian economy was breaking free of its former dependence on the state and that this process presaged the emergence of a liberal bourgeoisie capable of seizing power from the tsarist autocracy without falling victim to the radical left. In the words of Alexander Gerschenkron, "One might surmise that in the absence of the war Russia would have continued on the road of progressive westernization."[37] However, the present study leaves no doubt that the tsarist ministers clung to arbitrary methods in their administration of corporate law; and the contention that the state's influence in the economy gradually declined is disputed both by businessmen's statements at the time and by recent studies of heavy industry, especially the armaments sector.[38]

As for the alleged increase in oppositional attitudes among the manu-

---

[36] Mensheviks inclined to the view that Russian capitalists had no reason to complain about their treatment at the hands of the Ministry of Finance. The strongest statements are [Osip] A. Ermanskii [né Kogan], "Krupnaia burzhuaziia do 1905 goda," in L. Martov, P. Maslov, and A. Potresov, eds., *Obshchestvennoe dvizhenie v Rossii v nachale XX veka*, 4 vols. (St. Petersburg, 1909–14; reprinted The Hague, 1968), vol. 1, 313–48; A. Gushka [pseud. of Osip A. Ermanskii], *Predstavitel'nye organizatsii torgovo-promyshlennogo klassa v Rossii* (St. Petersburg, 1912); and Pavel A. Berlin, *Russkaia burzhuaziia v staroe i novoe vremia*, 2d ed. (Moscow, 1925), esp. 167, quoting Nikolai S. Avdakov's complacent statement in 1905: "Up to now no one has hindered us in any way; on the contrary, we have always enjoyed broad scope."

A useful corrective to the assumption of the capitalist's decisive influence on the political system is the comment by Joseph A. Schumpeter: "From where stems the influence or the power which most economists and historians attribute to him? I shall state frankly that I consider power to be one of the most misused words in the social sciences, though the competition is indeed great." So widely held is the idea "that entrepreneurs or else the capitalist class into which they merge are the prime movers of modern politics that it is very difficult to make headway against it and to point out how very little foundation there is to this opinion." "Economic Theory and Entrepreneurial History," in Hugh G. J. Aitken, ed., *Explorations in Enterprise* (Cambridge, Mass., 1965), 61. Schumpeter referred to Europe; his caveat has even greater relevance for Russia, where capitalist institutions remained far weaker. For a counterargument alleging the ability of business interests to exert power by defining the political agenda for their own benefit, see David Marsh, ed., *Capital and Politics in Western Europe* (Totowa, N.J., 1983).

[37] Gerschenkron, "Early Phases," 434.

[38] The AIT incessantly criticized state-owned railroads, forests, and other enterprises that gave private entrepreneurs serious competition. The best discussion of their views is Ruth A. Roosa, "Russian Industrialists and 'State Socialism.'" On the persistence of state influence in heavy industry, particularly armaments, see Peter Gatrell, *The Tsarist Economy, 1850–1917* (New York, 1986), 181, 186.

facturers and the creation of a united bourgeoisie intent on seizing power from the tsarist government, Ruth A. Roosa, the leading scholar of the AIT, recently concluded that such a version does not accord with the facts. Certainly its leaders felt "great bitterness" toward the regime for its "refusal to take the industrialists into its confidence and to allow them to participate in the formulation of economic policy" during the wartime emergency. However, the organization remained crippled by rivalries among personalities, industrial sectors, and geographical regions. It simply failed to create a meaningful bourgeois opposition. Even in the interregnum between the Romanovs and the Bolsheviks, "the industrialists as a class never rose to a position of political leadership, and it was left primarily to the Zemstvo agrarians and the intelligentsia to act out the role of the middle class as the bearer of liberal ideals."[39]

The main conclusion of recent studies of the Russian merchants in the late tsarist period is that although systemic conflict existed between the autocratic state and the capitalist elite, the latter nevertheless remained politically loyal to the tsar. The few liberal industrialists, like Konovalov, Riabushinskii, and Goujon after 1905, found themselves isolated culturally and politically both from the regime and from traditional merchants in the provinces. On the very eve of World War I, Pavel P. Riabushinskii and his small circle of liberal Moscow manufacturers tried desperately to ally various elements of the Russian merchant estate and associated business leaders, but their effort to create a national "bourgeois" organization failed completely.[40] Much research remains to be done on the political attitudes and behavior of business leaders in commercial and industrial centers outside Petersburg and Moscow, but certain patterns already can be discerned. It appears that business leaders from the Kingdom of Poland identified with the Polish faction (called the Kolo, or "circle") in the State Duma; that Jewish manufacturers and traders were preoccupied with the

---

[39] Ruth A. Roosa, "Russian Industrialists during World War I: The Interaction of Economics and Politics," in Guroff and Carstensen, eds., *Entrepreneurship*, 159–87, quotations from 186–7.

[40] Thomas C. Owen, *Capitalism and Politics in Russia: A Social History of the Moscow Merchants, 1855–1905* (Cambridge, 1981); Alfred J. Rieber, *Merchants and Entrepreneurs in Imperial Russia* (Chapel Hill, 1982); Jo Ann Ruckman, *The Moscow Business Elite: A Social and Cultural Portrait of Two Generations, 1840–1905* (De Kalb, Ill., 1984). The best account of the liberal Moscow manufacturers after 1905 is West, "Rjabušinskij." For a brief Soviet analysis of Riabushinskii's newspaper, *Utro Rossii* (Russian morn), see A. N. Bokhanov, "Iz istorii burzhuaznoi pechati," *Istoricheskie zapiski*, 97 (1976), 263–89. An informative Soviet work on the wartime period is Valentin S. Diakin, *Russkaia burzhuaziia i tsarizm v gody pervoi mirovoi voiny (1914–1917)* (Leningrad, 1967), supplemented by his *Samoderzhaviia, burzhuaziia i dvorianstvo v 1907–1911 gg.* (Leningrad, 1978).

issue of religious descrimination, which of course affected their business prospects; and that, except in Siberia, where merchants demanded zemstvos for the sake of the political autonomy of their region, the mass of provincial merchants of Great Russian stock kept alive the Moscow merchants' traditional disdain for zemstvo liberalism. Hardly a "ruling class" or even a partner in the political system dominated by bureaucrats from predominantly agrarian backgrounds, the Russian industrialists failed to break out of their cultural and legal limbo.

Thus, the record of tsarist intransigence favors the hypothesis of severe and unresolved social tensions even before World War I, of which labor unrest was only one major component. In contrast to Western Europe in the nineteenth century, the social and political institutions of the Russian Empire offered few prospects for peaceful change.[41] In this respect the issue of law deserves special attention. As Harold J. Berman has recently noted in his analysis of the medieval roots of modern ecclesiastical, municipal, commercial, and civil law, contemporary European and American legal institutions draw on centuries of prior evolution.[42] By the same token, the persistence of centralized rule from the early tsarist period to the 1980s owes much to the lack in Russian culture of institutional forces capable of challenging the state and preventing the reassertion of autocracy after brief periods of weakness, as in the crises of 1598–1613, 1730, 1825, and 1917. Recent comparative studies, such as those of Barrington Moore, Jr., Reinhard Bendix, and Theda Skocpol, have reiterated the peculiar resi

---

[41] Leopold Haimson, "The Problem of Social Stability in Urban Russia, 1905–1917," *Slavic Review*, 23, no. 4 (Dec. 1964), 619–42, and vol. 24, no. 1 (Mar. 1965), 1–21, stressed the growing social antagonisms prior to World War I. Without endorsing Haimson's contention that radical victory might have been possible in the absence of the economic chaos caused by the war, Geoffrey Hosking, *The Russian Constitutional Experiment: Government and Duma, 1907–1914* (Cambridge, 1973), vi, concluded that "there are really no grounds for supposing that the Tsarist system could ever have made a constitutional order work or could have achieved the peaceful modernization of Russia." This position is argued most vigorously by Von Laue, who cited geographical, cultural, and even psychological factors inimical to the development of liberalism in Russia; he quoted Miliukov's admission that "the 'plasticity' of the Russian character... was poor building material indeed for the self-reliant, rational, sovereign individual of liberal ideology." Theodore H. Von Laue, "The Prospects of Liberal Democracy in Tsarist Russia," in Charles E. Timberlake, ed., *Essays on Russian Liberalism* (Columbia, Mo., 1972), 164–81, quotation from 173. An unduly optimistic narrative of the growth of antiautocratic institutions under the tsarist regime, which alleges a growing liberal trend within the capitalist elite while admitting the lack of a genuine middle class, is Jacob Walkin, *The Rise of Democracy in Pre-Revolutionary Russia* (New York, 1962), esp. chaps. 6–9.

[42] Harold J. Berman, *Law and Revolution: The Formation of the Western Legal Tradition* (Cambridge, Mass., 1983).

lience of centralized state power in Russia in comparison with less autocratic political institutions elsewhere in the modern world.[43]

The utter lack of a legal framework to check the power of the Russian state helps to explain why European institutions such as the large corporation failed to assert their autonomy against the repression imposed by the tsarist bureaucracy in the nineteenth and early twentieth centuries. In the absence of the world war, a crucial catalyst for the triumph of radicalism in 1917–21, a military dictatorship in Russia – with or without the sanction of the Romanov dynasty – appeared at least as strong a possibility as a liberal democracy in the early twentieth century. Under the Soviet regime as well, the lack of a strong tradition of legal norms opened the way for unchecked arbitrary rule, against which the so-called socialist legality of Khrushchev's famous speech has carried pitifully little weight. The limited influence of the law, both in the economic realm as well as outside the marketplace, therefore becomes a subject deserving of careful treatment by historians of Russian politics and culture.

To study the inner life of a social group that met extinction more than seven decades ago may seem a project of dubious worth; but if historians are to succeed in explicating the social origins of the Russian Revolution and in charting the obstacles to the emergence of democratic institutions in regions of the world that Europeans in the era of Queen Victoria were pleased to call "uncivilized," the problem of the middle class in the Russian Empire commands our attention. As research into this complicated question proceeds, it may be useful to view economic behavior as an aspect of culture, in the sense that merchants in Russia from varying cultural backgrounds perceived economic opportunities differently and acted according to these perceptions. To the extent that such cultural patterns were kept alive and passed down to younger generations, as appears to have been the case despite impressive advances in education, then much of Russian economic history, even in the Soviet period, must be explained not purely in terms of the impersonal and universal aspects of finance, technology, and factory organization, but with due regard for the cultural context of economic behavior.

[43] Barrington Moore, Jr., *Social Origins of Dictatorship and Democracy: Lord and Peasant in the Making of the Modern World* (Boston, 1966), esp. chap. 9; Reinhard Bendix, *Kings or People: Power and the Mandate to Rule* (Berkeley, 1978), esp. chaps. 4 and 13; Theda Skocpol, *States and Social Revolutions: A Comparative Analysis of France, Russia, and China* (Cambridge, 1979), esp. chap. 6.

Selected bibliography

The sources listed here contributed directly to the elaboration of the main themes of this study: tsarist legislation affecting corporations, the evolution of corporations under the influence of such laws, and the role of the commercial-industrial leadership in the policy debates.

1. Archival documents

BAREEHC, Flige Collection, file 3: Memoirs of Nikolai N. Flige.
LOII, f. 202: Correspondence of Konstantin A. Skal'kovskii.
TsGIA, f. 20, op. 3, d. 2306: Printed version of Tsitovich Commission bill.
TsGIA, f. 23, op. 14, d. 205: Stenographic record of Timashev Conference.
TsGIA, f. 150: Materials of the Petersburg Society of Mill and Factory Owners.
TsGIA, f. 1261, op. 3, ed. kh. 69–1879: Report of Multiple Officeholding (*sovmestitel'stvo*) in Corporations by Governmental Officials.

2. Newspapers

Neftianoe delo (Baku).
Promyshlennost' i torgovlia (St. Petersburg).
Vestnik sakharnoi promyshlennosti (Kiev).

3. Government publications and documentary collections

Polnoe sobranie zakonov Rossiiskoi imperii (PSZ). Sobranie 1: 46 vols., St. Petersburg, 1830–9; Sobranie 2: 55 vols., 1830–84; Sobranie 3: 33 vols., 1882–1916.
Proekt polozheniia ob aktsionernykh obshchestvakh, sostavlennyi osoboiu kommissiei pri Ministerstve finansov. St. Petersburg, 1872.
Russia. Ministerstvo finansov. *Ministerstvo finansov, 1802–1902*. 2 vols. St. Petersburg, 1904.
Sidorov, A. L., ed. *Dokumenty po istorii monopolisticheskogo kapitalizma*. Moscow, 1959 [Vol. 6 of *Materialy po istorii SSSR*].
Sbornik deistvuiushchikh postanovlenii, izdannykh v poriadke stat'i 87 osnovnykh gosudarstvennykh zakonov: dopolnenie k Sborniku, izdannomu v 1913 godu. St. Petersburg, 1915.
Sobranie uzakonenii i rasporiazhenii pravitel'stva (SURP). 55 vols. St. Petersburg, 1863–1917.
Svod zakonov Rossiiskoi imperii, izdanie 1857 g. St. Petersburg, 1857.
Svod zamechanii na Proekt polozheniia ob aktsionernykh obshchestvakh, sostavlennyi osoboiu kommissiei pri Ministerstve finansov. St. Petersburg, 1872.

Trudy vysochaishe utverzhdennogo vserossiiskogo torgovo-promyshlennogo s"ezda 1896 g. v Nizhnem-Novgorode. 8 vols. St. Petersburg, 1897.

Viatkin, M. P., ed. *Monopolii v metallurgicheskoi promyshlennosti Rossii, 1900–1917 gg.: Dokumenty i materialy.* Moscow, 1963.

Volkov, N. E. *Ocherk zakonodatel'noi deiatel'nosti v tsarstvovanii Imperatora Aleksandra III, 1881–1894 gg.* St. Petersburg, 1910.

Zamechaniia na Proekt polozheniia ob aktsionernykh obshchestvakh, sostavlennyi osoboiu kommissieiu pri Ministerstve finansov. 2 parts in one pagination. St. Petersburg, 1872.

"Zhurnal zasedanii podkomissii iuridicheskogo obshchestva, obrazovannoi dlia obsuzhdeniia proekta postanovlenii ob aktsionernykh tovarishchestvakh," *Russkoe ekonomicheskoe obozrenie,* 4, no. 2 (Feb. 1900), 1–66. [Contains text of Justice Ministry reform bill of 1899, 42–66.]

Zhurnal zasedanii vysochaishe uchrezhdennoi kommissii po peresmotru deistvuiushchikh zakonopolozhenii o birzhakh i aktsionernykh kompaniiakh. St. Petersburg, 1896.

4. Contemporary brochures, books, legal manuals, and articles

Beable, William H. *Commercial Russia.* New York, 1919.

Bikerman, Iosif [Bickermann, Joseph]. *Cherta evreiskoi osedlosti.* St. Petersburg, 1911.

Biriukovich, V. "Birzha i publika," section "Khronika." *Vestnik Evropy,* 176, year 30, no. 6 (Nov. 1895), 337–65.

Braude, Iosif [L.]. *Aktsionernye obshchestva i tovarishchestva v torgovle i promyshlennosti.* 2nd ed. Moscow, 1926.

[Bunge, Nikolai Kh. Memorandum dated Sep. 20, 1880.] Reprinted as "Finansovaia politika tsarizma v 70–80-kh godakh XIX v." A. P. Pogrebinskii, ed. *Istoricheskii arkhiv,* 6, no. 2 (Mar.–Apr. 1960), 130–44.

Czarnomski, Francis B., ed. *The Polish Handbook, 1925.* London, 1925.

Dvadtsatiletie Kievskoi birzhi. Kiev, 1895.

Ely, Richard T. *Monopolies and Trusts.* New York, 1900.

Ermanskii, [Osip] A. [né Kogan]. "Krupnaia burzhuaziia do 1905 goda." In Lev Martov, P. Maslov, and A. Potresov, eds., *Obshchestvennoe dvizhenie v Rossii v nachale XX veka.* 4 vols. St. Petersburg, 1909–14; reprinted The Hague, 1968, vol. 1, 313–48.

Fenin, A. I. *Vospominaniia inzhenera: k istorii obshchestvennogo i khoziaistvennogo razvitiia Rossii (1883–1906 gg.).* Prague, 1938.

Firsov, Nikolai N. *Russkie torgovo-promyshlennye kompanii v pervuiu polovinu XVIII stoletiia.* Kazan, 1896.

Gal'perin, S. I. *Uchebnik russkogo torgovogo i veksel'nogo prava.* Ekaterinoslav, 1907.

Glivits, Ipolit [Gliwic, Hypolit]. *Zheleznaia promyshlennost' v Rossii.* St. Petersburg, 1911.

Gol'dshtein, I. M., ed. and trans. *Zakonodatel'stva raznykh gosudarstv o sindikatakh i trestakh.* St. Petersburg, 1910.

Gorbachev, Ivan A. *Tovarishchestva ... aktsionernye i paevye kompanii: zakon i praktika s senatskimi raz"iasneniiami.* Moscow, 1910.

Hume, George. *Thirty-Five Years in Russia.* London, 1914; reprinted New York, 1971.

Ivanovich, V., ed. *Rossiiskie partii, soiuzy i ligi: sbornik programm, ustavov i spravochnykh svedenii.* St. Petersburg, 1906.

Kaczkowski, Józef. "Towarzystwa akcyjne w państwie rosyjskiem: Studyum prawnoekonomiczne." *Ekonomista,* 8 (1908), no. 1, 81–128.

Kaminka, Avgust I. *Aktsionernaia kompaniia: iuridicheskoe issledovanie.* Vol. 1 [no more published]. St. Petersburg, 1902.

   Osnovy predprinimatel'skogo prava. Petrograd, 1917.

Selected bibliography

"Proekt polozheniia ob aktsionernykh predpriiatiiakh," *Zhurnal ministerstva iustitsii*, 3, no. 1 (Jan. 1897), 127–56.

Labry, Raoul. *L'industrie russe et la révolution.* Paris, 1919.

Lappo-Danilevskii, Aleksandr S. "Russkie promyshlennye i torgovye kompanii v pervoi polovine XVIII veka." *Zhurnal ministerstva narodnogo prosveshcheniia*, 320, no. 2 (Dec. 1898), part 2, 306–66; and 321, no. 2 (Feb. 1899), part 2, 371–436. [Also in monograph form, St. Petersburg, 1899.]

Levin, Isaak I. *Aktsionernye kommercheskie banki v Rossii.* Vol. 1 [no more published]. Petrograd, 1917.

"Rost Petrogradskoi fondovoi birzhi." In *Bankovaia entsiklopediia*, 2 vols. [no more published]. Kiev, 1914–16, vol. 2, 221–34.

Lose Blätter aus dem Geheim-Archiv der russischen Regierung. Leipzig, 1882.

Lur'e, E. S. *Predprinimatel'skie sindikaty po russkomu pravu.* St. Petersburg, 1914.

Maksimov, V. *O tovarishchestvakh.* 2nd ed. Moscow, 1911.

Mallieux, F. *La société anonyme d'après le droit civil russe.* Paris, 1902.

Mendeleev, Dmitrii I. "O vozbuzhdenii promyshlennogo razvitiia v Rossii." *Vestnik promyshlennosti* (Feb. 1884), 1–14. Reprinted, with restoration of full text of passages deleted by tsarist censor, but with new deletions by Soviet censor, in the following: Mendeleev, *Sochineniia.* 25 vols. Moscow, 1934–54, vol. 20, 74–93; Mendeleev, *Problemy ekonomicheskogo razvitiia Rossii.* Moscow, 1960, 173–88.

Miliukov, Paul. *Russia and Its Crisis.* 1905; reprinted New York, 1962.

Moscow. Birzha. *Zamechaniia na proekt polozheniia ob aktsionernykh obshchestvakh.* Moscow, 1872.

Naidenov, Nikolai A., ed. *Moskovskaia birzha 1839–1889 gg.* Moscow, 1889.

Vospominaniia o vidennom, slyshannom i ispytannom. 2 vols. Moscow, 1903–5; reprinted Newtonville, Mass., 1976.

Nikonov, Sergei P. *Iuridicheskaia priroda torgovykh i promyshlennykh predpriiatii po russkomu pravu.* Petrograd, 1917.

Ozeroff, Ivan [Ozerov, Ivan Kh.]. *Problèmes économiques et financiers de la Russie moderne.* Lausanne, 1916.

Pakhman [Pachmann], Semen V. *O zadachakh predstoiashchei reformy aktsionernogo zakonodatel'stva.* Kharkov, 1861.

Pavlov, Mikhail A. *Vospominaniia metallurga.* 2nd ed. Moscow, 1945.

Petrazhitskii, Lev I. *Aktsionernaia kompaniia.* St. Petersburg, 1898.

Pozner, M. "Spekuliatsiia i birzhevaia reforma." *Russkoe ekonomicheskoe obozrenie*, 2, no. 3 (Mar. 1898), 37–70; and no. 4 (Apr. 1898), 80–113.

Pros'bin, S. A. *Torgovo-promyshlennyi sbornik.* St. Petersburg, 1910.

Rozental', L[eon]. *Ocherk deiatel'nosti russkikh aktsionernykh obshchestv v techenii 1862 i 1863 gg.* St. Petersburg, 1865.

St. Petersburg. Birzha. *Zamechaniia S.-Peterburgskogo birzhevogo komiteta i komissii birzhevogo kupechestva na proekt polozheniia ob aktsionernykh obshchestvakh.* St. Petersburg, 1873.

Shakhovskoi, Vsevolod N. "*Sic transit gloria mundi*" (*Tak prokhodit mirskaia slava*), *1893–1917 gg.* Paris, 1952.

Shershenevich, G. F. *Kurs torgovogo prava.* 4th ed. 4 vols. St. Petersburg, 1908–12.

Shneerov, A., ed. *Voprosy promyshlennogo prava.* Moscow, 1928.

Skal'kovskii, Konstantin A. *Vospominaniia molodosti (po moriu zhiteiskomu), 1843–1869.* St. Petersburg, 1906.

Sodoffsky, Gustav. "Die Entwicklung der Aktiengesellschaften in Russland und die Bestimmungen von 21. Dezember (a. St.) 1901." *Jahrbücher für Nationalökonomie und Statistik*, 3rd series, 26 (1903), 54–81.

Spiridovich, L. [pseud.]. *Dela nashikh aktsionernykh kompanii.* Moscow, 1897.

Tarasov, Ivan T. *Uchenie ob aktsionernykh kompaniiakh.* Kiev, 1878.
Terner [Thörner], Fedor G. *Sravnitel'noe obozrenie aktsionernogo zakonodatel'stva glavneishikh evropeiskikh stran.* St. Petersburg, 1871.
Vospominaniia. Ed. M. G. Terner and E. G. Terner. 2 vols. St. Petersburg, 1910–11.
Timofeev, Aleksandr G. *Istoriia S.-Peterburgskoi birzhi, 1703–1903 gg.* St. Petersburg, 1903.
Verkhovskii, V. M., ed. *Istoricheskii ocherk razvitiia zheleznykh dorog v Rossii s ikh osnovaniia po 1897 g. vkliuchitel'no.* 2 vols. St. Petersburg, 1898–1901.
Vitmer, Aleksandr N. "Otryvochnye vospominaniia." *Istoricheskii vestnik,* 125, year 32 (Sep. 1911), 852–80.
Vol'tke, G. *Pravo torgovli i promyshlennosti v Rossii v istoricheskom razvitii.* 2nd ed. St. Petersburg, 1905.
Vrangel', Nikolai E. *Vospominaniia (ot krepostnogo prava do bol'shevikov).* Berlin, 1924.
Whishaw, James. *Memoirs of James Whishaw.* Ed. Maxwell S. Leigh. London, 1935.
Witte, Sergei Iu. *Vospominaniia.* 3 vols. Moscow, 1960.
Zaborin, Nikolai. "Trade Links: What the Law Says." *Moscow News,* July 1988, 14.

5. Secondary works

Amburger, Erik. "Das Haus Wogau & Co. in Moskau und der Wogau-Konzern, 1840–1917." In Amburger, *Fremde und Einheimische im Wirtschafts- und Kulturleben des neuzeitlichen Russland: Ausgewählte Aufsätze.* Ed. Klaus Zernack. Wiesbaden, 1982, 62–83.
Anan'ich, Nina I. "K istorii podatnykh reform 1880-kh godov." *Istoriia SSSR,* 1979, no. 1 (Jan.–Feb. 1979), 159–73.
Ball, Alan. "Lenin and the Question of Private Trade in Soviet Russia." *Slavic Review,* 43, no. 3 (Fall 1984), 399–412.
Bendix, Reinhard. *Kings or People: Power and the Mandate to Rule.* Berkeley, 1978.
Berlin, Pavel A. *Russkoe burzhuaziia v staroe i novoe vremia.* 2nd ed. Moscow, 1925.
Berliner, Joseph S. "Entrepreneurship in the Soviet Period: An Overview." In Gregory Guroff and Fred V. Carstensen, eds., *Entrepreneurship in Imperial Russia and the Soviet Union.* Princeton, 1983, 191–200.
Blackwell, William L. *The Beginnings of Russian Industrialization, 1800–1860.* Princeton, 1968.
Bovykin, Valerii I. *Formirovanie finansovogo kapitala v Rossii, konets XIX v.–1908 g.* Moscow, 1984.
Zarozhdenie finansovogo kapitala v Rossii. Moscow, 1967.
Bovykin, Valerii I., and Naumova, G. R. "Istochniki po istorii monopolii i finansovogo kapitala." In I. D. Koval'chenko, ed., *Massovye istochniki po sotsial'no-ekonomicheskoi istorii Rossii perioda kapitalizma.* Moscow, 1979, 120–60.
Buryshkin, Pavel A. *Moskva kupecheskaia.* New York, 1954.
Carstensen, Fred V. *American Enterprise in Foreign Markets: Studies of Singer and International Harvester in Imperial Russia.* Chapel Hill, 1984.
Diakin, Valentin S., and others, eds. *Krizis samoderzhaviia v Rossii, 1895–1917.* Leningrad, 1984.
Dijur, I. M. "Jews in the Russian Economy." In Jacob Frumkin, Gregor Aronson, and Alexis Goldenweiser, eds., *Russian Jewry (1860–1917).* New York, 1966, 120–43.
Fomin, P. I. *Kratkii ocherk istorii s"ezdov gornopromyshlennikov Iuga Rossii.* Kharkov, 1908.
Freeze, Gregory L. "The *Soslovie* (Estate) Paradigm and Russian Social History." *American Historical Review,* 91, no. 1 (Feb. 1986), 11–36.
Fursenko, A. A. "Materialy o korruptsii tsarskoi biurokratii (po bumagam K. A. Skal'kovskogo)." In N. E. Nosov and others, eds., *Issledovaniia po otechestvennomu istochnikovedeniiu.* Moscow, 1964, 149–56.

Gatrell, Peter. *The Tsarist Economy, 1850–1917*. New York, 1986.
Gefter, M. Ia. "Bor'ba vokrug sozdaniia metallurgicheskogo tresta v Rossii v nachale XX v." *Istoricheskie zapiski*, 47 (1954), 128–48.
"Tsarizm i zakonodatel'noe 'regulirovanie' deiatel'nosti sindikatov i trestov v Rossii nakanune pervoi mirovoi voiny." *Istoricheskie zapiski*, 54 (1955), 170–93.
Gerschenkron, Alexander. "The Early Phases of Industrialization in Russia and Their Relationship to the Historical Study of Economic Growth." In Barry E. Supple, ed., *The Experience of Economic Growth: Case Studies in Economic History*. New York, 1963, 426–44.
"Economic Backwardness in Historical Perspective." In Gerschenkron, *Economic Backwardness in Historical Perspective*. Cambridge, Mass., 1962, 5–30.
"Russia: Patterns and Problems of Economic Development, 1861–1958." In Gerschenkron, *Economic Backwardness in Historical Perspective*. Cambridge, Mass., 1962, 119–51.
Gindin, Iosif F. *Gosudarstvennyi bank i ekonomicheskaia politika tsarskogo pravitel'stva (1861–1892 gody)*. Moscow, 1960.
Goldberg, Carl A. "The Association of Industry and Trade, 1906–1917: The Successes and Failures of Russia's Organized Businessmen." Doctoral dissertation, University of Michigan, 1974.
Greenberg, Louis. *The Jews in Russia*. 2 vols. New Haven, 1944–51.
Grover, Stuart R. "Savva Mamontov and the Mamontov Circle, 1870–1905: Art Patronage and the Rise of Nationalism in Russian Art." Doctoral dissertation, University of Wisconsin, 1971.
Guroff, Gregory, and Carstensen, Fred V., eds. *Entrepreneurship in Imperial Russia and the Soviet Union*. Princeton, 1983.
Hartl, Johann H. *Die Interessenvertretungen der Industriellen in Russland, 1905–1914*. Vienna, 1978.
Hildermeier, Manfred. *Bürgertum und Stadt in Russland, 1760–1870: Rechliche Lage und soziale Struktur*. Cologne, 1986.
Istoriia Moskvy. 6 vols. Moscow, 1952–9.
Kahan, Arcadius. *Russian Economic History: The Nineteenth Century*. Ed. Roger Weiss. Chicago, 1989.
King, Victoria. "The Emergence of the St. Petersburg Industrialist Community, 1870–1905: The Origins and Early Years of the Petersburg Society of Manufacturers." Doctoral dissertation, University of California, Berkeley, 1982.
Kiniapina, Nina S. *Politika russkogo samoderzhaviia v oblasti promyshlennosti (20–50-e gody XIX v.)*. Moscow, 1968.
Kipp, Jacob W. "M. Kh. Reutern on the Russian State and Society: A Liberal Bureaucrat during the Crimean Era, 1854–60." *Journal of Modern History*, 47, no. 3 (Sep. 1975), 437–59.
Krimmer, Alexandre. *Sociétés de capitaux en Russie impériale et en Russie soviétique*. Tunis, 1934.
Krupina, T. D. "K voprosu o vzaimootnosheniiakh tsarskogo pravitel'stva s monopoliiami." *Istoricheskie zapiski*, 57 (1956), 144–76.
Laverychev, Vladimir Ia. *Gosudarstvo i monopolii v dorevoliutsionnoi Rossii*. Moscow, 1982.
"K voprosu o vmeshatel'stve tsarizma v ekonomicheskuiu zhizn' Rossii v nachale XX v." In I. M. Pushkareva and others, eds., *Samoderzhavie i krupnyi kapital v Rossii v kontse XIX–nachale XX v.: sbornik statei*. Moscow, 1982, 66–97.
Krupnaia burzhuaziia v poreformennoi Rossii (1861–1900 gg.). Moscow, 1974.
Liakhovskii, V. M. "K voprosu o fiktivnykh aktsionernykh kompaniiakh v Rossii 1860–1870-kh godov (kapitaly Riazansko-Kozlovskoi zh. d.)." *Istoricheskie zapiski*, 76 (1965), 276–91.
Lincoln, W. Bruce. *In the Vanguard of Reform: Russia's Enlightened Bureaucrats, 1825–1861*. De Kalb, Ill., 1982.

Löwe, Heinz-Dietrich. *Anti-Semitismus und Reaktionäre Utopie: Russischer Konservatismus im Kampf gegen den Wandel von Staat und Gesellschaft 1890–1917.* Hamburg, 1978.
McKay, John P. "Baku Oil and Transcaucasian Pipelines, 1883–1891: A Study in Tsarist Economic Policy." *Slavic Review*, 43, no. 4 (Winter 1984), 603–23.
 Pioneers for Profit: Foreign Entrepreneurship and Russian Industrialization, 1885–1913. Chicago, 1970.
Metzer, Jacob. *Some Economic Aspects of Railroad Development in Tsarist Russia.* New York, 1977. [Photoreproduction of doctoral dissertation, University of Chicago, 1972.]
Modern Encyclopedia of Russian and Soviet History (MERSH). Ed. Joseph L. Wieczynski. Gulf Breeze, Florida, 1976–89.
Moore, Barrington, Jr. *Social Origins of Dictatorship and Democracy: Lord and Peasant in the Making of the Modern World.* Boston, 1966.
Mosina, Iia G. *Formirovanie burzhuazii v politicheskuiu silu v Sibiri.* Tomsk, 1978.
Mosse, Werner E. "Russia and the Levant, 1856–1862: Grand Duke Constantine Nicolaevich and the Russian Steam Navigation Company." *Journal of Modern History*, 26, no. 1 (Mar. 1954), 39–48.
Owen, Thomas C. *Capitalism and Politics in Russia: A Social History of the Moscow Merchants, 1855–1905.* Cambridge, 1981.
Pełka, Bolesław. "Organizacja i historia łódzkiej giełdy pieniężnej i jej akta." *Archeion*, 46 (1967), 158–69.
Petrov, Iu. A. "Moskovskie banki i promyshlennost' k nachalu XX v." In I. M. Pushkareva and others, eds., *Samoderzhavie i krupnyi kapital v Rossii v kontse XIX–nachale XX v.: sbornik statei.* Moscow, 1982, 113–33.
Pintner, Walter M. *Russian Economic Policy under Nicholas I.* Ithaca, 1967.
Pogrebinskii, A. P. "Spornye voprosy izucheniia gosudarstvenno-monopolisticheskogo kapitalizma v dorevoliutsionnoi Rossii." In A. L. Sidorov, ed., *Ob osobennostiakh imperializma v Rossii.* Moscow, 1963, 124–48.
"Stroitel'stvo zheleznykh dorog v poreformennoi Rossii i finansovaia politika tsarizma (60–90-e gody XIX v.). *Istoricheskie zapiski*, 47 (1954), 149–80.
Pushkareva, I. M., and others, eds. *Samoderzhavie i krupnyi kapital v Rossii v kontse XIX–nachale XX v.: sbornik statei.* Moscow, 1982.
Queen, George S. *The United States and the Material Advance in Russia, 1881–1906.* New York, 1976. [Photoreproduction of doctoral dissertation, University of Illinois, 1941.]
Raeff, Marc. *The Well-Ordered Police State: Social and Institutional Change through Law in the Germanies and Russia.* New Haven, 1983.
Rieber, Alfred J. "The Formation of La Grande Société des Chemins de Fer Russes." *Jahrbücher für Geschichte Osteuropas*, N.S., 21, no. 3 (Sep. 1973), 375–91.
 Merchants and Entrepreneurs in Imperial Russia. Chapel Hill, 1982.
Roosa, Ruth A. "The Association of Industry and Trade, 1906–1914: An Examination of the Economic Views of Organized Industrialists in Prerevolutionary Russia." Doctoral dissertation, Columbia University, 1968.
 "Russian Industrialists and 'State Socialism,' 1906–1917." *Soviet Studies*, 23, no. 1 (Jan. 1972), 395–417.
 "Russian Industrialists Look to the Future: Thoughts on Economic Development, 1906–1917." In John S. Curtiss, ed., *Essays in Russian and Soviet History.* New York, 1963, 198–218.
Ruckman, Jo Ann S. *The Moscow Business Elite: A Social and Cultural Portrait of Two Generations, 1840–1905.* De Kalb, Ill., 1984.
Rudchenko, I. Ia. *Istoricheskii ocherk oblozheniia torgovli i promyslov v Rossii.* St. Petersburg, 1893.
Russkii biograficheskii slovar' (RBS). 25 vols. (incomplete). St. Petersburg, 1896–1918.

Rybakov, Iurii Ia. *Promyshlennoe zakonodatel'stvo Rossii pervoi poloviny XIX veka (istochnikovedcheskie ocherki)*. Moscow, 1986.
Shepelev, Leonid E. "Aktsionernoe zakonodatel'stvo Vremennogo pravitel'stva." In N. E. Nosov and others, eds., *Issledovaniia po sotsial'no-politicheskoi istorii Rossii: sbornik statei pamiati B. A. Romanova*. Leningrad, 1971, 369–80.
 Aktsionernye kompanii v Rossii. Leningrad, 1973.
 "Arkhivnye fondy aktsionernykh kommercheskikh bankov." *Problemy istochnikovedeniia*, 7 (1959), 58–104.
 "Chastnokapitalisticheskie torgovo-promyshlennye predpriiatiia Rossii v kontse XIX-nachale XX vv. i ikh arkhivnye fondy." *Informatsionnyi biulleten' Glavnogo arkhivnogo upravleniia MVD SSSR*, 1958, no. 10 (Oct.), 76–107.
 "Iz istorii russkogo aktsionernogo zakonodatel'stva (zakon 1836 g.)." In N. E. Nosov, ed., *Vnutrenniaia politika tsarizma (seredina XVI–nachalo XX veka)*. Leningrad, 1967, 168–96.
 "Tsarizm i aktsionernoe uchreditel'stvo v 1870–1910-kh godakh." In N. E. Nosov and others, eds., *Problemy krest'ianskogo zemlevladeniia i vnutrennei politiki Rossii: dooktriabr'skii period*. Leningrad, 1972, 274–318.
Tsarizm i burzhuaziia v 1904–1914 gg.: problemy torgovo-promyshlennoi politiki. Leningrad, 1987.
Tsarizm i burzhuaziia vo vtoroi polovine XIX veka: problemy torgovo-promyshlennoi politiki. Leningrad, 1981.
Solov'eva, Aida M. *Zheleznodorozhnyi transport Rossii vo vtoroi polovine XIX v.* Moscow, 1975.
Tolf, Robert W. *The Russian Rockefellers: The Saga of the Nobel Family and the Russian Oil Industry*. Stanford, 1976.
Tsyperovich, G. *Sindikaty i tresty v Rossii*. 2nd ed. Moscow, 1919.
Von Laue, Theodore H. *Sergei Witte and the Industrialization of Russia*. New York, 1963.
West, James L. "The Rjabušinskij Circle: Industrialists in Search of a Bourgeoisie." *Jahrbücher für Geschichte Osteuropas*, N.S., 32, no. 3 (Sep. 1984), 358–77.
Wortman, Richard S. *The Development of a Russian Legal Consciousness*. Chicago, 1976.

6. Studies of economic development and corporate law outside Russia

Aitken, Hugh G. J., ed. *Explorations in Enterprise*. Cambridge, Mass., 1965.
Berman, Harold J. *Law and Revolution: The Formation of the Western Legal Tradition*. Cambridge, Mass., 1983.
Chandler, Alfred, Jr. *The Visible Hand: The Managerial Revolution in American Business*. Cambridge, Mass., 1977.
Chandler, Alfred, Jr., and Daems, Herman, eds. *Managerial Hierarchies: Comparative Perspectives on the Rise of the Modern Industrial Enterprise*. Cambridge, Mass., 1980.
Clark, Rodney. *The Japanese Company*. New Haven, 1979.
Dodd, Edwin M. *American Business Corporations until 1860, with Special Reference to Massachusetts*. Cambridge, Mass., 1954.
Drucker, Peter F. *The Concept of the Corporation*. Mentor ed. New York, 1964.
DuBois, Armand B. *The English Business Company After the Bubble Act*. New York, 1938; reprinted 1971.
Fischer, Paul. *Die Aktiengesellschaft in der nationalsozialistischen Wirtschaft: Ein Beitrag zur Reform des Gesellschaftsrechts*. Munich, 1936.
Freedeman, Charles E. *Joint-Stock Enterprise in France, 1807–1867: From Privileged Company to Modern Corporation*. Chapel Hill, 1979.
Frommel, S. N., and Thompson, J. H., eds. *Company Law in Europe*. London, 1975.

Grange, William J., and Woodbury, Thomas C. *Corporation Law: Operating Procedures for Officers and Directors.* 2nd ed. New York, 1964.
Hirschmeier, Johannes, and Yui, Tsunehiko. *The Development of Japanese Business, 1600–1973.* 2nd ed. Boston, 1981.
Horn, Norbert, and Kocka, Jürgen, eds. *Recht und Entwicklung der Grossunternehmen im 19. und frühen 20. Jahrhundert.* Göttingen, 1979.
Hunt, Bishop C. *The Development of the Business Corporation in England, 1800–1867.* Cambridge, Mass., 1936.
Hurst, James W. *The Legitimacy of the Business Corporation in the Law of the United States, 1780–1970.* Charlottesville, Va., 1970.
McCloskey, Donald N. *Enterprise and Trade in Victorian Britain: Essays in Historical Economics.* London, 1981.
North, Douglass C. *Structure and Change in Economic History.* New York, 1981.
Rungta, Radhe S. *The Rise of Business Corporations in India, 1851–1900.* Cambridge, 1970.
Thomas, Philip A., ed. *Private Enterprise and the East African Company.* Dar es Salaam, 1969.
Tsurumi, Yoshi. *Japanese Business: A Research Guide with Annotated Bibliography.* New York, 1978.
Tucker, W. T. *The Social Context of Economic Behavior.* New York, 1964.
Weber, Max. *From Max Weber: Essays in Sociology.* Trans. Hans H. Gerth. Ed. Hans H. Gerth and C. Wright Mills. New York, 1958.
  General Economic History. Trans. Frank Knight. New York, 1927.
  The Theory of Social and Economic Organization. Trans. A. M. Henderson and Talcott Parsons. Ed. Talcott Parsons. New York, 1964.
Wiener, Martin J. *English Culture and the Decline of the Industrial Spirit, 1850–1980.* Cambridge, 1981.
Yushino, M. Y. *Japan's Managerial System: Tradition and Innovation.* Cambridge, Mass., 1968.

Index

Aksakov, Ivan S., 87
Alchevskii, Aleksei K., 207
Alexander I, 10, 25
Alexander II, 30–1, 77
Alexander III, 43
Amsterdam, 3
Amur region, 188
Anchor Insurance Company, 183–4
Anglo-Russian Bank, 64
Arkas, Nikolai A., 36
Armenians, 131
Association of Industry and Trade (AIT)
   and corporate bonds, 185
   and incorporation procedures, 170–1
   on law of April 18, 1914, 176–9
   ninth congress of (1915), 187
   and Provisional Government, 190
   and railroads, 205
   and Timashev Conference, 161, 165, 168
Association of Trade and Agriculture, 185
audit commission, 21, 66, 151
Austria, 56, 142, 182
Avdakov, Nikolai S., 160, 177, 212–13, 216 n36
Azerbaijanis, 131
Azov-Don Commercial Bank, 87

Babkin Woolen Textile Company, 102
Babst, Ivan K., 58, 87, 109, 110
Bakhshisaraitsev, 193
Baku, 112, 121
Baltic Railroad, 44
banks
   under Bunge, 109–10
   in Butovskii Commission bill, 70
   and conflict of interest, 87–8, 97, 151–2, 167
   development of, 98, 105–6
   nonprofit, 107
   under Reutern, 81, 105–9
   and State Bank, 97–104

   state supervision of, 188–9
   and Tsitovich Commission, 142
Bansa, Konrad K., 147 n72
Baranov, Aleksandr A., 9
Baranov Commission, 44, 80
Bark, Petr L., 174–5
Beilis, Mendel, 174
Belgium, 56, 120, 204
Beloretsk Iron Company, 183
Benckendorff, Aleksandr Kh., 117
Benckendorff, Dmitrii A., 89–90
Bendix, Reinhard, 218
Berliner, Joseph, 195
Berman, Harold J., 218
Bessarabia, 119
Bezobrazov, Vladimir P., 34
Billington, James H., 116
Birzhevye vedomosti (Stock-exchange news), 59, 73
Bloch, Jan, 92
Bludov, Dmitrii N., 16–18, 21, 24, 27
board of directors, 20–1, 66, 193
Boborykin, Petr D., 50
Bobrinskii, Aleksei A., 135
Bobrinskii, Andrei A., 135, 177
bonds, 29, 185
Brodskii family, 172–3
Brok, Petr F., 31, 33
Bunge, Nikolai Kh.
   and banks, 78, 104, 109–10
   and concession system, 57
   and corporations, 207–8, 210
   and railroads, 45
   and sugar cartel, 134
   training of, 80
Butovskii, Aleksandr I., 68–70, 87–8
Butovskii Commission, 68–74

capital, foreign, 41, 64, 118, 145, 148, 188
cartels, 117, 132–7, 170
Caspian Sea, 71, 119
Catherine the Great, 8–9, 97

228

Caucasus and Mercury Steamship Company, 46t, 72, 35 n14
Caucasus region, *see* Transcaucasus
Chaikovskii, Petr I., 42–3
chambers of commerce, proposed, 114, 159–60, 204
Chandler, Alfred D., Jr., 3, 213
Chauvin, George von, 184
Chevkin, Konstantin V., 85
Chistiakov, P. S., 164
Chizhov, Fedor V., 35, 83, 87, 89, 210
Cion, Il'ia F., 149
Colignon, 41
Commercial Bank, 17, 33
Commercial Council, 60, 66, 73
Commercial-Industrial Congress (1882), 114
company, *see* joint-stock company, share partnership
concession system
    abolition of, 190
    administrative nature of, 26, 27, 57, 119
    advantages of, 6–7
    and Butovskii Commission, 70
    disadvantages of, 64, 66, 69, 77, 138
    in law of 1836, 18–19
    reform of, 85, 105–6, 109
    under Soviet regime, 191, 193
    and Timashev Conference, 163–6
    and Tsitovich Commission, 142, 144–6
    in World War I, 185–7
Consultative Board of Gold and Platinum Producers, 159, 164
Consultative Board of Iron Producers, 159
corporation, *see* joint-stock company, share partnership
corporations, foreign, 120–2
Cossacks, 63, 160
Council of the United Nobility, 174
Council of Trade and Manufacturing, 59, 113 n80, 114 n81
Courland, 119

Delaware, 141
Del'vig, Andrei I., 35
Dement'ev, Petr A., 211–12
Demidov family, 8
Derwies, Pavel G., 42–3
Diakin, Valentin S., 175 n47, 176
Dnepr Steamship Company, 29
Dobrovol'skii, N. S., 170
Don Military Region, 63, 123, 188, 191
Doss, I. F., 146 n69
Doumer, Paul, 178
Dukhobors, 131

Ely, Richard T., 133 n37, 141
Emile Zündel Cotton Textile Company, 129
England, *see* Great Britain
Ermolov, Aleksei S., 212
exchanges, 47

Fedorov, Mikhail M., 162
Firsov, Nikolai N., 7
Flige, N., 104
Flige, Nikolai N., 104
foreigners, restrictions on
    under Shakhovskoi, 186
    in shipping companies, 71, 119
    and Timashev Conference, 165–6, 168
    in Turkestan, 128
    under Vyshnegradskii, 119–20
    under Witte, 121–2, 148–50, 156
France, 4, 27, 29, 56–8, 120, 162, 178–9
Freeze, Gregory, 60 n18, 209

Gagarin, Pavel P., 88
general assembly of stockholders, 20, 22, 66, 71, 150–1, 193
Gentry Land Bank, 101
Gerke, A. A. 146 n69
Germany, 20 n41, 56–7, 120, 161, 182–4, 193, 194, 203, 214
Gerschenkron, Alexander, 200–1, 216
Gindin, Iosif F., 52, 99–102
Gintsburg, A. G., 159
Girs, Aleksandr K., 73
Golitsyn, Grigorii S., 130–2
Golos (The voice), 73
Golubev, Viktor E., 131
Gorbachev, Mikhail S., 196–7
Goremykhin, Ivan L., 177, 179
Gosk'e, 92
Goujon, Jules, 168–70, 177, 217
Grauman, Leopold F., 159
Great Britain
    accounting profession in, 213
    corporate law of, 4, 56–8
    corporations in, 162
    economic conditions in, 213–14
    financial influence of, 64
    legal system of, 178
    reciprocity treaty with, 120
Great Iaroslavl Manufacturing Company, 138
Greece, 120
Greig, Samuil A., 94
Grinval'd, Iu. K., 161–2

Haimson, Leopold, 218 n41
Heehan, Thomas E., 116

Hermann, Rudolf, 184
Hosking, Geoffrey, 218 n41
Hume, George, 79
Hungary, 182, 185

India, 180, 200 n4
Italy, 56, 120
Izosimov, 87

Jews, restrictions on
  under Alexander II, 118, 122–3, 126
  under Alexander III, 122, 127
  Goujon and, 168–9
  under Nicholas II, 123–6, 129, 161–2, 171–5, 179–80, 217–18
  Shakhovskoi and, 186–7
  Timashev Conference and, 165, 168
  in Turkestan, 128–9
  Witte and, 148–50, 156, 158
joint-stock company, 12–13, 23, 51–2, 152, 167, 192

Kaczkowski, Józef, 55
Kahan, Arcadius, 171–2
Kakhanov, Mikhail S., 95
Kaminka, Avgust I., 76–7, 136, 143–4
Kankrin, Egor F., 15–18, 21, 24, 27, 29
Kharkov Coal and Iron Exchange, 47
Kharkov Exchange Committee, 140
Kharkov Land Bank, 107
Kherson Land Bank, 107
Khlopok (Cotton) Company, 129
Khrushchev, Nikita S., 219
Kierbedź, Stanisław, 35
Kiev, 122, 172, 174
Kiev Exchange Committee, 127, 140
Kiev Private Bank, 104
Kniazhevich, Aleksandr M., 31
Kobeko, Dmitrii F., 86
Kokorev, Vasilii A., 35, 83
Kokovtsov, Vladimir N., 170, 174, 178, 205
Kol'chugin Copper Company, 183
Konovalov, Aleksandr I., 155, 169–70, 189–90, 217
Kornilov, Fedor P., 85
Koshelev, Aleksandr I., 83
Kostroma Commercial Bank, 105
Kovalevskii, Vladimir I., 140, 148–50
Krestovnikov, Grigorii A., 147 n72, 177
Krivoshein, Aleksandr N., 173, 175
Kronenberg, Leopold, 104, 210
Kronstadt Commercial Bank, 105
Kuban region, 211
Kulomzin, Anatolii N., 43, 84–6, 88–9, 100, 149

Kul'zhinskii, 87
Kursk-Kiev Railroad, 42

Labry, Raoul, 202
Lamanskii, Evgenii I., 49, 88–9, 98–9, 101–4
Landau, L. A., 193
Latvia, 191
Latvian Credit Bank, 191
Laverychev, Vladimir Ia., 101, 128–9
laws (subject in parentheses)
  October 27, 1699 (trading companies), 7
  September 6, 1805 (limited liability), 10
  January 1, 1807 (corporations and partnerships), 10–13
  December 6, 1836 (corporations), 15–24, 26–8, 30, 34, 75, 77, 82
  June 14, 1848 (corporate shares), 27–8
  December 28, 1853 (financial procedures for incorporation), 28
  January 1, 1863 (commercial certificates), 60–3
  July 10, 1864 (landholding by Poles and Jews in western provinces), 122, 126
  December 10, 1865 (landholding by Poles and Jews in western provinces), 122, 126
  November 24, 1869 (stock ownership in Caspian Sea steamship companies), 71, 119
  May 31, 1872 (chartering of banks), 108–9
  May 22, 1880 (residence and landholding by Jews in Don Military Region), 123
  May 3, 1882 (restrictions on Jews), 123
  April 5, 1883 (chartering of banks), 109–10
  December 3, 1884 (conflict of interest), 96
  December 27, 1884 (corporate landholding in southwestern region), 122–3, 126
  January 23, 1885 (ban against non-Russians in Siberian gold mining), 119–20
  March 14, 1887 (ban against landholding in western provinces by foreign individuals and corporations), 119, 166
  June 2, 1887 (eminent domain for mining operations), 160

Index   231

December 24, 1888 (mining in Kingdom of Poland), 119
June 8, 1893 (futures trading in corporate securities), 138–9
November 29, 1893 (corporate landholding in Turkestan), 128
June 8, 1898 (business taxes), 123–5
November 24, 1898 (forfeiture of business certificates), 124
June 8, 1899 (ministerial comments on draft charters of corporations), 150
June 19, 1899 (restrictions on foreigners and Jews as corporate directors), 149 n74
June 15, 1901 (insurance companies), 152
December 21, 1901 (general assemblies and audit commissions), 150–4
May 10, 1903 (restrictions on ownership and use of rural land by Jews), 161
April 18, 1914 (limits on corporate landholding), 173, 175–9, 215
February 2, 1915 (restrictions on citizens of Austria, Hungary, Germany, and Turkey), 182
May 10, 1915 (liquidation of trading firms owned by German citizens), 182–3
July 1, 1915 (liquidation of corporations owned by German citizens), 182–3
April 5, 1916 (corporate landholding during war), 187
May 13, 1916 (corporate landholding during war), 188
May 13, 1916 (wartime landholding of corporations supplying armed forces), 188
March 10, 1917 (incorporation under Provisional Government), 189–90
April 10, 1923 (incorporation under Soviet government), 191
January 13, 1987 (joint ventures between foreign corporations and enterprises in USSR), 196
Levin, Isaak I., 103
liability, limited
  advantages of, 3
  under Alexander I, 10
  under Alexander II, 57–8, 79
  in Imperial Germany, 168
  in law of 1836, 18–19, 23
  under Nazi regime, 194
  under Peter I, 8
  in Prussia, 56
  under Soviet regime, 192
Libau Commercial Bank, 105
Libau Exchange Committee, 140
Libau-Romny Railroad, 42
Lincoln, W. Bruce, 36
Littauer, S. I., 159
Livonia, 119
Lopukhin, Prince, 100, 126

McKay, John P., 210
Mamontov, Savva I., 207
Manufacturing Council, 60, 66
Marc, Heinrich, 35
Marc, Hugo, 184
Marc, Mauritz, 184
Markov, Nikolai E., II, 174
Meck, K. F., 42–3
Meck, Nadezhda, 43 n32
Mel'nikov, Pavel P., 42
Mendeleev, Dmitrii I., 111–15, 209
merchant estate, 10–11, 13, 60–3, 87, 123, 214
Miliukov, Pavel N., 213
Miliutin, Ivan A., 101
Miliutin trading firm, 100
Ministry of Industry, proposed, 114, 159
Ministry of Trade and Industry, 160, 171
model charter, proposed, 107, 109, 150 n77, 186
Molokane, 131
Moore, Barrington, Jr., 218
Morozov, Timofei S., 101
Moscow Bank of Trade, 101
Moscow Commercial Loan Bank, 87, 102–3, 105
Moscow Electrolytic Company, 184
Moscow Exchange Committee (MEC)
  and Butovskii Commission, 71–2
  and corporate bonds, 185
  and incorporation by registration, 147 n72
  and metallurgical trust, 136
  and stock market, 47–8
  and Tsitovich Commission, 140
Moscow-Iaroslavl-Archangel Railroad, 44, 46t
Moscow Industrial Bank, 105, 108–9
Moscow Merchant Bank, 47, 52–3, 83, 88
Moscow-Riazan Railroad, 43, 44, 46t
Moscow-Saratov Railroad, 40
multiple officeholding, 86–97, 150–2, 167

Naidenov, Nikolai A., 101–3, 147 n72
Netherlands, 56
New Economic Policy (NEP), 191–4, 196
Nicholas I, 14, 23, 25

Nicholas II, 149, 175–6, 179
Nikolaev (city), 105
Nikonov, Sergei P., 183
Nizhnii Novgorod Exchange Committee, 140, 166
Nobel Brothers Petroleum Company, 152–3, 210
North, Douglass C., 5–6
Novoe vremia (New times), 174–5
Novoselov, S. S., 165
Novosel'skii, Nikolai A., 35–6

Odessa, 9, 105
Odessa Exchange Committee, 140, 143
Old Believers, 63–4, 127
Oliphant, Laurence, 30
Ozerov, Ivan Kh., 180, 208–9

Pakhman, Semen, 57–8, 69–70
Palen, Konstantin I., 67–8
Panic of 1873, 76
partnership, 3, 4, 11–13, 50, 56–8, 82, 168, 190, 192
Paul I, 9
Peretts, Egor A., 95
Permanent Council of Gentry Societies, 174
Peter the Great, 7–8, 79, 203
Peterhof Railroad, 40
Petrazhitskii, Lev I., 146 n69, 199–200
Petrograd Commercial-Industrial Union, 181
Pirvits, E. E., 145–6
Pleve, Nikolai V., 188 n12
Pobedonostsev, Konstantin P., 206–7
Pogrebinskii, A. P., 43, 88
Poland, 190
Poland, Kingdom of, 119, 123, 217
Poles, restrictions on, 122, 126–7, 144, 156, 158, 165
Polezhaev, Aleksei M., 101
Polezhaev, Mikhail M., 101
pollution, industrial, 25–6, 179
Pomerantsev, A. A., 164
Popov, V., 191
Portugal, 56
Pos'et, Konstantin N., 95
Potocki, Józef A., 157–8
Poznański family, 129
Prodameta (syndicate), 133, 135
Produgol' (syndicate), 133, 135–6, 170, 178
Prokhorov family, 129
Promyshlennost' i torgovlia (Industry and trade), 161
property rights, 5
Provisional Government (1917), 181–2
Prussia, 5, 29, 56, 73
  see also Germany
Putilov, Nikolai I., 101–2

Raeff, Marc, 203
Ragozin, Evgenii I., 73
railroads, 15–16, 35, 37–45, 83, 142, 152, 205–6
registration system of incorporation
  Association of Industry and Trade on, 168
  in Butovskii Commission, 70
  implementation of, 190
  Konovalov on, 169
  Ministry of Trade and Industry on, 163 n19
  Provisional Government and, 190
  State Duma and, 188
  Tarasov on, 77
  in Timashev Conference, 163–6, 176
  in Tsitovich Commission, 140–2, 144
  Witte's abandonment of, 145–50
Reutern, Mikhail Kh.
  and banks, 102–10, 117
  and corporate law reform, 67–8, 71, 75–7, 210–11
  and credit market, 41, 46, 47, 49, 118
  and Don Military Region, 63
  economic program of, 31, 64, 81–2
  and incorporation of small enterprises, 51
  and railroads, 39, 44, 94
  and tariff duties, 59
  training of, 80
Reval Commercial Bank, 105
Riabushinskii, Pavel P., 176–7, 204 n11, 217
Riazan Bank of Trade, 87
Riazan-Kozlov Railroad, 43, 44
Riga, 9, 67, 105, 210
Riga Commercial Bank, 104–5
Riga-Dünaburg Railroad, 40, 46t
Riga Exchange Committee, 66–7, 73, 140, 143, 146
Rittikh, Aleksandr A., 171, 175–6
Roosa, Ruth A., 217
Rostov-on-Don, 123, 196 n33
Rostov-on-Don Exchange Committee, 140
Rostow, Walt W., 195 n30
Rothschild, 92
Rothstein, Adolf, 90, 92
Rotwand, Stanisław M., 164
Rozenblium, D. Iu., 140–1
Rozental', Leon M., 73, 210
Rukhlov, Sergei V., 157
Rumania, 56

Russian-American Company, 9, 100
Russian Bank for Foreign Trade, 88
Russian Banking Association, 188–9
Russian Cotton Association, 179
Russian Industrial Society (RIS), 37, 48, 60, 72, 73, 147 n72
Russian Insurance and Annuity Company, 72
Russian Railroad Company, 39–42, 44, 46t
Russian Society of Sugar Producers (RSSP), 134–5, 177, 190
Russian Steamship Company (ROPIT), 36–7, 46t, 86
Russian Technical Society, 59
Russkaia mysl' (Russian thought), 212
Russo-Asian Bank, 183
Russo-French Trade Bureau, 202
Russo-Turkish War (1877–8), 44, 105
Rybinsk-Bologoe Railroad, 48, 93

St. Petersburg Discount and Loan Bank, 52, 87, 164, 183
 [Note: Petrograd replaced St. Petersburg in all organizational titles between August 1914 and January 1924]
St. Petersburg Exchange Committee (PEC)
 and Butovskii Commission, 69, 72–4, 110
 and corporate bonds, 185
 and stock market, 18, 47
 and Timashev Conference, 166–7
 and Tsitovich Commission, 140, 143
St. Petersburg Fire Insurance Company, 46t
St. Petersburg Grain Exchange, 47
St. Petersburg International Commercial Bank, 130, 183
St. Petersburg-Moscow Railroad, 37–8
St. Petersburg Mutual Credit Society, 48–9, 88
St. Petersburg Securities Exchange, 166–7
St. Petersburg Society of Mill and Factory Owners (PSMFO), 166–7, 170, 185
St. Petersburg Water Company, 92
Sankt-Peterburgskie vedomosti (St. Petersburg news), 73
savings and loan institutions, 107
Sazonov, Sergei D., 178
Schäffle, Albert E. F., 69
Schumacher, 183–4
Schumpeter, Joseph A., 216 n36
Shakhovskoi, Prince Vsevolod N., 181, 186–8
Sharapov, Sergei F., 149
share partnership, 12–13, 22–3, 51–2, 152–3, 167, 192

Shavrov, Nikolai A., 37
Shepelev, Leonid E.
 on Butovskii Commission bill, 75–6
 on concession system, 85, 170–1
 on conflict of interest, 96
 on interest rates, 32, 65
 on law of 1836, 16, 21, 22
 on law of April 18, 1914, 175–6, 180
 on Turkestan, 128
 on Witte, 145
Shepetovka-Proskurov Railroad, 157–8
Shipov, Ivan P., 135–6, 140
Shumakher, Dmitrii D., 87
Shuvalov, Petr I., 8
Siberia, 119, 159, 174, 218
Siberian Bank of Trade, 88
Siemens and Halske Company, 130
Siemens Brothers Company, 184
Singer Sewing Machine Company, 208
Skal'kovskii, Konstantin A., 84
Skocpol, Theda, 218
Sliozberg, G. B., 146 n69
Soldatenkov, Kuz'ma T., 101
Solzhenitsyn, Aleksandr I., 116–17
South Russian Coal and Iron Association (SRCIA), 146 n71, 160, 173, 187, 206 n14
South Sea Bubble, 4
Southwestern Railroad, 80, 86, 93, 140
Spain, 5, 56, 79
speculation
 Butovskii Commission and, 66, 70
 in 1850s, 34, 53
 in 1860s, 47–9, 81
 in 1890s, 138–40, 207
 law of 1836 and, 17–18, 21, 30–1
Speranskii, Mikhail M., 1
Spiridovich, L. [pseud.], 138, 153
Stackelberg Commission, 65
Stalin, Iosif V., 194
State Bank, 110
 and credit market, 33–5, 48–9, 97–9
 and conflict of interest, 87–8
 irregular loans of, 100–5, 126
 and Tsitovich Commission, 143
steamship lines, 36–7
Stieglitz, Alexander L., 40, 88, 98
Stieglitz, Ludwig, 40
Stolypin, Petr A., 157
Strogonov, Grigorii A., 84
Strol'man, K. A., 164
Strousberg, Bethel Henry, 102–3
Struve, Petr B., 198
Stundists, 131
Sukovkin, Akinfii P., 84
Sushchov, Nikolai N., 49–50, 211

Switzerland, 56
syndicates, *see* cartels

Taganrog, 105, 123
Tarasov, Ivan T., 77–8
taxation, 123–4, 185
Terner, Fedor G., 69–70, 83–4
Timashev, Sergei I., 163–4, 166, 171, 172, 187
Timashev Conference, 163–4, 168, 170
Times (London), 178
Times (New York), 200
Timiriazev, Vasilii I., 162, 164–5
Torgovo-promyshlennaia gazeta (Commercial and industrial gazette), 140
Torgovyi sbornik (The commercial reporter), 73
trading firm, *see* partnership
Transcaucasus, 128, 130–1, 171, 173
Trinity Railroad, *see* Moscow-Iaroslavl-Archangel Railroad
Tsarskoe selo Railroad, 37
Tsitovich, Petr P., 140, 142
Tsitovich Commission, 140–50, 154, 162
Turkestan, 128–9, 173
Turkey, 56, 182
Tverskoi, Petr A. [pseud.], *see* Dement'ev, Petr A.

Ukraine, 185
Ulmanis, Karlis, 191
Union of the Russian People, 157, 174
United States of America, 25 n51, 141
Ural region, 190, 214
Utin, Iakov I., 146 n69, 154 n87, 164

Valuev, Petr A., 87, 95
Vargunin, Ivan A., 101
Varpakhovskii, I. P., 84
Vestnik finansov (Financial herald), 140
Vilna, 122

Vinogradov, L. A., 193–4
Vitmer, Aleksandr N., 92–3
Volga-Don Horsedrawn Railroad, 37
Volga-Don Railroad, 40, 46t
Volga-Kama Commercial Bank, 88, 101
Vol'tke, G., 125
Von Laue, Theodore H., 201–2, 218 n41
Vorontsov-Dashkov, Ilarion I., 170–1
Voznesenskaia, Ninel', 196
Vyshnegradskii, Aleksandr I., 140, 188
Vyshnegradskii, Ivan A., 80, 91–3, 118–20

Walkin, Jacob, 218 n41
warehouse companies, 106–7, 109
Warsaw Exchange Committee, 140, 146
Warsaw-Vienna Railroad, 37–8, 44
Weber, Max, 13–14, 114 n82, 195 n30, 199, 207 n16
Whishaw, James, 121–2
White Sea, 8
Winans, William, 84
Witte, Sergei Iu.
    and corporate law reform, 137–8, 141–2, 145–50, 152, 210
    and foreign companies, 121–2, 125, 156, 204–5
    Golitsyn on, 130–1
    and Jews, 125, 156–8
    on Mendeleev, 112
    as railroad manager, 43, 80
    on speculation, 139
    training of, 80
    on Vyshnegradskii, 93
Wogau and Company, 183–4
Wortman, Richard S., 14
Wrangel, Nikolai E., 130–2, 211–12

Zakrevskii, Arsenii A., 26
Zolotarev, Aleksandr G., 69
Żukowski, Władysław, 165, 205

Studies of the Harriman Institute

Soviet National Income in 1937 by Abram Bergson, Columbia University Press, 1953.

Through the Glass of Soviet Literature: Views of Russian Society, Ernest Simmons Jr., ed., Columbia University Press, 1953.

Polish Postwar Economy by Thad Paul Alton, Columbia University Press, 1954.

Management of the Industrial Firm in the USSR: A Study in Soviet Economic Planning by David Granick, Columbia University Press, 1954.

Soviet Policies in China, 1917–1924 by Allen S. Whiting, Columbia University Press, 1954; paperback, Stanford University Press, 1968.

Literary Politics in the Soviet Ukraine, 1917–1934 by George S.N. Luckyj, Columbia University Press, 1956.

The Emergence of Russian Panslavism, 1856–1870 by Michael Boro Petrovich, Columbia University Press, 1956.

Lenin on Trade Unions and Revolution, 1893–1917 by Thomas Taylor Hammond, Columbia University Press, 1956.

The Last Years of the Georgian Monarchy, 1658–1832 by David Marshall Lang, Columbia University Press, 1957.

The Japanese Thrust into Siberia, 1918 by James William Morley, Columbia University Press, 1957.

Bolshevism in Turkestan, 1917–1927 by Alexander G. Park, Columbia University Press, 1957.

Soviet Marxism: A Critical Analysis by Herbert Marcuse, Columbia University Press, 1958; paperback, Columbia University Press, 1985.

Soviet Policy and the Chinese Communists, 1931–1946 by Charles B. McLane, Columbia University Press, 1958.

The Agrarian Foes of Bolshevism: Promise and Defeat of the Russian Socialist Revolutionaries, February to October, 1917 by Oliver H. Radkey, Columbia University Press, 1958.

Pattern for Soviet Youth: A Study of the Congresses of the Komsomol, 1918–1954 by Ralph Talcott Fisher, Jr., Columbia University Press, 1959.

The Emergence of Modern Lithuania by Alfred Erich Senn, Columbia University Press, 1959.

The Soviet Design for a World State by Elliot R. Goodman, Columbia University Press, 1960.

Settling Disputes in Soviet Society: The Formative Years of Legal Institutions by John N. Hazard, Columbia University Press, 1960.

Soviet Marxism and Natural Science, 1917–1932 by David Joravsky, Columbia University Press, 1961.

Russian Classics in Soviet Jackets by Maurice Friedberg, Columbia University Press, 1962.

Stalin and the French Communist Party, 1941–1947 by Alfred J. Rieber, Columbia University Press, 1962.

Sergei Witte and the Industrialization of Russia by Theodore H. Von Laue, Columbia University Press, 1963.

Ukrainian Nationalism by John H. Armstrong, Columbia University Press, 1963.

The Sickle under the Hammer: The Russian Socialist Revolutionaries in the Early Months of Soviet Rule by Oliver H. Radkey, Columbia University Press, 1963.

Comintern and World Revolution, 1928–1943: The Shaping of Doctrine by Kermit E. McKenzie, Columbia University Press, 1964.

Weimar Germany and Soviet Russia, 1926–1933: A Study in Diplomatic Instability by Harvey L. Dyck, Columbia University Press, 1966.

Financing Soviet Schools by Harold J. Noah, Teachers College Press, 1966.

Russia, Bolshevism, and the Versailles Peace by John M. Thompson, Princeton University Press, 1966.

The Russian Anarchists by Paul Avrich, Princeton University Press, 1967.

The Soviet Academy of Sciences and the Communist Party, 1927–1932 by Loren R. Graham, Princeton University Press, 1967.

Red Virgin Soil: Soviet Literature in the 1920's by Robert A. Maguire, Princeton University Press, 1968; paperback, Cornell University Press, 1987.

Communist Party Membership in the U.S.S.R., 1917–1967 by T.H. Rigby, Princeton University Press, 1968.

Soviet Ethics and Morality by Richard T. De George, University of Michigan Press, 1969; paperback, Ann Arbor Paperbacks, 1969.

Vladimir Akimov on the Dilemmas of Russian Marxism, 1895–1903 by Jonathan Frankel, Cambridge University Press, 1969.

Soviet Perspectives on International Relations, 1956–1967 by William Zimmerman, Princeton University Press, 1969.

Kronstadt, 1921 by Paul Avrich, Princeton University Press, 1970.

Class Struggle in the Pale: The Formative Years of the Jewish Workers' Movement in Tsarist Russia by Ezra Mendelsohn, Cambridge University Press, 1970.

The Proletarian Episode in Russian Literature by Edward J. Brown, Columbia University Press, 1971.

Labor and Society in Tsarist Russia: The Factory Workers of St. Petersburg, 1855–1870 by Reginald E. Zelnik, Stanford University Press, 1971.

Archives and Manuscript Repositories in the U.S.S.R.: Moscow and Leningrad by Patricia K. Grimsted, Princeton University Press, 1972.

The Baku Commune, 1917–1918 by Ronald G. Suny, Princeton University Press, 1972.

Mayakovsky: A Poet in the Revolution by Edward J. Brown, Princeton University Press, 1973.

Oblomov and his Creator: The Life and Art of Ivan Goncharov by Milton Ehre, Princeton University Press, 1973.

German Politics Under Soviet Occupation by Henry Krisch, Columbia University Press, 1974.

Soviet Politics and Society in the 1970's, Henry W. Morton and Rudolph L. Tokes, eds., Free Press, 1974.

Liberals in the Russian Revolution by William G. Rosenberg, Princeton University Press, 1974.

Famine in Russia, 1891–1892 by Richard G. Robbins, Jr., Columbia University Press, 1975.

In Stalin's Time: Middleclass Values in Soviet Fiction by Vera Dunham, Cambridge University Press, 1976.

The Road to Bloody Sunday by Walter Sablinsky, Princeton University Press, 1976; paperback, Princeton University Press, 1986.

The Familiar Letter as a Literary Genre in the Age of Pushkin by William Mills Todd III, Princeton University Press, 1976.

Russian Realist Art. The State and Society: The Peredvizhniki and Their Tradition by Elizabeth Valkenier, Ardis Publishers, 1977; paperback, Columbia University Press, 1989.

The Soviet Agrarian Debate by Susan Solomon, Westview Press, 1978.

Cultural Revolution in Russia, 1928–1931, Sheila Fitzpatrick, ed., Indiana University Press, 1978; paperback, Midland Books, 1984.

Soviet Criminologists and Criminal Policy: Specialists in Policy-Making by Peter Solomon, Columbia University Press, 1978.

Technology and Society under Lenin and Stalin: Origins of the Soviet Technical Intelligentsia by Kendall E. Bailes, Princeton University Press, 1978.

The Politics of Rural Russia, 1905–1914, Leopold H. Haimson, ed., Indiana University Press, 1979.

Political Participation in the U.S.S.R. by Theodore H. Friedgut, Princeton University Press, 1979; paperback, Princeton University Press, 1982.

Education and Social Mobility in the Soviet Union, 1921–1934 by Sheila Fitzpatrick, Cambridge University Press, 1979.

The Soviet Marriage Market: Mate Selection in Russia and the USSR by Wesley Andrew Fisher, Praeger Publishers, 1980.

Prophecy and Politics: Socialism, Nationalism, and the Russian Jews, 1862–1917 by Jonathan Frankel, Cambridge University Press, 1981.

Dostoevsky and The Idiot: *Author, Narrator, and Reader* by Robin Feuer Miller, Harvard University Press, 1981.

Moscow Workers and the 1917 Revolution by Diane Koenker, Princeton University Press, 1981; paperback, Princeton University Press, 1986.

Archives and Manuscript Repositories in the USSR: Estonia, Latvia, Lithuania, and Belorussia by Patricia K. Grimsted, Princeton University Press, 1981.

Zionism in Poland: The Formative Years, 1915–1926 by Ezra Mendelsohn, Yale University Press, 1982.

Soviet Risk-Taking and Crisis Behavior by Hannes Adomeit, George Allen and Unwin Publishers, 1982.

Russia at the Crossroads: The 26th Congress of the CPSU, Seweryn Bialer and Thane Gustafson, eds., George Allen and Unwin Publishers, 1982.

The Crisis of the Old Order in Russia: Gentry and Government by Roberta Thompson Manning, Princeton University Press, 1983, paperback, Princeton University Press, 1986.

Sergei Aksakov and Russian Pastoral by Andrew A. Durkin, Rutgers University Press, 1983.

Politics and Technology in the Soviet Union by Bruce Parrott, MIT Press, 1983.

The Soviet Union and the Third World: An Economic Bind by Elizabeth Kridl Valkenier, Praeger Publishers, 1983.

Russian Metaphysical Romanticism: The Poetry of Tiutchev and Boratynskii by Sarah Pratt, Stanford University Press, 1984.

Ruling Russia: Politics and Administration in the Age of Absolutism, 1762–1796 by John LeDonne, Princeton University Press, 1984.

Insidious Intent: A Structural Analysis of Fedor Sologub's Petty Demon by Diana Greene, Slavica Publishers, 1986.

Leo Tolstoy: Resident and Stranger by Richard Gustafson, Princeton University Press, 1986.

Workers, Society, and the State: Labor and Life in Moscow, 1918–1929 by William Chase, University of Illinois Press, 1987.

Andrey Bely: Spirit of Symbolism, John Malmstad, ed., Cornell University Press, 1987.

Government and Peasant in Russia, 1861–1906: The Prehistory of the Stolypin Reforms by David A.J. Macey, Northern Illinois University Press, 1987.

The Making of Three Russian Revolutionaries: Voices from the Menshevik Past, edited by Leopold H. Haimson in collaboration with Ziva Galili y Garcia and Richard Wortman, Cambridge University Press, 1988.

Revolution and Culture: The Bogdanov-Lenin Controversy by Zenovia A. Sochor, Cornell University Press, 1988.

A Handbook of Russian Verbs by Frank Miller, Ardis Publishers, 1989.

1905 in St. Petersburg: Labor, Society, and Revolution by Gerald D. Surh, Stanford University Press, 1989.

Alien Tongues: Bilingual Russian Writers of the "First" Emigration by Elizabeth Klosty Beaujour, Cornell University Press, 1989.

Iuzovka and Revolution, Volume I: Life and Work in Russia's Donbass, 1869–1924 by Theodore H. Friedgut, Princeton University Press, 1989.

The Menshevik Leaders in the Russian Revolution: Social Realities and Political Strategies by Ziva Galili, Princeton University Press, 1989.

Russian Literary Politics and the Pushkin Celebration of 1880 by Marcus C. Levitt, Cornell University Press, 1989.